Cameron and the Conservatives

Cameron and the Conservatives

The Transition to Coalition Government

Edited By

Timothy Heppell
Lecturer in British Politics, School of Politics and International Studies, University of Leeds, UK

and

David Seawright
Senior Lecturer in British Politics, School of Politics and International Studies, University of Leeds, UK

palgrave
macmillan

First published 2012 by
PALGRAVE MACMILLAN

Palgrave Macmillan in the UK is an imprint of Macmillan Publishers Limited, registered in England, company number 785998, of Houndmills, Basingstoke, Hampshire RG21 6XS.

Palgrave Macmillan in the US is a division of St Martin's Press LLC, 175 Fifth Avenue, New York, NY 10010.

Palgrave Macmillan is the global academic imprint of the above companies and has companies and representatives throughout the world.

Palgrave® and Macmillan® are registered trademarks in the United States, the United Kingdom, Europe and other countries

ISBN 978-0-230-31410-8

This book is printed on paper suitable for recycling and made from fully managed and sustained forest sources. Logging, pulping and manufacturing processes are expected to conform to the environmental regulations of the country of origin.

A catalogue record for this book is available from the British Library.

A catalogue record for this book is available from the Library of Congress.

10 9 8 7 6 5 4 3 2 1
21 20 19 18 17 16 15 14 13 12

Printed and bound in the United States of America
by Edwards Brothers Malloy

Contents

List of Figures and Tables

Figures

Tables

Notes on Contributors

Professor Tim Bale is a Professor of Politics within the Department of Politics and Contemporary European Studies at Sussex University. He is the author of *The Conservative Party from Thatcher to Cameron* (2010).

Christopher Bryne is a British Politics PhD student within the Department of Political Science and International Studies at the University of Birmingham.

Professor Valerie Bryson is a Professor of Politics within the Division of Criminology, Politics and Sociology at the University of Huddersfield. She is the author of *Feminist Political Theory* (2003) and *Gender and the Politics of Time* (2007).

Professor David Denver is a Professor of Politics within the Department of Politics and International Relations at Lancaster University. He is the author of *Elections and Voters in Britain* (2006).

Dr Emma Foster is Teaching Fellow within the Department of Political Science and International Studies at the University of Birmingham.

Professor Andrew Gamble is a Fellow of Queens' College at the University of Cambridge. He is the joint editor of *The Political Quarterly* and author of numerous books, including *Politics and Fate* (2000); *Between Europe and America: The Future of British Politics* (2006); and *The Spectre at the Feast: Capitalist Crisis and the Politics of Recession* (2009). In 2005 he was awarded the PSA Isaiah Berlin prize for Lifetime Contribution to Political Studies.

Dr James Hampshire is a Lecturer in Politics within the Department of Politics and Contemporary European Studies at Sussex University. He is the author of *Citizenship and Belonging: Immigration and the Politics of Demographic Governance in Post-war Britain* (2005).

Dr Richard Hayton is a Senior Lecturer in Politics within the Division of Criminology, Politics and Sociology at the University of Huddersfield. He is the author of *Reconstructing Conservatism: The Conservatives in Opposition 1997–2010* (forthcoming).

Dr Timothy Heppell is a Lecturer in British Politics within the School of Politics and International Studies (POLIS) at the University of Leeds. He is the author of *Choosing the Tory Leader: From Heath to Cameron* (2008) and *Choosing the Labour Leader: From Wilson to Brown* (2010).

Dr Michael Hill is a Lecturer in British Politics within the School of Education of Social Science at the University of Central Lancashire (UCLAN). His work on party political leadership has been published in journals such as *British Politics* and *Political Quarterly*.

Dr Victoria Honeyman is a Lecturer in British Politics within the School of Politics and International Studies (POLIS) at the University of Leeds. She is the author of *Richard Crossman: A Reforming Radical of the Labour Party* (2007).

Dr Peter Kerr is a Senior Lecturer in British Politics at the Department of Political Science and International Studies at the University of Birmingham. He is co-author of *Postwar British Politics in Perspective* (1999) and author of *Postwar British Politics: From Conflict to Consensus* (2001). His comparative examination of the modernisation approaches of Blair and New Labour and the Conservatives under Cameron will be published in 2012.

Dr Philip Lynch is a Senior Lecturer in British Politics at the Department of Politics and International Relations at the University of Leicester. He is the author of *Cameron and the Limits of Conservative Recovery* (forthcoming).

Dr Stuart McAnulla is a Lecturer in British Politics within the School of Politics and International Studies (POLIS) at the University of Leeds. He is the co-author of *Postwar British Politics in Perspective* (1999) and the author of *British Politics: A Critical Introduction* (2006).

Professor Lord Philip Norton is Professor of British Politics and Director of Centre for Legislative Studies, within the Department of Politics and International Studies at the University of Hull. He is the author of 27 books covering British politics, the constitution, the Conservative Party and legislatures in comparative perspectives. He was elevated to the peerage in 1998. He has served as chairman to the House of Lords Select Committee on the Constitution.

Dr Nick Randall is a Senior Lecturer in British Politics at Newcastle University. His work has been published in several edited collections and in journals including *British Politics, Political Quarterly* and *Parliamentary Affairs*.

Dr David Seawright is a Senior Lecturer in British Politics within the School of Politics and International Studies (POLIS) at the University of Leeds. He is the author of *The British Conservative Party and One Nation Politics* (2010) and *An Important Matter of Principle* (1999) about the post-war decline of the Scottish Conservative and Unionist Party.

Professor Kevin Theakston is Professor of British Government within the School of Politics and International Studies (POLIS) at the University of Leeds. He has published ten books including *Winston Churchill and the British Constitution* (2004) and *After Number Ten: Former Prime Ministers in British Politics* (2010).

Acknowledgements

The editors would like to thank the Centre for British Government in POLIS for providing funding to enable the 'Cameron and the Conservatives' event to take place at Leeds University in April 2011. Particular thanks must be given to the contributors, both for delivering their papers at the conference and for making our editorial role so straightforward. We would like to thank Amber Stone-Galilee and Liz Blackmore at Palgrave for their help and guidance throughout.

1
Introduction

Timothy Heppell and David Seawright

The Conservative Party has traditionally considered itself to be the natural party of government in British politics (Bale, 2010: 4), with an ability to successfully transform and renew itself as *the national party* (Seawright, 2010). The party's electoral dominance in twentieth century British politics was so absolute that it was defined politically as the Conservative century (Ramsden, 1999: 7–8). Between 1886 and 1997 they were in government for 77 out of 111 years, and between 1951 and 1997 they occupied power for 35 out of 46 years. In the post-war period Conservative election victories have often been substantial in parliamentary terms. They have secured three majorities of 100 plus (1959, 1983 and 1987); three majorities between 30 and 60 (1955, 1970 and 1979) and two majorities between 15 and 30 (1951 and 1992). Whereas Labour administrations, (prior to New Labour), tended to be relatively short-lived – 1945 to 1951, 1964 to 1970 and 1974 to 1979 – the Conservatives experienced two elongated periods in office. There was the three term period of governance under Winston Churchill, Anthony Eden, Harold Macmillan and Alec Douglas-Home between 1951 and 1964, and a four term period in office between 1979 and 1997 under Margaret Thatcher and John Major.

Statecraft: The art of winning elections and governing competently

For political historians explanations for the success of the Conservatives have been based on references to their 'appetite for power' and their willingness to 'subordinate' doctrinal considerations in that pursuit (see for example, Charmley, 1996; Davies, 1996; Ramsden, 1999). For political scientists, statecraft provides a more useful analytical framework. Statecraft refers to the method(s) by which the Conservatives seek to win office (the politics of support) and then governing competently (the politics of power) so as to then retain office (Bulpitt, 1986: 19–39). Understanding the statecraft model could be a considerable benefit as we assess the transition of the Cameron-led

Conservatives from opposition to government – they have (just) managed to win an election, but can they successfully manage the transitional period and then govern competently?

There are five dimensions to the cycle of statecraft analysis – successful party management, a winning electoral strategy, political argument hegemony, governing competence and then another winning electoral strategy – within which the starting point of analysis is as a party of opposition (Bulpitt, 1986: 21–2). Effective statecraft requires a convincing narrative of what Conservatism constitutes. Within an effective statecraft strategy, that core narrative enables the Conservatives to define the political terrain over which political arguments occur – that is ensuring that the Conservatives are perceived to be the more plausible party in terms of addressing the dominant issues of electoral concern (Taylor, 2005: 135).

Statecraft methods are dependent on circumstances and defeat and loss of office will require adaptation to the method. As Taylor notes adaptation is an 'intensely political process' which is 'seldom smooth or unproblematic because adaptation challenges the extant definition of what Conservatism is' (ibid: 133). If the process fails to deliver the party office – or it does but then fails to provide sufficient governing competence to secure re-election – then further adaptation will be required. Prior to their return to government in 2010, the Conservatives have manufactured three distinct adaptations in the post-war era: 1951, 1970 and 1979. Adaptation under Heath did provide electoral success in 1970 but failed to provide effective strategy. The absence of political argument hegemony and governing competence resulted in a failure to secure re-election in 1974. Taylor implies that the Conservatives have had two successful adaptations in the post-war era – first to the post-war settlement and consensus politics in the late 1940s; and, second, to the market (and what was to become defined as the politics of Thatcherism) in the late 1970s and early 1980s (ibid).

Thatcherism was geared towards the construction of a free economy and a strong state, through an amalgamation of neo-liberalism and neo-conservatism. It offered an appropriate and time specific mode of statecraft for the Conservatives. However, as Gamble had predicted as early as 1988 it was a mechanism of statecraft that would not be sustainable over the longer term (Gamble, 1988: 154). This was partly because the Thatcherite transformation of the economy undermined the relationship between the party and the middle classes, who had habitually turned to the Conservatives to provide personal economic security and political stability (Dorey, 2003: 142).

In the period between the fall of Thatcher and the rise of Cameron and the modernisers, the Conservatives have grappled with the legacy of Thatcherism and the need to construct a new mode of statecraft that reflected the reshaped political terrain created by the rise of New Labour. Addressing the conundrum of New Labour was to be hugely problematic. Previous modes of Conservative statecraft had been predicated on the compliance of the Labour Party by their continued adherence to electorally alienating positions and perceptions of governing incompetence. For example, Conservative strategy in the Thatcher/Major era was narrated around the memories of the Winter of Discontent in 1978–1979, and the fear of socialism and excessive trade union power (Hay, 2010: 446–70).

New Labour, however, was thus cloaked in electoral calculations of what was politically feasible, rather than what was ideologically desirable. Central to the New Labour rhetoric was the neutralisation of the perceived negatives around which the Conservative narrative could be constructed, within which the rhetoric of 'old' and 'new' was central (Buckler and Dolowitz, 2009: 16). Their combined emphasis on economic efficiency *and* social justice provided an external and contemporary electoral comparison (Gamble, 2010: 648). The emphasis on economic efficiency provided New Labour with an alternative strategy for growth, rooted in notions of stability and investment, which could be used as comparison with the 'boom and bust' economics associated with Thatcherism. The social justice dimension of their narrative allowed them 'to position themselves against an outmoded Conservative obsession with the free market', which they argued had 'blunted their ability to address problems with the social fabric'. This enabled New Labour to portray the Conservatives 'as socially regressive and lacking in compassion, particularly with respect to the excluded' (Buckler and Dolowitz, 2009: 24).

Through the politics of triangulation Blair and New Labour would deride the politics of Thatcherism for the economic instability and insecurity that it created. Such a strategy for undermining the Conservatives' statecraft strategy was aided by perceptions of incompetence (Black Wednesday) and disunity (European integration) which characterised the party in the Major era (Taylor, 2010: 492). The cumulative effect was the Conservatives could no longer narrate their appeal around the fears of a potential Labour administration. As Tim Bale concludes the triumph of New Labour was their ability to:

> tap into the widespread belief among the British that there *should not be a trade off* between social justice and economic growth; between fairness and efficiency, between quality public provision and higher net disposable incomes. At the same time, [they] also managed to persuade people that a *trade off does exist* between lower taxes and investment in the NHS and state education (Bale, 2010: 5).

Between 1997 and 2007, when operating in a favourable economic environment, Blair and New Labour thus framed party competition as being a choice between investment under Labour *or* cuts under the Conservatives. The 'cuts versus spending' strategy was a central explanation for their three election victories in 1997, 2001 and 2005 (Kavanagh and Cowley, 2010: 64). Reflecting prevailing voter preferences in an age of prosperity, and the intellectual climate of the times, New Labour had crafted a political and electoral strategy that Gamble suggests 'echoed in many ways the successful Conservative statecraft of the past' (Gamble, 2010: 644). In developing his comparison, Gamble noted that:

> At the heart of this conception of politics was the idea of the Big Tent, which was big enough to include almost everyone ... The Conservatives in the past had often conceived politics in this way, using ideas such as One Nation and the Middle Way, which played a similar role to the Third Way. This form of statecraft was always ideology-lite. Much greater attention was paid to responding to what voters found important rather than to sticking to party dogmas and principles (Gamble, 2010: 644).

A failure of statecraft: The conservative strategy 1997–2005

Between 1997 and 2005 the Conservatives would suffer three successive electoral reverses, two of which justify the term landslide parliamentary defeats. They would endure a dramatic collapse in their level of popular support since 1992. They secured over 14 million votes then, but in three successive election defeats in 1997, 2001 and 2005, their vote base fell to around eight to nine million. They suffered a ten per cent reduction in their vote share from 41.9 per cent in 1992 to 30.7 per cent in 1997. Two periods in opposition would produce limited improvements in vote share and parliamentary representation, with increases to 31.8 per cent and 166 seats in 2001; and 32.3 per cent and 198 seats in 2005 (Kavanagh and Cowley, 2010: 350–1).

That David Cameron would inherit a Conservative Party in such a calamitous position in 2005 was a reflection on the difficulties that they experienced in opposition in the 1997 to 2005 period – a failure of adaptation, reflecting their inability to construct a new and credible statecraft strategy. That inability or failure can be contextualised by recognition of the following three factors:

1. Within the party there were two conflicting explanations of their electoral meltdown. There was a school of thought which believed that New Labour was built on shallow foundations. Their popularity would wane and then the electorate would return to the tried and trusted policies of the Conservatives: that is, there was nothing fundamentally wrong with Conservatism. All that was required was a clear Thatcherite message of a small state, low taxation, Euroscepticism and social conservatism. The failure to be sufficiently Thatcherite explained their respective electoral reversals. The opposing school of thought advocated change as the emergence of New Labour amounted to a decisive shift in the mood of the British electorate, (that is, there was something fundamentally

wrong with Conservatism). The modernisers suggested that fundamental reform, and the adoption of a new narrative based around compassionate and inclusive conservatism, was essential to their strategy for electoral recovery (Dorey, 2003: 125; Seldon and Snowdon, 2005: 271).
2. This initial strategic dilemma was then compounded by the performance of New Labour in government and the response of the electorate to them. New Labour experienced a honeymoon period of electoral goodwill, aided by a benign economy, which was unparalleled in its duration. The Conservatives had a problem identifying government weaknesses that they could target (and thereby articulate an alternative Conservative narrative around) in an age of New Labour dominance (Beech, 2008: 1).
3. The Conservatives had lost dominance of elite political debate because the primary concern of the electorate was now public service delivery and issues relating to quality of life, in which Labour were in the ascendant. The electorate had switched their policy prioritisations and attitudes away from the primacy of tax reductions and privatisation, the very policy domains that had acted as the pillars of Conservative political argument hegemony in the age of Thatcherism (Dorey, 2003: 127; Seldon and Snowdon, 2005: 253).

Between 1997 and 2005 era the Conservatives failed to engage in a sustained rethink as had been the case between 1945 and 1950; 1966 and 1970 and 1975 and 1979. Without this, the party lacked a clear electoral strategy or political identity, and was unable to obtain the intellectual high ground or acquire political argument hegemony; the essential building block of electoral appeal (Norton, 2001: 79). Policy development evolved through two broad manifestations – 'reaching out' to reposition the party and attract new or lost voters, or 'shoring up' to ensure that the traditional core vote was mobilised. Within the literature, a general pattern can be identified which runs as follows:

1. Reaching out characterised the approach between 1997 and 1999 and again between 2001 and late 2002, in which the Conservatives aimed to compete with New Labour in the centre ground of British electoral politics. This approach subscribed to the point of view that Conservatism needed to transcend its Thatcherite legacy and modernise itself by adopting a more socially liberal identity (1997–1999 variant under William Hague) and/or concern for poverty and the public services (2001–2002 variant under Iain Duncan Smith). This broad, inclusive and mainstream strategy indicated a desire to shift party thinking towards reflecting the concerns of ordinary voters (Collings and Seldon, 2001: 628; Kelly, 2001: 197; Hayton and Heppell, 2010: 436–41).
2. The switch to shoring up would underpin the core vote strategy and core vote plus strategies for the 2001 and 2005 general election campaigns

> – strategies which were defined as sub-optimal. The shifts involved increasing the emphasis on traditionally Conservative owned issues. This involved building strategy around supposedly populist issues such as Europe, taxation, the family, law and order, and asylum and immigration (Norton, 2001: 79; Kelly, 2001: 199; Collings and Seldon, 2001: 628; Taylor, 2005: 149).

Thus after eight years in opposition and three different party leaders, the Conservatives were still wrestling with the same strategic conundrum – what does Conservatism stand for; what is the Conservative Party for, and how can they reclaim electoral support so that they can present themselves once again to the electorate as a credible alternative party of government? Writing in the year that Cameron became Conservative leader, Taylor concluded that the Conservatives current situation differed from that of the 1940s, 1960s and 1970s in that they seemed 'locked into a *systemic crisis*' (Taylor, 2005: 153).

It was argued that the systemic crisis could be addressed by the ideological repositioning of the party towards the centre-ground of British politics – that is embracing the reaching out strategy (as deployed in 1997–1999 and 2001–2002) and *sustaining* it. This thinking would inform the modernising strategy of Cameron and his supporters. Unlike Hague and Duncan Smith, the Cameron faction were determined to implement and maintain such a strategy and re-orientate the party's position to the centre ground and the location of the median voter (Taylor, 2010: 490).

Sanders argued that the general election of 2005 demonstrated two things for the Conservatives – first, they could increase their appeal if they abandon their identification with being the party of tax cuts and thus undermine the New Labour electoral strategy of defining party competition around New Labour investment and Conservative cuts; and, second by identifying a party leader who was 'not actively disliked' by the electorate. Cameron as an individual would fulfil that second issue. His programme of modernisation and strategic repositioning of the party aimed to address the first issue. However, what is critical to note is this. The simulations that Sanders constructed in 2006 concluded that the Conservatives would be able to increase their vote share by around 5 per cent. That would be insufficient to win an overall majority and a hung Parliament was thus the most likely outcome (Sanders, 2006: 170–94).

Given that surely Cameron did as well as could have been expected? Moreover, Cameron managed to overcome the disappointment of failing to secure a majority, and made that into an opportunity. As Gamble notes by constructing a Liberal-Conservative coalition:

> It allowed him to achieve what Tony Blair had failed to achieve, a realignment of British politics, a big tent involving the full participation of two of the three national parties. The realignment of the centre left which had

> been the aspiration of so many progressives had been transformed by Cameron into a realignment on the centre right. It allowed him to proclaim himself as a Liberal Conservative with more confidence than at any time since he had assumed the leadership (Gamble, 2010: 644).

Cameron and the Conservatives

There are two different schools of thought on how to view the performance of Cameron and the Conservatives at the general election of 2010. The defence case for Cameron runs as follows. With a parliamentary representation of 198 seats after the 2005 general election, Cameron inherited a worse position than the Labour Party after the 1983 general election, when under Michael Foot they secured 209 seats. After that Labour suffered two further defeats in 1987 and 1992 under Neil Kinnock. Whereas Kinnock increased Labour representation from 209 to 229 from 1983 to 1987, Cameron had seen the Conservatives representation increase from 198 to 307. It may not have been enough to propel Cameron into Downing Street as a majority administration, but it still represented a considerable achievement. After 1945, an increase of 109 seats for a party from one election to the next had only been achieved by Blair and New Labour (271 to 419) in 1997 (Kavanagh and Cowley, 2010: 350–1). Bale encapsulates the defence case by arguing that Cameron did 'pretty well' by ensuring that he became Prime Minister for 'he had to do in just four or five years what it had taken three Labour leaders some thirteen years to accomplish' (Bale, forthcoming).

However, critics of Cameron note that only 10.7 million people voted Conservative in 2010, which is only 1.1 million more than the Conservatives secured when they were humiliated at the general election of 1997. The Conservative vote in 2010 was around three million short of the 13 million plus that the Conservatives secured in 1979, 1983 and 1987 under Margaret Thatcher, and the 14.1 million secured by John Major in 1992. In percentage terms, whereas Thatcher and Major were able to secure votes shares of 41 to 44 per cent, Cameron was well short at 36.1 per cent. Thirteen years after losing office on 30.1 per cent, their vote share had slowly increased to 31.7 in 2001 and 32.4 in 2005. After a much trumpeted strategic re-orientation and rebranding exercise, why had Cameron secured only a 3.7 per cent increase as compared to 2005 (Kavanagh and Cowley, 2010: 350–1)?

Furthermore, such comparisons have to be viewed within the context of the economic environment. Whilst Labour had vulnerabilities when seeking their third term in 2005, notably the fallout from the Iraq war, they still benefitted from the enduring strength of the economy (Norton, 2009: 32, 43). Five years later Cameron found himself with political and economic circumstances that should have aided him as an opposition leader. The banking collapse and subsequent recession badly damaged the reputation of Labour for economic competence, which had been their trump card in their re-elections of 2001 and 2005. In Gordon Brown Labour were undermined by a leader with limited political communication skills. With there being constant speculation about attempts to replace Brown as their leader before facing the electorate, Labour gave the impression of being an incompetent, ideologically bankrupt and directionless administration (Denham et al, 2011: 155, 178; Dorey, 2010: 402–3). In the context of the aftermath of a deep recession and competing against a degenerating multi term Labour government led by a discredited Prime Minister, why did the electorates' desire for change and concerns about the competency of Labour fail to translate into trust in the Conservatives (Green, J., 2010: 680)?

The emergence of the coalition, rather than a majority Conservative administration, has encouraged political commentators and academics to want to analyse the relationship between the Conservatives and the Liberal Democrats, and to assess the performance of the government as a coalition, (see for example, Lee and Beech, 2011). There is a tendency within this to view the Liberal Democrats as the potentially problematic part of the coalition – an assumption given validity by the controversy surrounding tuition fees. In reality it is better to view the coalition as four parties rather than two – the Conservative and Liberal Democrats and their leaderships loyalists each forming two blocks; alongside two other blocks – the Conservative right and the Liberal Democrat left (Muir, 2010: 18–21; Paun and Hazell, 2010: 215).

Therefore, what is really intriguing about the coalition is the relationship between the Cameron modernising liberal conservative block (essentially leadership dominated) and his own parliamentary right block of traditional Thatcherites (mostly located within the backbenchers). Since becoming leader in 2005 the traditional Thatcherites on the right displayed a conditional relationship with Cameron. As the modernisation agenda developed – with its convergence with Labour on economic policy strategy in the 2005–2007 period running parallel to the detoxification of the brand by emphasising their socially liberal agenda – the traditional Thatcherites on the right tolerated rather than embraced Cameron. They were willing to swallow his modernising medicine if it was popular with the electorate and propelled the Conservatives back into power as a majority administration (Evans, 2008: 301).

The conduct of the Cameron leadership during the five days of negotiations with the Liberal Democrats, both in terms of decision-making and communication, intensified the internal party concerns about Cameron from within the traditional Thatcherites on the right. Cameron dismissed the idea of minority government immediately, even though it was favoured by many Conservatives (Kavanagh and Cowley, 2010: 223). At a relatively early stage in negotiations, Cameron issued a statement to his party, implying that they should be willing to concede political ground, 'both in the national interest and in the interest of forging an open and trusting relationship' with the Liberal Democrats (Fox, 2010: 611).

At this critical juncture, Cameron held two meetings, one with his shadow Cabinet and one with his newly elected Parliamentary Conservative Party (PCP). Without significant dissent, the shadow Cabinet agreed to Cameron's desire to offer the Liberal Democrats a referendum on the Alternative Vote (AV) for electoral reform. Cameron informed the PCP that Labour were offering the Liberal Democrats AV without a referendum, (a disputed claim), meaning that if they objected to a 'Con-Lib coalition government *with* a referendum on AV' then the Conservatives would be left 'with a Lab-Lib coalition and AV *without* a referendum' (Kavanagh and Cowley, 2010: 214). In securing his wishes, the methods that Cameron deployed would create resentment on the traditional Thatcherite right, as Kavanagh and Cowley conclude:

> For the Conservatives the coalition process had essentially been a top-down one, driven by a handful of Cameron's close confidants, and involving the Shadow cabinet and Parliamentary Party only sporadically, and only when the leadership needed it. On Tuesday night when Prime Minister Cameron went before Conservative MPs, it was essentially a *fait accompli*. It was difficult for Conservative MPs who harboured doubts about the coalition deal to air them openly in an atmosphere where the new Prime Minister was being paraded triumphantly in front of them. Nor were they shown a copy of the coalition agreement which had been drawn up between the two parties (ibid: 221).

Therefore, from an intra-party perspective political scientists should be focusing on the relationship between Cameron and the right wing of his own parliamentary party. That this was a problematic relationship was a factor in the calculations for establishing the coalition (Denham et al, 2011: 196). For Cameron there was little attraction in a minority administration, not just because of its instability, but because he feared becoming a hostage of his own parliamentary right. Forming a coalition enabled Cameron to minimise the impact of opposition from the parliamentary right by diluting it with the support of the Liberal Democrats. This issue was understood by Liberal Democrat negotiators. As David Laws noted a coalition gave Cameron:

> joint responsibility for tough decisions, not sole blame for the painful cuts to come; and an opportunity to change the entire perception of the Conservative Party and to reshape British politics ... the boldness of the coalition and the concessions on policy might act as a huge 'detoxifier' of a Conservative brand which had not quite been 'cleansed' by the Cameron team. Moreover, the position of the right wing of the Conservative Party would be notably weakened – they would no longer enjoy a blocking minority (Laws, 2010: 51, 200).

The transition to coalition government

Therefore, it is clear that there is a clear academic rationale for examining the coalition from a Conservative perspective. The component parts of the statecraft model help to inform the thinking that underpins this edited collection.

Statecraft dimension 1: A winning electoral strategy?

Chapters 2 to 4 aim to address that first question of why only coalition and not a majority government? In Chapter 2, Christopher Byrne, Emma Foster and Peter Kerr provide a critical deconstruction of the discourses and ideas which have informed the modernisation of the Conservatives under Cameron and demonstrate the need for a rigorous re-examination of the conceptual construct of 'modernisation' as it becomes inundated with an over-profusion of meaning. Focusing on the comparisons with the transformations under Tony Blair and New Labour, Chapter 2 also examines Conservative modernisation in terms of its distancing from a Thatcherite past but at the same time being an experiment in neo-liberal governmentality. Through such an analysis Byrne et al identify the drivers and limits to the strategic modernisation under Cameron, and how his political narrative relates to both the politics of Thatcherism and New Labour.

Having provided an analytical overview of the modernisation strategy adopted in the post-2005 period Chapter 3 focuses explicitly on the election campaign of 2010. Here David Seawright offers a critical interpretation of the conduct of a campaign dominated by the persona and supposed charisma of Cameron, but devoid of a clearly digestible and understandable narrative. Here Seawright argues that a successful campaign rests on the ability of the message to create clarity not confusion for the electorate, and that the Big Society narrative was singularly ineffective in this regard. Beyond the failure of the narrative, Seawright explains why the decision to participate in the Prime Ministerial debates was a strategic miscalculation.

In Chapter 4, David Denver analyses the electorate and their views on the Conservatives under Cameron. To understand fully the psephological position of the Conservative Party under David Cameron, Denver first examines the electoral history of the party since it was last in power. He examines the greater importance of the party leader in an age of 'valence politics', where the image of the leader is inextricably connected to the parties' characterisation as competent on a variety of universally approved goals, such as economic prosperity, reduction of crime or trustworthiness on national health. Denver addresses the crucial statecraft concern of the electoral cycle and examines the party's future prospects; in light of the extent to which it scaled the psephological mountain faced in 2010.

Statecraft dimensions 2 and 3: Governing competence and political argument hegemony

In attempting to assess the governing credentials, rather than examine their policy positions across themes which reflect the departmental apparatus of Whitehall – economic; education; health; welfare; home office; defence; foreign; international development – as in the case of Lee and Beech (2011), this edited collection includes particular themes around policy and governance for specific reasons. We have included policy domains that have been downplayed because they have been sources of internal division for the Conservatives and which Cameron has attempted to distance the party from – Europe and immigration. In addition, we have included women as an area of policy concern, as in opposition the Conservatives had deliberately prioritised this as a means by which to symbolise their detoxification. Finally, we have included policy areas in which the legacy from New Labour creates problems for the Conservatives as an incoming administration – for example, the unfinished business of the devolutionary settlement and the complexities that creates in terms of territorial management; and of course it was necessary to evaluate their ability to manage the New Labour inheritance in terms of welfare, foreign and economic policy.

Chapter 5 considers the economic policy pursued by the coalition government. Here Andrew Gamble outlines the strategy for eliminating the deficit in the public finances by 2015 and the assumptions that cuts on this scale can be delivered; that the fragile economic recovery will continue; and that inflation can be kept under control. Gamble compares the economic policy of the coalition with previous Conservative governments, and asks whether it is more or less radical as a result of having Liberal Democrats in the government. It also explores the tensions within the Conservatives over the nature of some of the spending cuts, and at whether it is ideology, or politics, which is driving the cuts agenda.

If Chapter 5 provides an opportunity to assess the adherence to Thatcherite neo-liberalism in the economic sphere, then Chapter 6 considers another aspect of the Thatcherite ideological inheritance: Euroscepticism. By examining policy developments on Europe through opposition, the coalition negotiations and then government policy on the European Union issues during its first year in office, Philip Lynch identifies the significance of the European Union Bill's referendum lock and sovereignty clause. The chapter examines the division between soft and hard variants of Euroscepticism in the Conservative Party, and evaluates the potential threat posed to the Conservatives' fortunes by an issue that has been described as 'a ticking time bomb'.

In Chapter 7, Tim Bale and James Hampshire consider the vexed issue of immigration. They explore and explain the Conservatives' position on immigration since 2005, setting it within the context of their traditional stance on the issue, their desire to undermine Labour, and modernisation of the party. It then looks in detail at the deal done with the Liberal

Democrats – and the difficulties that the new government will have in implementing that deal to the letter. It also considers the UK's situation with that of other advanced democracies in which centre right parties and governments are trying to balance their belief in economic dynamism with their supporters' concerns about migration and multiculturalism.

Extending the focus on the politics of identity, Chapter 8 examines how territorial politics has changed since the Conservatives were last in office. Here Nick Randall and David Seawright identify how the new constitutional arrangements established by New Labour, in particular through the setting up of the Scottish Parliament and Welsh Assembly, have created complexities for a Conservative Westminster government in terms of creating new solutions to its territorial politics problem. The chapter utilises Bulpitt's notion of an 'operational code' as a solution to the party's territorial management problem and the importance of such a code in securing governing competence. In assessing the implications for the future governance of the United Kingdom, this chapter also considers the Conservatives' approach to 'localism' for England and how the Conservatives have adapted to the realities of asymmetrical devolution and the potential that may exist that their territorial management may further endanger the very union that they wish to protect.

Just as territorial management concerns highlight the Conservatives' expedient relationship with the Liberal Democrats on questions of 'governing legitimacy', so Chapter 9 extends that focus by considering foreign policy. In this chapter Victoria Honeyman notes that often the guiding principle of foreign policy is pragmatism and bipartisan continuity and she examines how the realities of the coalition may be impacting on the Conservatives' traditional approach. Honeyman analyses the Hague/Cameron formulation of foreign policy based on the principles of 'Liberal Conservatism' and its similarities and differences with that of the approach of Blair and New Labour. However pragmatic the policy area though, Honeyman flags up the potential for division and splits within the coalition on the extent and level of interventionist projects.

In Chapter 10, Richard Hayton focuses on the welfare reform agenda of the coalition. Acknowledging that the genesis of this reform programme can be traced to their work in opposition (and notably the Centre for Social Justice under Duncan Smith), the chapter analyses the objectives the coalition have identified and their progress towards implementation in their first year of office. It weighs up the reality of this process against rhetoric emanating from government ministers, and assesses the likelihood of success of the programme as a whole and elements within it. The chapter argues that the coalition's social policy is being driven by the imperative to reduce the deficit in the public finances, and meet their self imposed target of eliminating the structural deficit, alongside the ideological commitment to fundamentally rebalance the relationship between the state, economy and society and to reduce the scope and scale of the state's role.

Chapter 11 considers the validity of the feminisation agenda that the Conservatives initiated in opposition to demonstrate symbolic change and to aid the detoxification of the brand. Here Valerie Bryson considers the evolution of Conservative thinking in terms of women and how policy developed post-2005. Whilst acknowledging that the rhetoric was more inclusive and there is evidence of a considerable shift in attitudes amongst Conservative elites on gender issues, the chapter develops a clear critique of the Conservatives in terms of their impact upon women once in office. The chapter concludes that the impact of the Comprehensive Spending Review and cuts agenda has and will impact upon women in a disproportionate manner, whilst the record of the government remains questionable in terms of issues such as rape anonymity; recognising marriage in the taxation system; and flexible working and the gender pay gap.

Moving beyond questions of governing competence and into political argument hegemony Stuart McAnulla (Chapter 12) examines particular aspects of this ideological trajectory from opposition and into office. He examines the efforts of leading figures to redefine the party's relationship with Thatcherism, and the attempt to articulate a sceptical approach to the state with a proclaimed commitment to social justice. The chapter also evaluates just how influential such ideas have continued to be during their first year in office, and argues that the approach to cutting the deficit remains consistent with pre-election ambitions to reduce state involvement in the economy yet also to give some relative protection to the most cherished public services. In assessing their attempts to secure dominance of elite debate, he considers to what extent coalition with the Liberal Democrats has compromised, or otherwise influenced, the ideological direction of the Conservatives. McAnulla concludes that whilst the notion of Liberal Conservatism does indeed capture important aspects of Cameron's approach, this owes at least as much to the revisions in Conservative thinking that occurred *before* the 2010 general election, as it does to the political dealing which ensued afterwards.

Statecraft dimensions 4 and 5: Party management and another winning electoral strategy

Chapters 13 to 15 examine the impact the new government has had on wider perceptions of party political competition – how cohesive and unified have the coalition been in parliamentary terms and specifically what evidence is there of Conservative rebellion; how effective has Cameron been as Prime Minister; and what has been the impact on New Labour as it adapts to opposition?

In Chapter 13, Philip Norton considers the significance of parliamentary dissent to the coalition government, and specifically amongst Conservative backbenchers. Here, Norton examines the development of two forms of dissent in the Parliament *within the coalition*: intra-party dissent and inter-party dissent. Focusing in on parliamentary rebellions, he notes that the new Parliament has seen an unprecedented level of intra-party dissent, Norton considers the nature and scale of the conflict within and between the coalition parties; the key issues generating dissent; and the means utilised by the coalition (in terms of established as well as novel mechanisms) to contain dissent. In noting this absence of behavioural cohesion Norton concludes that this offers the prospect of dissent in the first session being the norm for the Parliament.

In Chapter 14, Kevin Theakston examines the leadership style and political skills of Cameron as Prime Minister, against the background of his approach and methods during his five years as leader of the opposition. The impact of the move to coalition government on the structure and methods of policy-making and decision-making in Downing Street, the Cabinet system and in Whitehall is also analysed to provide an institutional context for the chapter. Comparisons are drawn with other recent Prime Ministers – notably Thatcher, Major, Blair and Brown – and with the experience and approach of earlier Prime Ministers who had to grapple with the problems and challenges of managing coalition governments. The central part of the chapter evaluates Cameron's governing style, strengths and weaknesses, and successes and failures under six headings: proficiency as a political communicator; organisational capacity; political skills; policy vision; cognitive style and emotional intelligence.

In Chapter 15, Timothy Heppell and Michael Hill consider how the demands of coalition government have impacted upon the dynamics of party political competition by examining the performance of Labour in opposition. To assess the transition to opposition, the chapter utilises two key issues to assess the performance of Labour in their first year of opposition. First, the chapter will consider the changes in personnel with particular reference to their leadership change and shadow Cabinet elections. Second, the chapter assesses the strategic issues facing Labour as they attempt to overcome the reasons for their eviction from government and distance the party from perceptions of a recent failed past.

Conclusion

The first paragraph of this introduction emphasised how the Conservatives have traditionally viewed themselves as the natural party of government. This assumption reflects their historical effectiveness at manufacturing time specific modes of statecraft. Their ability to recovery from defeat and recuperate speedily and effectively had been a traditional characteristic of the Conservatives after previous electoral reversals. Reconstructing Conservatism with a viable post-Thatcherite statecraft strategy did not gather real momentum in the 1997 to 2005 period, and coalition demonstrates that the Cameron configured statecraft between 2005 and 2010 had strategic limits (Taylor, 2010: 489). In assessing the prospect of the Cameron mode of statecraft working for the Conservatives longer term the following provides causes for concern: first, their long exclusion from office and limited ministerial and governing experience; second, the constraints created by the economic and political inheritance; and third, the added complexities of being politically constrained by being in coalition.

Perceptions of how effectively the Conservatives, and specifically Cameron, have adapted to the transition from opposition to government, will have huge implications for the future of British government and politics. This edited collection therefore aims to present an audit of their Liberal Conservative agenda at the point of its first anniversary (May, 2011). It provides us with an initial view on the viability of the Cameron statecraft strategy and the core narratives of Liberal Conservatism. It enables us to assess how Cameron's Conservatives have begun the process of trying to create a centre-right progressive hegemony (Taylor, 2010: 494). By reading this audit of the first year as Cameron and the Conservatives deal with the transition to coalition government, it will help students of Conservative politics to assess the validity of the following claim made by Hayton:

> Understood in terms of statecraft, the coalition agreement may be regarded as an astute piece of 'high politics' by Cameron. Whilst conceding some specific points to his junior partner (most notably a referendum on electoral reform) the Conservative leader secured for himself and his party all the key prizes: the major offices of state; control of the public finances and the direction of economic policy; and a large majority in the Commons to ensure the passage of the government's legislative programme. Statecraft would suggest a continued willingness on Cameron's part to compromise to hold the coalition together – at least until such a time as he adjudges it to be electorally rewarding to allow it to break down, prompting a general election. It also implies a governing approach driven by pragmatism rather than ideology, characterised, for example, by Cameron and Clegg's claims that they have no wish to slash public spending, but that cuts are simply 'unavoidable' because of the size of the government's deficit. If such an approach is successful, it could mark the beginning of a new Conservative century (Hayton, forthcoming, a).

2
Understanding Conservative Modernisation

Christopher Byrne, Emma Foster and Peter Kerr

Introduction

> *The changes we're making to the Conservative Party are modernisation with a purpose. That purpose is to make sure we can meet the big challenges of our age* (David Cameron, Speech launching Conservative Party Task Force, 6 February, 2006).
>
> *Modernisation is not an end in itself. It is for a purpose* (Tony Blair, Speech to the Annual Labour Party Conference, 30 September, 1997).

For the past two decades at least, 'modernisation' has formed a pivotal part of British political discourse. Tony Blair, who became the living embodiment of New Labour, characterised his political *raison-d'être* as a crusade to modernise the Labour Party before taking on the more sizeable task of modernising the whole of British society. The UK constitution was to be overhauled and modernised, as was the NHS, our education system, our economy, local government and our transport infrastructure. In fact, modernisation became the guiding principle in the formation of almost every area of government policy and Blair's public speeches were replete with references to the imperative of modernisation. Blair's references to modernisation, however, were not seminal. In one form or another, modernisation discourses have been prevalent in the rhetoric used by British politicians since the 1960s, spurred mainly by an acute perception of the UK's inability to keep apace with its major competitors both politically and economically on the international stage. However, since the election of the Thatcher government in 1979 and the subsequent transformation of the Labour Party into New Labour, the utilisation of modernisation discourses have accelerated to the point whereby the imperative of modernisation has become almost fetishised by modern UK politicians, with David Cameron being no exception. Indeed, the self-styled 'heir to Blair' has oftentimes been quite shameless in his plagiarism of Blair's political style and, in particular, in framing his ascent to the leadership of the Conservative Party in terms of the emergence of a moderniser willing and able to drag the party into the twenty-first century whilst at the same time making the British economy and welfare state fit for competition in the new global economy. Not only that, but at the recent general election, Cameron based much of his political appeal to the electorate on a promise to be the 'real' moderniser in British politics, despite echoing, as shown in the two quotes above, Blair's phrase 'modernisation with a purpose'.

In this chapter, we attempt to highlight the significance of modernisation discourses in Cameron's transformation of the Conservative Party in opposition as well as the central role they play in shaping his party's agenda whilst in office. Our aim is to show how modernisation rhetoric has functioned to enable Cameron to entrepreneurially reinvent and renew the neo-liberal state project which began under Thatcher and continued under New Labour. In this respect, we argue that modernisation discourses have been utilised by Cameron to facilitate continuity with broader trends in British politics over the past three decades whilst at the same time creating space for the invention of new technologies of government and more creative forms of neo-liberal governmentality. Finally, we conclude by speculating on some of the potential limitations of Cameron's modernisation project – a project which, we concede, could ultimately prove to be short-lived.

The zeitgeist of modernisation

Since the 1980s, the production and proliferation of 'modernisation' discourses has become something of an obsession for the two main UK political parties. David Cameron's attempts, whilst in opposition, to reconstitute the 'look, feel and identity' of the Conservative Party can be read as a somewhat distorted mirror image of the Labour Party's earlier 'modernisation' into New Labour during the 1990s. In both cases, the language of the 'modern' has served to define the logic of party change; implying the need for both parties to upgrade their product and throw off the shackles of the past in order to meet the needs of the present. But, the overlap between David Cameron's modernisation of the Conservatives and Tony Blair's reconfiguration of the Labour Party does not end with the deployment of the language of the modern. Both modernisation processes have involved similar key elements, including: changes in party leadership; changes to the organisational structure of the party; changes in policy selection; and, a rhetorical distancing of the party from its past (Bale, 2008b). In each case, party adaptation has been slow and 'modernisation' discourses have functioned to legitimise a movement towards the so-called 'centre ground'. Equally, for both parties, the modernisation process was triggered by a long spell in opposition and an attempt to refresh the party 'brand' for the purposes of regaining office.

But the production of modernisation discourses has not been confined solely to the conduct and aesthetic representation of political parties. It has flowed outwards from the arena of party change and circulated in and through a variety of interlocking changes to state practices and constitutional arrangements. At the level of the state, the discourse of modernisation has been deployed to encapsulate a plethora of changing patterns of regulatory procedures and practices generally associated with new and ascendant forms of 'governance' (Rhodes, 1997; Pierre and Peters, 2000; Newman, 2001). At the constitutional level, it has been coupled to the rhetoric of accountability and transparency in order to reshape institutionalised patterns of representation. As such, 'modernisation' discourses have been used to legitimise a myriad of changes, not only to Britain's two main political parties, but also to the state more generally. For that reason, modernisation has come to be imbued with such a variety of different meanings that it could be said to have acquired the status of an 'empty signifier'.

Empty signifiers are an important element in the work of Ernesto Laclau, who explains their function as key political slogans around which a number of interests can compete for power and influence. According to Laclau, empty signifiers – such as 'social justice', 'fairness' and 'accountability', to name a few examples which have proliferated contemporary British politics – function in discourse to represent something which is continually absent. In this respect, they signify a 'lack' of something which is ultimately impossible to fill. But the impossible fulfilment of this lack creates a set of conditions for political forces to 'compete in their efforts to present their particular objectives as those which carry out the filling of that lack' (Laclau, 1996: 44). In other words, empty signifiers represent an impossible and undeliverable ideal which political forces compete to deliver (Howarth and Stavrakakis, 2000: 8). Modernisation constitutes such an impossible ideal. Putting aside the futility of trying to reach a settled definition of 'modernisation', if modernisation is the quest to 'keep up' with, and adapt to, a political environment which is ever changing, then its fulfilment would appear impossible. Yet, it is the proposed fulfilment of this lack of 'keeping up' which has become a cornerstone for political contestation between Labour and the Conservatives over the past three decades.

It is perhaps unsurprising that the discourse of modernisation should have come to play such a pivotal role in defining the parameters of competition between the main political parties in the UK. Throughout the post-war period, Britain has been acutely aware of its declining status on the world stage, both politically and economically, and has been forced to reconcile itself with a retreat from its former hegemonic position. This has often been attributed to the UK's inability to modernise its economic infrastructure in order to compete with new, ascendant economic powers. At the same time, some of the blame for Britain's decline has also been attributed to the archaic nature of Britain's constitutional settlement. The highly centralised and top-down 'Westminster Model' which has historically underpinned the British political system has often been criticised for its inability to respond and adapt adequately to the needs of a modern, globalised economic context. As such, an overall perception that the UK has continually failed to 'keep up' in a fast-changing global environment has undoubtedly helped to shape the desire of political parties to be seen to be throwing off the legacies of past ideas and practices in order to make themselves 'fit for purpose' in the modern era. As a result, just as 'globalisation' has become the buzzword for changes that are occurring at the level of the international, 'modernisation' has emerged as its attendant bedfellow at the national and local levels.

The race to be modern

In the context of political party competition, modernisation becomes, to some extent, a self-perpetuating process. As one party succeeds in convincing the electorate that it has become 'fit for purpose', the other parties become inevitably drawn into a process of seemingly having to run to 'keep up'. Since as early as the 1960s, supremacy in this race to be more modern than one's competitors has oscillated between both Labour and the Conservatives. The 1964–1970 Labour government, under the leadership of Harold Wilson, emerged first out of the blocks in its attempts to harness the 'white heat of technology' in order to reverse Britain's economic decline. However, Wilson's modernisation drive was short-lived as it foundered amidst a series of economic difficulties and contradictory political objectives. From the late 1970s, the race to be modern picked up apace, with Mrs Thatcher's Conservative Party this time setting the pace in their attempts to seemingly overhaul the ideas, practices and political-economic settlement of the post-war era. Given the overwhelming electoral hegemony enjoyed by the Thatcher governments throughout the 1980s, the onus to 'keep up' inevitably switched back to Labour, which began its own long 'modernisation' process in the mid-1980s under the leadership of Neil Kinnock, continued under the stewardship of John Smith, before coming to fruition under Tony Blair.

Labour's modernisation imperative involved a number of contradictory pressures. On the one hand, the party had to be seen to have accommodated itself to the new neo-liberal agenda forged by the Thatcher governments and to the demands of a modern and de-regulated globalised economy (Hay, 1999). On the other, it had to demonstrate that it was able to respond to the perceived limitations of the Thatcher project. This entailed an 'upgrade' to the Conservatives' own brand of neo-liberalism in the form of a newly articulated set of 'Third Way' ideas, which attempted to reconcile neo-liberalism with Labour's broader tradition of social democracy (Driver and Martell, 1998). By the mid-1990s, with the Conservatives' project under the premiership of John Major beginning to run out of steam, Labour's ascendancy in the race to appear modern had become electorally overwhelming. New Labour, seemingly responsive to the social divisions created by the Thatcher and Major governments and slicker in its presentation of itself, appeared more attuned to the exigencies of the period and, as such, was able to confidently present a modernisation agenda which expanded far beyond the party arena into almost every aspect of British society. According to Finalyson, Labour's modernisation project was a 'big' project, aimed towards an attempted reinvention of Britain as a whole (2003).

For the Conservatives, the erstwhile modern and seemingly radical agenda laid down by the Thatcher governments, now appeared to be lagging a considerable distance behind the modernising momentum of New Labour. The major problem for the party was its inability to rid itself of the remnants of the Thatcherite legacy; a legacy which had been tarnished by its socially divisive approach, leaving the party wide open to criticisms that it had become intolerant towards a number of vulnerable societal groups, including foreigners, single mothers, same sex couples and ethnic minorities. Despite the attempts of party leaders – William Hague, Ian Duncan Smith and Michael Howard respectively to upgrade the party's brand, the story of the Conservatives' subsequent spell in opposition between 1997 and 2005, was one of failed modernisation (Denham and O'Hara, 2007). It is in this context that David Cameron took over the reins of the party in 2005, promising to finally adapt the party to the challenges of the present age; an achievement which has been met with only partial success, given the party's failure to secure an outright victory in the 2010 general election.

Elsewhere, we have argued that Cameron's modernisation agenda is both multi-dimensional and relatively coherent (Kerr et al, 2011). Broadly speaking, it can be argued to revolve around an attempt, at an ideological level, to present a more electorally friendly variant of the Thatcherite, neo-liberal agenda. This was achieved in opposition through the adoption of 'one nation' and liberal conservative discourse, signalling, on a rhetorical level at least, a return to a more traditional form of Conservative pragmatism (O'Hara, 2007; Dorey, 2007). Coupled with this seeming ideological shift were a number of symbolic gestures – such as a change to the party logo and attempts to reach out to various groups formerly excluded from Conservative Party discourse – aimed at widening the party's electoral appeal. At the level of policy and political strategy, the party has accelerated a trend towards depoliticising various aspects of the political agenda in the hope of increasing its own competence, whilst at the same time decreasing its responsibility, in dealing with a range of social problems contributing towards what it termed in its pre-election campaign strategy as 'broken Britain'. This has allowed the party to roll out newer and more creative forms of neo-liberal governmentality (Kerr et al, 2011). At the level of party change, Cameron's modernisation agenda, in combining depoliticisation with an attempt to narrow the political agenda, has exhibited some elements of what has been seen by some authors as a broader movement towards the 'cartelisation' of political parties (Katz and Mair, 1995).

For Cameron himself, Conservative Party modernisation is a process of upgrading the party to meet the challenges of the present age, and its contours can be mapped out as follows. Our public services are now one whole century out of date. They were designed in the middle of the twentieth century by politicians and civil servants under the influence of the generation which came before them, which took a Bismarckian model of centralised state welfare, and the Fordist model of mass production and mass consumption, as their template. The problem with this is that we now live in a new age – an age which Cameron calls the 'post-bureaucratic age' – in which new technology and the information revolution has made it possible for the state to share information with citizens, and for citizens to have more of a say over the ways in which they are governed (Cameron, 2007e). Although the Labour Party appears to understand this, as far as Cameron's Conservatives are concerned it is part of the party's DNA to look to the state for solutions to most social problems, making it incapable of carrying out the modernisation programme necessary in order to make our public services fit for this post-bureaucratic age (Cameron, 2010d). In Cameron's own words, the Labour Party has 'analogue solution[s] to the problems of a digital age' (Cameron, 2006h), which partly explains for Cameron why New Labour in government failed to achieve its goal of halving child poverty by 2010, why it spent so much on NHS consultants without seemingly improving the quality of service, and why it failed to achieve most of the other goals it set itself while in government. This is also why it was necessary for the Conservative Party to modernise itself; so that it could become a party fit for government in the post-bureaucratic age, and so, given its troubled spell in opposition, that its priorities became aligned with the priorities of the electorate of today, and not of 1979. This narrative, of Labour being hampered by an outdated approach to government, has allowed Cameron's Conservative Party to leapfrog their main competitors in the interminable race to be modern. However, as the result of the 2010 general election clearly demonstrated, the party's ability to lose sight of their opponents has been curtailed to some extent by an overall failure to secure an electoral hegemony around their modernising ambitions (Dorey, 2010).

The utility of modernisation discourses

The above point is important given that the modernisation of the Conservative Party has been primarily about making the Conservative Party electable once again. As noted previously, modernisation is a useful means of distancing Cameron's Conservatives from the Thatcherite inheritance which, due to its association with a socially divisive style of statecraft, became a burden to successive Conservative Party leaders. One only has to look to the experiences of William Hague, Ian Duncan Smith and Michael Howard to grasp the enormity of this burden. Hague was never able to shake off the image of himself as a teenager proselytising for the Thatcherite cause at the 1977 Conservative Party conference – an image which became indelibly etched on the collective psyche of the nation. Although Duncan Smith was initially successful in identifying himself with a more socially compassionate Conservatism, he quickly retreated back into the party's instinct of appealing to a core vote – that is, Thatcherite – strategy. Howard meanwhile found himself persistently associated with the hardest line of Thatcherite authoritarianism thanks to Anne Widdecombe's withering 'something of the night' epithet. During Cameron's spell in opposition, New Labour, being highly attuned to the importance of this kind of symbolic politics, sought to tar Cameron with the same Thatcherite brush, most notably through publicising the now infamous newsreel footage of Cameron at the Treasury on Black Wednesday during his tenure as one of Norman Lamont's key political advisors. Cameron, who was also not blind to the importance of this kind of symbolic politics, sought to prevent this association between himself and the failures of the Thatcher years in the public's mind through a number of statements which sought to draw a deliberate, though admittedly often ambivalent, distance between himself and his predecessor, most notably his oft-cited 'there is such a thing as society, we just don't think it's the same thing as the state' (Cameron, 2007e).

The attempt to throw off the Thatcherite inheritance, at least symbolically, has been one of the major reasons for Conservative Party modernisation, but it is also fair to say that, in a more general sense, throughout the 1990s and early 2000s the Conservatives suffered from being perceived as stuck in the past. In the eyes of many voters they were the 'right' party for the 1980s, capable of tackling the problems that Britain faced in that decade (to the Conservatives – irresponsible trade unionism, an overbearing state, the breakdown of law and order, and so on), but incapable of taking on the problems Britain faced at the turn of the century, to do with creating the infrastructure and education system demanded by globalisation, finding new ways of funding the welfare state in a globalised world and dealing with growing economic and political interdependence, especially in relation to Europe. Conservative Party modernisation can be seen as an attempt to undermine this perception and to portray the Conservatives as the 'right' party for here and now. This explains why the financial crisis, government indebtedness, cuts to public services, environmental problems, 'broken Britain', and so on, are all so important to Cameron; all of these problems, in the eyes of Cameron's Conservatives, require urgent attention and the Labour Party is a spent force, ill-equipped to deal with them. In contrast, Cameron's modernisation of the Conservatives allows the party to claim that it is they who are capable of dealing with these problems, making them the 'right' party for the present.

However, the fact that the appearance of modernisation has some obvious electoral benefits for the Conservative Party does not account for the full importance of this core element of Cameron's broader modernisation project. This is because a number of valuable benefits accrue to any politician that frames his or her politics in terms of modernisation, given some of the unique features of 'modernisation' as an empty signifier. The principle reason why modernisation works well as an empty signifier is related to its polysemous nature. Modernisation is one of those rare political terms which manages to appear to be a credible basis for a governing strategy, but which is also sufficiently vague so as to be able to mean almost anything. It seems to imply the enactment of a definite policy programme, but in actuality commits politicians to very few specific policies at all once they are in government. This has some obvious benefits for a politician like Cameron: by framing his politics in terms of 'modernisation' (or any of its synonyms, such as 'reform' or 'renewal') prior to the recent general election, he guaranteed for himself all the more leeway and flexibility upon becoming Prime Minister. In a similar vein, a second major benefit which accrues to any politician relying on a discourse of modernisation is its highly open-ended nature. For a politician like Cameron, and like Blair before him, a discourse of modernisation is extremely useful in practical political terms due to the fact that modernisation is a moving target. It is something which is never achieved once-and-for-all, but is only ever worked towards – an impossible ideal of sorts. It is something made necessary by globalisation, but because globalisation itself is a never-ending process – a kind of permanent revolution of the global economy and civil society – modernisation, as a response to this, is also a never-ending process. As such, it has no ultimate goal against which politicians can be judged to have either succeeded or failed and it is therefore all the more difficult to properly hold them to account.

Meanwhile, a third major benefit which accrues to politicians espousing a discourse of modernisation is the politically 'neutral' character of modernisation. One of the principal reasons for Blair having based his entire Third Way project around 'modernisation' as an empty signifier was the fact that modernisation came with no political baggage. Although one can relate it back to the Wilson governments of the 1960s and 1970s (Finlayson, 2003), it was nevertheless, in the public's mind, largely free from association with any one position along the left-right political spectrum, whilst still appearing to be a credible basis for a long-term governing strategy. As such, it allowed Blair to broaden the Labour Party's appeal without causing a mass desertion of traditional Labour Party voters, allowing him to form a winning electoral majority. Cameron has adopted the term as a central element of his political discourse for much the same reason. Cameron clearly realised upon winning the leadership of the Conservative Party that if the party was to ever win another general election it would have to appeal to a wider set of political constituencies without losing very many traditional

Conservative voters, and this is precisely what modernisation allowed Cameron to do.

The politically neutral character of 'modernisation' allowed Cameron to, without contradiction and whilst retaining sufficient credibility, retain the support of traditional Conservative Party voters interested in issues such as tax, the regulatory burden on small business and Europe, but also reach out to new constituencies which had never before been considered a natural fit with the Conservative Party, such as voters with environmentalist concerns, single mothers, same-sex couples, voters concerned with corporate 'social responsibility', and so on. If the information revolution and the globalisation of national economies is what leads us to 'the post-bureaucratic age', then modernisation seems to be an imperative. But it is a testament to the flexibility of this discourse that this can therefore be taken to imply that we need to both change our stance towards Europe so that we are much more wary of unnecessarily handing over more powers to what Eurosceptics regard as an excessively bureaucratic European Union *and* focus less on traditionally economistic measures of national success such as GDP and more on the 'quality of life agenda', with its emphasis on GWB (General Well Being) (Cameron, 2006i). Cameronism is full of these kinds of apparently contradictory elements taken from left- and right-wing political discourses, all wrapped up in a discourse of modernisation, and this is one of the principal reasons for the electoral success of Cameron relative to Howard, Duncan-Smith and Hague before him.

A final important benefit accruing to politicians such as Cameron who espouse a discourse of modernisation is related to the fact that 'modernisation' depoliticises the issue of party change. Modernisation discourse serves to depoliticise the wholesale transformation of Conservative Party policy and philosophy necessary in order to be able to appeal to a sufficiently wide spectrum of voters to win a general election. This is because, within a discourse of modernisation, there is no right or wrong, just or unjust; there is only that which is modern, and that which is outdated, and among that which is deemed modern, there are no incompatibilities. This kind of major transformation of an established political party is difficult to achieve if it has to be justified to the party at large, and to the voters who have traditionally aligned themselves with that party. However, modernisation serves to obviate the need to justify this transformation. Modernisation is not something we do because it is right. It is something we do because it is necessary and, as such, ethical considerations are of only secondary importance. Change has to happen, and to resist change – to go against modernisation – is to ally oneself with outdated modes of thinking. Whereas Blair often utilised this discourse and this line of reasoning to avoid having to justify the Third Way and the transformation of the Labour Party into New Labour, and in order to take the politics out of effectively abandoning social democracy (much of the non-academic discussion of the

Third Way simply focused on the necessity of the Third Way, not its merits), Cameron seems to use the same modernisation discourse to broaden the net – to conjoin traditional Conservative policy and philosophy with a variety of new elements in the formation of a viable and winning electoral strategy.

Cameron's neo-liberal modernisation

All of this accounts for the importance of 'modernisation' in hegemonic terms, as an empty signifier, but another way of looking at Conservative Party modernisation is to conceive of it in Foucauldian terms as a new stage in the unfolding of forms of neo-liberal governmentality (Kerr et al, 2011). Looked at in this way, Cameronism is an experiment in government which, in the first instance, consists of a range of elements borrowed from the Blairite form of neo-liberalism which preceded it (McAnulla, 2010), some of which have remained fully intact, and some of which have been transformed, often in quite radical ways, so that they serve new purposes and fit with Cameron's broader governing strategy; and in the second, a range of novel elements which represent Cameron's unique contribution to the project of neo-liberal governmentality. There are at least three key elements in Cameronite neo-liberalism. The first and most crucial element, and the one which is the most novel and distinctive, is the Big Society.

The Big Society

The Big Society is really what distinguishes Cameron's form of neo-liberalism from the Blairite form which has been dominant since the late 1990s. According to the official narrative provided by Cameron, the Big Society is about giving power to the people. It is about getting rid of the old ways of doing things, taking power away from politicians, and having the state step back so that the problems we face as a society can be tackled from the ground up by those best equipped to deal with them – namely, ordinary people. It is about fixing 'broken Britain' not by means of the 'inhuman, monolithic and clumsy' state, but by means of the hard work of ordinary people, working in friendly cooperation with one another to create a society in which people feel empowered, and in which many of the worst social problems we face cease to be problems any longer (Cameron, 2010d). Cameron aims to achieve this by promoting 'social action', which he defines as ordinary people 'giving their time, effort, even money, to causes around them' which benefit their community (Cameron, 2010e). However, disregarding the official narrative, we can say that the Big Society amounts to an attempt to inaugurate a more cost effective, stable and decentralised form of neo-liberalism in which control over the everyday activities of citizens is still maintained by the centre, but at a greater distance, and with less culpability when things go wrong. The Big Society is the centrepiece of a more cost-effective form of neo-liberal government because, although it holds out the possibility of many of the same goals which were important in Blairite and other previous forms of neo-liberalism being met, such as for example the provision of a range of social services, if the Big Society can be made to work in its ideal form, then the state is no longer primarily responsible for ensuring that these services are provided nor is its role to ensure that they are run in a socially responsible manner. The state's only responsibility is to step back; to let the agents of the Big Society do what they do best, which is to create the Big Society. Meanwhile, it also serves to insulate the central state from certain difficult-to-deal-with political pressures.

As things stand, in those areas in which the Big Society is due to take over from the big state, the central state is still culpable if things go wrong. If budgets are exceeded the state runs the risk of being seen by the electorate as profligate – carefree spenders of the taxpayers' money. If the quality of service provided does not meet the expectations of the consumers of these services the state risks being viewed as incompetent – incapable of properly managing its own affairs. However, if the state makes way for the Big Society then if things go wrong in these and other similar ways then the culpable party is none other than the people themselves, given that the Big Society is supposedly people power in action, and that the roll-out of the Big Society amounts to nothing more than the simple empowerment of individuals and communities.

Freedom of information

The second major plank of Cameron's governing strategy amounts to a co-optation and transformation of the Blairite discourse of 'freedom of information'. This discourse formed an important part of Blairism. On the one hand, it was simply one mechanism among many of ensuring better performance against the targets set by the central state for public sector workers as part of a modernised public service. In this regard, it can been seen as one of the drivers of the New Public Management, along with elements such as performance-related pay, incentive structures for public sector workers and regular auditing of departmental budgets. On the other hand, 'freedom of information' was also about empowering citizens. The centrepiece of the Freedom of Information Act 2000 was to enshrine the right for individual citizens to request information from any public body and to require public bodies to service these requests, in all but a handful of exceptional cases, at a minimal cost and in as timely a manner as possible. This is not how freedom of information works in Cameronism.

In his public speeches, Cameron talks about freedom of information in much the same way as Blair did: it is about creating a more open and less secretive form of government, and about recognising the fact that we now live in the 'information age', in which individual citizens are now not only much more demanding than they previously were, but also much more knowledgeable, thanks to the revolutionising power of the internet. However, the key difference in practical terms is that, whereas Blair sought to empower people, Cameron seeks to empower people *to do certain things*. For Blair, it was enough that people were given these new rights in relation to disclosure of sensitive information by public bodies. Cameron, meanwhile, has recognised the potential importance of freedom of information as a neo-liberal technology of government, and one which promises to allow for a more frugal and also more manageable form of neo-liberal government. This much is evident from even a cursory glance at the policing reforms Cameron has proposed in a number of his recent speeches. He has proposed divesting the central state of some of its responsibilities in relation to the regulatory oversight of the police force, but in such a way as to ensure that the goals it has set itself in relation to policing are still met, by publishing – under the guise of 'freedom of information' – statistics on the performance of local police forces, and by requiring representatives of those police forces to attend regular meetings of residents' associations and community groups to defend their performance (Conservative Party, 2010). The goal is still to meet targets in relation to reducing rates of a variety of crimes – from anti-social behaviour to burglary to violent crimes – but the mechanism for achieving reductions in these rates is no longer some kind of state-based regulatory framework. Rather, it is these regular meetings of community groups, in which the representatives of local police forces will undoubtedly be lambasted by those they are supposed to be serving if they fail to improve the quality of policing at the local level.

This is why it is more cost effective and also less politically troublesome for the central state. The responsibility for improving this service now rests with local residents themselves. 'Freedom of information' has effectively turned these local residents into disciplinary agents of neo-liberal control. Importantly, Cameron has proposed making similar reforms in other areas of government policy, including the education system (Cameron, 2009f) and the NHS (Cameron, 2009d), describing them as part of a shift from 'bureaucratic accountability to democratic accountability' (Cameron, 2009e). Also as part of this shift, and under the 'People's Right to Know' plan, Cameron has proposed publishing online details of every item of public spending over £25,000 and every public sector salary over £150,000 (Cameron, 2009d). Cameron describes this as 'a democratic check on wasteful spending' by government. What it amounts to is the co-optation of the Blairite discourse of freedom of information, and its reorientation in a Thatcherite direction. Effectively, what Cameron has done is to take the empowering capacity of Blairite freedom of information reforms and to transform them so that they 'empower' people to behave in ways which serve Conservative ends.

Depoliticisation

The third plank of Cameron's overarching governing strategy is another one which has been snatched from Blairite neo-liberalism, but in contrast to the treatment given to the discourse of 'freedom of information' after its appropriation by Cameron, this element has been preserved largely intact, and performs much the same function within Cameronism as it did within the New Labour project. This is depoliticisation. Burnham describes depoliticisation as 'the process of placing at one remove the political character of decision-making' and argues that the process is, besides being part of an effort to make government policy more credible to internationally mobile capital, designed primarily to shield government from the potentially hazardous consequences of unpopular policies (Burnham, 2001: 128). In a broader sense, depoliticisation can be understood in historical terms as a reaction to and an attempt to deal with what, in post-war America, became known as 'democratic overload' – a process in which the nation-state is argued to have become burdened with so many new responsibilities thanks to the lobbying efforts of a wide variety of interests groups which formed in the immediate post-war period that fulfilling all of them became an impossibility. In other words, a process in which '[t]he vitality of democracy in the 1960s raised questions about the *governability* of democracy in the 1970s' and subsequent decades (Crozier et al, 1975: 64).

Cameron, like Blair before him, can be seen as an agent of the reaction to this supposed democratic overload. Blair's most notable initiative in this regard was, of course, his 1997 decision to grant the Bank of England operational autonomy in the setting of interest rates. The most noteworthy initiative launched by Cameron thus far, and his most significant contribution to this longer-term historical trend towards depoliticisation to date, is the setting-up of the Office for Budget Responsibility (OBR) as part of the passing of the Budget Responsibility and National Audit Act 2011. The express purpose of the setting-up of the OBR was to provide an 'independent and authoritative' assessment of the likelihood of the government meeting its spending targets over the short and medium term. More specifically, the twofold goal is to balance the 'cyclically-adjusted current budget' five years ahead and to ensure that public sector debt is falling by the 2015–2016 financial year (Great Britain, 2011). This is evidently a continuation and, more importantly, institutionalisation of the line of policy first established with the setting-out of the so-called 'golden rules of fiscal policy' by Gordon Brown early on in his tenure as Chancellor (namely, that over the economic cycle the government should only borrow to invest and not to fund current spending, and that public sector debt should never exceed 40 per cent of GDP). As such, the OBR ought to be seen as Cameron's central bank independence moment, but for fiscal policy. Perhaps somewhat ironically, Cameron, once again like Blair before him, often frames this type of depoliticising initiative, which aims to take ever wider spheres of government policy out of the political realm and hand them over to groups of experts to decide, in terms of 'giving power back to the people' (Cameron, 2009g).

Potential problems for Cameron's modernisation agenda

However, if these are the general contours of a novel, neo-liberal governmental project, it is far from assured that Cameronism will be a success, or even last very long at all beyond the short term as a coherent form of statecraft. This is because there are a number of potential fundamental problems or contradictions built into the project which Cameron shows no signs of being able to adequately deal with. The most crucial of these problems relates to the centrepiece of the whole Cameronite enterprise: namely, the Big Society or, more accurately, the notion of 'social action'. Social action is a particularly problematic aspect of Cameronism due to the fact that, whilst the whole enterprise is entirely dependant upon it in the sense that the Big Society simply cannot function if people do not engage in social action in sufficiently large numbers to make a difference, the only means Cameron appears to have of ensuring that levels of social action do increase is exhortation – simply asking people to do more in their local communities so that the state can pull back. On the one hand, Cameron has stated numerous times in public speeches that the Big Society is about more than just the roll-back of the state, and that if it is to succeed the state will have to do more than to just ask people to take part in social action (Cameron, 2009f). However, on the other hand, in practice, Cameron has little else besides simple exhortation in place as a strategy to see that the Big Society does become a reality.

This is of such crucial importance because of the fact that so many of the initiatives Cameron has launched in government, or which he plans to launch within this parliament, are dependent upon social action. A notable example again, is the proposed reforms to policing discussed earlier. How are they supposed to work if, when they are put in place, nobody attends the regular meetings of the community groups designed to allow local residents to hold their local police force to account? What is more, how are they supposed to work even if local residents do attend, but fail to prosecute the representatives of their local police force in the manner expected of them by the central state, perhaps instead forming an alliance with their local police force against the neo-liberal re-organisation of the state apparatus by Cameron and his coalition partners?

Whilst it is true that Cameron has furnished a number of new identities or subject positions, the most notable of which are the 'social entrepreneur' (Cameron, 2009d) and the 'community activist' (Cameron, 2009f) – the Cameronite equivalents of Thatcher's 'business entrepreneurs' and Blair's 'life-long learners' – designed to encourage social action, and which if taken up in sufficiently large numbers could potentially serve to help make the Big Society a reality, it is unlikely that these subject positions – these new ways of being in the world – will prove popular enough to have any lasting effect given that Cameronite neo-liberalism lacks the widespread intellectual and cultural support enjoyed by the Thatcherite and Blairite forms of neo-liberalism which preceded it. In these latter two cases the ideas which underpinned the governing strategy by-and-large came from academia, the popular media and other parts of civil society such as independent think-tanks and research institutes. In Cameronite neo-liberalism the ideas have came almost exclusively from the centre – from Cameron's own speech writers and from Conservative Party-funded research – and they have not been taken very seriously almost anywhere else. In this regard, at the very least what the whole Big Society enterprise is likely to prove is the inadequacy of centralised reform of systems of neo-liberal governmentality.

What is more, the only other elements of the broader Big Society strategy set out by Cameron thus far – including the Big Society Bank, funded from unclaimed financial assets and designed to provide finance to groups willing to help promote or engage in social action (Cameron, 2010e); the National Citizen Service, a kind of Big Society 'boot camp' for young people, where they can 'learn what it means to be socially responsible' (Cameron, 2010d); the cooperatisation and mutualisation of some public services in an effort to give public sector workers a greater sense of ownership of the services they run (Conservative Party, 2010); and, more controversially, the prioritisation of research on the Big Society in the allocation of research council funding in UK higher education (Boffey, 2011b) – are unlikely to change this fact. Unlike Blair and even Thatcher before him, Cameron has seemingly displayed a lack of understanding of the fact that, first and foremost, every political reformer must work within the structural constraints he or she encounters upon entering office, and that it is very difficult, if not impossible, to re-organise an entire system of government from the centre according to one leader's whims; but he has also displayed a lack of understanding of the fact that many of these neo-liberal technologies of government – the Big Society, social action, freedom of information, depoliticisation, and so on – can only work if accompanied by what Foucault describes as a suitable 'politics of life', which furnishes citizens with a range of proclivities that are functional to his preferred brand of neo-liberalism (Foucault, 2008: 148). In other words, Cameron has potentially made the mistake of overlooking the need to change the context in which these novel technologies of government are to be embedded before actually embedding them.

As such, it is arguable that what Conservative modernisation in the medium to long term is likely to amount to is not much more than a re-branded form of Blairite neo-liberalism, with a few relatively minor additions and subtractions on the fringes, as the unworkable aspects of the Cameronite enterprise fall by the wayside. This implies an eventual return to a more statist and bureaucratic form of neo-liberalism based around a mixture of public sector reforms which entail further artificial marketisation, the expansion of a Blairite discourse of 'freedom of information', shorn of the more radical inflections it has thus far been given by Cameron, and the depoliticisation of even more areas of government policy, along the lines of the OBR and its New Labour precursors.

Conclusion

At the time of writing, and with the Conservative-Liberal Democrat coalition in only its second year of government, any speculation on the precise nature of the government's agenda, or indeed, its potential future prospects, is wrought with danger. What we have referred to here and elsewhere as 'Cameronism' may well prove to be a very short-lived and failed experiment in government. However, what does seem largely indisputable is that David Cameron's leadership of the Conservative Party has already contributed what is likely to be significant new twists to ongoing debates about the role, size and purpose of the state in the UK. Despite largely working within the parameters of the trajectory set by the Thatcher and Blair governments, Cameron has proved to be quite entrepreneurial in his modernisation and renewal of the neo-liberal project that has dominated the British political landscape for the past three decades. In so doing, he has set out new definitions of what a 'modern', 'fit-for-purpose' public sector should look like and what the role of government should be in relation to its citizenry. In this chapter, we have remained sceptical about the future prospects for David Cameron's modernising agenda and attempted to highlight at least some of its potential limitations. However, given that 'modernisation' remains and always will be an impossible ideal, the success of the Conservatives' strategy is unlikely to ultimately be measured in terms of quantifiable outcomes, but rather in its ability, as it was always intended to do, to win elections and keep the party in power.

3
The Conservative Election Campaign

David Seawright

Introduction

Well before the constituency declarations were complete for the 2010 general election, the Conservative Party realised that it had not done enough in order to govern alone. In effect the party came so agonisingly close, falling short of that overall target of 326 House of Commons seats by just 19. Indeed, one analysis established that just 16,000 extra votes, of the 29.7 million cast, distributed in the 19 constituency seats where the Conservatives had come closest to winning, would have secured the outright victory the party had so desired since it last won at Westminster in 1992 (Rallings and Thrasher, 2010). One has no difficulty in applying a positive gloss to the actual result, with the Conservatives obtaining a 4 per cent swing and a net gain of 97 seats, as undoubtedly the party had faced a psephological mountain, the size of which no other Conservative leader had overcome since the 1931 general election. However, much of the shine is lost when we consider the context of the 2010 election. In Gordon Brown Britain had one of the most disliked Labour Party Prime Ministers of all time and with the nation in the depth of an economic crisis the Conservative Party had the opportunity to exploit and utilise that most potent of campaign slogans: 'time for a change'. In a survey just weeks before the election was announced 68 per cent thought Britain needed a new government and prime minister. Unfortunately, throughout the campaign the Conservatives would never see this level of opinion translated directly into support for them or their leader David Cameron. There may have been only 19 per cent who thought Gordon Brown, and 11 per cent Nick Clegg, was 'campaigning best for the vote of people like you' but at 39 per cent the figure for David Cameron neatly illustrates the gap between the support for the Conservatives and that overall desire for change (Glover, 2010).

The very essence of the work of the political strategist (or if preferred spin doctor) is to construct the theme and slogans which effectively tap into and exploit such opinion as that desire for change; and quite often the more emotionally charged the better. Not for them the generally held colloquialism of 'familiarity breads contempt', in the sense that the taken for granted degenerates quickly into disregard. For the strategist 'familiarity breads favourability', through the essential political communication implements of repetition and consistency the developed theme and slogans of a campaign are successful if they are heavily symbolic of the national mood; surfacing what is already in the voter's mind, inviting them into an act of participation with the party or candidate (O'Shaughnessy, 2005: 911; Schwartz, 1974: 92–7). But, this chapter will show that similar to the election of 2005 the Conservative Party lacked definition in relation to the organised core meaning of its campaign and its theme and slogans (see O'Shaughnessy, 2005: 909–10). With regards to the 'message', a successful campaign creates clarity not confusion in the minds of the voters but unfortunately for the Conservative Party, the party activists and even parliamentary candidates appeared just as confused as the voter in 2010. Criticism from within the party was aimed at David Cameron's over reliance on a small core of advisers, 'an inner circle' which included: George Osborne, the shadow Chancellor who was in charge of the overall campaign; Steve Hilton, the director of strategy; Andy Coulson, the director of communications; Oliver Letwin, the party's policy chief; Michael Gove, the shadow education secretary and Ed Llewellyn, Cameron's chief of staff. There was also Lord Ashcroft, who had poured money into the marginal seats strategy, which looked to be working well with candidates in these seats having a considerable advantage in resources well before the election was even called. However, there was the question over Lord Ashcroft's tax status, was he or not a non-domiciled tax payer (a non-dom)? With a seat in the Lords, Ashcroft was to become the story, with a string of shadow ministers appearing embarrassingly to have no knowledge of his tax status; before William Hague confessed to having been in possession of such knowledge for 'some months' (Curtis et al, 2010; Snowdon, 2010: 393–4). Such ambiguity and garbled communication would be indicative of the campaign overall and a matter of weeks before the election was called it was reported in *The Times* that a number of Conservative MPs were describing the ideas underpinning the core message as 'over-complicated' or 'pretty uninspiring' and while criticising the 'control freakery' of Cameron's inner circle they also held the belief that 'you could have got colleagues to sit down and come up with something much simpler' (Coates, 2010). Similarly, by the end of the campaign the internal party verdict was one of 'what a mess' (Kite, 2010).

Thus, this chapter explores the lack of coherence and the inconsistency in the 'core meaning' of the 2010 Conservative Party campaign and in particular with that of the 'Big Society' theme. Such muddle would lead subsequently to the party losing control of its own agenda and the need to construct an impromptu strategy to address and counter the expected outcome of a 'hung parliament'. It also notes the exaggerated exposure of David

Cameron in the campaign, adding further weight to the candidate centric personalisation of politics thesis for the UK (Seawright, forthcoming). But, first the Prime Ministerial debates are examined, as they were to engulf all other aspects of the campaign, to the extent that it would not be an exaggeration to view them as *the* campaign. Undoubtedly, in such debates the party's message is presented through the public face of its leader and the first ever occasion of presidential type television debates in Britain quite obviously strengthens the argument for 'presidentialisation' but importantly they were to also contribute considerably to the effective derailment of the Conservative Party's campaign strategy.

Speak to the 'Great Ignored' Dave

Each and every UK general election of the television age has had a concomitant clamour for a US style Presidential leader debate. These appeals have been mainly from the broadcasters themselves but importantly the party who was trailing badly in the polls usually followed with one of their own. The reason such Prime Ministerial debates had failed to occur hitherto owed less to the argument that they were 'the epitome of Americanisation' than to the strategic calculation that no one in the lead in the opinion polls would be foolish enough to jeopardise it. For example, in 1979 when Jim Callaghan's acceptance of the broadcaster's offer for a debate was leaked, Gordon Reece, Mrs Thatcher's communications director, saw far too much risk in such an 'uncontrolled television appearance' and he also worried that the election would become far too focused on a single event. Thus, Mrs Thatcher was encouraged to reply with an outright rejection to the invitation: 'We should continue with the traditional broadcasting arrangements. ... Personally I believe that issues and policies not personalities decide elections. We are not electing a president' (Cockerell et al, 1984: 193–4). Similarly when Tony Blair was challenged by John Major to a debate, Alistair Campbell believed that New Labour would gain very little from it so he moved to kill the idea off while laying the blame at the door of the Tories for scuppering it (Campbell and Stott, 2007: 161, 167).

In light of the 2010 experience, Gordon Reece was right to be circumspect about such televised debates as the election did become far too focused on the broadcast events of 15, 22 and 29 April. As Dominic Wring rightly observed, once the parties had agreed to the debates the 'UK General Election of 2010 was always going to be a different kind of campaign' (Wring, 2011: 1). The ink was barely dry on the historic 76 point deal between the parties and the broadcasters when it was revealed that the Conservatives would be seeking the advice of Bill Knapp and Anita Dunn of the Washington-based political consultancy 'Squier, Knapp, Dunn Communications' to help Cameron with his preparation. Intriguingly, the Conservatives did not turn to an agency with Republican party sympathies as both Knapp and Dunn had a long history of aiding the Democrats and both had worked on the Obama campaign; where they had 'de-poshed' the Harvard educated Obama and enhanced his appeal to middle and working class women voters. The Conservatives were hoping that a similar trick could be performed for their Eton educated leader. Moreover, just as Dunn had persuaded Obama to project the role of his wife Michelle, so that women saw it was an equal marriage, it was also hoped that this could be emulated by Cameron with his wife Samantha (Seawright, forthcoming). Very rarely do such American consultants have to worry about third party candidates but one consequence of the first British debates would be the electrification of the Liberal Democrat, and in particular Nick Clegg's, campaign; which would make the defeat of Gordon Brown and Labour all the more difficult on election day. On the day of the first debate, Benedict Brogan was to correctly identify the inherent danger in giving such a platform to Nick Clegg and with it such a fillip to the third party campaign. Clegg it was assumed would portray himself as the representative of a 'new politics' exploiting the national mood of anger over the parliamentary expenses scandal with references to the culpability of the 'old parties', along with a seductive call to punish those politicians by giving no one overall power (Brogan, 2010a); and Clegg grasped the opportunity with alacrity.

In his opening statement to the first debate David Cameron offered an unequivocal apology for the expenses scandal and 'delivered hard lines on immigration and crime' but quite simply Cameron's message was to be drowned out by the media euphoria on the performance of Clegg. *The Times* reported that: 'Within minutes, 61 per cent of voters said he had won the night compared with 22 per cent for David Cameron and 17 per cent for Gordon Brown' (Watson, 2010). By the following weekend this media ebullience had reached such a crescendo that the *Sunday Times* claimed Clegg was nearly as popular as Churchill was at the end of the Second World War. Churchill had an 83 per cent approval rating then; by contrast Clegg had an almost unprecedented post-war approval rating of 72 per cent, compared to Cameron on 19 per cent and Brown on minus 18 per cent. More poignantly for the Tories, the electorate appeared to acquiesce in the invitation by the Liberal Democrats to participate in that seductive call for no overall power, with 53 per cent of respondents in the same survey saying that 'a hung parliament with the Lib Dems holding the balance of power would be a "good thing"' (Oliver and Smith, 2010). Notwithstanding the hired 'Washington expertise', there was to be no Obama magic for Cameron, the 'game changer' was to be one of Clegg appropriating the epithet of 'change candidate'; the very goal sought by Cameron and the Conservatives. And, although he was a former television industry communications professional, it was to be the very basics of TV presentation that would let Cameron down. Anita Dunn had told Cameron to 'project stability' by a 'forward looking gaze' (Owen and Lowther, 2010) but his bizarre 'statuesque pose' prior to the beginning of the first debate, which had him seemingly take a sweeping view of an imagined horizon had more in common with a Monty Python's sketch than the statesmanlike mien it was meant to represent. And, unlike Clegg he forgot to speak to the camera, which to the audience of millions at home gave the impression that they were indeed the 'great ignored'.

What became known as 'Cleggmania' would engross the rest of the campaign with the Conservative strategists now in reaction mode rather than successfully setting the agenda of the campaign. 'A week into the Nick Clegg phenomenon, Cameron's campaign pitch for the final fortnight was now refracted through the rise and rise of the man who was never supposed to be blocking his path to power' (Harding and Watson, 2010). In the second of the TV debates on 22 April, both Cameron and Clegg were reported as performing strongly in a much more adversarial debate; and seemingly dependent upon which party the newspaper endorsed, either Cameron just 'nicked it' (*The Times*, 23 April) or Clegg 'scored a narrow victory' (*The Guardian*, 23 April). There was no doubt that this was a much more assured performance by Cameron and he certainly did not forget to 'speak to the camera' while attempting to seize back the mantle of change from Clegg. But, undoubtedly from then on the narrative for the media was to be one of a 'hung parliament' and to which party Clegg would offer his support in a coalition government. The third and final debate of 29 April similarly threw up reports of Cameron and Clegg being 'neck and neck' in the debate polls and interestingly just days after the debates had come to a close the surge in support for the Liberal Democrats in the country had begun to ebb (Hennessy, 2010).

It must be said that Cameron had for some time championed the idea of the leaders' debates and was on record as saying: 'I've been pushing for two years for this to happen. I think debates can help enliven our democracy, help answer people's questions and help crystallise the debate about change this country needs' (Webster and Foster, 2010). However, such a view regarding the virtuous democratic components of TV debates is far from being an uncontested one. For example, it is argued that an aspect of the increasing personalisation of politics – and the debates undoubtedly reinforce such a trend, as evidenced by the American experience – can minimise the anchorage traditionally provided by the political parties, without which it is argued there can be no organised and coherent politics. And, moreover, it is also argued that substantive ideas must be trimmed in order to fit the Procrustean demands of television time limits (Jamieson and Birdsell, 1988: 163, 178). The Conservative commentator Charles Moore echoed such a cautionary note with regards to Britain: believing the 'three powers', the BBC, ITV and Sky, would set the agenda of the campaign in the sense that coverage would be set around their Thursday night broadcasts; and that the debates had not extended popular power as they had narrowed the field of argument turning 'the whole campaign into the quest for one thing (in three bits) – victory in a game show' (Moore, 2010). Brown's frustration was clear when he likened Clegg's performance in the debates to that of a TV games show host. This concern shown with the leader debates having resonances with such popular game shows as: 'The X-Factor'; 'Strictly Come Dancing' or 'Britain's Got Talent' should not have come as a surprise either, as just after the first US Presidential debate in 1960, Daniel Boorstin developed his conceptual construct of the 'pseudo-event' to explain such elaborately contrived situations. He believed the application of the 'quiz show format' to the so-called 'Great Debates' reduced great national issues to trivial dimensions and thus the debates were 'a clinical example of the pseudo-event, of how it is made, why it appeals, and of its consequences for democracy in America' (Boorstin, 1992: 41).

So why on earth did Cameron agree to undertake such a high risk strategy and more importantly the question may be asked of why he was allowed to by his advisers? After all, as Alistair Campbell has so clearly illustrated it is always possible to propose conditions with which to stall negotiations without being seen as the one scuppering them (Campbell and Stott, 2007: 161, 167). Cameron did concede that he underperformed in the earlier debates and that he wrongly treated them as if they were like one of his 'Cameron Direct' public meetings: 'there is a certain amount of artifice in them [that] you have to understand. It is not town hall debates which I sort of thought they were' (Oliver, 2010b). In a direct response to the reported internal party criticism that he and his key aides were at fault in giving the Liberal Democrats a massive strategic advantage, Cameron denied he had been naïve as he 'always knew that if you do debates you are going to give them a massive platform but I always thought it was worthwhile' (Elliot et al, 2010). Conversely, one 'insider account' of Cameron's 'inner circle' reported that despite the concerns it seemed that 'there was little discussion about how to deal with a strong performance from the Liberal Democrat leader' (Snowdon, 2010: 401). Importantly, many a Conservative failed to see the virtue in such trouble and effort and placed the decision to participate in the debates squarely at the door of Andy Coulson, the director of communications. Although an ex *News of the World* editor he still had close links to Murdoch and to *News International* and it is instructive that it was Sky who was the most proactive and belligerent in their advocacy of the debates; to the extent that in the same month that the *Sun* came out for Cameron, the head of Sky News threatened to set a date and time and let the cameras role on three empty chairs, if need be (Ryley, 2009). Just prior to the election being called Cameron praised such conduct: 'Well done to Sky, you held everyone's feet to the fire' (Sky News, April 2010).

However, the putative in depth analysis of the issues as offered by the leadership debates began to be swiftly questioned. For example, the day after the third and final debate the leader column of *The Times* opined: 'The television debates have been a great innovation but, granted the opportunity of an hour and a half to specify where spending cuts will come, all three pretenders to the office of the prime minister preferred not to say' (30 April 2010). The 'Elephant in the room' was undoubtedly the issue of the economy but again no one should have been surprised by the lack of specificity on the issue in the debates as experience in America had shown by 'requiring brief responses, and spreading discussions across a smorgasbord of topics, televised presidential debates sacrifice much of their power to educate the voters about the substance of issues' (Jamieson and Birdsell, 1988: 15). Thus, through the medium of the leaders' debates the voter would not be educated on the Conservative Party's theme and slogans, in particular on its 'big idea of the Big Society' – even if it were ever to get an airing in them – but in the next section we turn our attention to why it was highly unlikely in the first place that such 'an education' would ever take place.

Not big on the 'Big Society'

After three successive electoral defeats since 1992, and four leaders in that time, David Cameron appeared to be successfully addressing the crucial issue of party transformation and self-renewal. The Conservatives under Cameron asserted that they had made significant progress in decontaminating 'the brand'; utilising a number of interlaced themes of 'compassionate conservatism', 'progressive ends-conservative means' and 'social responsibility' in order to negate an image of it as the 'nasty' and 'singularly economics' party. Of course, there would be mistakes along the way, the 'the heir to Blair' claim and the appeals on the environment and crime that were parodied as 'hugging trees, huskies and even "hoodies"' (Seawright, 2010: 173). Part of the ideological claim of the Conservative Party is that it draws from the well of British tradition in order to safeguard personal freedom. In this context the 'Big Society-Not Big Government' theme worked perfectly well for the party's internal philosophical debate, which is crucial for its self-renewal and transformation, as it addressed the perennial fundamental discussion in the party concerning the relationship of the state to the individual and the optimum level of state intervention under a Conservative government (Seawright, 2010). But internal policy debates do not necessarily translate into core election messages that can give clarity of argument to the mass electorate. Powell identified, as early as 1959, what he termed the 'categorical imperative', the *sine qua non* for opposition success. 'There must be a great, simple, central theme, branching into all fields and subjects of debate, but in itself easily grasped, which runs through the words and actions of a successful opposition' (Powell, 1959: 340–1). But, as we shall see, in 2010 the central theme of the Conservative opposition would be anything but easily grasped.

It was the week of the manifesto launch when, in reality, we saw the elevation to prominence of the 'Big Society' theme. It was utilised by

Cameron in his Hugo Young memorial lecture in November 2009 but one party insider clearly identified the problem with its use in the campaign: 'To jump from one lecture in the autumn to the manifesto launch in April without it entering public consciousness much in between was asking a lot from the majority of voters' (Snowdon, 2010: 399). And, such 'concern was reinforced by polling that showed that even those voters who did not think it was simply a code for shrinking the welfare state were not sure what it meant' (Bale and Webb, 2011: 55). Thus, this was not to be the core message that could offer meaning to the campaign. As an election slogan many Conservatives on the stump found it to be woolly and lacking that very clarity of meaning that was to be the desideratum of the campaign. As one senior Conservative MP put it:

> Instead of this complete crap about Big Society we should have had a series of simple messages on crime, immigration, hospitals, schools, to repeat over and over again like Labour had with its pledge cards under Blair. If we had some clear themes we would have won a majority (Helm, 2010).

'Big Society-Not Big Government', as an election slogan, was unlikely to surface what was in the voters' minds and would not be symbolic of the national mood in the way, for instance, that 'Labour isn't working' was in 1979. *The Times* also warned of the dangers of the electorate not accepting such messages, as people were not used to being addressed in such a way and thus may see the whole thing as a gimmick: 'Not everyone will feel inclined to take up Mr Cameron's *Invitation To Join The* Government' (14 April 2010). This warning encapsulated the problem with the Conservatives 'core message'; quite simply, there wasn't one. Indeed, in that same edition of *The Times* we find a poll which showed that voters were confused over pledges; wrongly identifying as much as half of pledges with the party proposing them (ibid). Thus, if familiarity is to breed favourability it is essential that the message is consistent to allow for repetition, as it is hard 'to repeat over and over again' different slogans. The Manifesto itself gave just three pages to the ideas of the 'Big Society' (Conservative Party, 2010). But, as its title makes clear it also gave an *Invitation to Join the Government of Britain* and to confuse matters further, the slogan used for the image which would launch the manifesto at Battersea power station was: *We're all in this together*; which was an earlier theme for addressing the need for retrenchment in face of the economic crisis. Even earlier it had been: *We Can't Go On Like This*, then it was a nod to *Co-operatives* and with echoes of the 'Contract with America' a la Newt Gingrich, Mr Cameron, on the last day of April, unveiled and signed: *A contract between the Conservative Party and you*. *The Observer* mocked that even the Conservative bus displayed the Tory nerves, with time running out 'the proud slogan' on the side of the bus had changed from *Time For Change* to *Contract For Change* (McCrum, 2010). 'The Contract' was developed in urgent response to the first televised debate 'to crystallise the Conservative message' (Ashcroft, 2010: 69). But, rather than demonstrate consolidation it merely signposted the incoherent and fragmentary nature of the campaign. Moreover, with the disaster of the first TV debate in mind, as outlined above, we should note that on the day the election was called Cameron introduced the theme of the *Great Ignored* but as this plunged quicker than the proverbial runaway escalator it was to be quietly ignored itself. Is it any wonder then that voters would be confused in their reasoning with which party to give *A Vote For Change*?

Here then is evidence for a lack of coherence in the message which is of course the prerequisite for the repetition and consistency mantra of the successful election strategy but such muddle stretched to the organisational composition of the 'inner circle' itself. In March, in response to the almost universal lampooning of the 'We can't go on like this – airbrushed poster', which was placed in over a thousand sites costing nearly £400,000, the party turned back to M&C Saatchi for a more robust approach from an agency with the motto of 'brutal simplicity of thought' (Burgess, 2011: 187). Lord Tim Bell, who led the original Saatchi and Saatchi advertising team of 1979, described the poster as' rubbish'. Steve Hilton had conceived and designed the poster himself (Snowdon, 2010: 386) knocking up the 'airbrushed poster' on his laptop after discarding numerous proposals from the Euro RSCG agency (ibid). The Euro RSCG agency had been awarded the Conservatives' advertising contract in 2007 and would have been known to Coulson through its previous work for the *News of the World* (Burgess, 2011: 182). Steve Hilton was also identified as being the person behind the 'wackier elements of the party's rebranding, including the notorious "hug a hoodie" speech' (Oliver, 2010a). The indictment of crafting a message which failed to connect with voters is bad enough but more worryingly is the claim for little or no research on the 'Big Society' theme:

> Behind-the-scenes anecdotes are starting to emerge. One records how Bill Knapp, the US political consultant hired to help Cameron, had a simple question on the eve of the vital second television debate. What research had been done into what voters thought of the Tory campaign's key theme of the Big Society? The answer was an embarrassed silence. When results from a hurriedly convened focus group detailed a negative reaction at a subsequent meeting, Mr Hilton is said to have stormed out (Elliot and Watson, 2010; and see Snowdon, 2010: 400).

A clear coherent message required a consistent strategic approach from a coherent organised team but we find a 'party insider' identifying the problem as: 'It is not that we have two agencies, it is that there are none, and it is just Steve' (Coates et al, 2010).

Conclusion: The hung parliament party

There were times in 2009 when the Conservatives were registering leads of over 20 points in the opinion polls. But mixed messages on the economic crisis, of the level of retrenchment required in 'an age of austerity' – at the times of course when they were not denying retrenchment (Bale and Webb, 2011: 52) – and the concomitant fiasco over Cameron's 'cast iron guarantee' of a referendum on the Lisbon treaty were no doubt responsible in large part for the considerable reduction in support for the party. However, by the beginning of the campaign there was still an air of optimism that the single figure lead in the polls could reach into double digits. An impressive amount of money had been raised, with the party approaching the 2010 election in a far sounder financial footing than its two main political rivals; a financial advantage that the party maintained right up until polling day (Dorey, 2010: 411). Indeed, the year started well with a very positive poster and video campaign with the aim of reaching out to those sections of the electorate who had disproportionately avoided voting for the party in the past. One of the 'stars' of this campaign who would go on to feature in the manifesto and at its launch was Julie Fallon, a mother of two but importantly from Llandudno in Wales. She appeared under the caption: 'I've never voted Tory before, but I like their plans to help families'. There was also major support from the business sector in reaction to the party's pledge not to implement Labour's plan for an increase in National Insurance contributions; the Tories declaring this 'A Tax on Jobs'.

And, there was the massive own goal from the Labour Party in the poster-mock-up war. Due to financial constraints Labour had made a virtue out of holding a design competition amongst its supporters, with the Miliband brothers introducing the winning entry. Unfortunately, the poster was based on the non-politically correct and 'rakishly attractive' DCI Gene Hunt of the extremely popular TV programme *Ashes to Ashes*. The Conservatives were so delighted in Cameron being associated with Hunt, that the poster was quickly 'borrowed' with a change of caption from 'Don't let him take Britain back to the 1980s' to 'Fire up the Quatro. It's time for change' (for example, see the *Daily Mail* and *Daily Telegraph*, 4 April 2010). These poster mock ups, particularly the spoof versions on the web, gave 'the poster campaign' a new lease of life; just when so much had been pronounced on their terminal decline (Campbell, 2010). But, what such amusing events did show was that the election was still very much one of the 'old media'; the television was still the major facilitator of electoral communication; 'Twitter', 'YouTube' or other social media had not made the breakthrough for 2010 to be deemed the first UK web election (Wring and Ward, 2010); notwithstanding the attractiveness of Sam Cameron on 'Web-Cameron'.

However, optimism was to quickly turn to anxiety as the rise of that political phenomenon of 'Cleggmania' meant the party's electoral strategy would be derailed; losing control of setting the electoral agenda. In fact, in this concluding section we find that the Conservative Party Election Broadcasts (PEBs) were to be very much a microcosm of the actual campaign overall. In the main, these PEBs featured Cameron extensively, with a montage of shots of him in his garden or at his 'Cameron Direct' meetings or out on the stump. The first, broadcast on the 13 April, has Cameron in his back garden introducing swing voters, Julie from Llandudno, Danielle from Brighton and Ian who lives in Congleton, in the 'I've never voted Tory before' campaign but who are now voting Conservative for stronger families, for a nation of volunteers and to increase employment respectively. On the day that the manifesto was launched Cameron urges the millions at home to join them and him in creating a new kind of government, a 'Big Society'. The Big Society idea is mentioned in four of the five broadcasts but so are the ideas of *We're all in this together*; *An Invitation To Join The Government*; *A contract between the Conservative Party and you* and of course *A Vote For Change*. But, the Conservative campaign plan was effectively derailed as a consequence of the first television debate and in the second PEB on 19 April the fallout from Nick Clegg's challenge to that agenda of 'change' is painfully clear. *The Times* reported that the intended second broadcast, which would have attacked Gordon Brown's record, was junked in favour of 'urging voters not to be seduced by Mr Clegg' (20 April 2010). In his back garden again, Cameron begins by referring to the first TV debate and how it had shaken up the election campaign to the extent that people were looking at the parties in a way they weren't before and that he acknowledged that people were desperate for change and looking for anything different or new. But, due to the altered electoral landscape David Cameron now has to broadcast the warning, repeated on 23 April and in the last PEB on 3 May, that the only way of getting that change is through a decisive result for the Conservatives, any other result would lead to more indecision and more of the old politics with the danger that the country might even be left stuck with 'what we've got now, Gordon Brown and the same team running the country'.

The extent of the derailment could not be clearer in the content of the penultimate PEB broadcast on the evening of 27 April. The party's campaign strategy was to be blown so far off course that it was felt necessary to create a fictitious 'Hung Parliament party', with its own posters, rosettes, a party symbol of the 'hangman's rope' and its very own party election broadcast. In it the hung parliament party leader (uncannily resembling Mr Clegg) pledges to paralyse Britain, to undertake behind closed door politics and to have indecision and weak government. Promises are made on hiking interest rates and a guarantee of a run on the pound and for a brave new world of undemocratic processes. The Clegg lookalike states: 'and getting us in couldn't be easier, a vote for any party other than the Conservatives should do the job'. Thus, one of the most notable mistakes in the failure to gain an overall majority was the decision to participate in the first ever televised leader debates. Cameron did stress his long-standing support and encouragement for such broadcast events and the psephological reality might have been an 'undecided nation' but there is no doubting the benefit given to the third party and Nick Clegg as a consequence of this decision. A manifest direct consequence was in the redirection of resources away from the 20 or so Liberal Democrat target seats, as these were now believed to be a lost cause and out of reach (Snowdon, 2010: 405; Ashcroft, 2010: 83). It may well have been the vanity of Cameron and the arrogance of that coterie of advisers in 'Cameron Central' (*The Guardian*, 8 May 2010) or the felt need of 'Team Cameron' to ingratiate itself with *News International* through supporting the Sky News's campaign for such events but there was more than enough advice to avoid such a blunder; advice which was roundly ignored. Moreover, any policy initiative or big idea of the Big Society was to be comprehensively drowned out in the media euphoria surrounding Nick Clegg's performance.

Thus, the presidential style campaign, revealingly exhibited in the American style placards of 'Cameron 2010' (Seawright, forthcoming), fell rather short in more ways than one; with Cameron obtaining a new 'running mate' in Nick Clegg by virtue of that 'hung parliament party'. The creation of the coalition gave rise to questions regarding the next general election and with it the level of cooperation with the Liberal Democrats. In one survey nearly twice as many voters thought the Liberal Democrats had run a better campaign than the Conservatives (Bale and Webb, 2011: 54) and a few Tory MPs rushed enthusiastically to champion a full blown electoral pact between both parties (Boles, 2010: 131–2). But these MPs would always be a very small group within the parliamentary party. The future reality will probably see a return to 'the norm' as evidenced in the bitter Tory-Lib Dem battles of the Alternative Vote referendum campaign. In conclusion it is interesting to note that Michael Ashcroft was worried, with regards to the 'Brown bounce of 2007', that the Conservative Party would have to implement the 'inevitably imperfect general election campaign' (Ashcroft, 2010: 36) but unfortunately for the Conservative Party, the actual campaign of 2010 was to be just as imperfect.

4
The Conservatives and the Electorate

David Denver

The party and the electorate in context: 1997–2005

In order to appreciate fully the psephological position of the Conservative Party under David Cameron, we first need to examine the electoral history of the party since it was last in power. When David Cameron became its leader in December 2005 the Conservative Party had been in the electoral doldrums for 13 years and under three different leaders had been badly defeated in three successive general elections. The rot began shortly after an unexpectedly comfortable victory at the 1992 general election as the popularity of John Major's government declined very quickly and very markedly. The catalyst for this transformation was the forced withdrawal of the United Kingdom from the European exchange rate mechanism (ERM) in September 1992. Billions of pounds were wasted in trying to shore up the pound but in the end there was an effective devaluation of the currency. This shook the electorate's long-standing confidence in the ability of the Conservatives to manage the economy competently – a matter on which they had consistently outscored Labour for decades (see Denver, 1998). During the ensuing five years, Major and his party plumbed new depths of unpopularity in the opinion polls, lost thousands of council seats in local elections, failed to hold any of the eight constituencies that they defended in parliamentary by-elections and achieved their worst ever national election result (to that point) in the European elections of June 1994. Disaster loomed in the next general election and duly arrived in 1997 when Labour won an overwhelming victory. As Table 4.1 shows, the Conservatives were reduced to under a third of the votes cast (having won 42.8 per cent in 1992) and to their smallest number of Commons seats since 1906. The 'swing' from Conservative to Labour (10.3 per cent) was a post-war record.

Unsurprisingly, John Major rapidly departed the political scene (probably with some relief) and was succeeded as Conservative leader by William Hague in June 1997. By all accounts Hague performed creditably enough in the House of Commons but he simply failed to hit it off with the electorate

Table 4.1 General elections 1997–2005

	1997		2001		2005	
	Votes %	Seats	Votes %	Seats	Votes %	Seats
Conservative	31.5	165	32.7	166	33.2	198
Labour	44.3	418	42.0	412	36.1	355
Liberal Democrat	17.2	46	18.8	52	22.6	62
Other	7.0	12	6.5	11	8.1	13

Note: The figures are for Great Britain (i.e. exclude Northern Ireland).
Source: Adapted from Rallings and Thrasher, 2007: 55–7.

and the Conservatives suffered in consequence. Between 1997 and 2001 the party continued to wander in the electoral wilderness into which they had been cast by Labour's landslide. For the first time since regular opinion polling began, the governing party never once lost its lead in mean monthly voting intentions over the whole inter-election period (see Figure 4.1). It was hardly a surprise, therefore, that the Conservatives failed to make any significant

Figure 4.1 Levels of support for major parties 1997–2005

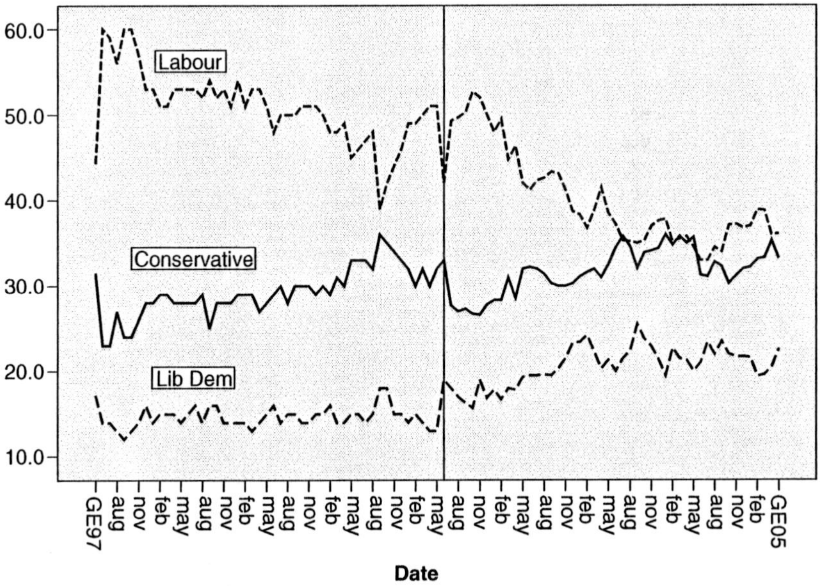

Note: For each month the graph shows the mean percentage in all published polls intending to vote for each party. The start point is the 1997 general election, the end point the 2005 general election and the vertical line indicates the 2001 general election.

progress in the 2001 general election. Their vote share inched upwards by 1.2 points but this resulted in a net gain of just one seat. Labour's majority in the House of Commons remained overwhelming.

Hague resigned the Conservative leadership on the morning after the election and three months later was succeeded by Ian Duncan Smith. Despite his evident decency, the self-proclaimed 'quiet man' proved to be something of an embarrassment as leader, being widely considered – not least among Conservative MPs – as simply not up to the job. Although his tenure actually coincided with a narrowing of the gap between Labour and the Conservatives in opinion polls, this was due more to the growing unpopularity of the government than to any new-found enthusiasm for the Tories. After losing a vote of confidence among his MPs, Duncan Smith resigned in September 2003 and was replaced by Michael Howard in the following month. Howard carried baggage from his time as a minister in Mrs Thatcher's government and was not thought by the electorate to be very likeable. On the other hand, he was certainly a substantial figure, commanding some respect. In the following general election (2005) the Conservatives at last made a little headway. The increase in their vote share (+0.5 points) was again very modest but, thanks to a sharp fall in Labour support (–5.9 points), the number of Conservative seats rose to 198. Even if this left them still a long way behind Labour, it was at least a move in the right direction.

Nonetheless, having been the most electorally successful party in Britain over the twentieth century, the Conservatives had been trounced in three consecutive general elections and between 1997 and 2005 they never once managed a significant lead in the opinion polls – as the party in opposition usually does. Four factors help to explain this unparalleled period of unpopularity. First, the loss of their reputation for economic competence referred to earlier continued to haunt the party for a number of years. At the time of the 1992 general election Gallup found that 49 per cent of poll respondents thought that the Conservatives could handle Britain's economic problems best while 36 per cent opted for Labour (despite the fact that the Tories had presided over a lengthy recession). In early September of the same year Labour still lagged five points behind the Conservatives on this question. In October, in the wake of the ERM crisis, Labour went into an 18 point lead and this stretched to 21 points in December. Thereafter, according to Gallup, the Conservatives trailed well behind Labour on economic competence in every single month until the firm withdrew from political polling in 2002. In the comparable YouGov series which began in January 2003, the Conservatives never established a sustained lead over Labour until the middle of 2008.

Second, during the Major government the Conservatives acquired a very unflattering image – being widely perceived as not just incompetent but also uncaring, selfish, sleazy, divided and out of touch (Denver, 1998). This 'toxic' mixture proved difficult to shake off. At the 2002 party conference, the party chair, Theresa May, startled the audience by asserting that many people thought of them as 'the nasty party' and three years later, after the 2005 election, Lord Ashcroft – a party vice-chairman – published influential research demonstrating the low esteem in which the party continued to be held by voters. The Conservative 'brand', it was suggested, needed to be 'decontaminated' (Ashcroft, 2005).

Third, throughout this period the Conservatives faced a thoroughly revitalised and modernised Labour Party. Having itself experienced a long period of unpopularity and lost four successive general elections (1979, 1983, 1987 and 1992), Labour had successfully reinvented itself as 'New' Labour, cast off its image as a 'tax and spend' party of the left in hock to the trade unions, shifted to the electorally fruitful centre ground and modernised its campaigning and media operations. Once in government, the party appeared to do a reasonable job with the Chancellor of the Exchequer, Gordon Brown, attracting particular praise for his management of the economy. Most importantly, however, Labour found a new leader in Tony Blair who – at least until the shine came off towards the end of his period in office – proved unusually popular with the voters (Denver and Fisher, 2009).

The fourth factor explaining the lengthy period of Conservative unpopularity, therefore, was their inability to find a leader to challenge Blair. Figure 4.2 shows which of the major party leaders was thought to be the best person for Prime Minister from July 1992 to the 2005 general election. Major's sharp fall from grace in late 1992 is apparent and for the rest of the parliament

Figure 4.2 Best person for Prime Minister (July 1992–2005)

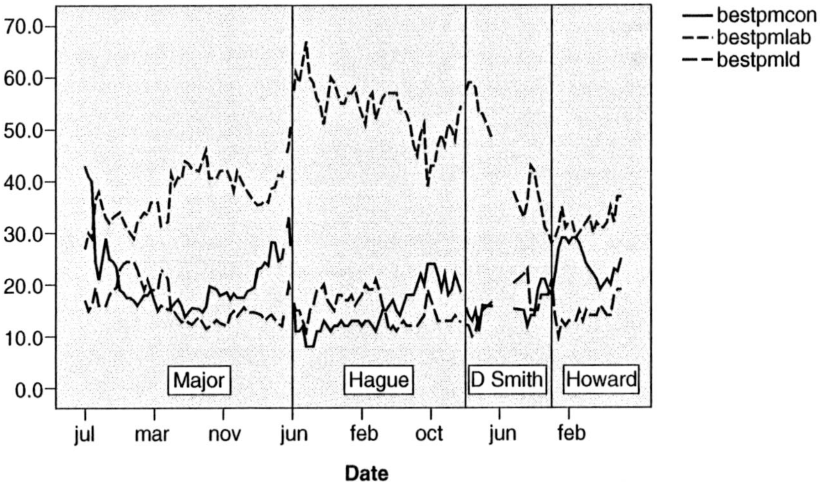

Notes: Data to January 2002 are from Gallup and from January 2003 from YouGov. Between these dates no polling firm asked the relevant question on a regular basis. There are other gaps when one of the parties was choosing a new leader. John Smith was Labour leader to May 1994 and Tony Blair thereafter. Liberal Democrat leaders in the period were Paddy Ashdown (to August 1999) and Charles Kennedy.

– although his ratings improved as the next election approached – he lagged well behind Blair in popularity. The next two Conservative leaders fared even worse, both vying with the Liberal Democrat leader for second place in the Prime Ministerial stakes while Blair was well out in front on his own. By the time Michael Howard became Conservative leader, Blair had become less popular, mainly due to the Iraq war, and Howard initially appeared to be in a position to challenge him. The gap between the two widened, however, as the 2005 election approached and, even if it was not as yawning as it had been over the previous years, it was enough to put the Conservatives at a significant electoral disadvantage. If the Conservatives had been wandering in an electoral desert, they had failed to find a Moses to lead them towards the Promised Land.

Valence politics

The importance of party leaders to electoral success (or failure) has been stressed by electoral researchers in recent years. From the 1950s to the 1970s, the influence of leaders on voters was generally played down (see Butler and Stokes, 1974). Party choice was largely a product of class position underpinned by party identification – a sense of being a party supporter – which voters acquired from family tradition, peers and community norms. To be sure, leaders were highly visible to the electorate and most voters had opinions about them but these opinions were determined to a great extent by the party supported by the voter. Labour supporters preferred Labour leaders and Conservatives preferred Conservative leaders. Party support preceded views on leaders, not the other way round. As nicely expressed by Bartle and Crewe, 'what mattered was what the parties stood for, not who stood for the parties' (2002: 75).

As class voting and the importance of party identification have declined, however, a different perspective on the role of party leaders has emerged. In their studies of the 2001 and 2005 elections the British Election Study team (Clarke et al, 2004, 2009) proposed and elaborated a new model of 'valence politics' for understanding party choice in the contemporary context. In brief, this suggests that the issues that most concern voters are ones about which there is broad agreement about the ends to be achieved – a strong economy, a good national health service, less crime and so on. So-called 'position issues', on which people do disagree about the end to be achieved – whether the railways should be in public ownership or not, for example – have declined in importance. The parties themselves try to avoid taking clear positions and instead try to associate themselves with generally approved goals (economic prosperity, being tough on crime) while associating their opponents with actions or inclinations which are widely disliked (being untrustworthy on the NHS, allowing large-scale immigration). In response, voters react by making judgements about the overall competence of the rival parties in achieving the goals that are widely shared. Making such judgements is time consuming and relatively difficult, however, and so voters use a convenient shortcut by substituting their evaluations of party leaders. This is a much simpler task since we can all react to people without necessarily knowing much about what parties have been doing or might do in future. Moreover, over the past 30 years or so the 'tabloidisation' of the press has meant that political coverage has become ever more focused on personalities – the strengths and weaknesses of party leaders (and even the clothes worn by their wives) – as has television coverage, culminating in the leadership debates during the 2010 election campaign. Although some analysts have remained sceptical of the importance of leaders once other factors are taken into account (Bartle and Crewe, 2002) and some evidence suggests that reactions to government performance remain more important than reactions to leaders (Denver and Garnett, forthcoming), media commentators, politicians and party campaign organisers certainly believe that leaders are key to electoral success or failure. To have a widely-liked leader has come to be thought almost a *sine qua non* of electoral appeal – perhaps even more important than having one who is respected.

The electoral impact of Cameron

Figure 4.3 suggests that the accession of Cameron had an immediate beneficial effect on the Conservative Party's ratings. This is not unusual when a fresh face takes over and within a few months the Conservatives had overtaken Labour in the polls. This lead – which proved to be the longest lasting

Figure 4.3 Trends in party support 2005–March 2010

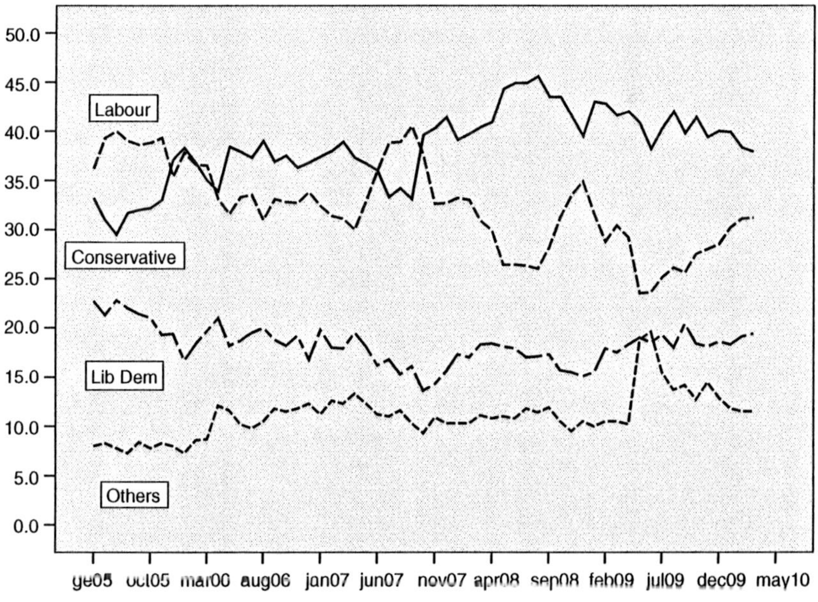

Note: For each month the graph shows the mean percentage intending to vote for each party on the basis of results from five firms which polled consistently throughout the period.

sustained Conservative lead since 1992 – was only briefly lost when Gordon Brown became Prime Minister in June 2007 but was then maintained until the start of the 2010 election campaign, even although the gap was narrowing as the election approached.

There were other indicators of electoral revival for the Conservatives. They successfully defended three seats in parliamentary by-elections between 2005 and 2010 and won two from Labour. The first of these (Crewe and Nantwich in May 2008) was their first by-election gain since 1982. In each round of local elections after 2005 the Conservatives easily outpolled the other parties, gaining numerous seats and councils in the process. After the 2009 elections, they were by far the largest party in local government in England and Wales, holding 48 per cent of all council seats (compared with 23 per cent for Labour and 21 per cent for the Liberal Democrats) and controlling 209 of the 373 councils (Rallings and Thrasher, 2009).

To a considerable extent, no doubt, the Conservative recovery is directly attributable to the personal appeal of Cameron. Figure 4.4 shows that immediately upon being chosen he began to challenge Tony Blair as the electorate's choice of best person to be Prime Minister whereas the previous four leaders had lagged well behind the Labour leader in this respect. When Gordon Brown replaced Tony Blair in June 2007, he made a very favourable impression at first and easily led Cameron in the polls. Impressions of Brown soon became negative, however, and Cameron's lead was restored by the autumn of 2007. Although Brown's ratings were temporarily boosted by the onset of

Figure 4.4 Best person for Prime Minister 2005–March 2010

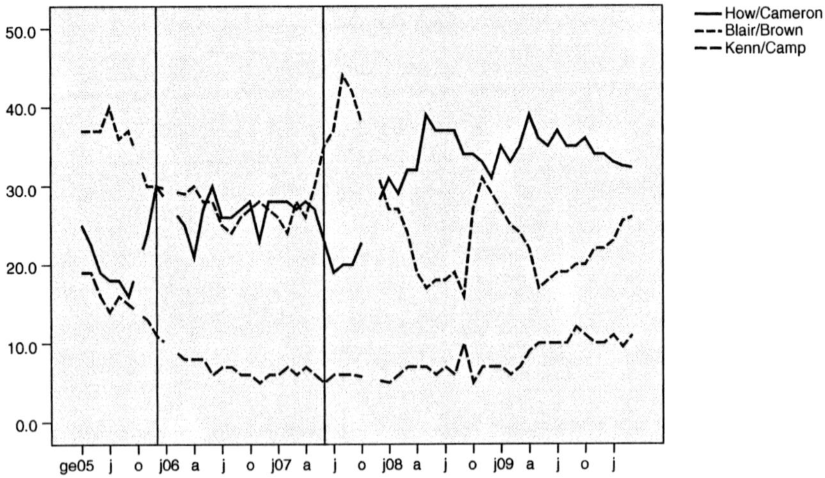

Notes: Data are from YouGov. The first vertical line (December 2005) marks the point at which Cameron became Conservative leader and the second (June 2007) when Gordon Brown became Prime Minister.

the economic crisis in late 2008 and were slowly improving as the election approached, Cameron maintained his lead as the most-preferred Prime Minister up to the beginning of the 2010 election campaign.

Another measure of Cameron's appeal comes from the regular Ipsos Mori opinion polls which ask respondents whether they are satisfied or dissatisfied with the way the leader of the opposition is doing his or her job. Although it seems likely that few voters would actually have much idea of what the job of opposition leader entails, these data can be interpreted as indicators of the popularity of the politicians concerned. Over their period as Conservative leader net ratings (% satisfied – % dissatisfied) for Hague, Duncan Smith and Howard were all negative, averaging –24.8, –16.4 and –11.7 respectively. Cameron, on the other hand, averaged +5.0 over 50 months. This is not a spectacular figure but it is positive and it must have made a pleasant change for rank and file Conservatives to have a relatively popular leader.

In addition, however, Cameron could have had an indirect effect on Conservative prospects by seeking to modernise the party's image (see Bale and Webb, 2011). In broad terms, 'team Cameron' set out to move the party towards the centre of the political spectrum – emphasising their commitment to the National Health Service (NHS), for example, and disavowing any intention to extend selective education in schools. The party image was also to be freshened by encouraging the selection of women and ethnic minority candidates, claiming green credentials and so on. In fact these initiatives were not entirely successful. The virtual imposition of 'A list' candidates in some cases caused major rows in the party and the composition of the list (mocked as 'Tatler Tories') attracted some derision. More generally, by the time of the election the party was seen as only very slightly less right wing that it had been in 2005 under Michael Howard and Bale and Webb cite a poll which suggested that whereas 46 per cent of voters thought that David Cameron had changed the party, 50 per cent thought it had not changed very much. As they comment, 'the party had only partially succeeded in throwing off old reputations' (2011: 56–7). Even partial success is something, however, and the Conservatives certainly entered the 2010 election in a stronger position than had been the case in the previous three elections.

The 2010 election

The 2010 election campaign was marked by the first ever televised debates between the leaders of the three major parties. It would not be going too far, indeed, to say that the debates defined the campaign. Figure 4.5 charts the trend in voting intentions, according to the daily polls undertaken by YouGov, from the day that the election date was announced through to the actual result on polling day. The first week was generally thought somewhat lacklustre by commentators and saw little change in support for the major parties, although there appears to have been a slight improvement in

Figure 4.5 Trends in voting intentions during the 'short' campaign

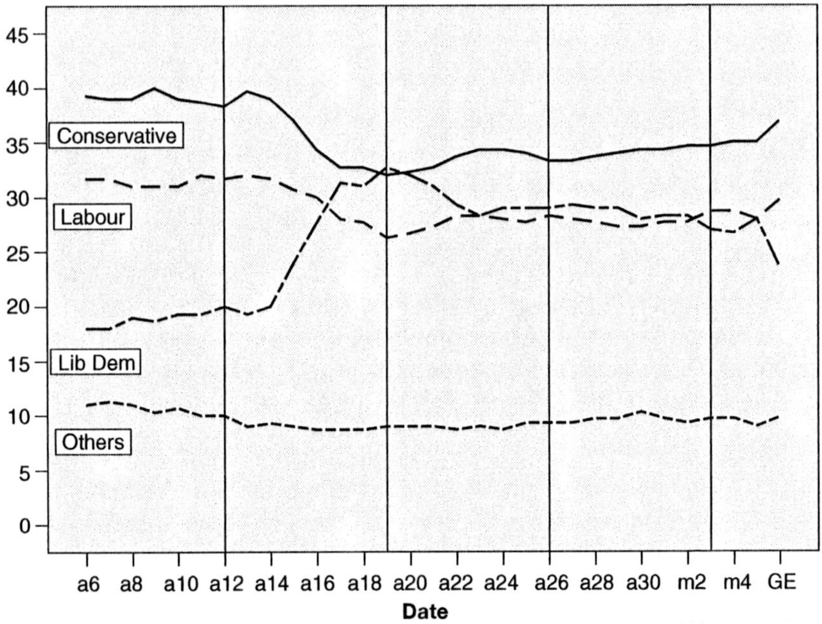

Note: The data are three-day moving averages of figures reported in YouGov's tracking polls for the *Sun* and *Sunday Times*. The vertical lines mark each Monday of the campaign.

the position of the Liberal Democrats and a slight decrease in support for others. In the second week, however, the first televised leaders' debate shattered the somnolent atmosphere. By general consent the Liberal Democrat leader, Nick Clegg, made the best impression and, as the graph shows, the impact on public opinion was immediate and dramatic. Two YouGov polls over the weekend following the debate even put the Liberal Democrats in the lead. Cameron, some suggested, had made a significant tactical error in agreeing to the debates and, in addition, seemed under-prepared and nervous (Chapter 3 and Kavanagh and Cowley, 2010).

The Conservative ship steadied somewhat in the following week and there was no clear 'winner' in the second leaders' debate. It was widely thought however that David Cameron came off best in the third. Whether as a result of this or not, the Conservatives inched forward in the penultimate and also the last week of campaigning while the other parties remained close together, stuck in the high twenties. In the event, both the Conservatives and Labour did better than predicted by the final polls as Liberal Democrat support evaporated.

Table 4.2 shows the results of the election for Great Britain. (In Northern Ireland, the Conservative strategy of entering into a formal alliance with the Ulster Unionist Party proved to be a flop; see Chapter 8.) The increase

Table 4.2 The 2010 general election (Great Britain)

	Share of votes (%)	Change 2005–10	Number of seats	Change 2005–10
Conservative	36.9	+3.7	306	+97
Labour	29.7	–6.4	258	–90
Liberal Democrat	23.6	+1.0	57	–6
Other	9.9	+1.8	11	–1

Notes: The Speaker, who was not opposed by the Conservatives, Labour or Liberal Democrats, is treated as an 'other'. The change in seats is calculated on the basis of 'notional' 2005 results in England and Wales due to boundary changes.

in the Conservative vote share (+3.7 points) was relatively modest and, although they advanced in every region of the country, was particularly poor in London (+2.6) and Scotland (+0.9). Labour's decline was larger (–6.4) but the net swing to the Conservatives was not large enough to ensure an overall majority for the party in the House of Commons for which 20 more seats would have been required.

There is little doubt that David Cameron continued to provide an electoral bonus to his party in the election. As already seen, he clearly led Gordon Brown and (even more clearly) Nick Clegg as the most preferred Prime Minister going into the election and, as reported by the British Election Study (BES) rolling campaign survey (http://bes2009-10.org/), he maintained a comfortable lead on this question throughout the campaign, despite the outburst of 'Cleggmania' following the first leaders' debate. In the final campaign week, YouGov reported that Cameron was the preferred choice of 32 per cent of voters compared with 26 per cent for Brown and 22 per cent for Clegg. In both the pre- and post-election surveys by the BES, respondents were asked to rate the party leaders in terms of likeability, competence and trustworthiness. In each case, Cameron scored better than either of his rivals. It is hard to escape the conclusion that had the election been decided on the basis of personalities alone then Cameron would probably have won a decisive victory.

However, the performance of the government more generally and the prospective performance of the other competing parties are also aspects of valence politics and in this respect the electorate continued to harbour doubts about the Conservatives. Perhaps the best evidence of this is the failure of their campaign to convince the voters that they were clearly the best party to deal with the problems facing the country. The BES rolling campaign survey shows that the Conservatives maintained only a narrow lead over Labour as the party best able to deal with the issue nominated by respondents as the most important. On the key valence issue of the economy (rated as by far the most important by the electorate), Labour had steadily whittled away the Conservatives' lead as the 'best party' so that, by the time of the election, the two parties were running neck and neck (see Green, J., 2010). More generally, although the Conservatives' standing with the electorate had improved, they had not managed to generate much enthusiastic or committed support. Although more people were willing to vote for the party there was little recovery in terms of party identification. There were still more people thinking of themselves as Labour supporters than as Conservatives. As Jane Green (2010) observes, the Conservatives won 'some minds but few hearts'. Although Gordon Brown and the Labour government were clearly unpopular, the electorate as a whole was not convinced that the Conservatives would do a great deal better.

The electoral system

The foregoing brief discussion attempts to explain why the Conservatives did not receive as large a boost in voting support as they might have hoped for in 2010. Even so, the gap in vote share between them and Labour would normally have been enough to ensure a comfortable majority of seats were it not the case that, relative to Labour, the Conservatives are disadvantaged by the operation of the electoral system. Thus, in 2005 Labour obtained 56.5 per cent of the seats in Britain with 36.1 per cent of the votes; in 2010 the Conservatives had a slightly larger vote share (36.9 per cent) but got only 48.4 per cent of the seats.

This bias in the system arises from five features (see Johnston et al, 2009). First, Scotland and Wales are over-represented in the House of Commons given their electorates and both are very weak areas for the Conservatives. In 2010 there were 59 Westminster constituencies in Scotland of which the Conservatives won only one while in Wales they took eight of the 40 seats. Second, the seats in which the Conservatives do well tend to have larger electorates than those in which Labour is stronger. Thus, in 2010 the average electorate in seats won by the Conservatives was over 72,000 while Labour seats averaged under 70,000. Third, Conservative seats have higher turnouts (a mean of 68.3 per cent in 2010 compared with 61.1 per cent in Labour seats). As a consequence of these two points, the Conservatives amassed many more votes than Labour for every seat won. Fourth, the Conservatives have suffered more from the advances made in recent elections by the Liberal Democrats. Of the 57 seats won by the latter in 2010 the Conservatives came second in 38 and Labour in 17 (with the SNP as runners up in the other two). Finally, the geographical distribution of the Conservative vote is simply less 'efficient' (in terms of converting votes into seats) than that of Labour. Across constituencies, the Conservatives tend to 'win big and lose small' and, under first past the post, that kind of vote distribution does not yield seats as efficiently as 'winning small and losing big' – which is more characteristic of Labour's performance.

Conservative strategists as well as media commentators were well aware of these facts of electoral life in advance of the election. Assuming uniform swing across constituencies, the Conservatives needed a lead of almost six percentage points over Labour to become the largest party in the Commons. To get an overall majority, the lead required was almost 11 points. It was little wonder, then, that before the election Conservative leaders stressed that they had a mountain to climb and they could not have been altogether surprised when they fell short of a majority and were forced to enter into a governing coalition with the Liberal Democrats. The latter was the outcome of intense negotiations immediately after the election (see Kavanagh and Cowley, 2010) and resulted in David Cameron becoming Prime Minister with Nick Clegg as his deputy and several Liberal Democrats being given key positions in the government.

The electoral consequences of a year in office

Given the perilous state of the British economy and the enormous deficit in public finances inherited by the new government, it was apparent that some harsh decisions would have to be taken and that these would result in significant unpopularity for the Conservatives. In several areas, however, government policies appeared to be almost deliberately designed to outrage core Conservative supporters. Child benefit was summarily removed from families paying the higher rate of income tax. Such people, by definition, are not poor but they are by no means invariably affluent. The overseas aid budget was protected from cuts and was even set to increase. University student tuition fees were tripled and ministers persistently argued that 'top' universities should discriminate in favour of applicants from 'deprived' backgrounds (and hence against those from solidly middle class families). Following a speedy defence review the armed services were subject to severe cuts in personnel and equipment with soldiers serving in Afghanistan reportedly receiving notices of potential redundancy. The police too were subject to budget cuts and at the same time the Justice Secretary (Kenneth Clarke) embarked on a policy of reducing the number of criminals being sent to prison.

In the face of this onslaught on traditional Conservative values, the letters pages of the *Daily Telegraph* fairly bristled with indignation. Indeed, following another slap in the face to his supporters – when the Prime Minister on a visit to Pakistan 'apologised' for Britain's past role in allegedly causing various problems around the world – one correspondent asked: 'When will he apologise to the millions who voted for him thinking that he was a Conservative?' (*Daily Telegraph*, 7 April 2011).

More generally, while some aspects of the government's performance attracted praise (for example, welfare reform) the programme of public spending cuts generated the anticipated negative reactions from those likely to be affected. Perhaps more seriously, the government's plans for reforming the NHS rapidly began to unravel. The NHS is very clearly a valence issue. It is strongly supported by almost everyone and is an institution of which British people as a whole are very proud. 'Don't mess with the NHS' would be a sensible posture for any prudent government to adopt – or at least 'don't be seen to mess too much with the NHS'. On this occasion, however, having promised that there would be an end to top-down re-organisations, the government set out plans for wholesale change. Anything that smacks of threatening the ethos of the NHS – or can be portrayed as doing so – is, to say the least, electorally perilous. In the spring of 2011 the government's plans for the NHS were put on hold to allow for a further period of consultation. In other words the government realised the danger and began to backtrack.

In these circumstances – and even although the Labour opposition was having problems of its own as the new leader, Ed Miliband, struggled to make a positive impact (see Chapter 15) – it is not surprising that Conservative popularity, as well as that of David Cameron, tailed off fairly quickly after the election (Table 4.3). In terms of voting intentions, the Conservatives initially had handy leads over Labour after the election but by November they were trailing and in 2011 the deficit widened. To be fair, there was no great slump in Conservative support. In the first three months of 2011 the party was still receiving more than 35 per cent of voting intentions. The problem was that support for the Liberal Democrats dropped like a stone while that for Labour (and others) rose, leaving the Conservatives relatively worse off.

Table 4.3 The popularity of the Conservatives, the government and David Cameron, 2010–2011

		Conservative lead over Labour	Net approval of government record	Net satisfaction with Cameron
General election		+7.2	–	–
	Jun	+7.6	+16.3	+41.5
	Jul	+4.3	+6.1	+26.6
	Aug	+4.6	+2.0	+20.3
	Sep	+2.0	–2.0	+18.0
	Oct	+1.9	–1.6	+18.0
	Nov	–0.1	–8.0	+7.0
	Dec	–0.9	–13.1	+1.0
2011	Jan	–5.7	–20.8	–3.5
	Feb	–5.0	–24.6	–6.3
	Mar	–4.5	–25.6	–7.8
	Apr	–4.8	–24.0	–7.0

Notes: The Conservative 'lead' in voting intentions is derived from monthly averages in all published polls. The other two columns are monthly averages from YouGov's regular tracking polls.

On the other hand, there was a steep decline in the electorate's satisfaction with the government's performance and by early 2011 large negative scores were being recorded. David Cameron's personal ratings initially held up well and he was consistently more popular than either his party or the government. Nonetheless, he too entered negative territory at the start of 2011.

The first major electoral test for the Conservatives came in May 2011 when there were widespread local elections in England (outside London) as well as elections to the Scottish Parliament and Welsh Assembly. To no one's surprise, the Conservatives fell back in Scotland where their share of the vote in constituency contests declined by 2.7 points to 13.9 per cent as compared with the previous election in 2007. In England and Wales, however, the party did surprisingly well. Their vote share in Wales increased to 25 per cent (+2.6) in the constituency contests and they gained two additional seats in the Assembly. In the English local elections the Conservatives were braced for large losses since they had made many gains in 2007 when the seats at stake had last been contested (see Chapter 8). In the event, the number of Conservative councillors actually increased by 85 and the party took control of four additional councils. The big losers in all of these elections were the Liberal Democrats. The 'national equivalent' vote shares (according to Rallings and Thrasher in the *Sunday Times*, 8 May 2011) were Conservative 38 per cent, Labour 37 per cent and Liberal Democrats 16 per cent. Given the tough decisions that had been taken by the government and the unpopularity of some of its policies, this was something of an achievement for the Conservatives. The electorate, it appears, were still willing to give them the benefit of the doubt in their efforts to do something about the deficit in public finances bequeathed them by Labour.

There was more good news for Conservatives. On the same day as these elections there was a referendum on a proposal to change the method of electing the House of Commons to the Alternative Vote (AV) system. This was one of the prices paid by the Conservatives in negotiations to secure Liberal Democrat agreement to participation in the governing coalition in 2010. Change was strongly backed by Nick Clegg and the Liberal Democrats while David Cameron and the Conservatives campaigned strongly for a NO vote. The result was a massive victory for the 'NO' side (68 per cent to 32 per cent). The issue had imposed some strains on the coalition but the outcome clearly strengthened Cameron's position.

Prospects

Despite the relatively good performance of the Conservatives in the May 2011 elections, it almost goes without saying that electorally rough waters lie ahead for the Conservatives. All governments become unpopular. There is a well-established inter-election cycle of government popularity whereby, after an initial 'honeymoon', support for the governing party declines and the government suffers from 'mid-term blues' while the opposition does very well in polls, by-elections, local elections and so on. As another general election approaches, however, support for the governing party tends to pick up and the gap narrows. In explaining the electoral cycle, analysts have frequently focused on the economic cycle (Sanders, 2005) although some have offered more directly political explanations (Miller and Mackie, 1973).

The electoral cycle doesn't always conform to expectations, however, and there is obviously no guarantee that when support for the Conservatives declines it will then improve enough to win the next general election, due in 2015. At the same time, that election is some way distant and there is no need for excessive pessimism after just a year in office. Much depends on how successful and competent the government will be seen to have been in handling the key valence issues that concern the public – the deficit and the economy, the NHS and, perhaps to a lesser extent, immigration. If things go well in these areas then there is every prospect that the Conservatives could win the election especially given that – currently at least – the electorate appear to be more impressed by David Cameron than by Labour's leader, Ed Miliband (see Chapter 15).

The electoral system remains a problem for the Conservatives, however. In their first year in office, the new government initiated a review of parliamentary constituency boundaries and revised the rules for redistribution. The total number of seats in the House of Commons is to be reduced from 650 to 600 and (with some minor exceptions) the electorates of all constituencies have to be within 5 per cent of the average. This is a major innovation, which gives a higher priority to more equal electorates than to other considerations – such as community ties – which can be taken into account in drawing boundaries. The Boundary Commissions are to report in time for new arrangements to be implemented at the next general election. The new emphasis on equal electorates applies across the United Kingdom and thus the number of seats in Scotland and Wales will decrease. This, together with equalisation within England will reduce somewhat the disadvantage suffered by the Conservatives but will certainly not eliminate it. It is more than likely that Conservative seats will continue to have higher turnouts, that the Conservatives will suffer more from Liberal Democrat successes (even if the vote of the latter is sharply reduced) and, most crucially of all, the geographical distribution of Conservative support will once again see votes piled up in strong areas while falling short in more marginal areas. If there is not quite a mountain to climb in order to achieve an overall majority, then there is certainly a very steep hill.

5
Economic Policy

Andrew Gamble

The economy in context

The Conservatives were in government between 1979 and 1997 and then in opposition until 2010, their longest spell in opposition in their modern history. The period of the 1980s was associated with the aftermath of the stagflation of the 1970s and the implementation of the new ideas of Thatcherism aimed at reversing British decline and restoring a pathway of growth. The 1980s was a period of considerable economic turmoil and political strife. The government presided over a very deep recession in 1980–1981, which saw unemployment rise sharply as what remained of the traditional heavy manufacturing base largely disappeared. It peaked at three million, and remained there for most of the decade. At the same time inflation rose sharply because of another spike in the price of oil fuelled by the breakdown of pay restraint. The Thatcher government abolished foreign exchange controls and announced a major deflationary budget when the economy was still in recession, which signalled the government's determination to make major cuts in public expenditure. The government was keen to continue the monetarist experiment begun by the Labour government but to make it much more rigorous (Maynard, 1988).

In the middle of the 1980s inflation began to fall sharply and growth revived. Following the defeat of the miners in a long battle over pit closures, major tax cuts in personal incomes and the Big Bang in 1986, which freed the City from previous regulatory restrictions, the economy boomed in 1986–1987, helping the Conservatives to win a third election victory in 1987. By this time the main themes of Conservative economic policy – a tight monetary framework, public expenditure restraint, trade union curbs, privatisation, deregulation, and lower taxes – were all firmly established. The Conservative manifesto in 1987 was suitably ecstatic about the turn-round of the British economy, and openly proclaimed an economic miracle and the end of British decline. This was rather spoiled immediately after the election when the economy, with inflation soaring, plunged back into recession. The

Conservatives under John Major had to fight the election of 1992 against a very difficult economic background, but still managed to win, although with only a small majority.

One of the reasons why the Conservatives were able to win again in 1992 was that there was confidence that the government had once more got a firm financial framework in place, this time as a result of the decision to join the Exchange Rate Mechanism (ERM). By linking the pound to the ERM the government thought that it would benefit by being connected to the strongest currency in Europe, the Deutschmark (DM), and that this would help hold inflation down and create the right financial climate for growth (Stephens, 1996). It was a major misjudgement, partly because of the implications of German reunification on the stability of the DM had not been foreseen. The major strains that erupted in the ERM straight after the 1992 general election culminated in Black Wednesday, 16 September 1992. Sterling was forced out of the ERM but not before the government had sought to defend the £ by raising interest rates (briefly) to 15 per cent. The widespread perception that the government had lost control of the situation and been proved incompetent deepened with the severe austerity and tax increases which the government was forced to impose as a result of leaving the ERM. That was the moment at which the government lost its lead over Labour for economic competence, which it had enjoyed since the 1970s. It was not to regain it until the long boom in the British economy which began in 1993 finally ended with the financial crash of 2008. The Conservatives felt aggrieved because the long boom began in 1993 after the ERM exit, so they argued that under the Chancellorship of Ken Clarke they had laid the foundations on which Labour then built, but the electorate was not listening, and though the economy was performing well by 1997 the Conservatives went down to one of the biggest electoral defeats in their history.

Although the Conservatives lost in 1997 during their 18 years in power they had presided over a transformation of the British economy, a major move from industry to services, a sharp decline in trade union membership and strikes, and privatisation of the greater part of the public utilities and other productive enterprises in the public sector. The share of government spending in GDP was much what it had been in 1979, but both the private and the public sectors were now structured very differently (Owen, 2000). One of the problems the Conservatives bequeathed to their successors was that the economy had become very reliant on financial services, consumer credit and housing for growth, and the destruction of low-skilled jobs in the 1980s had made large numbers of people reliant on benefits, and had created a significant dependency culture, concentrated in particular parts of the country (Coates, 1994). But by 1997 both the official count of people unemployed was falling and the rate of inflation was low. Britain like the rest of the advanced economies was benefiting from the flood of cheap

Chinese imports which had begun to arrive and which exerted downward pressure on many prices.

The growth model which the Conservatives bequeathed to Labour was to prove highly successful, at least in generating consistent growth, which made economic management extremely benign for 15 years, a marked contrast to all previous eras of economic management in the post-war period. Colin Crouch has called the policy 'privatised Keynesianism' because of the extent to which it relied on consumers reducing their savings and being prepared to borrow ever larger sums to fund house purchase and personal consumption (Crouch, 2008). Britain acquired one of the lowest household savings ratios in the western world, and one of the most rapidly growing house price bubbles. Inequality had widened sharply in the 1980s reversing the trend established over a long period since 1945 during which it had narrowed, and this combined with the large number of long-term unemployed and disabled meant that large numbers were left behind. But for most citizens this was a time of increasing prosperity.

The success of this growth model gave the Conservative leadership after 1997 a difficult political problem. They kept predicting that the wheels would fall off, that Labour would not be able to keep the growth going, that Labour would tax too much, spend too much, intervene too much, and that the British economy would plunge back into recession. But this did not happen. There were recessions elsewhere in the international economy, notably in 2001–2002, when the dotcom bubble burst. Britain was affected, but although growth dipped the economy did not go into recession. At the beginning Labour also convinced the City that it could manage the economy successfully by handing over operational control of interest rates to the Bank of England and its Monetary Committee, and at the same time by sticking for two years to the rather tough spending plans which the Conservatives had announced before the election (Driver and Martell, 2002).

The failure of Labour to conform to Conservative expectations and begin spending extravagantly as soon as it entered office proved disconcerting, and the electorate's relative judgement of the two main parties' economic competence did not alter very much for the first ten years. Labour was trusted with the economy more than the Conservatives, and there seemed to be nothing the Conservatives could do to shift that perception, especially since it was receiving confirmation in the irresistible rise of living standards, personal consumption and house prices.

After the Conservatives' third defeat in 2005 at the hands of Tony Blair, the Conservatives elected David Cameron as their leader. George Osborne became shadow Chancellor. Their arrival brought a fundamental shift in Conservative strategy. Cameron and Osborne decided to copy what New Labour had done before 1997, and endorse the policy of the incumbent government. Osborne committed the Conservatives to adopting the same spending plans as Labour. He wanted an even lighter touch regulation of the banks in order to attract still more banks to London and he argued that the Conservatives would redistribute the 'dividend of growth' in the future differently from Labour, by allowing a greater proportion to take the form of tax cuts rather than public expenditure rises. But the Conservatives were still committed to public spending increases, and to Labour's increases, particularly in areas such as the NHS. This was deemed necessary to reassure voters that the Conservatives could be trusted with key public services (Bale, 2010).

The financial crisis which began in 2007 and erupted into a major financial crash in 2008 caught both government and opposition by surprise. This was not in the script as the growth model on which both relied appeared punctured beyond repair. Some of Britain's major banks, including RBS and Lloyds had to be wholly or partly nationalised, and the rest of the financial sector bailed out with huge sums of taxpayers' money to prevent a complete financial collapse. The crash plunged all the major economies in Europe and North America into deep recession, and raised serious questions about the long-term prospects for recovery and growth, given the extent of toxic debt overhanging so many economies, and the severe danger of a spiral of deflation, of the kind Japan had suffered in the 1990s, following the collapse of its property boom (Mason, 2009).

The Conservatives at first felt their way carefully, and were at times wrong-footed by the speed of the crisis, and the fact that Gordon Brown and Alistair Darling, the Labour Chancellor, received some domestic credit for the way the government responded, particularly when it appeared that Britain was setting the international agenda and was being praised by other countries for its leadership. However as the scale of the crisis became clearer, the general effect on Labour's reputation for economic competence proved profoundly negative, and the inability of the government to foresee it or prepare for it. The opposition parties were equally culpable but had not been in office, so were not blamed in the same way. (The same had been true in 1992. Labour had been enthusiastic supporters of Britain joining the ERM but had avoided blame when the policy was shipwrecked.) Labour as the incumbent party took the hit in 2008–2010, and was unable to shift perceptions before the election. The Conservatives overtook Labour for economic competence, and remained ahead in the general election campaign and into the transition period to coalition government.

The Conservative reaction to the crash was different in one important respect from that of the government. Cameron and Osborne dropped their policy of shadowing the government's policy. Instead they reverted to fiscal conservatism, opposing bank bailouts and calling for tougher cuts from the beginning to bring order back to the public finances. This allowed them politically to distance themselves from the government and to begin to develop the narrative that the crisis was due to Labour profligacy and incompetence, and that Labour was continuing to spend far too much and not take the decisive measures needed to resolve the crisis. If the Conservatives had been in government themselves it is extremely unlikely that they would have done anything very different to Labour, because of the severe risk in 2008–2009 of a complete financial collapse. That was the real moment of crisis. Averting that crisis and the recession which followed was achieved through concerted international action, a combination of bailouts, lowering of interest rates and fiscal stimulus packages, as well as reliance on the traditional automatic Keynesian stabilisers. These policies were adopted by most of the leading economies including the United States, and proved enough to stabilise the Organisation for Economic Cooperation and Development (OECD) economies that were badly affected. But it was done at a high cost. As revenues plunged and expenditure soared so too did deficits, which were covered by borrowing which increased long-term debt and the debt interest charges associated with it. The end of growth and greatly increased expenditure turned the banking crisis quite swiftly into a fiscal crisis and then also fairly quickly threatened to turn it into a sovereign debt crisis, as the banks and the financial system which had just been rescued by taxpayers, now insisted that governments had either to raise taxes or slash spending in order to keep their confidence, and ensure their solvency by being permitted to keep borrowing at affordable interest rates.

The Conservatives were able to turn this situation to their political advantage, by presenting themselves as the more fiscally responsible party. However they were cautious at first about how tough they wanted to be, because they were nervous about associating the Conservatives once again with cuts, as they had been in the 1980s and again at the beginning of the 1990s. Since assuming the leadership Cameron and Osborne had been determined that the party should dissociate itself from the image it had acquired in the Thatcher years and particularly in the great debacle of 1992. It was a key aspect of their plan to decontaminate the Conservative brand, to associate the party with growth and high spending, both public and private. In the run-up to the 2010 election, although they stuck to the line that the Conservatives would cut harder and faster than Labour, they were careful to give specific spending pledges in some areas, for instance they pledged to ring fence spending on the NHS (the biggest single spending programme) as well as foreign aid, and to preserve universal benefits such as the winter fuel allowance and free travel passes for the elderly. They were also committed to many infrastructural projects, including new high speed rail lines.

The coalition negotiations

In the election the Conservatives made substantial gains but fell just short of an overall majority. Cameron responded to this situation by issuing an open invitation to the Liberal Democrats to discuss the formation of a coalition government with seats for several Liberal Democrats in the Cabinet. The negotiations that followed over that weekend after the election hammered out a coalition agreement, which allowed Cameron to become Prime Minister on 10 May 2010. Osborne became Chancellor but with a Liberal Democrat, initially David Laws, later Danny Alexander, as Chief Secretary, and with Vince Cable installed as Business Secretary and Chris Huhne as Energy and Climate Change Secretary.

The coalition agreement incorporated more pledges from the Liberal Democratic Manifesto than from the Conservative Manifesto. This was the sweetener to tempt the Liberal Democrats in. But the Conservatives maintained their red lines, one of which was their general stance on the economy, and their right to set the overall strategic direction for economic management. The Liberal Democrats were forced to accept the Conservative policy that the deficit should be eliminated in one Parliament, and that the bulk of the reduction should be achieved by spending cuts rather than tax increases. This was a significant break from Labour's strategy which had been planning to cut the deficit by half during the next Parliament. Labour's approach to the reduction of the deficit had been shared by Vince Cable, and the Liberal Democrats had been very critical before the election of the Conservatives' harder stance, because the Conservatives were unwilling to specify in any detail where they would make the cuts, but instead appealed for a general mandate to bring down the deficit. The other two parties were equally vague, but they were clear that they would cut at a slower pace. The deficit would take longer to be eliminated. Borrowing would be allowed to rise further, and the exchange rate to weaken until it was clear that the recovery was firmly established.

This was the position which was now abandoned by the coalition agreement. The huge benefit of this for the Conservatives was that the Liberal Democrats were bound by the agreement and were therefore obliged to support the Conservative line on deficit reduction and to criticise Labour. Two of the main parties would therefore line up against the third and accuse it of creating the mess which the coalition was now seeking to clear up. Fast deficit reduction was the only responsible way to do this. The Liberal Democrats had not believed that before the election, but after the coalition agreement, and some conversations with the Governor of the Bank of England, they were converted, and became willing contributors to the major narrative of the coalition.

The coalition agreement

Both in the preface and in the text of the coalition agreement the importance of deficit reduction is stressed: 'We recognise that deficit reduction, and continuing to ensure economic recovery, is the most urgent issue facing Britain' (HM Government, 2010a: 15). The next paragraph then signals the acceptance by the Liberal Democrats of the Conservative position on the speed of deficit reduction: 'We will significantly accelerate the reduction of the structural deficit over the course of a Parliament, with the main burden of deficit reduction borne by reduced spending rather than increased taxes' (ibid). The detailed plans it was agreed would be set out in the emergency budget promised for June. The new Office for Budget Responsibility (OBR) was to be charged with making new forecasts of growth and borrowing for this emergency budget. £6 billion of cuts to non-front-line services would be made within the financial year 2010–2011, but the bulk of the cuts would start from 2011–2012 following a full Spending Review in the autumn. Apart from a few specifics, such as reducing spending on the Child Trust Fund and on tax credits for higher earners, and a reduction in the number and cost of quangos, this was all the coalition agreement had to say about the reduction of the deficit. The details were all to be worked out in the Treasury in the run-up to the Spending Review.

In return for their cooperation on the big strategic picture, the Liberal Democrats did get some of their policies accepted elsewhere in the agreement. This was the fairness agenda. In the section on taxation there was a clear commitment to increase the personal allowance for income tax to help 'lower and middle income earners' (HM Government, 2010a: 30) with the eventual goal of increasing the personal allowance to £10,000. The agreement states that this goal will be given priority over other tax cuts, including cuts to inheritance tax, and that it will be funded through increases in Capital Gains Tax and by not implementing the Conservative policy to increase employee National Insurance thresholds (ibid). The parties pledged to tax non-business capital gains at similar rates to those applied to income, with exemptions for entrepreneurs. There were also pledges on tax avoidance, non-doms, environmental taxes and air travel. What received no mention in the agreement was the coalition's policy on VAT, which the Chancellor announced in his emergency budget in June 2010, this would be increased to 20 per cent from January 2011, its highest level ever in the UK.

In the section on banking there are commitments to reform the banking system 'to avoid a repeat of the financial crisis' (HM Government, 2010a: 9) and to increase the flow of lending to small businesses, but there are few specifics in the agreement apart from the plan to give the Bank of England responsibility for regulating the financial system again. Joining the euro was ruled out for the duration of the agreement (another Conservative red line). The section on business promises major cuts in red tape to lift the burden of regulation, and to encourage new enterprise. The coalition pledged itself to create 'the most competitive corporate tax regime in the G20, while protecting manufacturing industries' (HM Government, 2010a: 10).

Another area of economic policy where the Liberal Democrats put their imprint on the coalition was on energy and climate change. The agreement makes many specific pledges which reflect Liberal Democrat commitments, for example on renewable energy sources, including wind power, carbon capture, a green investment bank, and energy from waste. The coalition committed itself to supporting an increase in the EU emission reduction target to 30 per cent by 2020. On nuclear power they agreed to disagree. The government was to be allowed to take the legal steps to make new nuclear construction possible, but Liberal Democrats would be given the right to oppose the Planning Statement and to abstain in the vote.

In areas of social policy the agreement made a number of pledges, such as maintaining the goal of ending child poverty in the UK by 2020 (HM Government, 2010a: 19), focusing Sure Start on the neediest families, creating a single welfare to work programme in place of the existing schemes, continuing the minimum wage, guaranteeing that health spending 'increases in real terms in each year of the Parliament' (HM Government, 2010a: 24), restoring the earnings link for the basic state pension from April 2011, phasing out the default retirement age, and protecting key benefits for older people, such as the winter fuel allowance, free TV licences, free bus travel, and free eye tests and prescriptions (HM Government, 2010a: 26). The agreement also pledges to maintain Britain's overseas aid budget, to fund a significant premium for disadvantaged pupils 'from outside the schools budget' (HM Government, 2010a: 28). On infrastructure there are pledges to establish a high speed rail network and to go ahead with Crossrail (HM Government, 2010a: 31).

Like many political documents the coalition agreement is rather stronger on the extra spending it proposes than on the cuts it requires to fund them and to reduce the deficit. David Cameron and Nick Clegg declared in the Foreword to the agreement that they did not come into politics to tackle the deficit, and similar words have been uttered many times since by coalition ministers. The urgency of cutting the deficit was to become the main mantra of the coalition and was laid out with great skill in the Emergency Budget speech in June 2010 by George Osborne, but the deficit is rather downplayed in the coalition agreement, which is all about the positive things the two parties can achieve together, and most of them unsurprisingly involve higher government spending not less. To that extent the coalition agreement has a rather large foot still placed in the pre-election rather than the post-election world. These are politicians still running for office, and trying to ensure that as many of the good things they promised in their manifestos are included in the coalition agreement.

The coalition government's first year

In the first year of the coalition government economic policy largely followed the script laid down, at least on the points covered by the agreement. Some Conservative policies were put on ice, such as getting rid of the 50p income tax rate, increasing inheritance tax thresholds, as well as cutting the basic rate. The Treasury Team quickly swung into action and George Osborne announced a package of measures in his June 22 Emergency Budget, and set out the strategy for the Parliament. VAT was increased to 20 per cent, personal allowances by £1000; council tax and public sector pay were frozen for two years, capital gains was increased (although not by as much as had been planned) and child benefit was cut for wealthier families. But more important than any of these specific measures was the development of the argument which was to be hammered home at every opportunity during the coalition's first year in office. All coalition ministers, both Conservative and Liberal Democrat, included in every media interview, every article and every speech a reference to the mess that they had inherited from Labour. The rationale for the formation of the coalition was presented constantly as necessary because of the seriousness of the economic situation which required the Conservatives and the Liberal Democrats to put aside their differences on economic policy and work together in the national interest to heal the national finances and rebalance the economy. The political advantage of this narrative was obvious since it placed all the responsibility for the financial crash on blunders and incompetence by Labour ministers, rather than on the regulatory regime and the financial growth model which went back to the 1980s and which no party had seriously questioned before the crash. The Conservatives had as noted shifted to a harder position on the deficit at the end of 2008, but the Liberal Democrats had not.

Now in government the Liberal Democrats endorsed the Conservative position and denounced Labour for the way it had responded to the recession, including the fiscal stimulus in 2009. What had formerly been seen as the necessary means to avoid financial collapse and restart growth; was now redefined as the problem which had to be removed before growth could resume. Certain figures were constantly repeated by coalition ministers. It was said that the deficit was the largest structural deficit in Europe, that the government was borrowing one pound for every four that it spent, that the government was paying £120 million pounds a day in debt interest, £43 billion a year, and that under the plans of the previous government the ratio of debt to GDP would still be rising in 2014. It was alleged that in May 2010 the UK faced being caught up in the sovereign debt crises sweeping through the eurozone if nothing was done. 2010 was turned into the real crisis rather than 2008. Labour had created the current crisis by its response to the crash, and by the mistakes it had made in its economic policy, and in particular in its regulation of the City before 2008. Ministers adroitly used the change of government to suggest that a line could now be drawn on the mismanagement, waste, and profligacy of the previous government, and that the coalition could be trusted to apply a new fiscal discipline to restore the economy and the public finances to health.

The strategy on the deficit was largely shaped by the Conservative Treasury team but endorsed by the Cabinet. The aim to eliminate the deficit in one five year Parliament implied steep tax increases or major public expenditure cuts. The government announced that it would put the emphasis on public spending cuts, with 78 per cent of deficit reduction being achieved in this way, and 22 per cent through tax increases. This implied a major adjustment to public expenditure programmes with many departments facing 20 per cent cuts or higher, and only a few programmes, notably health and overseas aid, being ring-fenced. These priorities were endorsed by the Liberal Democrats but health and foreign aid were also specific Conservative manifesto pledges. Analysis of the red book accompanying the budget showed that although the cuts appeared draconian the share of public spending in GDP in 2015 was planned to be roughly the same as in 2007, around 41 per cent. The reason why the cuts appeared so large in some departments was because the recession had permanently reduced GDP by approximately 6 per cent. A very large adjustment of public spending plans and expectations needed to be made if taxes were not to have to be increased substantially to maintain existing levels of spending. As in previous public expenditure crises, the short-term ballooning of the deficit was due to the contraction of the economy, the impact of automatic stabilisers such as welfare benefits paid to workers who lost their jobs, and the fiscal stimulus which had included measures such as the temporary VAT reduction. The political judgement was that as soon as economic conditions allowed and there were clear signs that the recession was over the deficit should be rapidly reduced and public expenditure programmes brought back into balance with private expenditure, to reflect the level of taxation the government was prepared to impose. Much of the argument between the government and the Opposition was over the timing of the deficit reduction not on whether there should be deficit reduction at all. George Osborne wanted rapid deficit reduction to reassure the markets that Britain had the political will to impose financial control and discipline, and thinking ahead it also made political sense to get the cuts over as quickly as possible in the hope that a growing economy in the second half of the Parliament would allow taxes to be reduced in the run-up to the next election scheduled for 2015.

The public spending cuts were agreed between the spending departments and the Treasury over the summer and published in the Comprehensive Spending Review in the autumn on 20 October 2010. The ease with which departments signed up to the cuts attracted some comment, since it appeared to indicate either that new ministers did not understand how difficult it might be to implement the size of cuts they were agreeing to make, or that the government was not serious in pushing through major reductions, and would wait for a combination of growth and inflation to reduce the scale of the problem. As in deficit reductions in the past the political symbolism is sometimes more important than the actual measures. governments intent on deficit reduction need to shift political perception and to persuade their electorate that there is no alternative. In reality there are always alternatives, such as tax increases, but these are generally judged politically less palatable than spending cuts, although often easier to implement. Governments are prone to exaggerate the situation they face in order to establish a new definition of political reality and a new set of policies. It is often convenient to put the blame on external agencies. In 1976 the IMF served this function, but research has shown how the real initiative for the cuts came from within the Treasury and how the IMF were on the whole reluctant participants, acting as a lightning rod to deflect public anger. In 2010 the excuse for urgent action has been the bond markets, who if not satisfied with the government's plans might precipitate a sovereign debt crisis. Before the adoption of the cuts programme, however, there was no evidence that the bond markets were in fact alarmed about the British economy. British bonds were still long-dated, in sharp contrast to the terms offered to Greece and other struggling economies in the eurozone. The political decisions to protect certain major budgets, particularly health, but also defence, showed that the government did have considerable flexibility in how it implemented its plans. There was no immediate crisis (Wolf, 2011a).

The cuts stirred up a great deal of controversy, but in the first year of the coalition government very few were actually implemented. The pain was prospective rather than immediate. Some of the decisions which attracted most attention, and most tension within the coalition, such as the withdrawal of most teaching funds to universities and their replacement through a trebling of student fees, gave little benefit to the public finances, since the fees were not to be paid up-front but only when students were earning, so the Treasury still bore the financial burden. Other cuts like the proposed sell-off of some of the forests owned by the Forestry Commission stirred up such opposition that the government had to abandon them. The sums were trivial in relation to the totals that the cuts were designed to save, but there were a number of similar retreats by government, so that by the end of its first year some analysts were already beginning to forecast that the government was unlikely to meet its targets for reducing the deficit over the Parliament (National Institute of Economic and Social Research (NIESR), 2011).

This was not the view however of the Office for Budget Responsibility (OBR). The OBR was a major institutional innovation launched by the coalition government in May 2010. The aim behind setting up such an agency was to create more transparency about government fiscal planning, and to increase credibility about government targets and figures in the markets. It can be compared with the decision by the Labour government in 1997 to give operational freedom to the Monetary Policy Committee of the Bank of England to set interest rates. The OBR does not have an equivalent role in fiscal policy, but it audits government targets and estimates, and makes judgements about whether the government's plans are likely to achieve its fiscal objectives. It does not comment on the fiscal objectives themselves and whether they are desirable, only whether the government is providing the means to achieve them.

In its Economic Outlook for April 2011 the OBR noted various changes in the economy since its previous report, notably an unexpected drop in output of 0.5 per cent in the final quarter of 2010 (OBR, 2011). But while noting the uncertainty around all its predictions its central forecast was that government had a greater than 50 per cent chance of meeting its two medium-term fiscal targets – eliminating the budget deficit (balancing the cyclically-adjusted current budget) and seeing the public sector net debt (PSND) falling by 2015–2016. It predicted that the level of debt would peak at 70.9 per cent of GDP in 2013–2014, leading to a slight fall in debt interest by the end of the period. Debt interest would however remain a substantial component of public spending, at over £40 billion per annum. Public sector net debt is forecast to be 60 per cent of GDP in 2010–2011 and rises in the following three financial years. This makes the fiscal consolidation a long-drawn out gradual process rather than the short sharp shock which some Conservative columnists such as Christopher Booker in the *Sunday Telegraph* would prefer. What is feared by many of these critics on the Right is that as the cuts really bite over the next few years, the opposition to them will grow, and the government will not have the political strength to impose them. Public sector net debt might still be rising not falling as a consequence by the end of the period, and there would still be a sizeable budge deficit, making scope for tax cuts much less.

The argument of Conservative supply-siders has been that the government should be much bolder in reducing spending immediately and at the same announce tax cuts to stimulate the economy. The government has not adopted this advice, but it is vulnerable to seeing its fiscal targets slip if it cannot deliver the spending cuts it has set out. Such slippage is not uncommon, and afflicted both the Thatcher government and the Reagan administration (Pierson, 1994). Apart from the failure to carry through an ambitious cuts programme, the government's plans might also be derailed if growth in the UK economy and in the world economy is less than forecast. But it could also benefit if that growth turned out to be higher than expected. What many commentators have noted however is that the government's strategy requires at least 2 per cent growth to be achieved, and many independent commentators are sceptical as to whether this is possible (Wolf, 2011b); in part because of the fiscal consolidation, and the danger that Britain could be trapped as Japan was in a long period of very slow growth.

Economic growth

The strategy for fiscal consolidation dominated the first year of the government, but it is intimately intertwined with the government's strategy for growth. The destruction of the growth model on which Britain had relied for 20 years in the financial crash of 2007–2008 raises important questions about what kind of growth Britain can expect in the future. The coalition has talked a great deal about rebalancing the economy. Rebalancing in this context has two main aspects – it can mean rebalancing the economy by shrinking the public sector and expanding the private, but it can also mean rebalancing the private sector by shrinking financial services and expanding manufacturing. In both cases there is a vague idea that Britain should lose some of its dependence on financial services, and revive its manufacturing. Export-led growth is the goal, on the model of Germany, which has suddenly started being praised again by British politicians, after 20 years when it was the model not to follow, and there was a great deal of praise for the Anglo-Saxon model from Conservative politicians. Michael Howard for example as Conservative leader, addressing News International Corporation in Cancun in 2004 declared:

> America has created the most successful form of capitalism in the free world ... [but] Western nations have developed two competing models of capitalism. For several decades, the governments of mainland Europe have chosen not to emulate the more liberal economic policies of the United States. They have chosen to adopt a much more regulatory, and in some cases corporatist, approach. This has sometimes been referred to as the 'German' model, although Germany is far from unique in adopting this approach. ... It has made the European economies less flexible and therefore less competitive. This has had a real cost in terms of jobs and growth. Labour costs and taxes are much higher in Europe than in the US. Growth and job creation is much lower. There are more unemployed people in Europe and they are out of work for longer. In fact, if Europe had followed the American model, it would have created 28 million more jobs and its workers would have produced £5000 more a year in output (Howard, 2004).

The UK variant of the Anglo-Saxon model has been much more dependent on financial services than the United States. Even then the role of financial services should not be exaggerated – it is an important sector, making up about 10 per cent of the UK economy, and employing more than one million people. It does produce very high tax receipts for the Treasury and it makes a major contribution to British exports. It has also spearheaded the financialisation of the British economy, and has provided the means for individuals and households to take on ever greater levels of personal debt. Growth in this model has been consumer-led rather than export-led, dependent on an expanding domestic market. A great deal of government policy in the last ten years has been aimed at improving skills of UK workers and investing in the science base, but there remains a substantial productivity gap, and the UK does not have the kind of manufacturing capacity for this sector to provide the lead in a growth surge.

In the absence of a clear alternative growth strategy the coalition is trusting to a *laissez faire* approach and the appearance in due course of green shoots of recovery as it did in the 1980s and 1990s. It hopes the economy will find a way to rebalance itself, if the government provides financial stability and keeps the burden of taxation low. There is strong continuity between the general fiscal policy of this government and its Labour predecessor, not least in budgetary policy. The second budget of George Osborne was very similar in style to Gordon Brown's budgets, tinkering with allowances, incentives and special schemes. It was fiscally neutral but contained some minor changes to the tax system, such as the one pence reduction in petrol duty, which appeared to be designed mainly for short-term political effect rather than for any long-term strategic purpose. The OBR had made its forecasts before the budget but it decided that the budget made little difference to any of them.

The main strategic growth policy of the coalition lies in the plans to develop green industries and set exacting targets for emissions. Both parties in the coalition were committed to these policies in their manifestos, and they are an important part of the coalition agreement. Chris Huhne, the Climate Change Secretary, published a bill in May 2011, reaffirming these commitments, but there was doubt about whether these could be delivered, because of opposition within industry, within the Conservative Party and within the government to give such a high priority to the green strategy in a period of financial hardship, particularly when other countries seemed unlikely to do the same.

Conclusion

It is difficult to make an accurate assessment of how the new government may perform after only one year, but the terms on which it will eventually be judged have become clear. In part it has set these terms itself. The judgement on whether it succeeds or fails in meeting its medium-term fiscal targets will be made by the OBR. The government inherited a difficult financial situation because of the financial crash and the recession. It adopted a particularly ambitious plan for reducing the deficit, choosing to label the position it inherited as one in which the finances were out of control and needed urgent remedial attention. The actual deficit reduction plan announced does not quite match the government's presentation of its predicament, but politically it has been highly successful, particularly for the Conservatives, and has allowed them to consolidate their new-found reputation for economic competence, and to hang the financial mess around the neck of the Labour Party.

The strategy for reducing the deficit has risks, which many independent commentators have pointed out, but the government clearly feels these are risks worth running, and it hopes with reasonable luck to have a story by the end of the Parliament which will enable the return of a majority Conservative government. The plans may come unstuck if opposition to the cuts in certain key areas mean that the savings required cannot be delivered. The government could resort to tax increases to meet its fiscal targets, but this would be very unpopular inside the Conservative Party, and would damage the government's credibility with its voters. The government's plans are also threatened by what happens in the world economy, particularly in the eurozone, and in the British economy. Events in the first are largely outside its control and it only has limited capacity to influence the second. The government needs strong international growth to help lift off the British economy, and if such growth materialised the British government would be very tempted to encourage the revival of the financial growth model, since this is a political economy which is tried and tested, and for which all the elements are still in place. A significant uplift in house prices would be a good backdrop for a general election. The government has commissioned reports on the financial sector, and major changes may be recommended. It will be an important decision for the government as to how radical it chooses to be in for example breaking up the big banks, or separating investment and retail banking. The more the government becomes worried about the strength of the recovery in the British economy, the less likely it is to be radical in reforming the financial sector. The real threat to the government's political prospects in the spring of 2011 was not another major downturn, but the possibility that British growth might prove much more sluggish than most other advanced economies, and that this might put extra strain on the public finances and on public support for such a long drawn out process of fiscal consolidation. The government's official stance, however, remained optimistic. A corner had been turned, and the British economy was set once more for growth and financial stability, with only minor changes to the way the British economy had been configured under Blair, Brown and Major.

6
European Policy

Philip Lynch

The issue of European integration caused significant divisions in the Conservative Party when it was last in power in the 1990s and these contributed to the party's general election drubbing in 1997. In opposition, the Conservatives became more Eurosceptic as European integration deepened, but the party leadership also enjoyed some success in both detoxifying the issue and managing internal dissent. With the Conservatives back in office, in a coalition government with the pro-European Liberal Democrats, the European issue is posing problems once more. Ideological differences between the Conservatives and Liberal Democrats are more pronounced on Europe than on most other issues. The Conservatives are a 'soft' Eurosceptic party (Taggart and Szczerbiack, 2008: 247–8) that supports membership of the European Union (EU) but opposes key areas of integration such as Economic and Monetary Union (EMU) and the extension of EU competence in social policy, justice and home affairs, and foreign and security policy.

Cameron and Conservative policy on Europe

Europe was not as high a profile an issue in the 2005 Conservative Party leadership election as in previous contests, but it was nonetheless significant in David Cameron's victory. A number of Eurosceptic MPs sought to maximise their influence by agreeing to support a candidate who made a firm commitment to pull Conservative MEPs out of the European People's Party-European Democrats (EPP-ED) group in the European Parliament (Lynch and Whitaker, 2008). This was a symbolically important issue for Eurosceptics and one that could be delivered by the party leader in opposition. Cameron pledged to leave the EPP-ED, a decision borne from conviction rather than just electoral calculation, as did Thatcherite Eurosceptic Liam Fox. But frontrunner David Davis did not because he feared that it would be difficult to implement. Cameron's pledge enabled him to broaden his support by adding votes from the Eurosceptic right, move ahead of Davis on the second ballot of MPs and beat him in the vote of party members.

The pledge to remove Conservative MEPs from the EPP-ED was Cameron's most significant early initiative on Europe. Group membership had been a thorny issue in opposition. William Hague had negotiated special status for Conservative MEPs in the European Democrats section of the EPP-ED, with the Conservative Party free to pursue its own position. But critics argued that the link with the federalist EPP muted the Conservatives' distinctive position on Europe. Iain Duncan Smith planned to leave the EPP-ED but the search for potential allies was not concluded during his brief spell in the leadership in 2001–2003. Michael Howard then sought to close the issue down by negotiating greater autonomy for the European Democrat section and requiring all Conservative candidates for the 2004 European elections to agree to respect the leader's decision on group membership.

Cameron did not deliver on the promise to leave the EPP-ED until after the 2009 European elections because of the reluctance of many Conservative MEPs and some potential allies to leave their groups. The Conservatives became the largest party in the new European Conservatives and Reformists Group, which initially included 55 MEPs from eight member states. The Polish Law and Justice Party and the Czech Civic Democrats were economic rather than socially liberal, and were not the largest centre right parties in their respective countries but had recently been in government (Bale et al, 2010). Tensions over the group leadership and the failure to recruit more mainstream parties limited its impact, but its votes did give the group some weight in the European Parliament (for example on the re-election of Jose Manuel Barroso as Commission President) and Conservative MEP Malcolm Harbour chaired the influential Internal Market committee.

There was greater consistency in European policy during the Conservative Party's spell in opposition than in many other areas, with Cameron maintaining and developing broad objectives and policy commitments that initially took shape under Hague, Duncan Smith and Howard. Continuity is also evident in discourse on Europe and in the relatively low salience afforded to the issue. Cameron broadly maintained the 'in Europe, not run by Europe' position developed during Hague's spell as leader, as well his commitment to hold a referendum on a future EU treaty transferring powers to Brussels.

The Conservatives have continued to promote a deregulatory agenda, urging the completion of the Single European Market, further liberalisation of protected sectors and a more rigorous competition policy. Criticism of EU social and employment policy is another consistent theme of Conservative policy. EU enlargement is another long-standing goal, with Cameron supporting, in principle, the membership applications of Turkey and the Balkan states.

In his first major speech on the EU in 2007, Cameron stated that it should focus on three issues – globalisation, global warming and global poverty (Cameron, 2007a). Concerns about the costs of the Common Agricultural Policy (CAP) to farmers in the developing world and to the environment were added to long-standing British criticism of its inefficiency. Cameron urged member states to tackle climate change through the EU's Emissions Trading Scheme, but did not propose any extension of EU competence. His focus on global poverty as an EU priority marked a departure from the position taken under Howard when international aid was identified as a competence to be repatriated to nation states. Under Duncan Smith, the Conservatives had adopted a more pronounced Eurosceptic position on EMU by ruling out membership of the euro. Following the unsuccessful 2001 general election 'save the Pound' campaign, the party leadership reduced the salience of the issue. Opposition to euro entry was reiterated under Cameron, with the government claiming that Britain's position outside the eurozone left it in a better position to tackle the recession and national debt. Conservative opposition to the EU Constitutional Treaty under Howard had focused on issues of democracy and trust rather than traditional Tory themes of sovereignty and nationhood. Cameron maintained the argument that, because Lisbon was essentially the same as its predecessor, Labour's manifesto commitment to hold a referendum on the Constitution should also apply to Lisbon. The Conservatives also claimed that the additional safeguards secured by Labour on its 'red lines' – on the EU foreign policy post, criminal justice, the Charter of Fundamental Rights, and unanimity – were insufficient.

Cameron's claim that his commitment to a referendum on Lisbon was a 'cast iron guarantee' (Cameron, 2007b) would prove problematic. If Lisbon had not been ratified by all 27 Member States when the Conservatives entered office, the party promised to suspend ratification and campaign for a 'No' vote in a referendum. But if it had been ratified, the Conservatives said only that they would 'not let matters rest there'. After the treaty was ratified by Ireland and the Czech Republic, Cameron announced that a Conservative government would not hold a 'made-up referendum' (Cameron, 2009b). The party would instead use the forthcoming general election deliberately to seek a mandate to negotiate further 'British guarantees' on the application of the Lisbon Treaty and 'restore key powers to Britain'. A Conservative government would seek a 'full opt-out from the Charter of Fundamental Rights' and 'greater protection against EU encroachment into the UK's criminal justice system' (Cameron, 2009b). Support for the repatriation of social and employment policy did not necessarily mean a rolling back of existing policy, with Cameron seeking 'guarantees over the application of the Working Time Directive in our public services' rather than to overturn it (Cameron, 2009b).

Cameron also pledged domestic action to prevent further powers being ceded to the EU. The Conservative election manifesto thus proposed a 'referendum lock' to ensure that any future treaty handing over further powers to the EU would be subject to a referendum, and a Sovereignty Bill would confirm that ultimate authority resides with the Westminster Parliament (Conservative Party, 2010). Both had their origins in policies first developed during Hague's leadership.

The coalition and Europe

The Conservatives failed to secure a parliamentary majority at the 2010 general election. An alliance with the Eurosceptic Democratic Unionist Party would also leave them short of a majority. Rather than seek to govern without a majority, the Conservatives swiftly opened coalition negotiations with the Liberal Democrats. The Liberal Democrat manifesto had a strong pro-European flavour, albeit tempered by the economic crisis. The party believed that it was in Britain's long-term interest to join the single currency, subject to approval in a referendum, but recognised that 'Britain should only join when the economic conditions are right, and in the present economic situation they are not' (Liberal Democrats, 2010: 67). The Liberal Democrats pledged to remain part of justice and home affairs initiatives such as the European Arrest Warrant and supported EU regulation of financial services and banking. The manifesto recognised, however, that the EU 'is not perfect' and sought reform of the EU budget and CAP, and an end to European Parliament sessions in Strasbourg.

The Liberal Democrats also promised an 'in-out' referendum the next time that a British government signed up to 'fundamental change in the relationship between the UK and the EU' (Liberal Democrats, 2010: 67). The party had supported a referendum on the Constitutional Treaty in 2005 but then argued that a referendum on Lisbon was not required. Menzies Campbell advocated an in-out referendum, a policy that his successor as leader Nick Clegg maintained. When a Liberal Democrat amendment on an in-out referendum was not selected during the parliamentary debate on Lisbon, Clegg ordered his MPs to abstain on a Conservative amendment on a Lisbon referendum. Three members of his shadow Cabinet – David Heath, Alistair Carmichael and Tim Farron – resigned and 15 Liberal Democrats supported the Conservative amendment (Cowley and Stuart, 2010a: 143–4).

Europe was one of the Conservatives' red lines in the coalition negotiations. They were unwilling to concede ground on the referendum lock and opposition to further European integration. But senior Conservatives were prepared to drop demands for the repatriation of powers and further guarantees on Lisbon, recognising that these were unpalatable for the Liberal Democrats and would strain relations with the EU. The Liberal Democrats were keen to ensure that Britain would play a constructive role in the EU but had little problem in accepting that membership of the euro would not happen over the next five years. Their key concession was an acceptance that there would be no further transfers of power in this period. The referendum lock survived and the agreement promised to 'examine the case' for a Sovereignty Bill.

The Programme for government claims that the coalition's European policy 'strikes the right balance between constructive engagement with the EU to deal with the issues that affect us all and protecting our national sovereignty' (HM Government, 2010a: 19). Positive statements on EU action on global competitiveness, global warming and global poverty echo those in the Conservative manifesto. Compromises are evident on policy competences, where the coalition will 'examine the balance of the EU's existing competences' and 'work to limit the application of the Working Time Directive'. European Commission proposals to amend the latter may address British concerns about the impact of its rules concerning on-call time and rest periods in the NHS. Participation in a European Public Prosecutor system is ruled out, but other criminal justice legislation will be handled on 'a case-by-case basis, with a view to maximizing our country's security, protecting Britain's civil liberties and preserving the integrity of our criminal justice system' (ibid). Coalition policy is not radically different from that of recent governments which sought to play a positive role in the EU whilst defending the national interest, supported the single market and enlargement, demanded reform of the CAP and EU budget, and were cautious about EU competence in social policy, criminal justice and defence.

William Hague became Foreign Secretary, but the appointment of the pragmatic Conservative David Lidington, a former Foreign Office adviser, as Minister for Europe rather than the Eurosceptic Mark Francois, who had been the shadow minister, soothed Liberal Democrat nerves. Cameron had been a pragmatic Eurosceptic in opposition. In his first year in Downing Street, his pragmatism became more apparent and his Euroscepticism less so. Cameron described himself as a Eurosceptic, but a 'practical, sensible one at the same time' (Kirkup, 2011c). Even before the coalition took office, Hague spoke of a 'strategic decision' to avoid early conflict: 'We have enough on our hands without an instant confrontation with the EU. ... It will not be our approach to go and bang on the table and say immediately "we demand A, B, C"' (Parker and Pignal, 2010). The Conservatives would be 'active and activist in the European Union from day one, energetically engaging with our partners' (Hague, 2010a). Relations between Cameron and German Chancellor Angela Merkel had been strained since the former's announcement that the Conservatives would leave the EPP-ED, but suggestions that Merkel would cold-shoulder Cameron in government were far-fetched. The new prime minister secured German and French support for his call for spending restraint. He also secured the backing of states in northern, central and eastern Europe for the British position on the single market. However, the development of multiple bilateral relationships with states on a variety of issues could not disguise the tensions between the UK and some allies on issues such as the CAP and British budget rebate.

EU policy developments

There were reasons for believing that relations with the EU would be relatively quiescent during the coalition's first months in office. No major treaty revision was on the horizon and the Franco-German motor of integration had been spluttering. Nonetheless, the dynamism of European integration means that problems were unlikely to be far away. This was particularly true of two key areas of EU policy activism, economic governance and justice and home affairs, which will be examined below. The Lisbon Treaty, which the Conservatives had opposed, was in force and accepted by ministers as political reality. The European External Action Service (EEAS) was, for example, launched in late 2010 as a diplomatic service for the EU, speaking on behalf of common positions on foreign policy and managing the EU's foreign relations, security and defence policies. Moreover, annual negotiations on the EU budget would also create tensions. With Britain's contribution to the EU budget reaching £9 billion in 2010, the government rejected the European Parliament's proposal for a 5.9 per cent budget increase for 2011. Cameron led calls for the budget to reflect the public spending cuts being made across Europe, a position supported by 11 other member states including France and Germany. If no deal was reached, the 2011 budget would remain at the previous year's level – an appealing prospect for Eurosceptics. The government's initial demand for a budget cut or freeze did not achieve sufficient support so a compromise of 2.9 per cent increase was agreed that cost the UK an additional £450 million. Cameron had talked tough, raising Eurosceptic expectations, then settled for a deal which others were already willing to accept. Months later, the UK also opposed a proposal from the European Commission for a 4.9 per cent increase for the 2012 EU budget.

Negotiations on the EU's multiannual financial framework for 2014–2020 began in 2011. Britain, France, Germany, Finland and the Netherlands agreed to a text in December 2010 calling for the 2012 and 2013 budgets to reflect national spending cuts and for a real term freeze for 2014–2020. Cameron claimed that he was leading the initiative but the search for allies is complicated by opposition from other states to the British budget rebate, which the Conservatives are loathe to give up. The Commission has proposed that the annual rebate is replaced by a lump sum payment made in 2014 for the 2014–2020 period, with cuts in the rebate occurring when the EU budget increases. The government continues to press for reform of the CAP but Britain's unwillingness to give ground on the EU budget and its rebate makes this less likely.

Economic governance

Chancellor George Osborne abolished the Treasury's Euro Preparations Unit on taking office. But this was primarily a symbolic measure as the prospects of British entry had all but disappeared since Gordon Brown's announcement in 2003 that only one of his five economic tests had been met. While the Conservatives and Liberal Democrats were locked in coalition negotiations, outgoing Labour Chancellor Alasdair Darling committed the incoming government to take part in an EU bailout for Greece. The EU established a temporary European Financial Stability Mechanism (EFSM) funded by all member states, and a smaller European Financial Stability Facility to which only eurozone states contribute. Side tracking the 'no bailout' clause (Article 125), member states agreed to use Article 122(2), which allows financial support in exceptional circumstances, to help Greece. The UK will contribute 8.6 per cent of the EFSM funds and remain part of the temporary bailout mechanism until 2013. Cameron opposed this at the time but, in office, said that his government would have to live with it. Britain contributed to the bailout for Ireland through the EFSM, the International Monetary Fund (IMF) and an additional £3.25 billion bilateral loan, and to a bailout for Portugal through the EFSM and IMF. But the UK will only contribute to a second bailout for Greece through the IMF, with the EU contribution coming only from eurozone states.

In December 2010, Member States agreed to establish a permanent European Stability Mechanism from 2013 which may be used to bail out states, subject to 'strict conditionality', if their debt problems threaten the stability of the eurozone. The government accepted a German demand for an amendment to Article 36 because this will only apply to member states whose currency is the euro and will not involve a transfer of power from the UK to the EU. Treaty change will occur through the Simplified Revision Procedure and ratification will require an Act of Parliament but not a referendum. In March 2011, 23 member states signed up to the Euro Plus Pact which proposes further European action to foster competitiveness, employment, sustainable public finances and financial stability. Participating states are expected to translate the fiscal rules of the EU Stability and Growth Pact into national law and pursue further coordination of their tax systems, notably through a common corporate tax base. Nine member states supported a British document, 'Let's Choose Growth', proposing further action to complete the Single Market and cut regulation. But with only the UK, the Czech Republic, Hungary and Sweden staying outside the Euro Plus Pact, the prospect grew of Britain being left outside new economic decision-making bodies in a two-speed Europe.

Member states have also agreed to greater economic surveillance. They will send their national budgets to the Commission each spring, which will check that their plans are consistent with European guidelines on fiscal policy and deficit reduction. The Commission will then issue an opinion and draft budget plans will be discussed at Ecofin in early summer before approval by national parliaments. The coalition agreed to this, but insisted that the budget would be heard first by the House of Commons and warned that it would veto any proposal requiring the British budget to be cleared by the Commission. The UK is exempted from the sanctions and enforcement measures because of its EMU opt-out. But Eurosceptics warned that the measures marked a significant expansion of EU economic policy.

Justice and Home Affairs

Justice and Home Affairs (JHA) is an expanding field of EU activity, as seen in the five-year Stockholm Programme. The Lisbon Treaty extended EU competence in police and criminal justice, but Britain retains an opt-in arrangement. Once a proposal is tabled, the government has three months to decide whether to opt-in or opt-out, and may also opt-in to the legislation at a later date. By 2014, the UK must decide whether to opt-in *en masse* to existing EU justice and home affairs measures adopted under the old third pillar.

In its first six months in office, the government opted-in to six JHA proposals (Home Office, 2011), including the draft directive on the European Investigation Order (EIO). Home Secretary Theresa May stated that the latter was a practical measure that would help to tackle cross-border crime and provide a speedier and more efficient system of obtaining evidence from overseas (Hansard, 27 July 2010, col. 881). Other police forces would not be permitted to instruct the British police on what operations to conduct, nor allow them to operate with law enforcement powers in the UK. But Eurosceptics and civil liberties groups warned that British police could be compelled to collect evidence on individuals for conduct that is not regarded as criminal in the UK. By opting-in while the directive was still at draft stage, the government hoped to persuade other Member States to accept a proportionality test and additional safeguards on the collection of evidence. But the final decision on the directive will be taken by qualified majority voting, and the UK cannot then reverse its decision to opt-in.

The coalition had opted-out of five JHA measures by December 2010, including a draft directive on seasonal workers. The government had initially chosen not to opt-in to an EU directive on human trafficking, with ministers claiming that much of what it proposed was already in operation in the UK. In March 2011, the Minister of State for Immigration, Damian Green, stated that the government would now apply to opt-in to the directive (HC Hansard Written Answer, 31 March 2011, col. 459W). The government was also expected to opt-in to an EU directive on Passenger Name Records, having persuaded other states to apply its provisions on the collection of data on air travel to intra-EU flights. Meanwhile, Sir Scott Baker is chairing an independent review of Britain's extradition laws, including the operation of the European Arrest Warrant (EAW). More than 1000 people had been detained and extradited by British police under the EAW in 2009–2010.

The main European challenge to the government's home affairs agenda came not from the EU but from the European Court of Human Rights (ECHR), which falls within the remit of the Council of Europe. The ECHR had ruled in 2005 that the UK had breached the European Convention on Human Rights by denying a convicted rapist the right to vote. In November 2010, the Court gave the UK six months to comply with its verdict. Conservative Eurosceptics seized on the case as an opportunity to assert the sovereignty of Parliament against European judicial decisions. With David Davis and former Labour Home Secretary Jack Straw mobilising opposition to the Court's decision, Cameron spoke of his revulsion at the decision. Ministers were ordered to abstain and backbenchers given a free vote as the House of Commons voted by 234 to 22 to maintain the blanket ban on prisoners voting. However, the Court rejected the government's subsequent appeal. Ministers will do the minimum to comply with the ruling but prisoners could pursue claims for compensation. The coalition established an independent commission to examine the case for a British Bill of Rights, while Conservative backbenchers continued to urge the government to defy the Court.

The European Union Act 2011

The European Union Act 2011, originally introduced in the House of Commons in autumn 2010, enacts three key commitments in the coalition programme: (i) a referendum lock, (ii) addition controls on the use of the ratchet clauses in the EU treaties, and (iii) a restatement of the sovereignty of parliament. The referendum lock will ensure that any future treaty that transfers power from the UK to the EU will be subject to a referendum before the government can agree to it. Ministers must issue a statement to parliament setting out whether a treaty change involves a transfer of power, with their decisions subject to judicial review if challenged. A referendum will occur after the treaty had been approved by parliament and its result would be binding – it could not come into force unless a majority of those voting in the referendum were in favour of ratification. Separate questions will be required for each treaty change or decision requiring a referendum. No referendum will be required if the government of the day blocks proposed changes to the treaties in EU negotiations. Given that the coalition programme rules out further integration, it is unlikely that there will be a referendum on a new treaty in the near future – unless an accession treaty incorporates new transfers of power.

A referendum will also be required before the government can agree to certain decisions provided for in the treaties that transfer competence or power to the EU. The treaties set out the competences of the EU (that is the ability of the EU to act in a given way) but do not define its 'power'. The Act thus stipulates that a transfer of power occurs when unanimity is replaced by qualified majority voting and when an EU institution gains the power to impose an obligation or sanctions on the UK. The treaties include various procedures that permit Member States to modify the existing treaties without recourse to formal treaty change. The Simplified Revision Procedure allows decisions currently taken by unanimity (except on defence) to be decided by a majority vote if all Member States agree by unanimity and all national parliaments give their approval. Enabling clauses and *passerelles*, known as 'ratchet clauses', which allow the transfer of an area of competence to the EU without treaty change.

The European Union Act includes additional controls on the use of the Simplified Revision Procedure and specified ratchet clauses. As there is no clear definition of what constitutes a ratchet clause, the Act lists the treaty articles and stipulates the action to be taken before the government can use them. Some will require an Act of Parliament and a referendum, some an Act of Parliament, and others a vote in both the House of Commons and House of Lords. A referendum will be required before a decision to give up the veto in a 'significant' area. This qualification angered Eurosceptics. The European Scrutiny Committee concluded that the exemptions in the Bill would allow the government to support some major changes, such as the strengthening of the eurozone or the accession of Turkey, without requiring a referendum (European Scrutiny Committee, 2011: 33). A referendum will be required on the removal of any of some 44 national vetoes and on a dozen other decisions, including membership of the euro, participation in a European Public Prosecutor system and the removal of UK border controls. The accession of new Member States will not trigger a referendum. Where the use of a ratchet clause would alter what can be done in an existing area of EU competence (for example on criminal law), approval by an Act of Parliament will be necessary. A vote in both Houses will be required where, for example, a ratchet clause modifies the rules of procedure or composition of EU institutions.

Sovereignty clause

Clause 18 of the Act states:

> Status of EU law dependent on continuing statutory basis
> Directly applicable or effective EU law (that is, the rights, powers, liabilities, obligations, restrictions, remedies and procedures referred to in section 2(1) of the European Communities Act 1972) falls to be recognised and available in law in the United Kingdom only by virtue of that Act and where it is required to be recognised and available in law by virtue of any other Act.

This is a declaratory clause that does not change the relationship between the UK and the EU or affect the primacy of EU law. By creating a statutory point of reference for the principle that EU law only takes effect in the UK through the will of parliament, the government argues that the clause counters claims that EU law constitutes a higher autonomous legal authority derived from the EU treaties which has become an integral part of UK law independent of statute, and thus assist the courts by providing clarity about the intentions of parliament (David Lidington, Hansard, 11 January 2011, cols 243–52). The latter claim had been made in *Thoburn v Sunderland City Council [2002]* but was rejected by Lord Justice Laws. Clause 18 would, the government claims, put the matter beyond speculation (Lidington, 2010).

The European Union Scrutiny Committee, chaired by veteran Eurosceptic Bill Cash, conducted pre-legislative scrutiny on the sovereignty clause. It considered the original version of which began with the words 'It is only by virtue of an Act of Parliament that...'. The final version set out above was agreed by both Houses after the Commons rejected a Lords amendment that sought to rewrite the clause so that it stated that EU law is recognised in the UK solely 'by virtue of the European Communities Act 1972' rather than through the wider reference point of 'an Act of Parliament'. Constitutional experts who gave evidence to the Committee agreed that the clause was not required in a legal sense and had no practical effect. Clause 18 reaffirms the principle of dualism – that a treaty agreed by the executive does not come into effect domestically until incorporated into law by parliament – but does not, the Committee claims, say anything about the relationship between UK and EU law in the event of a clash between the two. The House of Lords Constitution Committee agreed that the clause 'restates, but does not change, the law' (Constitution Committee, 2011: 16). The European Scrutiny Committee warned that the government's assertion in the Explanatory Notes to the Bill that the legislative supremacy of parliament originates from common law leaves it open to revision by the courts. As Clause 18 only concerns EU law, the report also warned that the courts may interpret legislative supremacy in this narrow sense. The Committee concluded that 'Clause 18 is not a sovereignty clause in the manner claimed by the government, and the whole premise on which it has been included in the Bill is, in our view, exaggerated' (European Scrutiny Committee, 2010: 31). Ministers subsequently amended the Explanatory Notes to make it clear that the government did not endorse the opinion that parliament's authority derives from common law.

The coupling of the sovereignty clause and the referendum lock is an uncomfortable one. The doctrine of parliamentary sovereignty states that parliament cannot bind its successors – a future parliament may amend or repeal any existing legislation. However, the European Union Act attempts, if not to bind its successors, to at least make it difficult for a future government to overturn the requirement to hold a referendum if powers are transferred to the EU. This might, in time, become a constitutional convention but no previous EU treaty has been put to a popular vote. As the House of Lords Constitution Committee notes, it marks 'a radical step-change in the adoption of referendum requirements' as it requires referendums on a range of issues that are not fundamental constitutional matters (Constitution Committee, 2011: 11).

Eurosceptic dissent

The European Union Bill passed its second reading without a vote, but the debate had highlighted the unease felt by Eurosceptic Conservatives about both it and coalition policy on Europe in general. They argued that the

Bill's provisions on sovereignty were toothless and that the referendum lock was too restrictive because a referendum would not be required if a transfer of power was not judged 'significant'. There were five rebellions on the Bill at Committee of the Whole House stage. Twenty-seven Conservative MPs supported an amendment that would have added a statement to Clause 18 reaffirming the sovereignty of Parliament, and 20 backed an amendment providing for an in-out referendum should a 'No' vote be registered in the referendum on a transfer of competence.

Eurosceptic dissent had been relatively muted at the outset of the coalition but soon gathered momentum. Seven Conservative MPs voted against a motion in July 2010 taking note of EU documents establishing the European External Action Service. The House debated the draft 2011 EU budget in October when a majority backed a motion supportive of the government's efforts to maintain it at a level equivalent to the 2010 budget. Also approved, with the support of the whips, was an amendment by Bill Cash calling for the government to reject the European Parliament's proposal to increase the budget. Economic Secretary to the Treasury Justine Greening stated that she shared the sentiments behind an alternative amendment proposed by Douglas Carswell which urged the government to reduce Britain's contribution to the EU, but could not support it because withdrawing money would be illegal (Hansard, 13 October, col. 410). Despite intensive activity by the whips, the Carswell amendment was supported by 37 Conservative MPs and 12 others had signed the amendment but abstained or were absent from the vote. The following month, MPs approved a motion supporting the government's position that sanctions proposed by the Task Force on Economic Governance should not apply to the UK but 25 Conservatives opposed it, registering their concern about the extension of EU powers. Ahead of the proposed bailout for Portugal, 30 Conservatives voted against the government on financial assistance to the eurozone in May 2011. A motion approving an increase in the UK subscription to the IMF was approved in July but 31 Conservatives joined Labour in voting against it, and more might have done so had the vote not been held late on a Monday night.

Senior Eurosceptics estimate that more than 100 Conservative backbenchers are unhappy with coalition policy on Europe. A total of 63 different Conservative MPs had rebelled on European votes (including votes on the loan to Ireland and an increase in the UK's contribution to the IMF) by July 2011. Among the rebels were veteran Eurosceptics like John Redwood and Richard Shepherd, plus members of the 2005 intake such as Carswell who had quickly established a reputation for independence. The 2010 intake is primarily Eurosceptic, with most favouring the repatriation of powers and a significant minority advocating withdrawal. By July 2011, 31 of the new intake had defied the whips on Europe. Eurosceptic rebels (and potential rebels) fall into three broad groupings. First are serial rebels on Europe, and other issues, who support withdrawal from the EU (Taggart and Szczerbiack, 2008: 247–8) and have criticised the leadership for dropping commitments to a referendum on Lisbon and the repatriation of powers. Carswell captured their anger when he described the coalition as 'the most pro-integrationist administration since Ted Heath's' (Carswell, 2011). Many in this grouping, including Carswell, Philip Davies and Philip Hollobone, are supporters of the Better Off Out campaign. The second grouping consists of Eurosceptics who support a significant rebalancing of the relationship with the EU – including the repatriation of powers in areas of social policy, and justice and home affairs – and are unhappy that the manifesto commitment to repatriation was dropped. MPs in this grouping, like John Redwood and Bill Cash, regard the European Union Bill as too timid and have criticised the government for accepting treaty change on economic governance without demanding a repatriation of powers or further opt-outs in return. They want the European integration process to be reversed rather than stalled, and are unlikely to be won over by compromise deals on EU issues. The final grouping includes Eurosceptics who initially accepted the coalition's position on Europe, albeit with reservations, but are concerned that its pledge that there would be no further integration during the current parliament is not being adhered to rigorously and that the coalition has not used the eurozone debt crisis to win concessions on other issues. An indication that these pragmatic Eurosceptics were beginning to flex their muscles came with the publication of a letter in the *Financial Times* (23 June 2011) by Chris Heaton-Harris and 13 other Conservative MPs from the 2010 intake opposing further bailouts and arguing that the eurozone crisis provided an opportunity for the UK to push for reform of the EU. It will be a cause for concern to the whips that many MPs from the second grouping have already rebelled; if those from the third grouping lose patience with the government's approach, serious dissent on Europe is likely.

Current Conservative divisions on Europe are, then, different from those of the 1990s when there was a clear fault-line in the party between pro-European and Eurosceptics. Now, the divisions reflect the differing degrees of Euroscepticism within the party. Pro-Europeanism is a minority position in today's Conservative Party and those who remain have accepted its Eurosceptic position, with Kenneth Clarke the prime example. Previously vocal pro-Europeans like Stephen Dorrell have tempered their enthusiasm, while the small number of pro-Europeans in the 2010 cohort, such as Robert Buckland and Laura Sandys, are unlikely to rock the boat. All three spoke in favour of the European Union Bill at second reading. Not a single Liberal Democrat MP rebelled on Europe in the first year of the government. In the House of Lords rebel Liberal Democrat and pro-European Conservative peers, including Lords Brittan, Heseltine and Howe, combined to defeat the government on key areas of the European Union Bill. These would have set a referendum turnout threshold of 40 per cent of the electorate to ratify treaty changes, introduced a 'sunset clause' that would have seen the referendum requirements lapse at the end of the current Parliament, and restricted the number of policy areas on which a referendum would be held. The defeats were overturned in the Commons and the Lords then relented.

Hague has reportedly described Europe as a 'ticking time bomb' for the Conservatives (Robinson, 2008). The first year of the coalition provided a reminder that the bomb remains live, but it does not yet appear set to explode. Dissent in this period did not exhibit the organisation and coherence of the Maastricht rebellions. Conservative Eurosceptics have not formed an organised group and, with the new cohort not automatically falling into line behind the older generation, does not have clear leadership. They also differ on objectives and strategy. While some Eurosceptics, for example, supported Cash's amendment to the sovereignty clause in the European Union Bill, others regarded the Bill as a welcome, albeit imperfect, step in the right direction. Some also felt that rebellion on as complex an issue as parliamentary sovereignty would not capture the public imagination and might revive perceptions that the Conservatives have an unhealthy obsession with the issue. It is also worth noting that some convinced Eurosceptics, such as former Referendum Party member Priti Patel and Better Off Out signatories David Davies and Laurence Robertson, did not register any dissenting votes on European issues in the first year of the coalition. The repatriation of powers and a referendum on Britain's relationship with the EU are the core Eurosceptic demands. But picking the right fight is a challenge as, with no defining moment such as major treaty change on the horizon, it will be difficult to mobilise sufficient numbers to defeat the government. And, Labour resisted the temptation to side with Conservative rebels to inflict defeat on the early stages of the European Union Bill. Labour did, though, vote against a significant increase in the UK contribution to the IMF designed to help fund bailouts of eurozone states.

Conclusions

The European policy of the coalition government has not been as different from that of the previous Labour government as some had expected. Its policy on the euro, the EU budget, CAP, the Single European Market, social policy, EU foreign policy, and justice and home affairs is broadly consistent with that of recent British governments. The Conservatives were far from enthusiastic about the European External Action Force, British participation in the European Financial Stability Mechanism, and an increase in the EU budget for 2011, but were prepared to live with these rather than provoke an early confrontation with the EU. The coalition does, however, appear more relaxed about the prospect of the UK's non-participation in future EU action on economic governance than its predecessor. Following the second Greek bailout, Cameron stated that these moves towards economic governance mean that 'there will be opportunities for Britain to maximise what we want in terms of our engagement with Europe' (Forsyth and Nelson, 2011).

The most significant break in European policy has come in the domestic arena with the European Union Act's provision for a referendum lock. Domestically, the requirement for a referendum on future treaty change and on the transfer of powers in a range of areas goes well beyond the current expectation that referendums are only held on issues of major constitutional significance. Within the EU, the provisions in the Bill will strengthen perceptions of British exceptionalism and cause future governments to think twice about supporting further integration given the potential difficulties of winning a referendum. However, given the coalition's opposition to further integration, a referendum looks unlikely during the current Parliament.

The pragmatic approach adopted by the coalition in its European policy reflects the compromises required for agreement between the soft Eurosceptic Conservatives and the pro-European Liberal Democrats. But the Conservative leadership had already determined that it would avoid confrontation with the EU in its first months in office. As in opposition, Cameron's instinctive Euroscepticism was trumped by his political pragmatism and desire to detoxify the issue. Significant efforts were made to forge effective working relations with other Member States. Managing the European issue was, however, going to be more difficult in government than in opposition because the Conservatives, given that they were uncomfortable with key aspects of the EU, would also have to deal with proposals for further integration. The escalation of Conservative dissent shows the difficulty that faces Cameron in striking the right balance between pragmatism and Euroscepticism.

Further difficulties in Brussels and at Westminster await the government. It is unlikely to gain significant CAP reform or a budget freeze for the 2014–2020 financial framework, especially if it is refuses to give ground on the British rebate. Eurosceptics will continue to press ministers to use the negotiations to seek one or both of their core objectives: policy repatriation and a referendum on Britain's relationship with the EU. The financial situation in the EU remains bleak and with the bailout of Portugal, Britain remains liable for payments until 2013. The Euro Plus Pact will see most Member States agree to further economic coordination and new EU taxes. Most Conservatives are happy for the UK to remain outside these arrangements and will hope that the UK will continue to rally support from economically liberal Member States on Single Market issues. Liberal Democrats who harbour long-term ambitions to join the euro have kept their counsel on European issues within the coalition, but will be concerned if Britain is left outside an inner core of eurozone states moving apace towards further integration.

Acknowledgment

Research for this chapter was supported by the Leverhulme Trust (grant number F/00212/AD).

7
Immigration Policy

Tim Bale and James Hampshire[1]

Since their agreement to form a coalition government in May 2010, the Conservatives and Liberal Democrats have set about the difficult task of making good on the former's electoral promise to cut immigration from 'hundreds of thousands' to 'tens of thousands' by the end of this parliament. This represents a *volte face* on Labour's demand-led system, which saw net migration rise to over 200,000 per annum, and, if successful, will see a major change in migration flows to the UK. The promise to more than halve immigration in the space of five years, however, has set the government on a collision course with a broad range of organised interests, including businesses ranging from international banks to curry houses, universities, trade unions, and migrant NGOs.

It is not difficult to explain the electoral logic behind the immigration cuts: the political salience of immigration has increased over the last decade, many voters want numbers to be reduced, and immigration was one of the few issues on which the Conservatives enjoyed a consistent lead over Labour during the latter's pomp (Bale et al, 2011: 398). However, making a popular, if not populist, promise to cut numbers at election time is easier than actually cutting numbers once in power. While many policy proposals can fairly be characterised as 'easier said than done', immigration policy is especially prone to reality checks because the electoral dividends of talking tough are so at odds with the functional imperatives of migration management in advanced capitalist economies (Hampshire, forthcoming). This tension is especially acute in the UK, a country on the one hand, with relatively high levels of anti-immigrant sentiment (Transatlantic Trends, 2011) and ferociously anti-immigrant newspapers, and, on the other hand, an economy that has become particularly reliant on migrant labour.

As well as opposition from vested interests outside government, the coalition also faces intra-party divisions and inter-party tensions. The intra-party divisions within the Conservative Party reflect some core contradictions in centre-right ideology towards immigration. To paraphrase Andrew Gamble (1988), a free economy requires openness towards immigration, while a strong nation state mandates closure. Thus centre-right parties are often divided between the 'business right', which supports liberal immigration policies, and the 'identity right' which does not (Bale, 2008a: 324). This generic centre-right dilemma is exacerbated by David Cameron's modernisation agenda, which has led the party to downplay its more obvious anti-immigrant rhetoric following the 2005 election defeat. For many of the Tory grassroots, there is a suspicion that the party elite are not willing to be tough enough on immigration (as a perusal of Conservative Home threads on immigration will reveal). Yet for more liberally-minded Conservatives the imposition of a quota sits uneasily with a pro-business approach and commitment to free markets, as the reservations of Education Secretary Michael Gove and Universities Minister David Willets show.

All of this is further exacerbated by inter-party tensions with the Liberal Democrats. The cut is a Conservative policy, clearly at odds with the Liberal Democrats' campaign promises. While the latter apparently had very little impact on the immigration section of the coalition agreement – both in terms of agreeing to drop most of their policies and accepting most of the Tories' plans – senior Liberal Democrats, including at least two of their ministers, have since tried to push policy in a more permissive direction. One of the most vocal critics of the immigration cap has been the Business Secretary, Vince Cable, who has won some significant concessions on economic migration and also on student visas.

Thus the Conservatives and, by extension, the coalition, face an uphill struggle in making good on their promise to reduce immigration. This chapter briefly outlines the Conservatives' traditional stance on immigration, assessing how their policy evolved under Cameron and then through the coalition negotiations. The chapter then discusses immigration policy-making since May 2005, showing how the government has proposed to cut numbers, the opposition it has encountered, and concessions that have been made in response. The chapter concludes by reflecting on the economic and political risks of the coalition's immigration policy.

Conservative immigration policy December 2005–May 2010[2]

David Cameron's election as leader in late 2005 triggered the first sustained and serious attempt by the Conservative Party to reposition itself since losing office in 1997. His immediate predecessors, desperate to find issues on which the Party had something in common with voters who were unimpressed with its policies on the economy and public services, were tempted into exploiting widespread anxiety over immigration in predictably populist fashion. Cameron's initial silence on the issue, his appointment of a moderate as the Party's immigration spokesman, and an attempt to shift the focus onto the economic impact of migration were but one way in which Cameron tried to 'decontaminate the Tory brand' in order to gain 'permission to be heard' by middle class, small-l liberals who were crucial to the Party's electoral recovery but who were alienated by hard-line stances. Immigration, however, was never entirely left out of the equation even in this early period: it was always seen – as long as it was carefully handled – as an issue capable of damaging Labour by casting doubt on its competence and on the extent to which it was in touch with what the British people really wanted. As such, it was skilfully factored back into the carefully-balanced offer that the Party presented to the electorate from late 2007 onwards.

The May 2010 general election thus represented a change in tone on immigration and asylum policy from the Conservative Party, especially when compared to its efforts in 2001 and 2005. The Party's previous fixation with bogus asylum seekers, for instance, had completely disappeared. On the other hand, its manifesto still contained a promise to limit numbers and expressed a particular and apparently new-found concern about the abuse of student visas. And while these policies were scarcely mentioned in the Party's campaign in the national media, they featured quite heavily in its 'under the radar' direct mail operation aimed at target voters in marginal constituencies. The Conservatives also relied on its friends in the media to exploit concerns about the Liberal Democrats' apparent support for an amnesty for illegal immigrants, not least in order to halt the alarming rise in support for Britain's 'third party' following its leader's commanding performance in the first televised debate.

Whether the Lib Dems or the Conservatives got most out of the coalition agreement overall will continue to be debated for some time to come. When it comes to immigration, however, there can be little doubt that it was the Tories who trumped their junior partners. Not one of the policies outlined in their manifesto in that area was dropped: all that was added was the inclusion of a Lib Dem promise to end the detention of children in asylum cases – a promise that even many 'mainstream' Conservatives could live with. All accounts of the formation of the coalition suggest that immigration was a non-negotiable 'red-line' for the Tories and that the Lib Dems were made aware of this from the off. It is also notable that the issue figured prominently in Cameron's concerted effort, following the formation of the coalition, to reassure both Party members and voters (and probably MPs as well) of his Tory credentials. As he stressed repeatedly, he was still a Conservative PM delivering an agenda all Conservatives could be proud of on Europe, on spending cuts, on public service reform and, of course, on immigration.

The numbers game

The coalition thus came into office with a promise to reduce net migration. Ever since David Cameron broke his silence on immigration with his 2007 speech, saying that the level of immigration must be reduced to a 'sustainable' level, the Conservatives had refused to put precise figures on what they thought that level should be. Instead, they repeatedly referred to reducing immigration from the 'hundreds of thousands' to the 'tens of thousands'. This was obviously intended to create some wiggle room, but at the same time it effectively set an upper limit of 100,000, which, given that net migration stood at 215,000 in 2010, meant reducing it by over 50 per cent.

It was somewhat surprising that the coalition's very first announcement on immigration had nothing to do with cutting numbers and was, moreover, a progressive move. Indeed, it was the only significant Lib Dem policy commitment that had made it into the agreement. On 15 May, just three days after the coalition was announced, the new Immigration minister, Damian Green, affirmed the government's commitment to end the detention of children for immigration purposes and announced a review of alternatives. In Parliament, Nick Clegg denounced the previous government's policy as a 'moral outrage' and claimed that the proposed end to child detention showed the Liberal Democrats' influence on coalition policy, a refrain that would become increasingly questionable in the months to come.

The announcement on child detention met with applause from children's charities, as well as migrant and human rights NGOs, but it must have bemused the Tory faithful. However, if some worried that the government had gone soft on immigration, there was no need. It has proven much more difficult than expected to develop a workable alternative to child detention and after considerable debate the government has had to row back on its original commitment. The latest proposal is that families and children will be detained for immigration purposes only as a last resort, and in separate facilities, but detention will not be stopped altogether.

Rewind back to June 2010, and it becomes clear that the initial liberal phase was short-lived. Shortly after the announcement on child detention, the coalition got down to the business of cutting numbers. The centrepiece of the immigration cut was a proposal to impose an annual limit, or cap, on economic migration. The government soon realised, however, that restricting economic migration – which means restricting highly-skilled and skilled workers through Tiers 1 and 2 of the Points Based System (PBS)[3] since the Tier 3 low-skilled route for non-EU workers was never opened by Labour – would not be sufficient on its own. Given the diversity of migration flows to the UK, achieving a net reduction of over 100,000 would require what Theresa May later described as a 'comprehensive package' focusing on all aspects of the immigration system to put 'steady downward pressure on each of the main routes into the UK' (May, 2010). To this end, the government instructed the Home Office to conduct research on possible areas for restriction, which was published as *The Migrant Journey* on 7 September 2010 (Achato et al, 2010). As a result of this and other deliberations, the government committed itself to reducing numbers across all four of the main routes for non-EU nationals: economic migrants, international students, family migration, and the 'settlement link' through which temporary migrants acquire permanent residency. The cap on economic migrants remains at the heart of the policy – and has certainly received ample media coverage – but it is now just one part of a much wider strategy.

Politics trumps economics? Capping work-related migration

The government announced its intention to impose a cap on work-related migration on 28 June 2010. Economic migration accounts for around 20 per cent of total immigration to the UK. Therefore, assuming all else is equal, even a modest reduction of 5 per cent in total immigration would require a cut of 25 per cent of work-related immigration; and since the low-skilled Tier 3 route is closed, this would mean 25 per cent of *highly-skilled* and *skilled* migration through Tiers 1 and 2 – a tall order with low returns. Despite this, on 28 June two consultations were launched, one by the UK Border Agency (UKBA) on the mechanism for limiting non-EU economic migration (UKBA, 2010a), the other by the Migration Advisory Committee (MAC) on the numerical level of the annual limit (MAC, 2010). The proposals included a pool system for highly-skilled migrants; raising the minimum criteria for qualification under Tier 1; a first-come-first-served monthly system for skilled workers under Tier 2; a merger of the Shortage Occupation and Resident Labour Market Test routes; raised English language requirements for Tier 2; and the inclusion of intra-company transferees within the cap. Whatever shape it would eventually take, the annual limit would come into effect from April 2011.

In the meantime, there was an interim cap of 24,100 skilled work visas announced, a reduction of 1,300 or 5 per cent on the previous year. The intention was to avoid what the government called a 'closing down sale', as employers and migrants brought forward applications in an attempt to beat the April 2011 deadline. The interim cap met with immediate opposition from employers, especially those dependent on overseas staff. A joint briefing for the House of Lords by Universities UK, the Wellcome Trust and the Association of Medical Research Charities, argued that 'arbitrary' numerical limits 'work directly against' attracting the 'best and brightest' to work in science and medical research (UUKA et al, 2010). The interim cap was successfully challenged in the courts by the Joint Council for the Welfare of Immigrants (JCWI) for by-passing parliamentary scrutiny, but re-instated in December following a ministerial statement to the Commons by Green.

In fact, opposition to the interim cap was just the curtain-raiser on the main event. The government's proposals for an annual limit starting in April 2011 came under sustained attack by employers' organisations and companies across almost every major sector. The individual firms who lined up to criticise all or some of the proposals reads like a who's who of blue chip companies, covering financial services (JP Morgan, Deutsche Bank), pharmaceuticals (GlaxoSmithKline), computing (Microsoft UK), the automotive industry (Honda, Nissan, Toyota), technology and telecommunications (BT, General Electric, Siemens), retailers (Asda), and engineering (Arup).

The concerns of business were forcefully articulated within government by Vince Cable, the new Business Secretary, who became increasingly open about his misgivings. In its July 2010 Strategy for Sustainable Growth, the Department for Business Innovation and Skills (BIS) warned that 'while it is important that the public has confidence that we are controlling net migration, it is equally important that the migration system allows business to make best use of global talent' (BIS, 2010: 10). Cable was supported in this debate by fellow Liberal Democrat and Energy Secretary, Chris Huhne, as well as Conservative ministers Michael Gove and David Willets, who voiced their concerns at a Cabinet committee chaired by Nick Clegg (Parker and Boxell, 2010).

Nor was opposition limited to the domestic sphere. Cameron's visit to India in late July, leading a trade delegation that included the chief executives of Barclays, Vodafone, and the English Premier League, risked being overshadowed by controversy about the cap (BBC News, 2010a). A week before the trip, Anand Sharma, India's Commerce Minister, expressed his concerns to the Prime Minister at Downing Street and also went public telling the *Daily Telegraph* that the UK government's immigration proposals 'would affect adversely the professionals, Indian doctors, engineers and nurses, who have made a notable contribution to the UK economy' (Nelson, 2010). When Cameron arrived in India, the Indian government again raised its concerns, Sharma warning that the cap could have an 'adverse effect' on trade relations. Vince Cable tried to reassure the Indian media, telling them that:

> it's no great secret that in my department, and me personally, we want to see an open economy, and as liberal an immigration policy as it's possible to have. ... We are arguing, within Government, about how we create the most flexible regime we can possibly have (quoted in Barker, 2010).

Another member of the trade delegation, Jo Johnson, Conservative MP and Deputy Chair of the Indo-British All Party Parliamentary Group, expressed concern about 'contradictory messages' on immigration (Watt, 2010a). Keen to contain the damage, David Cameron promised that India would be consulted on the cap, and just a few weeks later Damian Green was dispatched to reassure the Indian government and IT firms that the 'best and brightest' would not be excluded (Home Office, 2010a, 2010b).

Back at home things weren't going much more smoothly. If the public statements of business weren't enough, the results of the consultation, which received 3,201 responses, revealed substantial opposition (UKBA, 2010b). During the autumn, ministers went on a charm offensive to try and allay business fears. In a speech to the Royal Commonwealth Society on

7 September, Damian Green insisted on the need for 'sustainable immigration levels' to 'relieve pressure on public services, and stop immigration being such a delicate political issue', but acknowledged that 'at the same time, we must be confident enough to say Britain is open for business and study to those who will make this a better country, and a more open society' (Green, D., 2010). At the CBI annual conference in October, David Cameron made conciliatory noises, telling the assembled business elite that 'as we control our borders and bring immigration to a manageable level, we will not impede you from attracting the best talent from around the world' (Kirkup and Whitehead, 2010).

In a speech to the Policy Exchange think-tank in November, the Home Secretary, Theresa May, insisted that 'we can reduce net migration without damaging our economy. ... We can attract more of the brightest and the best at the same time as we reduce the overall number' (May, 2010). May acknowledged business opposition to inclusion of intra-company transfers within the cap, and signalled that this would be addressed; and she also stressed that the limit would be reviewed annually by the MAC. While she recognised employers' concerns about the changes to Tier 2, she insisted that the skills levels must be raised to ensure that people coming in under this route were doing skilled work. Tier 1 would also be subject to more stringent requirements. Employers had lobbied less vociferously on Tier 1 (which is a route for highly-skilled migrants without a job offer) and May claimed there was evidence that many who came through this route were in fact working in low paid jobs. Tier 1 would be tightened up to focus on 'investors, entrepreneurs, and people of exceptional talent'.

A few weeks later details of the cap were announced (UKBA, 2010c, 2010d). From 1 April 2011, an annual limit of 20,700 would be introduced for those coming to the UK under both Tiers 1 and 2. A monthly quota of visas would be available, starting with 4,200 for April then 1,500 thereafter. If the allocation is oversubscribed, applicants will be ranked using the points system, with preference for those jobs on the shortage occupation list, published by MAC, as well as scientists and high earners. Tier 1 General Route will be closed and Tier 1 restricted to entrepreneurs and investors, plus an extra 1,000 visas for the 'exceptionally talented'. All jobs under Tier 2 (General) will be raised to graduate level and the minimum salary for those coming under the intra-company transfer route for more than 12 months (but no more than five years) would be raised to £40,000; those earning between £24,000 and £40,000 would be able to enter for up to 12 months.

Despite the imposition of limits, several important concessions were made. In response to lobbying from banks and law firms, migrants earning more than £150,000 were exempted from the annual limit. The numbers involved are relatively small, but this is nevertheless a major concession to the City, meaning it can continue to bring in as many high-flyers as it wishes. In response to lobbying from scientists and medical researchers, who had argued that while weighting highly-paid jobs might work for finance and law it would exclude many highly-skilled scientists and researchers, the latter will be given a 'significant advantage' through the points system. Most significantly of all, in a deal brokered by Cable and May, intra-company transfers were exempted from the annual cap following fierce lobbying from multinationals, including Indian IT firms such as Infosys. And the decision to allow those earning under £40,000 to enter for up to 12 months will allow multinational companies to rotate staff on moderate salaries. These are numerically significant concessions as intra-company transfers accounted for about 22,000 of 36,490 non-EU skilled workers who came to the UK in 2009.

While many business leaders have said that they welcome the government's more 'business friendly' approach, others remain sceptical. On 24 January 2011, the outgoing Director of the CBI, Sir Richard Lambert, launched a stinging attack on the coalition's economic record, singling out the immigration cap:

> when it comes to micro policy initiatives, politics appear to have trumped economics on too many occasions over the past eight months. ... I'm thinking of the immigration cap, which is still a source of concern for companies and institutions, like universities, that need to bring international talent into the UK (Lambert, 2011; though see also CBI, 2011).

The government continues to insist that the UK is 'open for business', for example issuing a press release on the only aspect of the new arrangements that are intended to incentivise migration to the UK, entitled 'Government rolls out red carpet for entrepreneurs and investors' (UKBA, 2011).

'Some unpleasant things have crawled out': Cutting international students

The second, equally controversial, part of the coalition's package is the reduction of the number of student visas under Tier 4 of the PBS. If the coalition is to stand any chance of reducing net migration this is essential as students are now the largest single group of migrants. Approximately 273,000 international students (plus 30,000 dependants) came to the UK in 2009, about two-thirds of the total number of migrants. As one of the leading markets for education – second only to the United States – the UK economy receives a significant contribution from international students, over £5bn if off-campus spending is included. In addition to English language colleges whose market is obviously overseas students, the further and higher education sectors have become increasingly dependent on non-EU overseas students; indeed this has been one of the few areas for income growth in recent years. No surprise, then, that the government's plans provoked a robust response from those whose interests were affected, nor that those ministers involved once again strained the doctrine of collective responsibility.

While acknowledging the importance of the international student market, the government insists – not implausibly – that there are high levels of abuse, or 'non-compliance'. Indeed, it argues that one of the reasons why student numbers have grown so much is that Tier 3, for low-skilled workers, was never opened, and that many migrants coming through the student route are in fact looking for work, either for themselves or their dependents. Hence the idea of 'bogus students': those who are under-qualified, or who work outside the terms of their study visa, or who over-stay after their course has finished. Home Office data suggest that they constitute a significant problem, especially at the sub-degree level. About half of Tier 4 visas are issued to students studying at this level, including independent schools, public further education institutions, private further education colleges, and English language schools. It is the private sector that is of most concern to the government.

Given the absolute numbers involved, and the apparent levels of non-compliance, students are an essential element of the cuts package. It took the government a while to come round to this view, however. Having initially focused on the immigration cap for Tiers 1 and 2, it only signalled its intentions on Tier 4 in November 2010, when Theresa May suggested in Parliament that the number of student visas could be cut by up to 120,000, or 40 per cent (Morris, 2010). Although the government subsequently stated that it does not want to impose an annual cap as it has done for work-related migration, it has committed to a large-scale reduction.

A public consultation launched on 7 December 2010 sought views on mechanisms for achieving such a reduction. Proposals included raising the level of courses that students could come to the UK to study; tougher entry criteria and English language requirements; ensuring students return home after their course is completed; limiting entitlements to work for both students and their dependants; and stricter accreditation procedures for education providers in the private sector (UKBA, 2010e). The consultation was nothing if not bold. It proposed largely restricting Tier 4 to degree-level courses, and closing the 'post-study work route', through which 38,000 overseas students found jobs following graduation in 2009.

The hostile response was even more remarkable than the earlier consultation on work-related migration. By the deadline of 31 January 2011, the government had received more than 31,000 responses – one of the highest ever figures for a UK government consultation on any matter. The responses revealed widespread opposition to the proposals: universities, colleges, and schools voiced their concerns; as did a wide range of interests including the governments of India, China, Japan, and Canada.

Faced with widespread criticism, the government tried to play down the impact its proposals would have on 'genuine students' and 'legitimate courses'. And as with work-related migration, it sought to reassure critics that it does not want to cause economic damage with its policy. Indeed, every time the subject came up, the Home Secretary and Immigration Minister insisted that they do not want to deter bona fide students, particularly in the higher education sector. In her speech on 5 November, when the consultation was still open, the Home Secretary said that the government wanted to attract the 'best and brightest ... the top students to our top universities'. Damian Green has made similar reassurances, saying that 'universities, all of whom are highly trusted sponsors of foreign students, should not worry', though with regard to other parts of the education sector, particularly private colleges, he was distinctly less reassuring, at one point employing (uncharacteristically for him) imagery reminiscent of the tabloid Conservatism the Party had seemed so keen to put behind it: on 1 February he confided to a think-tank audience 'I have been turning over stones in this area. I have to report that some unpleasant things have crawled out' (Green, 2011).

Despite his reassurances, Green's stone-turning left not only private colleges but the whole education sector distinctly worried. In addition to the intrinsic effects on private colleges of cutting sub-degree level visas, a major concern was the effect that this, and any tightening of post-study opportunities, would have on the recruitment of degree-level students. As Essex University's Vice Chancellor, Colin Riordan, told *The Times* in December 2010:

> it is looking as if there may be a real risk that we make ... a big mistake on student visas. ... Unfortunately, there seems to be a belief that if you restrict visas at the sub-degree level outside universities (in language colleges, pathway colleges), that will end up as a restriction on net migration without affecting universities too severely. ... In fact, if you took our case, about half of our students who come in as overseas students are already resident in this country (Morgan, 2010).

This claim is reinforced by Universities UK, whose research shows that approximately 40 per cent of international degree students begin on below degree-level courses – the 'pre-university pathway courses' that, according to Green, are crawling with unpleasant things (APPG, 2011). In addition, the proposal to tighten up post-degree opportunities through the closure of the post-study work route would impact on student recruitment if it undermined the perceived desirability of studying at a British university.

This caused further wrangling between the Home Office/UKBA on the one hand, and BIS and Education on the other. The Universities Minister, David Willets, met with Green on several occasions, and made public some of his misgivings to the House of Commons Home Affairs Select Committee (Travis, 2011). That Committee's subsequent report on student visas cautioned that the proposals could have 'serious unintended consequences' and 'damage the UK's thriving educational export sector' (HASC, 2011). Similarly, the All Party Parliamentary Group on Migration expressed unanimous concern about the impact cutting student numbers would have on the higher education sector and the wider economy. Lord Boswell, a Conservative Peer and former Education Minister, put it succinctly when he said that the proposals are 'not geared towards economic arguments but the spur of public anxiety towards immigration' (quoted in MRN, 2011).

The government showed its hand on 22 March 2011. In keeping with the concessions made to business on work-related migration, the new student visa policy is significantly less draconian than many feared. On the one hand, the government has increased the English language requirements for degree-level students and from April 2012 any institution wanting to sponsor students will have to go through a tougher accreditation procedure to be classified as a 'Highly Trusted' sponsor. There will also be some tightening of work rights and only postgraduate students will be allowed to bring dependants. However, in a major concession, the government agreed to retain post-study work opportunities, albeit in a more restricted form. Tier 1 (post-study work route) will be closed, but graduates will be able to stay on through Tier 2 if they have a graduate-level job offer from a sponsoring employer. The government also acknowledged arguments about 'pathway' colleges, and private further education institutions will be able to recruit students so long as they meet the new accreditation requirements. Universities UK announced that it was 'pleased' the government has listened to its concerns on these issues (UUK, 2011). The Home Secretary told the House of Commons that the proposals should see a reduction of up to 80,000 student visas, a sizeable number, but significantly less than the original intention.

Family migration and the settlement link

The third component of the coalition's attempt to reduce immigration is family migration and the so-called 'settlement link' – the routes by which those on short-term visitor visas move to permanent residency. The government plans to tighten both of these routes. It estimates that family migration accounted for nearly 20 per cent of non-EU migration in 2009 and, as with students, it argues that there is significant abuse of the system, especially through 'sham marriages'. To date there has been just one major policy announcement in this area, although it was the very first concrete proposal to reduce numbers. On 9 June 2010, the government announced that it would impose an English language test for marriage migrants. This had previously been proposed by the Labour government in 2007, but downgraded to a 'medium-term goal' after 68 per cent of respondents to the consultation expressed opposition (UKBA, 2008). The coalition did not consult again – possibly expecting similar levels of opposition – and as of 29 November

2010, applicants for marriage visas have had to pass an English language test from an 'approved provider' before they can come to the UK. The tests are set at the basic A1 Common European Framework of Reference (CEFR) standard but, despite this relatively low bar, one Conservative MP estimated that they will lead to a 10 per cent reduction in marriage visa applications (Rosindell, 2010). The English language requirement was opposed by migrant NGOs but, unsurprisingly given the relative weakness of this lobby group compared to business and education, they did not secure any concessions.

One interesting aspect of the language test policy is the ambiguity about its official rationale. When the policy was first announced, it was justified on integration grounds: 'the new English requirement for spouses will help promote integration, remove cultural barriers and protect public services' (Home Office, 2010c). However, in a speech on 6 September, which set out options for reducing numbers, Damian Green implied more restrictionist motives: 'we have started to take action in this area by requiring, from November, a minimum level of English from those applying for marriage visas' (Green, D., 2010). As the Immigration Law Practitioners Association (ILPA) has pointed out, these are quite distinct, and potentially contradictory, rationales (JCWI, 2010). This ambiguity has persisted, with both integration and limitation rationales hinted at, but independent of whether the test will have positive integration effects, it seems clear that reduction of numbers is the main driver. Aside from the wider context of government's aim to cut immigration, this assessment is supported by the fact that spouses already have to learn English within two years of entry if they are to remain in the UK, and by the apparent lack of consideration given to providing information about how or where the new tests could be taken overseas. The government has promised further tightening of family visas, with a consultation on 'cracking down on sham marriages' (Green, 2011) due in 2011.

The final component of the cuts package does not directly address the numbers of immigrants admitted to the UK, but rather the routes through which persons admitted on a temporary basis 'quietly drift' (Green, 2011) to permanent residency status. The Home Office's *Migrant Journey* research (Achato et al, 2010) reported that in 2009, 81,000 people who had originally entered the UK for employment on a time-limited basis were granted settlement, while over a fifth of students who entered Britain in 2004 were still resident five years later. The government wants to reduce these figures. As Theresa May put it, 'it is too easy, at the moment, to move from temporary residence to permanent settlement' (May, 2010). Some aspects of the proposals on work-related migrants and student visas are already aimed at breaking the settlement link (for example, the time limits on intra-company transferees). But the government plans to consult on all routes to settlement in 2011, with the intention of making policy 'much clearer about those who are coming here for a time, and those who are coming here to settle' (Green, 2011). This is unlikely to be straightforward.

'Change is seldom easy'

Although the above developments clearly represent a restrictionist shift in policy, it is worth pointing out that the coalition has not entirely broken with Labour's legacy. The government has not sought to overhaul the PBS, but is rather using it to tighten up access to the UK. Perhaps more surprisingly, the government has retained the Migration Advisory Committee (MAC), a panel of economists who provide advice to the government on work-related migration. This is part of a wider continuity, namely the new government's commitment to a New Labour mantra of evidence-based policy-making. Finally, the coalition has adopted an essentially moderate, technocratic discourse on immigration, so much so that it is hard to see a significant shift from the Labour years and as with Labour, 'bogus' immigrants are loudly denounced but the 'best and brightest' are almost equally loudly championed (especially on overseas trade visits).

The government's moderation of tone, and the real concessions made in the face of opposition from organised interests, helps to explain why, despite the promise to more than halve net migration, there are already some grumblings of discontent from the right. While the *Daily Mail* remains mercifully on side, for some grassroots Tories the government is not going far enough fast enough (something which dovetails with a distrust of David Cameron's leadership) and for anti-immigration campaigners, such as MigrationWatch-UK's Sir Andrew Green, there is concern that the Conservatives may cave in to 'special pleading from employers and academics together with Liberal Democrat opposition to any significant measures' (Green, A., 2010), even if (perhaps surprisingly) there has been precious little evidence of the latter. While the odd bone has been thrown to assuage anti-immigrant opinion, overall the government has gone about halving immigration using fairly temperate language.

The most significant obstacle to the immigration cuts has been the resistance of organised interests. The coalition has quickly discovered that immigration has become so embedded in the British economy that any attempt to cut numbers meets with fierce opposition. There is nothing particularly unusual about this: established models of immigration politics show how well-organised client groups are able to influence policy in a more expansive direction than numerous, though diffuse, groups who oppose it (Freeman, 1995). But given that a lot of what has unfolded was eminently predictable, what is surprising is that the Conservatives didn't (or possibly didn't want) to see it coming, and that the Liberal Democrats have gone along for the ride.

For there is a clear conflict between the political objective of cutting immigration and the economic imperatives of an advanced capitalist economy and the minister who has come closest to admitting this is Vince Cable; who told Indian reporters at Heathrow that '*we're trying to reconcile two different objectives*, one of which is to reassure the British public that immigration is under control, and the other is to have an open economy where we can bring the talents from around the world' (quoted in Barker, 2010. Emphasis added.) What Cable didn't say is whether he believes these two objectives are indeed ultimately reconcilable. If not, the government faces a difficult choice: face down business and accept potential damage to the UK economy; or offer so many concessions that the numbers remain above 100,000. The concessions that have already been made, such as the exclusion of intra-company transfers from the immigration cap or the revised post-study work route, suggest that the latter is more likely.

The effect of both intra-party divisions and inter-party conflict between the coalition partners has largely operated as a function of this underlying tension. On the one hand, there is no doubt that the coalition immigration policy is essentially a Conservative policy. The only major Liberal Democrat campaign promise that made it into the coalition agreement was an end to child detention, and as we have seen this has been watered down. Other policies that the Liberal Democrats campaigned for, including regularisation and the suggestion of regional immigration policies that earned Clegg such derision from both Brown and Cameron in the third leaders' debate, were dropped quicker than you can say amnesty. Immigration was a Tory 'red line' and the party faithful (in common, it must be said, with most voters) would never have accepted such 'soft' policies.

Yet for all this it is hard to escape the impression that disagreements within the coalition have been as much intra-governmental as inter-party, tending to reflect ministerial portfolios and individual beliefs as much as party allegiance. Certainly, Vince Cable has been critical of the cuts, both behind closed doors and increasingly in the media. After the Prime Minister gave a major immigration speech in the run up to the local elections, calling for 'good immigration, not mass immigration' and reiterating the promise to cut immigration from hundreds to tens of thousands, Cable openly attacked him, calling the speech 'very unwise' and arguing that though the reference to tens of thousands was Conservative policy it was not in the coalition agreement and was not therefore government policy. The media certainly played this as a sign of growing conflict between the parties, but it was arguably as much a reflection of Cable's role as Business Secretary than as a Liberal Democrat. Indeed, internal criticisms of the cuts have come as much from Conservative ministers, such as David Willets and Michael Gove, who have both warned of the potential damage that could be done to education and the wider economy. The most plausible analysis is that the coalition arrangements have heightened the centre-right dilemma by lending a party political dimension to a predictable tension between the Home Office and Business departments. With Vince Cable as Business Secretary, and both the Home Secretary and Immigration portfolios held by on-message (albeit 'modernising' and moderate) Conservatives, the very different imperatives of these departments have been intensified, even though it would probably have existed in a purely Tory government. Thus while there clearly are differences between the two parties on immigration, and the Conservatives have made the running, intra-party divisions and departmental conflicts appear more fundamental to immigration policy-making dynamics than coalition tensions.

Conclusion

While it is hardly surprising to see a shift to a more restrictive immigration regime under a Conservative-led coalition, it nevertheless throws up an interesting paradox. In its effort to bring down numbers, the government is imposing constraints on Labour's demand-driven and employer-led system. With an irony that is little short of delicious, a centre-left government's *laissez faire*, pro-business policy is being replaced by a centre-right government policy based on state planning and opposed by big business.

This exposes the coalition to political risks in both directions. Cutting numbers by half risks damaging the economy, undermining the recovery, and alienating business interests; all of which could be damaging at election time. Not cutting numbers by half will expose the government to political flak and possible loss of public confidence, which could be every bit (indeed possibly more) damaging.

The government tries to gloss over this with a rhetorical blend of openness and control – as the Home Secretary put it in her 5 November speech, 'I want to attract more of the best and the brightest at the same time as we reduce the overall numbers' (May, 2010) – but it strains to hide the basic contradiction.

It is too early to tell what effect the policies will have on numbers. However, if, as seems likely, the government struggles to meet its target of 'tens of thousands', there is a real chance of an initially vague promise becoming an electoral albatross. If numbers stay above 100,000 the government can expect criticism from the right-wing media and from the right of the Tory Party. Indeed, there is already some evidence of this happening. Following his spat with Vince Cable over his 14 April immigration speech, David Cameron appeared to water down his commitment in a BBC interview, describing the tens of thousands target as an 'ambition' and refusing to state whether it was government policy. This drew fire from *The Sun* newspaper which accused him of 'backtracking' on his 'vow to slash immigration', quoting Tory backbencher Philip Davies as saying: 'The people don't want wishy-washy talk of ambitions. And they do not want the Lib Dem tail wagging the dog. David Cameron has to deliver on his promise' (Wilson, 2011). Failure to get numbers down is also likely to be attacked by MigrationWatchUK and the far right parties – the BNP of course, but more importantly UKIP, which draws its support from Tory heartlands and is increasingly as much anti-immigrant as Eurosceptic (Cutts et al, 2011). Labour, too, will treat the coalition to a taste of its own medicine by attacking them on competence grounds and accusing them of failing to meet their promises (indeed, this was exactly their strategy following the Cameron-Cable row). Whether voters respond to such criticisms will depend in part on how important the issue is relative to others – the economy, public services, etc. – which in turn will depend partly on the media. The right-wing tabloid press was more than happy to use the failure to control immigration as a stick with which to beat the previous Labour government; whether they will equally be keen to wield it against a Conservative-led administration will be interesting to see.

Notes

1 The authors gratefully acknowledge the research assistance of Erica Consterdine.
2 This section relies heavily on the more detailed treatment of the period contained in Bale et al (2011: 398–404).
3 The PBS was created in 2008 by the Labour government. It rationalised the then myriad immigration routes into five 'tiers' for managing migration: Tier 1 for highly-skilled workers; Tier 2 for skilled workers with a job offer; Tier 3 for low-skilled workers (never opened); Tier 4 for students; and Tier 5 for temporary workers and youth mobility. Potential immigrants apply through the appropriate tier, accruing points according to various factors such as education, income, qualifications, and so on.

8
Territorial Politics

Nick Randall and David Seawright

Introduction

As Jim Bulpitt noted, 'for the Conservative Party the United Kingdom is, and always has been, a particularly difficult piece of political real estate to manage' (1982: 144). The party nevertheless historically negotiated these difficulties with such skill that its territorial politics were regarded as 'one of the most consistently successful aspects of its statecraft' (Gamble, 1995: 14). During the Thatcher and Major premierships however, the Conservatives encountered increasing difficulties in their management of territorial politics. The result was the destruction of the party's base in local government (Rallings et al, 2002), followed by electoral annihilation in Scotland and Wales in the 1997 general election.

In the interregnum between the Major and Cameron premierships the challenges of managing the UK's 'political real estate' changed significantly and in this chapter we consider the Conservative Party's response. We do so with reference to Jim Bulpitt's characterisation of UK territorial politics and, in particular, his notion of a territorial 'operational code'. Thus, a summary of Bulpitt's approach is this chapter's first consideration. We then outline the evolution of the Conservative approach to territorial management after 1997. This leads us, in turn, to specify the challenges presented to the Conservatives upon returning to office. We then review the relationship between central and sub-central tiers of government during the Cameron government's first year in office. We conclude by reviewing the Conservative's operational code as it stands at the end of that year and consider its future prospects.

Bulpitt's characterisation of UK territorial politics

In a sequence of works, centred upon his 1983 book *Territory and Power in the United Kingdom*, Jim Bulpitt presented a distinct interpretation of territorial politics. For Bulpitt territorial politics concerns 'that arena of political activity concerned with the relations between central political institutions in the capital city and those interests, communities, political organisations and governmental bodies outside the central institutional complex' (2008: 19). His principal focus was upon how elites at the centre manage these interests, communities, organisations and bodies in the periphery and he suggested they had several potential strategies available to them. They could attempt to manage the periphery by *coercive power*. This would necessitate use of, or threats of, coercion against peripheral interests, communities and governing bodies. Alternatively, a *central authority* model of territorial management would allow the centre to secure cooperation on the grounds that its legitimacy and authority was recognised in the periphery. A model of *capital city bargaining* would emerge where peripheral elites were able to penetrate and negotiate at the centre. Finally, there was the *central autonomy* model. This sought, above all, 'the peace, order and tranquillity of the realm' (2008: 81). Conflict between the centre and the periphery was to be avoided and territorial management should be depoliticised, ideally via a system of indirect rule by cooperative local elites. This corresponded to a distinction between 'High Politics' and 'Low Politics'. 'High Politics' were matters the centre regarded as its domain and where it wished to preserve its autonomy to act and typically included matters of foreign and defence policy, taxation and macro-economic policy. 'Low Politics' concerned all other matters, for which the centre was generally content to offload responsibility to the periphery.

In Bulpitt's view it was this central autonomy model which emerged as the dominant 'operational code' for territorial management in the period after 1688. This held even in the late twentieth century. Although the Thatcher governments found themselves forced to intervene in the periphery, principally to secure their 'High Politics' objective of macro-economic stability, the centre hoped to draw back once reliable local collaborators had been established (Bulpitt, 1989; Carmichael, 1996). Bradbury (2006) has also shown how Bulpitt's analysis remains relevant to New Labour's period in office. On this account New Labour's devolution programme ultimately rested upon the same desire to secure the centre's autonomy. New Labour's statecraft sought to secure reliable local collaborators in the devolved institutions and amongst providers of public services. This was coupled to a conscious effort to minimise intergovernmental conflict between the centre and the devolved institutions. The objective was to permit the centre to concentrate upon the tasks of improving economic performance and public service delivery that were central to New Labour's social democratic 'High Politics'.

However, Bulpitt's account of territorial politics says little about the motives of central elites beyond their desire to promote stability, order and the centre's capacity for autonomous action. As Bradbury (2010: 329) suggests, by integrating this account with Bulpitt's later work on statecraft we broaden the range of motivations of those at the centre. And as we saw in Chapter 1 and can stand recapitulation here, statecraft is 'the art of winning elections and achieving some necessary degree of governing competence in office' (Bulpitt, 1986: 21) and requires that party leaders address a sequence of problems. Firstly, they need to attend to *party management*: their relations with back-benchers, constituency organisations and pressure groups that support or are affiliated with the party. Secondly, they need to devise a *winning electoral strategy*. Party leaders need an image and policy package sufficiently attractive to voters to initially secure office. Once in office they will need to devise a further strategy to secure re-election. Thirdly, they need to secure *political argument hegemony* by 'achieving an easy predominance in the elite debate regarding political problems, policies and the general stance of government' (1986: 21). Fourthly, the party leadership has to secure *governing competence* by devising policies that can be successfully implemented. We could therefore envisage an optimal operational code for territorial management as addressing the following considerations:

(a) the preservation of the territorial integrity of the United Kingdom,
(b) guaranteeing the autonomy of elites at the centre to act in 'High Politics',
(c) securing reliable collaborators in the periphery,
(d) enabling effective party management on matters of territorial politics,
(e) maximising electoral benefits for elites at the centre,
(f) gaining political argument hegemony on issues of territorial politics and,
(g) demonstrating governing competence by effective territorial management

The evolution of the Conservative operational code, 1997–2010

The Conservative approach to territorial management has proven surprisingly flexible. For example, the Conservatives response to the SNP's breakthrough in the late 1960s saw the party abandon its historic opposition to legislative devolution with its 'Declaration of Perth', subsequently ignore these proposals in office under Heath before conducting a *volte face* under Margaret Thatcher as Leader of the Opposition which returned the party to opposing Scottish and Welsh devolution. Flexibility is also evident after 1997 as changing circumstances triggered the revision of its previous commitments. The party initially maintained the Major's government's hostility to anything beyond administrative devolution for Scotland and Wales. In Scotland it campaigned, albeit without much gusto, for a No/No vote in the 1997 referendum. It also opposed the creation of a Welsh Assembly, although it deliberately kept a low profile in the No campaign. The success of both referendums triggered a speedy reappraisal whereby the party committed itself to make devolution work in both nations. As William Hague told the 1998 party conference:

> We are not going to leave the battleground to nationalist parties who want to destroy our country and a Labour Party which has played into their

> hands. We are going to invest the time and the energy and the resources to make sure the Conservative voice is heard in Edinburgh and Cardiff (Hague, 1998).

In practice, reconciliation to the new settlement proved easier in Scotland. For example, the party chose to participate in, and endorse the recommendations of the Calman Commission. The party's commitment to Welsh devolution proved rather more tentative and ambivalent. In the 2001 election the party proposed an independent commission to examine the workings of the Assembly. By the next election it advocated a 'preferendum' with options to maintain the status quo, abolish, or enhance the powers of the Assembly. This was abandoned in January 2006 but dissent continued between Conservative Assembly Members (AMs) and MPs over the powers of the Assembly. A party review only fudged the issue by proposing that an incoming Conservative government conduct 'a root-and-branch examination of the system of governance in Wales' (Conservative Party, 2008a: 1). Rather it took the imminent report of the All Wales Convention in November 2009 for the party to retreat further from 'devoscepticism' by declaring that it would not block a referendum on further legislative powers for the Assembly.

The party's approach to local government underwent a relatively early reappraisal as the Conservatives rediscovered their localist credentials. For example, by July 1997 the party had abandoned its opposition to a London Mayor. By the 1999 local elections William Hague had retreated further from the policies of his predecessors with a commitment to 'increase the independence and accountability of local authorities, with the objective of abolishing central controls on local government like capping' (Hague, 1999). By the 2001 general and local elections the party had a programme of reducing ring-fencing and national targets, increasing transparency and accountability and of local referendums on council tax increases above inflation. These proved enduring commitments and accompanied the party into office in 2010. However, following a leadership campaign in which localism played a prominent part (Denham and O'Hara, 2007: 2) David Cameron was keen to revive the party's Chamberlainite tradition. The result was a deeper and broader prospectus of decentralisation. This included granting the councils a 'general power of competence', allowing residents to petition for local referendums and an increasing enthusiasm for directly elected mayors (Conservative Party, 2009, 2010). The corollary was a deep hostility to regionalism. The party maintained a consistent opposition to regional chambers and regional assemblies throughout its period in opposition. Although there was some prevarication under both Duncan Smith and Cameron, the party also advocated the abolition of Regional Development Agencies.

In such policies it is plausible to see a desire to re-peripheralise 'Low Politics' even if, in the case of Wales, party management dictated a tentative approach. Acceptance of Scottish and Welsh devolution also seemed the minimum necessary for the party to rebuild its electoral credibility in the periphery. While some on the right, for example Simon Heffer, saw a greater electoral prize in becoming an English nationalist party the party's leadership refused to countenance compromising the Union for electoral advantage. Rather, as David Cameron clearly articulated, preservation of the Union is essential to an operational code that is focused on the centre's capacity to act autonomously in 'High Politics'. For Cameron,

> standing up for the Union isn't just about expressing our important feelings about our shared heritage. It's also a rational argument based on mutual interest. Together, we are the fifth largest economy in the world. Together, we have a seat at the top table and are listened to in a way that other countries can only dream of. Together, we have one of only five permanent seats of the United Nations Security Council. Together we are a major player in the EU, in NATO and other international organisations. And together, we have the British military – one of the most respected armed forces in the world (Cameron, 2008a).

Consequently, Conservative leaders after 1997 felt compelled to address at least some of the anomalies left by devolution. With a section of the party critical of England's position following devolution, this represented prudent party management. But in addition there has been a fear that such anomalies, if left unattended, could generate protest from English voters and place the Union in jeopardy. Chief amongst these has been the 'West Lothian question'. William Hague regarded this as a 'ticking time-bomb under the British constitution' and considered advocating an English Parliament or establishing an English select committee before taking up a policy of 'English votes on English Laws' in July 1999. This envisaged Scottish MPs losing any right to vote on English legislation and featured in the 2001 and 2005 manifestos. David Cameron, in contrast, referred the matter to the party's Democracy Task Force (2008). This proposed a diluted form of Hague's policy in which Scottish MPs would only lose the right to vote on 'English' Bills at the committee and report stages.

However, the party proved rather more circumspect during its period of opposition on other issues left unresolved by devolution, not least the future of the Barnett formula. Cameron, for his part offered general reassurances that while 'We all know that families can fall out bitterly over money. I'm determined that won't happen to the British family. We're bigger and better than that' (Cameron, 2006b). Such sentiments were entirely in keeping with Cameron's broader pragmatic Unionism. As he told a Scottish audience in 2007, 'if it should ever come to a choice between constitutional perfection and the preservation of our nation, I choose our United Kingdom. Better an imperfect union than a broken one. Better an imperfect union than a perfect divorce' (Cameron, 2007d).

Yet if the Conservatives were unwilling to trade the Union for electoral success they also recognised that their plausibility as a Unionist party meant addressing their electoral position in the periphery. Under David Cameron's leadership this had several dimensions. Firstly, he concluded an electoral pact with the Ulster Unionists in July 2008. This burnished the Conservatives Unionist credentials by permitting them to stand candidates in all nations of the UK, it represented an effort to normalise Northern Irish politics and, if successful, could mean additional MPs taking the Conservative whip. Elsewhere, the party renewed its efforts to revive its fortunes in northern England (Randall, 2009) while its efforts to 'detoxify' its image also meant addressing memories of the party's past territorial politics. Accordingly, Cameron lamented that 'provoked by crazy Leftwing local politicians in the 1980s – the Conservative government had to increase the levers of central control' (Cameron, 2007c), while in Scotland he confessed that 'A series of blunders were committed in the 1980s and 90s of which the imposition of the Poll Tax was the most egregious' (Cameron, 2006b). But in addition to dealing with the past, Cameron was also anxious to offer assurances regarding his and his party's future conduct. This took the form of a 'respect agenda' toward the devolved institutions. In Scotland Cameron pledged to 'be a Prime Minister that respects and listens to the voice of the Scottish people ... I will work tirelessly for consent and consensus' (Cameron, 2007d). In Wales Cameron sought 'to make the politics of the principality about progress, not politically inspired grievance. And one way we can do that is to make the relationship between Cardiff and Westminster one of co-operation, not confrontation' (Cameron, 2009a). Thus a Cameron government would formalise intergovernmental relations between Westminster and the periphery, particularly by reviving the Joint Ministerial Committee and would present its ministers for questioning before the devolved institutions.

Pandora's box: The problems of territorial management following the 2010 election

Bulpitt understood that lurking behind the centre's territorial operational code was a 'Pandora's box of trouble waiting to get out' (2008: 143) and as the outcome of the 2010 election became clear, two major problems presented themselves to the Conservatives. The first was associated with the party's electoral performance. While the Conservatives recovery in English local government meant that they now controlled 57 per cent of English councils, elsewhere in the periphery, in Scotland and Wales, the party confronted entrenched, legitimate and potentially uncooperative local elites. In addition, the party at Westminster remained strikingly Anglocentric. As Table 8.1 demonstrates, this was not unusual. The Conservatives last won a majority in Scotland in 1955 and thereafter witnessed a profound deterioration in its electoral position (Seawright, 1999). In Wales, the party had not

Table 8.1 The Conservative and Unionist percentage share of votes and seats in England, Scotland, Wales and Northern Ireland, 1955–2010

	England		*Scotland*		*Wales*		*Northern Ireland*	
	Vote	*Seats*	*Vote*	*Seats*	*Vote*	*Seats*	*Vote*	*Seats*
1955	50.6	57.1	50.1	50.7	33.5	16.6	68.5	83.3
1959	50.2	61.6	47.6	43.7	33.8	19.4	77.2	100
1964	44.1	51.1	40.6	32.9	29.4	16.6	63.0	100
1966	42.8	42.9	37.6	28.2	27.9	8.3	61.8	100
1970	48.4	57.1	38.5	32.4	27.7	19.4	54.2	66.7
1974F	38.9	51.9	24.7	29.6	23.9	22.2	–	–
1974O	40.2	48.8	32.9	22.5	25.9	22.2	–	–
1979	47.2	59.3	31.4	31.0	32.2	30.6	–	–
1983	46.0	69.2	28.4	29.2	31.0	36.8	–	–
1987	46.2	68.3	24.0	13.9	29.5	21.1	–	–
1992	45.5	60.9	25.7	15.3	28.6	15.8	–	–
1997	33.7	31.2	17.5	–	19.6	–	1.2	–
2001	35.2	31.2	15.6	1.4	21.0	–	0.3	–
2005	35.7	36.7	15.8	1.7	21.4	7.5	0.4	–
2010	39.6	56.0	16.7	1.7	26.1	20.0	15.2	–

Notes: 1955–1974 figures refer to Ulster Unionist Party MPs who were affiliated to the National Union and who took the Conservative whip in Parliament. UUP MPs ceased to take the Conservative whip following the Sunningdale agreement (although the party maintained its affiliation to the National Union until the 1985 Anglo-Irish Agreement). 1992 to 2005 results refer to Conservative Party candidates in Northern Ireland. 2010 results refer to Ulster Conservatives and Unionists – New Force (UCUNF).

won a majority of seats since 1868 (McLean, 2010: 172). However, as Table 8.2 shows, the reliance of the Conservatives on English votes and seats became particularly marked following Margaret Thatcher's third electoral victory and in 2010 the party did little to remedy this general trend. The Conservatives under Cameron's leadership remained a party of southern and middle England.

In Scotland, the Conservatives made no advance despite considerable campaigning effort. The party registered a slim increase in its vote share but still fell short of the 17.5 per cent of Scottish votes won by John Major 13 years earlier. It returned just a single Scottish MP to Westminster for the third election in a row. In Northern Ireland, the party's electoral alliance could not even deliver a single MP. In Wales the party's recovery from its 1997 nadir continued with the party securing a quarter of Welsh votes and a fifth of its seats. However it was in England where the party made its

Table 8.2 Composition of the Conservative Parliamentary Party

	England		*Scotland*		*Wales*		*Northern Ireland*	
	N	*%*	*N*	*%*	*N*	*%*	*N*	*%*
1955	293	84.9	36	10.4	6	1.7	10	2.9
1959	315	86.3	31	8.5	7	1.9	12	3.3
1964	262	86.2	24	7.9	6	2.0	12	4.0
1966	219	86.6	20	7.9	3	1.2	11	4.4
1970	292	88.5	23	7.0	7	2.1	8	2.4
1974F	268	90.2	21	7.1	8	2.7	–	–
1974O	253	91.3	16	5.8	8	2.9	–	–
1979	306	90.3	22	6.5	11	3.2	–	–
1983	362	91.2	21	5.3	14	3.5	–	–
1987	358	95.2	10	2.7	8	2.1	–	–
1992	319	94.9	11	3.3	6	1.8	–	–
1997	165	100	0	–	0	–	–	–
2001	165	99.4	1	0.6	0	–	–	–
2005	194	98.0	1	0.5	3	1.5	–	–
2010	298	97.1	1	0.3	8	2.6	–	–

greatest advance (91 out of 96 gains) and to which it owed its status as largest party in Parliament. However, success was rather more qualified in northern England where the party still only won 30.7 per cent of the vote and 27.2 per cent of northern seats.

The outcome was, as Table 8.2 shows, that 97.1 per cent of Cameron's parliamentary party represented English constituencies and it carried the danger of increased politicisation of territorial management. Given this pattern of representation, one is even more reliant upon the representatives of English constituencies than the governments led by Margaret Thatcher and John Major; a minority Conservative government could have found its legitimacy to govern for the whole of the UK questioned.

Such criticism would probably have been more muted than that which met the 1992 and 1997 election results. After all, the devolved institutions were designed to address such a legitimacy deficit (Mitchell, 2006). But, in the event, the creation of a coalition with the Liberal Democrats forestalled even if it did not wholly dismiss such questions of legitimacy. As Table 8.3 shows, the coalition parties could stake a convincing claim to legitimacy in England with a combined vote share that surpassed even the National coalition in 1931. In Wales, the Liberal Democrats contributed relatively few seats to the coalition total but their votes meant that the coalition claimed a greater share of the vote than Labour (36.2 per cent).

Table 8.3 Coalition parties' percentage share of votes and seats in England, Scotland and Wales in the 2010 general election

	England		*Scotland*		*Wales*	
	Vote	*Seats*	*Vote*	*Seats*	*Vote*	*Seats*
Conservatives	39.6	56.0	16.7	1.7	26.1	20.0
Liberal Democrats	24.2	8.1	18.9	18.6	20.1	7.5
Coalition Total	63.8	64.1	35.6	20.3	46.2	27.5

In Scotland however, Alex Salmond asserted that 'The Tories languish in fourth place in Scotland, while the Lib Dems came third in share of the vote. Clearly, from a Scottish perspective, a Tory-Lib Dem government lacks legitimacy' (Salmond, 2010). Yet, at the time the SNP could scarcely claim a more convincing mandate with just 19.9 per cent of the 2010 general election vote. Labour, with 42 per cent of the vote and 70 per cent of Scottish seats, were better positioned to criticise the legitimacy of the coalition. However, the party chose not to dispute the coalition's right to govern Scotland, seeking instead to position itself as Scotland's best defence against the coalition government's expected austerity measures.

The distribution of territorial portfolios and responsibilities among the coalition partners provided the Conservatives with another means of defusing potential criticism. The Scotland Office was one of just three government departments allocated to a Liberal Democrat Secretary of State. This recognised the Liberal Democrats relative electoral strength in Scotland but also gave them the primary responsibility for selling the coalition's policies north of the border. The Wales Office remained under a Conservative Secretary of State and while Labour drew attention to the fact that Cheryl Gillan represented a Buckinghamshire constituency, she was at least born and raised in Wales (unlike Conservative holders of the post after 1987).

The second challenge facing the new coalition government was related to the broader programme that it now sought to implement. As Bulpitt's work recognises, periods of economic constraint have, in the past, tended to generate dissent in the periphery and the coalition's programme to accelerate reduction of the deficit could not disguise that 'Hard Times' had returned. Although both parties sought to 'tackle the deficit in a fair and responsible way' (HM Government, 2010a: 15) public spending cuts would be the principal means of driving down the deficit. This, as Cameron had indicated in an interview with Jeremy Paxman during the 2010 general election campaign, would have a particular impact on those parts of the periphery most dependent upon the public sector. In territorial terms, the coalition confronted a considerable challenge to demonstrate that all parts of the United Kingdom would be 'in it together'.

Local government and the English regions

The Conservative 2010 manifesto held that the party's 'fundamental tenet is that power should be devolved from politicians to people, from the central to the local' (Conservative Party, 2010: vii) and the first year of the coalition saw movement toward that objective. Eric Pickles, as Secretary of State for the Department of Communities and Local Government, moved quickly to remove a swathe of central government targets and inspection regimes including Comprehensive Area Assessments and Local Area Agreements. The extent of ring-fencing of grants diminished and a 'power of general competence' was advanced in the government's Localism Bill. In addition, the entire regional tier of governance – Government Offices of the Regions and Regional Development Agencies (RDAs) – was quickly dismantled with RDAs replaced by Local Enterprise Partnerships founded upon cooperation between businesses and local councils.

In these respects it appeared that the government was seeking to re-peripheralise 'Low Politics' and restore the autonomy of the centre. As Pickles told the Local Government Association, 'I'm not going to tell you what to do any more. So you don't have to keep running and asking me what you should be doing'. However, while the same occasion may have seen Pickles testify that 'I absolutely trust local government to deliver' (Pickles, 2010) a number of his measures suggested an underlying mistrust and a need to reform local government into a more reliable collaborator. Consequently the government sought to foster greater transparency in local government, for example, by disclosure of senior staff salaries and spending on items over £500. Concomitantly, the Localism Bill sought to empower residents to petition for referendums on local issues and to permit them to veto excessive council tax increases by referendum. In the longer term, the government's Big Society agenda offered the prospect of by-passing local government by devolving power to communities, neighbourhoods and individuals. However, like his predecessors in the governments of the 1980s, Pickles soon found himself unable to wait for such reforms to take their course and was forced to contemplate a more coercive approach that would ensure that local authorities did not disrupt the government's broader agenda. For example, faced with the prospect that the Big Society might be undermined, the Secretary of State threatened to take statutory powers to prevent councils from making disproportionate cuts to the funding of voluntary sector organisations (Pickles, 2011a).

Indeed, local government was an early and heavy target of the government's austerity measures. A £1.165 billion in-year budget cut was announced in June 2010 and a 16.2 per cent cut in the formula grant followed in the 2011–13 financial settlement announced in December 2010. The government sought to present these cuts as a progressive settlement. However, the most deprived local authorities faced the biggest cuts in their finances (Berman and

Keep, 2011: 19–20). Ministers also argued that efficiency measures such as merging back-office functions and cutting council executive's pay could protect front-line jobs and services. But considerable doubts emerged whether such measures could deliver savings on the scale required (New Local Government Network, 2011; Local Government Association, 2011). With these arguments having failed to gain traction, ministers turned to accusing Labour councils of making political capital out of the cuts by means of a 'bleeding stump' strategy (Pickles, 2011b). But opposition was not confined to Labour councillors. Freedom of information requests revealed that a number of prominent Conservative figures in local government had also privately articulated their dismay over the cuts (Ridge, 2011) and 92 Liberal Democrat council and group leaders wrote to *The Times* in February 2011 to protest at the extent and the timescale of local authority spending cuts. However, it was Liberal Democrat, rather than Conservative councillors who faced electoral retribution in the May 2011 council elections where the Liberal Democrats lost 748 councillors and control of nine councils; the Conservatives made a net gain of 86 councillors and gained control of three further councils.

Devolutionary bona fides and English resentment

The Scottish Conservatives may have been reconciled to the new devolution settlement but they continued to be perceived by Scots as an 'anglicised party' with a coercive potential towards peripheral interests (Seawright, 2002) and the party had the 'most to do to establish its devolutionary bona fides' (Aughey, 2011: 168). James Mitchell encapsulates such resistance to the Conservative Party with the view that 'The whole point of the parliament was that it was meant to insulate Scotland from a Tory government' (Barnes, 2011). Thus, David Mundell, the sole Scottish Conservative MP and Parliamentary Under-Secretary of State for Scotland, thought it vital that the Conservative Party in Scotland had a strong voice at Holyrood 'to fight against this twisted sense of what devolution is about'. He held that that particular chapter of divisive Scottish politics had been closed with the help of the government's mutual respect agenda between Westminster and Holyrood and by working alongside the Liberal Democrats in 'a broad based government that enjoys a bigger electoral mandate in Scotland than the SNP Government in Holyrood' (Mundell, 2010). However, Table 8.4 illustrates the difficulty for the Conservatives in developing a strong voice at Holyrood. The level of support for the party in Scotland shows a consistency in an already depressed one-sixth of the vote acquired at both Westminster and Holyrood elections since 1997 (compare with Table 8.1); until the latest Holyrood election when it fell even further to just under 14 per cent. And, Mundell's claim for legitimacy in Scotland is also rather undermined with the Liberal Democrat support in the 2011 Scottish parliamentary election halving to just below 8 per cent with a concomitant loss of over two-thirds of their Scottish parliamentary seats.

Table 8.4 The Conservative and Unionist percentage share of votes and seats for the devolved institutions in Scotland, Wales and Northern Ireland, 1999–2011

	Scotland		*Wales*		*Northern Ireland*	
	Vote	*Seats*	*Vote*	*Seats*	*Vote*	*Seats*
1999	15.6	13.9	15.8	15.0	–	–
2003	16.6	13.9	20.0	18.3	–	–
2007	16.6	13.1	22.4	20.0	–	–
2011	13.9	11.6	25.0	23.3	13.2	14.8

Note: The percentage vote is for the constituency vote in the Additional Member System for Scotland and Wales and for First Preferences in the Single Transferable Vote for Northern Ireland.

Conversely, the SNP was the first party in Scotland to gain an overall majority of seats at Holyrood by obtaining 45.4 per cent of constituency ballots in 2011 (up from 32.9 per cent in 2007). A comparison of Tables 8.1 and 8.4 suggests that it is highly unlikely that the Conservative Party will be the beneficiary any time soon of the trend that sees voters in Scotland switching allegiances depending on which parliament they are electing.

Similarly the electoral climate for the Conservatives looked just as bleak in Northern Ireland. The restoration of the historic relationship that was billed as a dynamic new political force and named the Ulster Conservatives and Unionists – New Force (UCUNF) had even more of a lacklustre performance than that of their Scottish counterparts. Indeed, in response to this electoral pact Lady Sylvia Herman resigned from the Ulster Unionist Party (UUP) months before the 2010 general election and stood as an Independent, winning nearly two-thirds of the vote in her North Down constituency compared with that of the UCUNF on 20 per cent. Not only had the UCUNF lost their only Westminster MP but the Unionist political mould in Northern Ireland would now be shaped more by the dominance of the Democratic Unionist Party (DUP), with the 2011 Assembly election resulting in 38 DUP Members of the Legislative Assembly (MLAs) to the 16 MLAs of the UUP. In contrast, although after the 2011 Welsh Assembly election Labour had 30 of the 60 Assembly Members (AMs), with 14 AMs the Conservatives managed to successfully push the nationalist Plaid Cymru into third place. Quite clearly the peripheral elites of the devolved institutions could not be secured on the basis of their Conservative allegiance and the idea of Richard Rose on effective territorial management from Westminster, that 'Policy unites what geography divides' (Aughey, 2010a: 270), would now require unprecedented levels of elasticity. However, the provisions of the Scotland Bill, which gave effect to the recommendations of the Calman Commission, were meant to be the very embodiment of such a goal.

The Bill proposed yet further transfers of financial power from Westminster to Holyrood. The Scottish Parliament would be allowed to set its own rates of income tax and the level of stamp duty, along with an ability to levy taxes on areas that are deemed 'Scotland specific'. Moreover, going further than Calman, it was also proposed that Holyrood would have a borrowing requirement of £2.7 billion. In addition, competence in other areas would be transferred, including speed and drink driving limits (HM Government, 2010b). In a similar fashion the Yes vote in the Welsh Referendum meant that Cardiff now had legislative competence for 20 policy areas including that of health and education. The Welsh Tory leader of the Assembly admitted that in the past he had got devolution wrong but was pleased that the Assembly now had 'the tools to do the job' (de Bruxelles, 2011). Less it be overlooked the Northern Ireland Affairs Committee published a report on the 24 May 2011 which it asserted made a convincing case for the reduction of the corporation tax rate in Northern Ireland; in effect halving the rate to 12.5 per cent which would allow it to compete more effectively with the Republic in attracting business (UK Parliament, 2011). A long-term aspiration of these reforms was the strengthening of the fiscal and monetary accountability of the devolved institutions and importantly also the depoliticisation of financing them as an issue; as the expectation was that the Westminster block grant would be reduced by equivalent amounts to the money raised by them in taxation.

However, part of the invisible bonds securing the Union were felt to be the uniformity of standards across the United Kingdom as a whole (Aughey, 2010a: 270) and a number of Conservatives were known to be distinctly uncomfortable with the Scotland Bill's proposals believing they contribute to the further fracture of the UK. The erstwhile Tory Secretary of State for Scotland, Lord Michael Forsyth, warned of the dynamic towards separation that such proposals would facilitate in further nationalist claims. And, there was a certain irony to his apparent vindication as the call for corporation tax to be lowered in Scotland to the level proposed for Northern Ireland came from the Scottish Conservative finance spokesman in the run up to the Scottish parliamentary election (MacNab, 2011). Of course, after their impressive victory at the 2011 parliamentary election, this equalisation of corporation tax was to be just one of six demands put forward by the SNP for augmenting the autonomous measures in the Scotland Act; the other five were the devolving of broadcasting powers, excise duty and Crown estates property, in conjunction with additional borrowing powers for the Scottish parliament and a greater role for Scottish parliament ministers in European Union discussion. In addition, David Cameron also faced concerted pressure from sections of the party at Westminster with regards to the uniformity of standards for their English constituents with particular reference to the role of MPs from the 'devolved nations'. In short, the legitimacy deficit had been displaced not removed (Mitchell, 2006). The Conservative Party manifesto claimed it would address this 'question' (2010: 84) but the coalition negotiations had deliberately sent it into the long grass (Laws, 2010) with a 'commitment' to 'establish a commission to consider the West Lothian Question' (HM Government, 2010a: 4). Likewise, the coalition was also hesitant to reconsider the Barnett formula. The coalition agreement stated that 'at this time, the priority must be to reduce the deficit and therefore any change must await the stabilisation of the public finances' (HM Government, 2010a: 28); while subsequent pledges to establish a 'Calman-style commission' for Wales did not suggest that the issue would be resolved with any greater alacrity.

That the Cameron government temporised on a mechanism that underfunds Wales but which over-rewards Scotland, was indicative of a broader asymmetry in relations between the UK government and the devolved institutions. Not surprisingly, relations with all devolved institutions exhibited strain at various points during the Cameron government's first year in office. Some events, not least the failure to consult upon the scheduling of the AV referendum on the same day as the devolved elections, alienated elites across all institutions. Other decisions, such as the tax increase on North Sea oil and gas profits in George Osborne's second budget, generated dissent in particular parts of the periphery. But, reflecting a well-established pattern (McLean and McMillan, 2005), the Cameron government generally accorded greatest 'respect' to those parts of the periphery able to summon the most credible threats to the Union. Consequently, Scotland secured significant concessions. For example, Scottish ministers were permitted to represent the UK in EU discussions for the first time (on disputes over mackerel quotas). In contrast, Welsh ministers had to settle for much more limited concessions and became more accustomed to Westminster rejecting its requests, for example on the devolution of energy policy, with the result that the rhetoric between Westminster and Cardiff grew increasingly confrontational.

Conclusion

To what extent do the actions of the Cameron government in its first year of office correspond to the optimal operational code of territorial management that we set out at the beginning of this chapter? As we have argued, David Cameron is a committed, but pragmatic Unionist and *preservation of the Union* remains central to the doctrine and ethos of the contemporary Conservative Party. Such a commitment, as we have seen, draws upon a belief that the Union enhances the capacity of elites at Westminster to pursue 'High Politics' in areas such as economic and foreign policy. This *prioritisation of 'High Politics'* by Cameron's government has led, although not wholly consistently, to efforts to re-peripheralise 'Low Politics' to local government. The same emphasis upon 'High Politics', coupled with a desire to avoid the centre-periphery conflicts characteristic of the Conservative's last period in office, saw the Cameron government seek to implement a 'respect agenda' with the devolved institutions. This was pursued most fully in regard to Scotland. The government's broader desire to avoid unnecessary politicisation of territorial politics was confirmed by its deferral of both the 'West Lothian question' and the Barnett formula.

In implementing this agenda, the Cameron government avoided high-profile errors and u-turns of the kind that placed its *governing competence* under question in other policy areas such as education and healthcare in its first year. Nevertheless, the breakneck speed at which the government implemented its territorial policies did generate concern. For example, Vince Cable reflected that the scrapping of RDAs had been 'a little Maoist and chaotic' (Stratton, 2010a) while the bidding process for Local Enterprise Partnerships was also disorderly, prompting the Director General of the CBI to describe it as a 'bit of a shambles' (Groom and Rigby, 2010). The frontloading of cuts to local government also meant that the biggest savings were required in the financial year 2011–12. This raised doubts about whether changes of this magnitude and pace could be successfully delivered (CIPFA, 2011).

Several aspects of the Cameron government's territorial policies generated dissent within Conservative ranks. Conservative councillors registered their alarm regarding cuts to local government expenditure. The Scottish party questioned the strategy underlying the Cameron's government efforts to preserve the Union, attacking in particular, the devolution of tax raising powers. Concerns were evident across the party about postponing resolution of the anomalies generated by devolution. Given the issues involved, it would have been inconceivable that such disagreements did not surface but, from a perspective of *party management*, such dissent remained within relatively manageable bounds during Cameron's first 12 months in office. However, the government's efforts to secure *political argument hegemony* on territorial issues remained incomplete. For example, despite a consensus on the virtues of 'localism' between the major parties, the government's 'Big Society' failed to convince commentators and the public despite repeated high-profile re-launches. Similarly, the Cameron government's measures to deal with 'Hard Times' met with a uniformly hostile response in the periphery, prompting the first ministers of Scotland, Wales and Northern Ireland to issue an unprecedented joint declaration in October 2010 that the cuts were 'too fast and too deep' (Northern Ireland Executive, Scottish Government and Welsh Assembly Government, 2010).

Electorally, the first year of the coalition delivered asymmetric electoral verdicts on the two parties. The Liberal Democrats sustained the greater electoral damage in Scotland, Wales and in local government. The Conservatives fell back in the Scottish Parliament but they arguably maximised the *electoral benefits* that were realistically available to them elsewhere; their trajectory of electoral improvement continued in the Welsh Assembly and the party's representation in English local government was bolstered. However, these electoral developments had contradictory implications for territorial management.

Given Liberal Democrat losses, *reliable collaborators* with the coalition in local government diminished. Moreover, the government's first year had shown it could not wholly rely upon the cooperation of councillors representing the coalition parties. Yet Eric Pickles could remain relatively untroubled by Labour's local government gains in the short term; Labour's recovery was from such a low base that it still remained far weaker in local government than at any point during the 1980s and 1990s. The formation of a Labour single-party administration following the Welsh Assembly election of May 2011 did not significantly alter the prospects for collaboration facing Cheryl Gillan given that the 'respect agenda' had been faltering even under the One Wales Government.

However, the formation of a majority SNP government did present the Cameron government with a new set of challenges after 6 May 2011. Given the need for the Scottish Parliament's legislative consent, this immediately meant revisiting the provisions of the Scotland Bill. Beyond this, and with a referendum on independence promised for the second half of its term, the SNP was well positioned to test the parameters of the 'respect agenda' by pressing much more forcefully for concessions from Westminster. This could place the Cameron government in a particularly invidious position. If Westminster refuses to meet SNP demands it risks strengthening the nationalist case in an independence referendum. To accede to SNP demands poses different hazards. Firstly, it risks further infuriating those Conservatives who regard each concession as a further step down the slippery slope towards independence, thus creating a problem of party management. Secondly, it risks generating resentment elsewhere. While there is little evidence of an English backlash to devolution as yet (Curtice, 2009), the Cameron government will be anxious not to further jeopardise the Union by facilitating the transformation of English nationalism from a mood to a movement (Aughey, 2010b). Solutions to the West Lothian question and the Barnett formula might forestall such a prospect. But it remains doubtful how feasible the Conservatives preferred solution to the West Lothian question is (see, for example, Bogdanor, 2010: 161–5); while any revision to the Barnett formula would almost certainly be unfavourable to Scotland, thereby providing the SNP with a further potent example of Westminster's perfidy. In this respect, as it enters its second year, the Cameron government would be wise to anticipate that the UK is likely to continue to be a particularly challenging piece of political real estate to manage.

9
Foreign Policy

Victoria Honeyman

Introduction

This chapter will focus on one of the most pragmatic areas of British politics – foreign policy. This is generally, in practice, an ideology free zone where pragmatism rules. Only occasionally are tricky notions of conscience and ethics introduced into foreign policy, such as when Robin Cook made his rather well-received but largely ignored call for an 'ethical dimension to foreign policy' (*Guardian*, 1997). Cameron (2008b) argued that: 'the conduct of international affairs must always be tempered by realism. But these great international challenges of the 21st century are moral questions, not just questions of realpolitik'. The need to ensure continuity in policy and demonstrate unity to both our international friends and enemies alike means that, unlike other policy areas where the parties often adopt strong opposing positions, foreign policy tends to be dominated by continuity and nuance. Often, the main difference in the foreign policy aims and objectives of the three main parties is in terms of their rhetoric. There are, however, exceptions to this rule with the conflict in Iraq being perhaps the most notorious recent example. Whilst both the Conservative and Labour parties supported the invasion of Iraq, in order to defend Britain (largely due to Blair's 45 minute claim and the allegedly 'sexed up' dodgy dossier), the Liberal Democrats opposed it vehemently. While the Lib Dems could make great political capital out of their opposition to the war, it is likely that their status as the third party allowed them greater scope to be idealistic in their foreign policy-making; far more than could be afforded to either of the two other parties. Political parties that are likely to form the next government are largely unable to pursue such idealistic approaches to foreign policy, particularly with the danger of being hostages to fortune in their next period in office. Such a situation is compounded once British troops are deployed, when any dissention over their aims and achievements can be construed as disloyal. However, the political fallout over Iraq should not be seen as typical of foreign policy-making, where continuity is generally paramount.

The focus here then is on several key elements of foreign policy as pursued by the Conservative–Liberal Democrat coalition government, starting by focusing on the views behind these policies. Indeed, the Conservative Party approach has been described by both William Hague and David Cameron, prior to the 2010 election, as 'Liberal Conservatism'. The situation in Iraq and the war in Afghanistan are not as salient as they once were as issues for both parties. In terms of Afghanistan, the main area of debate within the British government is over the withdrawal of troops on the ground, rather than discussing the merits of increasing or maintaining Britain's commitment any further. It will be argued that the foreign policy which has been pursued by the coalition government is almost exclusively driven by Hague and, inevitably as Prime Minister, David Cameron. The approach taken since the creation of the coalition government in May 2010 and the entry of Hague to the Foreign and Commonwealth Office (FCO) has been consistent with that outlined by Cameron and Hague since 2006, suggesting that the Liberal Democrats have had very little impact on foreign policy-making. It seems probable that the reason for this is due to the preoccupation of the Liberal Democrats with domestic policy, with their most high-profile foreign policies being centred on the EU and the Iraq war. The Liberal Democrat 2010 manifesto focused on weapons, Afghanistan and particularly Britain's relationship with the EU; with very little detail on other policy areas. And, Justin Morris noted that 'the coalition's Programme for Government provides very little insight into how the new government view Britain's role in the world' (2011: 13). However, William Hague thought that 'our foreign policy is more effective and better understood abroad when it is bi-partisan and pursued consistently over the long-term by both main political parties' (Hague, 2007b).

'Liberal Conservatism'

In 1999 in Chicago, Tony Blair outlined his six principles for foreign policy in a speech usually referred to as his 'Doctrine of the International Community'. The six principles were fairly detailed and outlined his style of policy-making and were loosely called 'Liberal Interventionism':

1. In global finance, a thorough, far-reaching overhaul and reform of the system of international financial regulation.
2. A new push on free trade in the WTO.
3. A reconsideration of the role, workings and decision-making process of the UN, and in particular the UN Security Council.
4. For NATO, a critical examination of the lessons to be learnt, and the changes we need to make in organisation and structure.
5. In respect of Kyoto and the environment, far closer working between the main industrial nations and the developing world as to how the Kyoto

targets can be met and the practical measures necessary to slow down and stop global warming; and
6. A serious examination of the issue of third world debt (Blair, 1999).

Cameron appointed William Hague as shadow Foreign Secretary early in his leadership, safe in the knowledge that he could utilise his knowledge and experience without him being a threat to his own position due to Hague's own ill-fated tenure as leader. And, Hague was still seen as a political big hitter with an understanding of foreign policy and a thorough knowledge of the history of the Conservative Party. Hague argued that:

> during that time in Opposition it became increasingly apparent to me that the previous Government had neglected to lift its eyes to the wider strategic needs of this country, to take stock of British interests and to determine in a systematic fashion what we must do as a nation if we are to secure our international influence and earn our living in a world that is rapidly changing (Hague, 2010b).

Hague and Cameron worked very closely together to formulate a specific approach to foreign policy, which they termed 'Liberal Conservatism', and this was repeatedly discussed in speeches by both Cameron and Hague from 2006 onwards. Dodds and Elden argued that 'the "conservatism" comes not only from a scepticism but also recognition of "the complexities of human nature"; yet the "liberal" comes because he [Cameron] supports "the aims of spreading freedom and democracy, and supports[s] humanitarian intervention"' (2008: 357).

Although vaguer than Blair's doctrine, due no doubt to being in opposition, five principles of foreign policy were developed:

1. That we should understand fully the threat we face.
2. That democracy cannot quickly be imposed from outside.
3. That our strategy needs to go far beyond military action.
4. That we need a new multilateralism to tackle the new global challenges we face.
5. We must strive to act with moral authority (Cameron, 2006c).

Although five and not six, there were certain similarities between the principles of Cameron and Blair, with perhaps the most obvious omission being the lack of any discussion of the Kyoto protocol and the environment in Cameron's five principles – a little odd for a leader who used the environment as a key issue during his first year in office. One possible explanation is that Cameron and Hague wanted to treat issues surrounding the environment as distinct from wider foreign affairs, avoiding a possible muddying of the waters where possible. However, there is no clear evidence as to why the Kyoto protocol was excluded from Cameron and Hague's 'Liberal Conservatism'.

A key critique of Blair's foreign policy approach was the style and method employed in the decision-making itself. Hague criticised Blair's 'sofa-style decision-making' arguing that it was leading to poor decisions being made and would be avoided by the Conservative government when they returned to power (Hague, 2007a). The implication being that the style was too casual and informal, and with Iraq in mind, leading to some rather dubious judgements. Vickers points out that 'both Cameron and Hague came into power believing that British foreign policy not only required a new vision, but also needed to be overhauled in terms of policy-making, which under New Labour had become too informal and disjointed' (Vickers, 2011: 207). Hague and Cameron both committed themselves to a more formal decision-making process, taking advice and opinion from all quarters (Hague, 2007a). In conjunction with considerations over the style of decision-making, point four of Hague's 'Liberal Conservatism' indicates that multilateralism is important, meaning that Britain should not act alone. Hague and Cameron both discussed the importance of the UN and NATO to Britain and how these can be developed to reflect the twenty-first century world. The lack of a UN resolution in regard to Iraq led to concerns of legitimacy, and this was a problem which Cameron did not want to face in relation to Libya. The No Fly Zone and measures to protect the rebels in Libya were introduced only after the passing of UN resolution 1973 legitimising actions to protect civilians. This is discussed further below.

Although Blair did not explicitly make reference to it in his 1999 speech in Chicago, the labelling of his principles as 'Liberal Interventionism' suggested that the developed world (or the UN or NATO depending on the circumstances) would be justified and willing to intervene in various international disputes and internal wars. The international actions in Kosovo, and those that followed in Afghanistan and Iraq demonstrated just how far Blair was willing to intervene to protect citizens, pursue terrorists and insurgents and protect the financial interests of the UK and its allies. Dodds and Elden characterise Blair's foreign policy as 'a form of idealism moderated by realism' (2008: 359). His critics argue that Blair actually went too far. However, there was no discussion of this in the original principles and it seems likely that interventionism was dealt with on a case-by-case basis and that the issues surrounding it were not solidified by Blair in 1999, only becoming more thought out in the light of 9/11. Cameron and Hague's 'Liberal Conservatism' also makes no direct reference to interventionism, although it does indicate that democracy cannot be imposed from outside, meaning that interventionism would need to be accompanied by mediation and multilateral action. These principles seem to owe a great deal to the Iraq war and its repercussions and the desire not only to disassociate themselves from it, but also from the desire to learn from previous mistakes.

The events in various Middle Eastern nations, including Tunisia and Egypt, suggested that the coalition government had learnt from previous mistakes, allowing democracy to develop from within nations in order to overthrow long-serving dictators; with Britain offering not much more than supportive words. However, in Libya where the leader had less compunction about turning his arsenal on his own people, supportive words were not enough to ensure Gaddafi's defeat and the international community became involved militarily. This issue will be discussed in further detail below, but it does suggest that, like Blair, Hague and Cameron are developing their principles in the light of circumstance and the realities of being in office. While hazy principles might be suitable for opposition, power requires difficult decisions and sometimes principles have to be adapted, or even abandoned, to deal with international problems. Perhaps, as Dodds and Elden argue, 'the new British conservatism is not so different from Blair' (2008: 360).

The special relationship

The close relationship between British Prime Ministers and American Presidents has been at the heart of Conservative Party policy since it was forged during the Second World War. The relationship has tended to be at its strongest when the Conservatives have been in power – Thatcher and Reagan, MacMillan and Kennedy, Churchill and Roosevelt. There have been notable exceptions, such as Blair's close relationship with Bush Jnr and Major's relationship with Clinton which was not particularly close, but that has not decreased the importance of the relationship to Britain or to the Conservative Party. However, the political realities of the twentieth century have meant that increasingly Britain has become the junior member and the increasingly good relationships between the USA and Germany and with the EU have meant that there have been fears over how special the 'special relationship' actually is. The close relationship between Blair and Bush Jnr initially allayed some of these fears, cementing Britain's position as the US's closest ally, but this was quickly overtaken by fears, in the light of the Iraq war, that Britain had become too close to the US and had sacrificed her independence to secure the relationship. Indeed, Blair was labelled 'Bush's poodle', a label which undoubtedly damaged him and his party. This reflected the popular perception that the relationship between Blair and Bush was not an equal one and that while Britain often shares similar values and objectives with the US, there should still be room for Britain to pursue its own aims, regardless of whether they dove-tailed with those of the US (Cohen, 2001).

Thus the Conservative Party had a tricky balancing act to perform in opposition as one of its main planks of foreign policy had been tainted by the Blair–Bush relationship. And the Liberal Democrats advocated a much stronger relationship with the EU, with the individual European nations acting as a counterweight to such an extremely strong relationship with the

US. This policy reflects, to some degree, the inherent view within large sections of the British political elite that in foreign policy terms, Britain either interacts and supports the US or the EU, but doing both in a balanced relationship is not possible. And even more so for the Conservative Party, historically so riven by the anti-European Union stance of its MPs, members and supporters, a strong relationship with the EU that would rival the 'special relationship' is simply anathema. Additionally, due to the nature of the EU and its foreign policy (Common Foreign and Security Policy – CFSP), which is largely dealt with on an intergovernmental basis rather than a supranational footing, it would be extremely difficult for such a relationship to be forged and to work effectively. Beech argues that 'given their [the Conservative Party] lack of affinity for the European Union – a supra-national, intergovernmental, political, economic and diplomatic power bloc – they are compelled to steer Britain into the sphere of influence of the US' (2011a: 6). Therefore, the US remains Britain's closest ally, meaning that the key question for the Conservative Party is how far are they willing to go in order to maintain this most important of relationships?

The Conservative Party was keen to have a different relationship with the US than Blair had cultivated. Therefore the party had to ensure that they supported a strong relationship with the US while ensuring that the public was informed of the limitations of that relationship and that the Conservative Party was not willing to simply acquiesce to the will of the US. That is exactly what the party did, and both Hague and Cameron have tread a careful line between being a strong supporter of the US and the Anglo-American relationship, while still maintaining the independence of the UK to act as it wishes, rather than simply follow the US in their battles and disputes. In September 2006, less than a year after becoming party leader, Cameron spoke of the importance of the Anglo-American 'special relationship' to the modern day Conservative Party. He argued that: 'anti-Americanism represents an intellectual and moral surrender. It is complacent cowardice born of resentment of success and a desire for the world's problems simply to go away' (Cameron, 2006c). But this support for the 'special relationship' has been tempered by Cameron and Hague, and their repeated use of the key phrase 'solid, but not slavish' (Cameron, 2006c; Hague, 2006).

This careful balance, while not at odds with the policy of the Liberal Democrats, who recognise the importance of the 'special relationship' even if they are not gushing in their rhetoric with regards to the US, certainly does not seem to have been an issue for debate when the coalition government was being formed. In reality, it would be political suicide for Britain (or the Conservative Party) to turn away from the US, and it seems that the Liberal Democrats recognised this. The policy with regards the 'special relationship' has not altered from the approach taken in opposition. With Obama in the White House, and the difficult Bush affiliations fading, Cameron was already in a stronger position than he would have been had Bush still been President. Relations with the US have been cordial and friendly, and the joint action on Libya has certainly suggested that the relationship is still strong and Britain is still willing, with the important addition of a UN mandate, to work with the US to achieve certain foreign policy aims. The killing of Osama Bin Laden by the US in Northern Pakistan in May 2011 has secured Obama's warrior leader status, and the actions of the US, while not universally supported, were strongly backed by the British government and Cameron specifically. While the rhetoric of the party might not have been as strident as it was under previous leaders, such as Thatcher, the will was still to support the US where possible, although only time will tell as to whether the rhetoric and the actions of the coalition government will remain constant.

International organisations and international development

The UN (United Nations) and NATO (North Atlantic Treaty Organisation) have been key organisations in British post-war politics. Both of these organisations were co-created by the British and have tended to be at the very heart of British foreign policy. NATO has formed a key plank in defence policy and has often been at the heart of British military action, while the UN has been crucial to justify and legalise military action, such as in Libya, as well as organising and coordinating aid and peace-keeping. However, the UN Security Council has tended to maintain a very elite membership, reflecting the settlement at the end of the Second World War, while NATO has a membership based on its geographical limitations. All of the three main political parties in Britain have called for the maintenance of both of these organisations and the expansion of the membership of the UN Security Council to reflect the changing world, although discussion on how this should be accomplished has tended to lack clarity.

The Conservative Party's proposals for reform of the UN Security Council, which they have carried into government with them, have a lot in common with those of the previous Labour government, reflecting perhaps a wider movement within the international community for change in the UN Security Council. In 2007, Hague stated that 'Britain should be a powerful advocate of its [the UN Security Council] reforming, giving, for instance, Japan, India, Germany and Brazil permanent seats on the UN Security Council and arguing for similar reforms of the International Monetary Fund' (Hague, 2007a). However, as the Labour government discovered, it requires more than encouraging words from the British government (or opposition) to make this change happen. The Blair and Brown governments were both unsuccessful in pushing this reform through, and currently the Cameron government does not seem to be having any greater success. But, making these calls will undoubtedly encourage stronger links between Britain and these nations, regardless of whether the calls are successful or not. Without wider agreement within the existing UN Security Council members, all calls for reform are futile and action is impossible. Apart from a call to the UN 'to see that international law is respected and upheld' (Hague, 2009c) there have been no concrete suggestions on further aims but the structure of the UN suits the British government well, in that its members can opt out of any action which they feel is inappropriate or would damage their national interests.

Hague and Cameron have been rather tight lipped on the future of NATO and their aims for that organisation, although unsurprisingly the Conservatives have tried to encourage it to take a more active role in Afghanistan, allowing the British to withdraw their troops at a much faster rate. In 2007 Hague stated that:

> we have to do our utmost to galvanise NATO into doing what is necessary to make a success of the deployment in Afghanistan, persuading other countries to summon the political will to make a major contribution to what is, after all, their defence, rather than always relying on British, Canadian and American forces to take on the greatest dangers (Hague, 2007a).

There has been little other discussion on the future of NATO, although there seems no doubt that it will remain at the heart of the British approach to foreign policy for some time yet, and the lack of debate and criticism may well reflect a general contentment about its current form and activities in contrast to Conservative views on relationships such as the European Common Foreign and Security Policy.

It is worth mentioning here also the role of international aid in Conservatives foreign policy aims. When Gordon Brown was Chancellor in Blair's government, he believed strongly that international aid was crucial and should be maintained and increased, regardless of Britain's own financial situation. As Chancellor, Brown massively increased the budget of the new Department for International Development (DFID) and encouraged Blair to commit to the UN Millennium Development Goals to improve the lives of those living in developing nations. 'In the case of Tony Blair and Gordon Brown ... their interest and commitment to improving conditions in developing nations, particularly those in Africa, is driven partially by their personal religious views' (Honeyman, 2010a: 88). However, the Conservative Party did not automatically have to pledge its support for this policy, but the 2001 general election manifesto contained a promise to *work towards* the UN target of 0.7 per cent on international aid (Conservative Party, 2001a). This commitment was also made in the 2005 manifesto, which stated that 'we will support further action on debt relief and will work to meet the UN target of spending 0.7 per cent of national income on overseas aid by 2013' (Conservative Party, 2005: 27). The 2010 election manifesto, despite the worsening economic conditions after the credit crunch in 2007 also committed the party to the UN aid target of 0.7 per cent of national income by 2013 (Conservative Party, 2010: 117). The reasons behind these commitments have not been widely discussed, but it seems likely that the same moral issues which contributed to the Blair and Brown government's actions were also experienced by the Conservative Party. It is worth mentioning that the Liberal Democrats were also committed to the 0.7 per cent UN aid target (Liberal Democrats, 2010: 57).

The Commonwealth

The Commonwealth is often viewed as a slightly redundant international organisation. It was originally established to create links between the nations which had previously been members of the British Empire. Rather than allow these nations to simply drift apart, the Commonwealth was a way to ensure that strong links were maintained between these nations and that they could pursue common goals. In addition, it allowed Britain to pursue its own needs once the empire had collapsed; the Commonwealth was an empire without the financial or political complications. However, the principle and the practice were rather different. Firstly, not all the previous members of the empire joined the Commonwealth, so for example Pakistan (which had previously been part of India before the British had left and the country had been partitioned into India and Pakistan) declined to join the Commonwealth. Secondly, the British were, on occasion, unable to directly influence the Commonwealth countries, such as over the issue of apartheid in South Africa during Mrs Thatcher's tenure. Thirdly, and perhaps most importantly for the coalition government, the Commonwealth has become something of a talking shop, with only limited ability to act, even when events have required it, such as in the case of Robert Mugabe and his human rights violation in Zimbabwe.

The Commonwealth, despite being one of a handful of global organisations of which Britain is a member, has become rather sidelined in terms of British foreign policy. William Hague made several speeches while in opposition about the importance of the Commonwealth and what it could achieve. In 2009 he stated that:

> it is not a mini-UN or an alternative to the WTO [World Trade Organisation] or regional groupings such as the EU, AU or CARICOM; but it can provide a unique perspective and forum in world affairs and should be a source of strength and opportunity for its members (Hague, 2009a).

He also commented, rather dismissively, that under the previous Labour government the only mention of the Commonwealth within an FCO strategic plan was in the FCO emblem on the top of the release, being keen to ensure that the Commonwealth is a source of strength for Britain and arguing that 'relinquishing our Commonwealth commitments is incredibly short-sighted and ultimately detrimental to the prosperity and sphere of influence of our country (ibid). He thus set out a plan for developing the role of the Commonwealth, with an outline for five improvements:

1. The expansion of membership
2. Enhance the Commonwealth's role in conflict prevention and resolution
3. Take a leading role where appropriate in addressing state failure
4. Extend its influence to areas outside the domain of its traditional membership and build bridges where its expertise would be welcomed
5. To tackle issues which cross divides and national boundaries and its efforts should be given more recognition (ibid).

While Hague has discussed his desire to build upon the diverse membership of the Commonwealth and utilise it to its full potential, there has been no practical measures implemented to achieve this since the coalition government gained power in May 2010. It is difficult to see how such a diverse organisation as the Commonwealth would be able to achieve the single-mindedness required to achieve real political movement in foreign policy on numerous diverse and over difficult policy areas covering many geographical territories. This demonstrates at this juncture the Commonwealth does not appear to be a leading priority in foreign policy terms.

The quest for democracy in the Middle East – The Arab spring

While preaching that democracy is the best form of government, it has suited the developed world for numerous Middle Eastern and African countries to be ruled by tyrants and dictators. Many Middle Eastern leaders would support the cynical Churchillian view that the best argument against democracy is a five-minute conversation with the average voter. Democracy can lead to some rather difficult bedfellows, as has been seen by the election of Hamas on the West Bank. However, in the volatile areas of the Middle East and large parts of Africa, dictators and tyrants, who are friendly to the US and the west generally, have been supported and even 'propped up' by their friends in the west, due to fear of the alternative. This has meant that several nations have had leaders for several decades that lack democratic mandates and are willing to use their armies and weapons against their own people or at the very least convincingly threaten it. However, in December 2010 the Jasmine revolution began in Tunisia after a man who had been beaten by the police set himself on fire. The President, Zine el-Abidine Ben Ali was overthrown in a peaceful revolution with the public demanding democracy and presidential elections (Al Jazeera, 2011). There were then moves in several countries, such as Yemen, Bahrain and Jordan which forced concessions from the ruling elite and the introduction of more democracy into their political systems. The next nation to experience a peaceful revolution and perhaps the most influential was Egypt, where Mubarak was pressured to leave power after nearly 30 years by the peaceful protests in Cairo and the unwillingness of the army to intervene on his behalf.

After this peaceful Egyptian revolution, there was a temporary lull before the next casualty from 'the rise of the people'. This time, the state in question was Libya in Northern Africa, ruled by Colonel Muammar Gaddafi for over 40 years. Gaddafi had been no friend of the west, particularly after the bombing of the Pan Am flight 103 over Lockerbie in Scotland on 21 December 1988, which killed over 250 people, largely US and UK citizens. However, during Blair's time in power, Gaddafi had renounced his weapons of mass destruction and turned away from nuclear weapons research, meaning he was welcomed back into the international community. However, Gaddafi was still a military figure who had come to power in a military coup in 1969 and had no democratic mandate. He was also rather a volatile figure and this was certainly shown by his reaction to the uprising in the east of Libya in early 2011. Rather than appease the public uprising or offer concessions, Gaddafi threatened to turn his arms against his own people, and then sent his army to the east to retake the rebel held towns and cities. This caused real concern within the international community, not only because Gaddafi was attacking his own people, who were seriously outgunned and like lambs to the slaughter, but also because Libya is a large oil-producing nation and with each threat the supply of oil from the country decreased and the price of oil increased.

Rather than follow the path of Iraq, Cameron, with the enthusiastic support of the French President Nicolas Sarkozy, began to push for a no-fly zone over Libya and muted that this should be pursued at the UN and a resolution sought. While Cameron's motivation for this seems to have been ethically motivated, Sarkozy's sympathies were tangled up with a practical consideration. France is one of the largest buyers of Libyan oil, and 'France's *Total* and Italian companies *Eni* and *Saras* were regular buyers of Libyan oil in the past' (Energy-pedia, 2011). It is not the first time that the French and the British, traditional enemies of old, have cooperated with each other in defence policy. In November 2010, Sarkozy and Cameron agreed to a 50-year treaty on defence 'including a shared aircraft carrier, a 10,000-strong joint expeditionary force and development of joint nuclear testing facilities' (Wintour, 2010a). This cooperation, largely motivated by monetary constraints in both nations, was possible in large part to France's willingness to re-join NATO. While the Eurosceptics within the Conservative Party were unhappy with this agreement, with one describing the French as 'duplicitous' (ibid), Cameron argued that the French and British often found themselves united in military action, and that this agreement would not interfere with the ability of either nation to act independently. However, Patrick Wintour, writing in the *Guardian* noted that 'the agreement required intensive explanation to Washington, but has won

Pentagon agreement on the basis that Britain would remain dependent on US nuclear technology' (ibid). It is interesting that the British government felt it necessary to get 'agreement' from the Pentagon for this action, a move designed to ensure that this treaty did not interfere or degrade the 'special relationship'. While Sarkozy and Cameron have built a strong working relationship over the Libyan issue, this should not be seen to interfere with the 'special relationship', certainly not for the British, who prize their alliance with the US very highly, certainly more highly than that with the French, however cordial relations may be.

It was approximately three weeks after Cameron began calling for a no-fly zone that UN mandate 1973 was agreed which allowed 'all necessary measures' to be pursued to protect the citizens of Libya. While this resolution was passed, there were five abstentions – China, The Russian Federation, India, Germany and Brazil (UN Security Council, 2011). This mandate was crucial for Cameron and his government. There could be no suggestion that this would become another Iraq. Instead a mandate was sought, and granted, and multilateral action was necessary. The day after the resolution was granted Cameron said:

> It was right to take a lead, right to help marshal concerted international effort and right to bring forward the action to stop this slaughter. All along we have been clear about what was required before action could take place ... a demonstrable need on the ground, strong regional support, and a clear legal basis for anything proposed. These three conditions have now fully been met (Cameron, 2011a).

It was imperative that this action would not be seen as Britain and the US (even though the French were actively participating in the military action) again marching into a nation, particularly an oil rich nation, as this would be hugely unpopular in both the UK and the US. Cameron and Obama wanted to ensure that they were not mistaken for Blair and Bush and this also meant that ground troops, while a useful threat, were unlikely to be deployed. President Obama has stated that US ground troops will not be deployed in Libya, although the British government has sent approximately a dozen troops to assist the rebels with their organisation, rather than train them or, perhaps even more inadvisably, provide them with arms (BBC News, 2011). Sarkozy, perhaps driven by his nation's interest in Libyan oil deposits, along with Cameron, has really driven Obama on this issue, but it would be foolish to suggest that the US has been forced into any action which they did not wholeheartedly support.

The actions of the coalition in relation to the quest for democracy in the Middle East have been markedly different to those of the Blair government over Iraq, and it has been important for the coalition government that this distinction be very clear in the minds of the British public. Among the general public, there seems to be very little appetite for any action, whether it be to protect citizens or encourage democracy, but the coalition appears to believe that it is both morally necessary and economically advisable to prevent Libya becoming a rogue state again, and hopefully encouraging the appointment of a democratic leader with whom a good relationship could be built. Cameron and Hague have been very keen to encourage democracy, although this falls far short of imposing it from outside, something which they argued was not advisable in their Liberal Conservatism principles. The Conservative-Liberal Democrat government have, except in the case of Libya, refused to intervene, a course of action which seems to be very sensible. However, the prevailing view of the British establishment, that Britain retains some kind of role as the policeman of the world, continues despite the decreasing influence of Britain and its financial hardship in the light of the credit crunch. While there may have been less direct intervention than was seen during the leadership of Blair, it is true to say that Cameron and Hague's 'Liberal Conservatism' is showing some unexpected signs of interventionism in the Middle East. Unfortunately Beech was incorrect when he wrote:

> where this [Liberal Conservatism] differs from Blair's doctrine of the international community – a muscular form of liberal interventionism – is that Cameron's Conservatives appear less willing to use robust rhetoric and they are likely to employ a more cautious approach to utilising military instruments for humanitarian ends (Beech, 2011a: 360).

Perhaps Robin Cook's desire for an ethical dimension to British foreign policy has found its way into the fabric of the government and the Foreign and Commonwealth Office.

Conclusions

Blair's 'Liberal Interventionism' had led Britain to take part in several contentious conflicts across the world. Rather than simply defending Britain's interest, British foreign policy began to focus on what was morally 'right' and the protection of people far outside of Britain's traditional scope. While this certainly sounded good in theory, in practice it led to accusations of Britain becoming involved in issues which were simply nothing to do with her, and often the intervention itself might have caused more problems than it solved. The most glaring example of this is the war in Iraq. These interventions also led to Blair having to deny that Britain's increased military actions were not causing danger to the British public by inspiring or encouraging those with a specific interest in Iraq to turn their attention to the 'invaders'. Blair's successor, Brown, certainly dampened down the flames of interventionism, focusing instead on international aid and encouraging business links while reducing the number of troops in Iraq and Afghanistan. However, the Conservative-led coalition had a real opportunity when it gained power to follow its 'Liberal Conservatism' agenda and intervene less in global affairs: 'On the one hand it seeks to distance itself from traditional conservative policies; on the other to temper the more aggressive neo-conservatism of the Bush administration' (Dodds and Elden, 2008: 359–60).

While it was always going to be difficult for the Conservative Party to accept a smaller role for Britain in global affairs, due to its militaristic background and slightly jingoistic history, the agenda of 'Liberal Conservatism' coupled with their Liberal Democrat bedfellows, traditionally a party who have followed a less interventionist line, protecting the rights of people in all nations, could have signalled a far less interventionist foreign policy and perhaps even some recognition of the decreased role of Britain in the world. Finally, Britain could have recognised that she was 'punching above her weight' and reflected that in her foreign policy. However, that was not to be the case, and 'Liberal Conservatism' was to be short-lived in power. Perhaps it should come as no surprise that a radical rethink has not been forthcoming as in 2008, Cameron noted that 'Britain has a valuable role to play in the world, standing on the side of those who are struggling for democracy and justice. This is our continuing duty and responsibility' (Cameron, 2008b). And, Dodds and Elden (2008) argued that 'Liberal Conservatism' was in a difficult position.

The actions of the coalition government in Libya have tested the five elements of 'Liberal Conservatism' to the limit. The first element, that we 'should understand the threat we face' is fairly obvious and really adds nothing to our discussion of foreign policy. The second element, that 'democracy cannot quickly be imposed from outside' was, in my opinion, included as a direct response to the war in Iraq. While there has not currently been any serious discussion of imposing democracy from outside (by force presumably), with the focus instead on encouraging the seeds of democracy within the nation which already exist, the preoccupation with pushing the importance of democracy does not seem to have diminished with the departure of the Blair government. The third element that 'our strategy needs to go far beyond military action' was also a little misleading. While the Blair governments may have been criticised for their foreign policy actions, it would be misleading to suggest that they only focused on military action, when instead the governments did pursue non-military actions in order to further their foreign policy aims, such as the strong and vocal support of both Blair and Brown for the UN Millennium Goals. In terms of Libya, it could be argued that due to the time frame involved, there has not been a great deal of opportunity to pursue non-military aims, although the government has been rather lukewarm about pushing for sanctions against Libya, which might well take time to work, but would almost certainly have a sizeable impact. The fourth element that 'we need a new multilateralism to tackle the new global challenges we face' could be seen to have been adhered to in relation to Libya. The government has sought, and achieved a UN mandate and is supported, at least in terms of rhetoric if not in terms of action, by numerous NATO nations and members of the African Union. Again, it could be argued that this specific point was included as a direct result of the Iraq war, where there was no international mandate and the Blair government was dogged by questions over the legality of war. Cameron and Hague clearly did not want to follow this path and the UN mandate has enabled them to sidestep the issue of legality. The fifth element, that 'we must strive to act with moral authority' speaks to Robin Cooks' 1997 speech where he called for 'ethical dimensions to foreign policy', the desire to act morally rather than simply pursue British interests without regard for others (*Guardian*, 1997). Again, it could be seen that this was a reaction to the war in Iraq, but almost certainly has longer roots than that.

While the actions of the Conservative-Liberal Democrat coalition government have not completely contradicted the principles of 'Liberal Conservatism' they certainly seem to be more interventionist than the principles themselves suggest. Hague and Cameron have pursued a policy in relation to Libya which is fairly hawkish, increasing Britain's foreign policy obligations further and increasing the pulls on the military, leading confirmed budget cuts within the Army, Navy and Air Force to be re-examined and delayed. Any hopes that British foreign policy might have been re-examined following the Blair/Brown years was perhaps a little naïve, but the Cameron government has been in power for only a year, and has been rather overtaken by events. However, foreign policy generally tends to be a rather pragmatic policy area, driven by events rather than ideology in many instances. The Conservative-led coalition will struggle to remain united if the problems in Libya, or in another as yet unknown nation (perhaps Syria), become the focus of discussion on the deployment of ground troops. Cameron and his government will struggle to survive if their actions in Libya are unpopular amongst the British public, or if their actions come to closely resemble those of Blair in Iraq. As Vickers points out: 'the new government does not wish to change the world, but does wish to maintain Britain's global reach across it at a time of economic constraints' (2011: 204).

10
Fixing Broken Britain

Richard Hayton

The contention that British society was broken and in need of repair, was a leitmotif of David Cameron's tenure as leader of the opposition. In his victory speech accepting the party leadership, he identified the need for 'social action to ensure social justice, and a stronger society' and declared that the Conservatives could 'mend our broken society'. Cameron identified a number of key indicators of social breakdown which he would return to over the next five years: 'drug abuse, family breakdown, poor public space, chaotic home environments [and] high crime' (Cameron, 2005). He also alluded to the essential element of the broken society critique, that these problems could not be addressed by the state, but required community action through charities, voluntary organisations and social enterprises.

The focus on social problems such as these was part of a deliberate strategy aimed at convincing the electorate that the Conservative Party was changing, and was serious about addressing contemporary social issues. As such it was a key element in Cameron's modernisation agenda to transform his party's image, by concentrating attention on issues not traditionally associated with the Conservatives. Other issues which were also central to this brand decontamination strategy were the environment and climate change (Carter, 2009) and the politics of the family, where Cameron sought to strike a more liberal and inclusive tone than his predecessors (Hayton, 2010). However, while the focus on 'broken Britain' marked an important shift of emphasis and rhetoric by the Conservatives, this chapter argues that it drew in substantial part on the Thatcherite ideological legacy. In this sense it did not mark a radical overhaul of Conservative thinking, but a more coherent effort to reformulate it as a critique of New Labour's record in office.

In its first 12 months in power the Conservative-Liberal Democrat coalition government embarked upon an ambitious programme of social policy reform. This chapter analyses the social policy objectives the coalition identified, and progress towards implementation of them in its first year in office. It also considers the reality of this process against rhetoric emanating from government ministers, and weighs up the likelihood of success of the programme as a whole and elements within it. The chapter argues that the coalition's social policy is being driven by three main pressures. Firstly, the overriding imperative identified by the politicians involved to reduce the deficit in the public finances, and meet their self-imposed target of eliminating the structural deficit within the lifetime of the current parliament. This perceived need derives from both the neo-liberal framework which prevails in economic discourse in the United Kingdom in general and the Conservative Party in particular, and the constraints of the integrated global economy. Secondly, there is an ideological commitment to fundamentally rebalance the relationship between the state, economy and society; to reduce the scope and scale of the state's role. In this respect, the deficit has provided an opportunity for the coalition to present a picture of a crisis in the public finances, and pursue this ideological objective on seemingly pragmatic grounds. Thirdly, the form and nature of specific policy proposals within the broad field of social policy is being shaped by the dynamics of coalition, namely the need to negotiate positions acceptable to both parties. A related aspect of this is a desire held by both Nick Clegg and David Cameron that the government be able to present its reforms as 'progressive'.

The chapter focuses particularly on welfare policy. Under the direction of the Secretary of State for Work and Pensions, Iain Duncan Smith, the coalition stated that it planned to undertake the most radical reform of the welfare state since the implementation of the Beveridge Report after World War II. The changes proposed included restrictions on entitlement to the previously universal child benefit; cuts to housing benefit; reform to disability benefits; and the phasing-in of a system of 'universal credit' to replace all current means-tested benefits for job seekers. The genesis of this reform programme will be traced through an examination of the policy work undertaken in opposition; notably that by Duncan Smith's Centre for Social Justice and the related policy group which he chaired.

In exploring these issues, the chapter first identifies traditional Thatcherite positioning on social policy. It then turns to the Conservatives' policy agenda in opposition, identifying the main elements of the 'broken society' critique. The extent to which this has been carried forward into government is then assessed, and the impact of the coalition considered. Finally, the prospects for this agenda are reflected upon.

Thatcherite Conservative positioning on social policy

The rise of the New Right in the 1970s and the election of the first Thatcher government in 1979 marked a pivotal moment in British social, economic and political life. The ideological legacy of Thatcherism continues to have an enduring significance in Conservative Party politics, both as a reference point against which contemporary debates over policy, electoral strategy and modernisation are often framed, and for neo-liberal Conservatives, as a roadmap which still offers the most compelling set of directions for the party to follow. The implications of Thatcherism for Conservative positioning on social policy were far-reaching, although they took time to unfold in practice. In fact, it was not until Thatcher herself had left office that many of the more radical aspects of Thatcherite social policy were realised (Hickson, 2010).

The New Right was a reaction against the post-war consensus that dominated British politics between 1945 and 1970, and which had as one of its central features an acceptance of comprehensive welfare provision by the state. One Nation Conservatism enjoyed its greatest influence as part of this consensus, and during a lengthy period of government (1951–1964) the Conservatives did not seek to unpick the general principles of the welfare settlement established by Clement Attlee's administration. This did not, however, indicate 'any new and significant commitment to social justice and tackling poverty' on the part of Conservatives (Bochel, 2010: 123). Rather, the key concern of One Nation Conservatives was the preservation of order and social harmony, meaning that a pragmatic case for limiting inequality could be made (Hickson, 2009). Advocates of the New Right offered a critique of One Nation Conservatism which argued that the acceptance of Keynesian welfarism had damaged both the economy and British society. The moment of 'crisis' was reached in the Winter of Discontent of 1978–1999, which was successfully narrated by the New Right as demonstrating that the state had become overextended to breaking point and was in need of a dose of neo-liberal retrenchment (Hay, 2010).

The central concern of Thatcherism was the reversal of relative national decline. For Thatcher and her followers this was about more than the economy and Britain's role in international affairs, but also required a moral rejuvenation of the nation based on a revival of individualistic 'vigorous virtues' (Letwin, 1992) reminiscent of the Victorian era. The welfare state attracted particular enmity as it was blamed for creating a culture of dependency and idleness which eviscerated the moral fibre of the nation (Hickson, 2010: 138). However, as Hickson has noted, tackling the welfare state was not an immediate priority for Thatcher on entering office in 1979, who concentrated her efforts on a neo-liberal economic policy of monetary control, fiscal conservatism and assailing the trade unions. The resultant doubling of unemployment increased the cost of welfare dependency and obstructed the government's desire to reduce overall state expenditure (Hickson, 2010: 139–40). The Thatcher administrations took some measures to try and restrict the growth in welfare spending, notably de-linking state pension increases from the rate of average earnings (a policy reversed by the coalition government in 2010) and cutting the value of the State Earnings Related Pension Scheme (SERPS). As well as being driven by a desire to save money, these policies were also informed by a wish to encourage self-reliance and private provision, and people were encouraged to opt out of SERPS in favour of individual or company pension schemes.

More radical measures to reform social security on Thatcherite lines were taken by John Major's government between 1990 and 1997, again motivated by both ideology and cost. Between 1980 and 1989 the number of lone parents in receipt of income support had more than doubled from 330,000 to 770,000 (Nutt, 2006). In an effort to address this, the government created the Child Support Agency (CSA), which was charged with pursuing absent fathers and enforcing the payment of child maintenance. The CSA was beset with operational problems and became symbolic of the Major government's disastrous 'Back to Basics' initiative, which was launched at the 1993 party conference (Hickson, 2010: 142). This blighted campaign was an attempt to revive the Conservatives' fortunes by seizing the initiative on social policy following the calamitous events of Black Wednesday in September 1992, which had destroyed the party's reputation for economic management. This moral posturing quickly came to haunt the Conservatives however, as allegations of sleaze against various Tory MPs appeared in the newspapers and the party attracted the charge of hypocrisy (Hayton, 2010: 492). A moralistic tone also accompanied other key social policy changes under Major, notably the replacement of unemployment benefit with Job Seeker's Allowance in 1996. Thatcherite social policy reforms consequently took a significant amount of time to develop between 1979 and 1997, but 'were ultimately decisive and enduring' (Hay and Farrall, 2011: 8). Elements of this agenda would be carried forward by New Labour in office, particularly in terms of the focus on welfare to work (Driver, 2008).

The Thatcherite legacy: Conservative policy positioning in Opposition

After losing the 1997 general election, the intra-party debate about how the Conservatives should seek to modernise in order to revive their electoral appeal was often characterised as a battle between socially liberal 'mods' and traditionalist 'rockers' who favoured an authoritarian approach more in tune with the Victorian values admired by Thatcher. Modernisers such as Michael Portillo saw the next logical step for Conservatives as to build on the economic liberalism they had advocated in the 1980s with a similarly radical agenda of social liberalism. This would have entailed a repudiation of a key element of Thatcherite ideology, something the party was not ready to countenance in 1997. Having lost his seat at the general election, Portillo was not in a position to stand for the party leadership, and the mantle passed from John Major to William Hague. Hague's pitch for the leadership was that the party needed a 'fresh start' and that he was the man to deliver it, and he was successful in attracting the support of modernisers such as Alan Duncan, who managed his campaign (Driver, 2009: 85). However, this message was tempered by the endorsement of his candidature by Margaret Thatcher, which helped him secure the support of voters on the right of the party, but also reinforced the caricature of Hague as a Tory Boy unable to step out of her shadow.

After an initial dalliance with social liberalism under Hague's leadership the Conservatives soon retreated to a core-vote electoral strategy located firmly within Thatcherite ideological parameters (Hayton, 2010: 493–5). Following the 2001 general election defeat, the selection of Iain Duncan Smith as Hague's successor appeared to signal the strengthening hold of the traditionalist right on the party. Despite securing the backing of most of the shadow Cabinet, Portillo was unable to convince even a third of his parliamentary colleagues of the merit of his agenda for modernisation in the leadership election, and following his third place finish withdrew to the backbenches. Although he firmly rejected the notion of modernisation (which he associated with Portillo's social liberalism) Duncan Smith surprised many with his efforts as Conservative leader to re-orientate the party's electoral strategy and renew its policy agenda. Although the language used was different, 'the approach he adopted until early-2003 presaged much of the Cameron modernisation agenda' (Hayton and Heppell, 2010: 436).

Duncan Smith sought to downplay the core vote issues of Europe, immigration and taxation and attempted to demonstrate that the Conservatives were engaged in developing policies to improve the public services and to address broader social problems. This was a two part strategy: firstly to identify the Conservatives with the electorate's priorities, and secondly to challenge negative preconceptions about the party by focusing attention on the poorest sections of society (Hayton and Heppell, 2010: 430). In a series of speeches Duncan Smith pledged to 'champion the vulnerable' and argued that Labour did not have 'a monopoly on compassion' (Duncan Smith, 2004). The party held a conference on compassionate conservatism, and Duncan Smith even wrote the introduction to a book on the subject entitled *There is such a thing as society* (Streeter, 2003). In a wilful attempt to dissociate from the Thatcher era the Conservatives began to talk about social justice (a concept that Thatcher's favourite guru, Friedrich von Hayek, had labelled a mirage).

The compassionate conservatism agenda did not, however, mark a return to a form of one nation conservatism of the kind seen in Britain during the post-war consensus. Nor did it mark a move towards a socially liberal stance as advocated by the modernisers. Rather it took its inspiration from the US Republican Party, where compassionate conservatism had been championed particularly by George Bush in the 2000 presidential election campaign. This view sought to combat the idea that conservatism was not concerned about the poor, but also argued that tackling poverty required more than government action and advocated 'a more holistic approach in which voluntary organisations and faith groups would be accorded the lead role' (Page, 2010: 148). In other words, obligation is placed on the shoulders of individuals, families and communities, not on the state. As such compassionate conservatism is compatible with the Thatcherite desires for both a smaller state and a strong sense of collective social morality. The difficulty for British Conservatives was that while US Republicans might hope that the glue of religious morality would help bind society together, in the increasingly secular UK other civic institutions between the state and the market would have to be nurtured (Willetts, 2005). In arguing for a 'civic conservatism' David Willetts attempted to address this issue, and it also informed Oliver Letwin's vision of a 'Neighbourly Society' which he articulated as shadow Home Secretary under Duncan Smith. Letwin argued that empowering local communities was essential for solving social problems such as crime and anti-social behaviour. These ideas can also be found in much of the localism agenda (for example, Direct Democracy, 2005) and ultimately informed Cameron's Big Society narrative.

Duncan Smith's leadership failed because of his own shortcomings in terms of party management, political communication, and an inability to establish his authority as leader (Hayton, forthcoming, b). His successor Michael Howard was stronger in these respects, but did little to push forward the social policy agenda Duncan Smith had tried to develop, and which he continued to pursue at the Centre for Social Justice (a think-tank he established in 2004). Although a self ascribed moderniser, as Conservative leader David Cameron adopted and built on Duncan Smith's legacy in this policy area. One of his first acts on becoming leader was to announce the establishment of six policy review groups, and Duncan Smith took on the social justice brief. The work carried out by the Social Justice Poverty Group underpinned and developed the assertion that British society was broken, which was a key theme of Cameron's tenure as leader of the opposition. The capacity of the 'broken Britain' narrative to appeal to a wide spectrum of Conservative opinion is illustrated by the fact that the phrase was first used in the 2005 leadership election by Liam Fox, who told the 2005 conference:

> And under this Labour government, we can all see what I call a broken society. I'm sure you know what I mean: more marriages breaking down, rising levels of violent crime, record truancy rates from schools, more domestic violence, increasing numbers of suicides, too many young people, especially young men with no role models, running wild in our communities (Fox, 2005).

While Cameron's modernising stance was associated with the socially liberal left of the party, Fox appealed firmly to the traditionalist Thatcherite right (Heppell and Hill, 2009). Nonetheless, the issues highlighted by Fox proved to be broadly in line with those that would be stressed by Cameron and by the Social Justice Policy Group (SJPG) he established. Fox realised that this social and moral agenda would play to his core constituency on the right of the party, something which might also partly explain Cameron's interest in it, as he sought to build a cross-party appeal (he also emphasised his Euroscepticism during the leadership campaign). However, Cameron's commitment to developing policy in this area also reflected a broader concern amongst Conservatives that they had allowed themselves to be caricatured as having little to say on social issues and as only being interested in the economy and money. It also signalled a growing confidence that they could effectively challenge Labour on this territory, as the intractability of problems such as antisocial behaviour suggested to some Conservatives that the government was failing and that more radical solutions needed to be devised. Cameron thus argued that his brand of 'modern conservatism' offered the opportunity to 'combine the preservation of the Conservative economic inheritance with the resolution of the social problems which were left unresolved at the end of our time in government, and which remain unresolved after a thousand short-term bureaucratic initiatives' (Cameron, 2006d). On this reading Blair had identified the post-Thatcher zeitgeist, but New Labour had struggled to address it effectively in office.

At the launch of the Centre for Social Justice in December 2004 Duncan Smith presented a paper entitled *Britain's conservative majority*. Drawing inspiration from the recent electoral success of George Bush in the USA and John Howard in Australia, Duncan Smith argued that 'moderate social conservatism' could strike a chord with mainstream public opinion in the UK. He claimed that the 'small c conservative majority' was committed to social justice issues, but also looked for 'moral purpose' in policy platforms (Duncan Smith, 2004: 4–5). While the parallels with Fox's account of the broken society are clear, this belief in the need for a greater sense of moral direction also informed the policy work carried out by the SJPG for Cameron. Two substantial reports were produced: *Breakdown Britain* (SJPG, 2006) and *Breakthrough Britain* (SJPG, 2007). Together these critiqued the growth of the welfare state and 'the weakening of the welfare society' (SJPG, 2006: 14) and argued that the state had not only failed to recognise the importance of the third sector organisations which help make up the latter, but had actually caused substantial damage to them. *Breakthrough Britain* claimed to offer a middle way to fight poverty, rejecting both *laissez faire* and state-centred approaches. Instead:

> Our approach is based on the belief that people must take responsibility for their own choices but that government has a responsibility to help people make the right choices. Government must therefore value and support positive life choices. At the heart of this approach is support for the role of marriage and initiatives to help people to live free of debt and addiction (SJPG, 2007: 7).

This emphasis on responsibility and marriage contained echoes of John Major's failed 'back to basics' campaign (Driver, 2009: 88), and ran through the policy recommendations made by the SJPG. However, a key difference was the weight of evidence the SJPG presented in an effort to substantiate its recommendations, which gave it the confidence to claim it was 'not about preaching to people about how they should live their lives. It is about what works' (SJPG, 2007: 10). Similarly in his repeated affirmation as leader of the opposition of the importance of marriage and family values, Cameron was 'careful to base this support on evidence rather than morality' (Kirby, 2009: 246). Combined with a more liberal tone than his predecessors on social issues such as gay rights, this helped Cameron accommodate the politics of the family within his modernisation strategy (Hayton, 2010).

The *Breakdown Britain* report identified five pathways to poverty (family breakdown, worklessness and economic dependency, addiction, debt and educational failure) and *Breakthrough Britain* made 190 recommendations based on these (Page, 2010: 150). Amongst the most striking was the suggestion of transferable tax allowances for married couples, a policy that had previously featured in the 2001 manifesto. The report also argued for tax credit reforms to remove the 'couple penalty' it identified in the current system (ibid). It also suggested that there is 'overwhelming evidence that the cycle of disadvantage starts very early' (SJPG, 2007: 8) and suggested a number of measures such as better childcare provision and improved nursery education aimed at enhancing early years support. In terms of welfare to work, *Breakthrough Britain* noted the poverty trap for those on benefit seeking to move into work (or from part-time to full-time work), as the withdrawal of benefit left some facing a marginal tax rate of 90 per cent. This was investigated in greater detail in a further report published in 2009, and the SJPG proposed the creation of a Universal Credit scheme to replace a range of means-tested benefits, to be withdrawn at a rate of 55 per cent as claimants move into work (Page, 2010: 151).

Although the 2010 Conservative Party manifesto did not commit to a Universal Credit system, it did draw substantially on the work carried out by the SJPG. It promised to reduce welfare dependency through a new work programme which would involve private providers and oblige the unemployed to participate and accept job offers, with the sanction of a loss of benefit for up to three years if they refused (Conservative Party, 2010: 15–16). Family policy also occupied a prominent place in the document, as the Conservatives pledged to make Britain 'the most family-friendly country in Europe' (2010: 41) through enhanced rights to flexible working; tax credit reform; and through a recognition of marriage and civil partnerships in the tax system (although the mechanism was not specified).The emphasis placed on early intervention by the SJPG also appeared in the manifesto with a promise to focus Sure Start on the 'neediest families' (2010: 43).

The key narrative of the manifesto was the promise to build the Big Society. Although this remained poorly defined it was presented as the alternative to 'big government' (2010: 36) and as the answer to the social problems identified by the broken society critique:

> The size, scope and role of government in the UK has reached a point where it is now inhibiting, not advancing, the progressive aims of reducing poverty, fighting inequality, and increasing general well-being. We can't go on pretending that government has all the answers. Our alternative to big government is the Big Society: a society with much higher levels of personal, professional, civic and corporate responsibility; a society where people come together to solve problems and improve life for themselves and their communities; a society where the leading force for progress is social responsibility, not state control (2010: 37).

The nebulous nature of the Big Society facilitated its use as a theme to link policy proposals across a range of areas including local government, health and education, as well as the welfare state. It was also an attempt to offer a message of hope, as although British society was said to be broken, the Conservatives promised that 'together we can mend it: we can build the Big Society' (2010: 35). At the core of the idea is a belief in community involvement and a more active citizenry, encapsulated in Cameron's suggestion of a National Citizen Service (Mycock and Tonge, 2011). As Kisby (2010) has argued however, it also implies the hollowing out and retreat of the state from the provision of core public services, in the hope or expectation that communities, voluntary groups and families will fill the void. As such it suggests that a Thatcherite desire to reduce the size and scope of the state remained firmly embedded in Conservative thinking at the time of the 2010 election, and that the party was keen to pursue these ideas in relation to social reform as well as the economy.

Social policy in practice: The first year in government

Analysing Conservative social policy development in 2009, Stephen Driver predicted that in office Cameron's administration 'would be a government largely of mods not rockers' and characterised Conservative social policy as 'post-Thatcherite' (2009: 95). However, research by Bochel and Defty (2010) suggested that Conservative MPs retained firmly Thatcherite views on the appropriate role of the state in welfare provision, with 36 per cent agreeing it should be a 'safety-net only for those most in need' and a further 18 per cent seeing its function as to support the extension of private provision as (no Liberal Democrats were placed in either of these categories). By contrast 50 per cent of Liberal Democrat MPs believed in a 'high national minimum level of services/universal provision' and a further 7 per cent saw the function as to redistribute wealth. No Conservatives appeared in either of these categories and although there was some movement on both sides towards a centre ground, the results clearly aligned Liberal Democrat and Labour parliamentarians on the left of the political spectrum and Conservatives on the right (Bochel and Defty, 2010: 80). This implied that social policy could be a divisive issue for the coalition. In practice however, welfare reform did not prove to be a contentious area in the 2010 coalition negotiations. This can be explained by the fact that it had not been a prominent issue in the election campaign, with the three major parties sharing 'a broad policy consensus around work-orientated welfare reform' (Driver, 2011: 106). This view is supported by research that suggests that the New Labour era saw the emergence of a cross-party consensus on welfare reform in the UK (Taylor-Gooby, 2001).

The coalition agreement between the Conservatives and Liberal Democrats in May 2010 certainly indicated some important areas of continuity with the policies of the previous Labour administration, notably retention of the national minimum wage and the goal of ending child poverty by 2020. Although the document promised to replace the existing welfare to work schemes with one new programme the principle was essentially the same, and the proposed reassessment of incapacity benefit claimants was something that had previously been suggested by Labour's James Purnell during his time as Secretary of State for Work and Pensions. The coalition agreement also made two mentions of the Big Society. It promised to 'use funds from dormant bank accounts to establish a Big Society Bank, which will provide new finance for neighbourhood groups, charities, social enterprises and other non-governmental bodies' (HM Government, 2010a: 29–30). It also attempted to use the notion of a Big Society as a unifying theme for the two parties in coalition, claiming: 'when you take Conservative plans to strengthen families and encourage social responsibility, and add to them the Liberal Democrat passion for protecting our civil liberties and stopping the relentless incursion of the state into the lives of individuals, you create a Big Society matched by big citizens' (2010a: 8).

After the coalition was formed Cameron appointed Iain Duncan Smith as Secretary of State for Work and Pensions. The priority placed on deficit reduction and the size of the welfare budget meant that Duncan Smith was under immediate pressure to bring forward plans to reduce his departmental spending. In the June 2010 emergency budget, Chancellor of the Exchequer George Osborne noted: 'It is simply not possible to deal with a budget deficit of this size without undertaking lasting reform of welfare' (Osborne, 2010: 23). He announced plans to up-rate benefits in line with the consumer price index rather than the (usually higher) retail price index; cuts to tax credits for families earning over £40,000; abolition of the Health in Pregnancy Grant; and a three year freeze of child benefit. Housing benefit entitlements would also be restricted to save £1.8 billion per year, and the pension age increased to 66 sooner than originally planned. Osborne also made it clear that Duncan Smith would be asked to look for further savings and that additional reductions in welfare spending would 'greatly relieve the pressure' on other departments, which on average were being asked to make a 25 per cent cut (2010: 20).

Deficit reduction had been established as the overriding priority of the new government in the coalition agreement, which argued that it was 'the most urgent issue facing Britain' and promised to 'significantly accelerate the reduction of the structural deficit over the course of a Parliament, with the main burden of deficit reduction borne by reduced spending rather than increased taxes' (HM Government, 2010a: 15). This represented a victory for Conservative economic policy over that of their new partners, Vince Cable and Nick Clegg having spent much of the election campaign warning of the risk to growth of cutting too far and too fast. The proposed ratio of spending cuts to tax increases (approximately four to one) also signalled the triumph of fiscally conservative neo-liberal orthodoxy, with severe implications for big spending departments such as Work and Pensions (DWP) which were offered no protection (unlike the Department of Health, which had its budget ring-fenced).

In spite of the pressure to make cost savings, Duncan Smith was also keen to reiterate his determination to push forward with substantive reform (*Guardian*, 26 May 2011). However, he faced the problem that his desired system of universal credit (as proposed by the SJPG) carried significant upfront cost, and was consequently viewed with scepticism by the Treasury. However, Duncan Smith received Prime Ministerial backing for his proposals and a deal was reached: universal credit would be introduced, albeit with a higher rate of withdrawal than favoured by the SJPG plans (65 per cent rather than 55 per cent). Duncan Smith was consequently able to announce the government's commitment to universal credit at the Conservative Party conference in October 2010, and the details were fleshed out in a White Paper published the following month. The new payment would replace six existing means-tested benefits and come with a start up cost to the government of £2.1bn (BBC News, 2010b). To recoup this cost other benefit cuts were also announced. Most controversially, also at the Conservative conference, George Osborne announced that entitlement to the previously non-means tested child benefit would be removed from families where one or more earners paid higher rate tax. This policy was widely attacked as it would create a significant anomaly in the tax and benefit system: a one earner household just over the higher rate tax threshold would lose out substantially, whereas a two earner household with both earners just below the threshold would lose nothing, despite having a considerably higher family income. This apparent attack on families who conformed to the model of parenting generally most favoured by traditionalist Tories (two parents, with one going out to work and the other looking after the children) incurred the wrath of the *Daily Mail* and bloggers on the influential Mumsnet website, and appeared to contradict Cameron's professed desire to support family life. Rattled by the backlash, Cameron felt the need to hold out the prospect of a tax-break for married couples being introduced by 2015 (*Daily Telegraph*, 6.10.2010) – a pledge that had been made by the Conservatives before the election, but downgraded in the coalition agreement due to Liberal Democrat opposition.

October 2010 also saw the announcement of substantial cuts in housing benefit, aimed at saving £2bn per year. The proposals included a cap on claims of £400 per week (lower for smaller properties) which led Conservative Mayor of London Boris Johnson to warn that the policy would result in 'Kosovo-style social cleansing' of the poor from the capital (*Guardian*, 28 October 2010). The government also proposed a 10 per cent cut in payments for claimants who had been out of work for more than one year, although this plan was dropped from the Welfare Reform bill in February 2011 after 'a last minute intervention by Nick Clegg' (*Guardian*, 17 February 2011). This episode highlighted growing unease on the Liberal Democrat benches about the impact on the poorest of the welfare cuts, which in time could develop into a noteworthy source of tension between the coalition partners. As Driver noted, in the coalition's first year 'while Duncan Smith might have got his universal credit, the Treasury had got its cuts' (2011: 110), and as the effects of these roll out over the course of the parliament they could prove too much for some Liberal Democrats to stomach.

Conclusion: Austerity politics and social reform

In its first year in office, the coalition has embarked upon a radical programme of welfare reform. The most pressing factor behind this programme has been the government's commitment (derived from its neo-Thatcherite economic policy) to eliminate the structural deficit within the lifetime of the parliament. However, another key influence has been the strategic repositioning and policy work carried out by the Conservatives in opposition, particularly by Iain Duncan Smith. This began during his tenure as party leader but gained credibility and traction through the Centre for Social Justice (and the policy group it hosted) under the auspices of Cameron's modernising leadership agenda. The coalition in office has consequently taken on the challenge of implementing a far-reaching programme of welfare reform during a period of unprecedented public sector austerity. These circumstances present an opportunity in that they provide a justification for uncompromising reform, but also act as a constraint on any measures which cost money (even if this is merely an up-front cost which could reasonably be expected to be recouped over the medium term). In securing the introduction of a Universal Credit, Duncan Smith has achieved a central part of the package of measures recommended by his policy review group in opposition. However, the long-term effectiveness of this is brought into question by the compromise on the rate of benefit withdrawal which is higher than under previous arrangements for tax credits, which could mean that for some benefit recipients incentives to work (or work more) are actually reduced (Brewer et al, 2010: 67).

In opposition under Cameron, the Conservatives also persistently argued that Britain was afflicted with a 'broken society' which they would repair in office. Leaving aside the counter argument that there is cornucopia of evidence available to contradict that claim (see for example *The Economist*, 2010a and 2010b) there remains unanswered the question of whether the coalition's social policy agenda will alleviate or exacerbate the issues they had identified. A victim of the coalition agreement was the Conservatives' commitment to prioritising tax-breaks for married couples, and the child benefit cuts noted above (both in terms of the rate freeze and removal from higher rate taxpayers) also directly contradict the rhetorical emphasis on the importance of supporting families to aid social cohesion. The key symptoms of the broken society identified by the SJPG – family breakdown, worklessness and economic dependency, addiction, debt and educational failure – all seem unlikely to be eased by a programme of fiscal austerity and public sector cuts, which is liable to result in higher unemployment and less support being available for the most vulnerable in society. The government has also struggled to put flesh on the bones of its Big Society vision. An opinion poll in early-2011 found that 50 per cent of people regarded it as 'a gimmick' and 41 per cent saw it as 'merely a cover for spending cuts' (Rentoul, 2011), illustrating the difficulty the coalition has had in defining what, beyond deficit reduction, it actually wants to achieve.

The coalition's social policy agenda is fundamentally an ideological one in two key respects. Firstly, it is part of a broader neo-Thatcherite project defined by the government's economic policy, which exhibits a commitment to the neo-liberal ideals of a smaller state intervening less in the economy, lower taxes, and a highly cautious fiscal policy. The Big Society agenda fits into this schema through its stress on encouraging third sector organisations to take on roles previously carried out by the state. In this respect, the 2010 general election re-exposed a deep divide between the Conservatives and Labour in terms of their views on the appropriate role of the state and its relationship with society (Smith, 2010). Secondly, as discussed in this chapter the coalition's social policy agenda itself draws substantially on the Thatcherite ideological legacy in Conservative politics, notably in the sense of the responsibility placed on individuals and families, rather than the state. Whether this proves problematic in terms of party management within the coalition will depend on whether the Liberal Democrats rediscover their social liberalism and have the capacity to reaffirm it, or whether the occasional policy compromise (such as on housing benefit) will keep them onside while the essentially Conservative social policy programme is implemented.

11
Women and Feminisation

Valerie Bryson

When David Cameron became its leader in 2005, he appeared determined to 'feminise' the Conservative Party, both by increasing women's political representation and by addressing their interests and concerns. The first section of this chapter explores the reasons for this move by placing it in the context of the gender environment and policy agenda inherited from 13 years of Labour government; this generated powerful pragmatic political motivations for change. The second section identifies pressures and counter-pressures for feminisation within the Conservative Party, the third outlines Cameron's key promises to women and the fourth assesses what the coalition government has delivered in practice. The chapter concludes that Cameron's commitment to feminisation seems largely cosmetic, and that it is incompatible with the policies his government has pursued.

The inheritance from Labour

The policies of a new political leader and a new government are inevitably conditioned by the political and ideological situation that they inherit from previous leaders and governments. When Cameron became party leader, two terms of Labour government had apparently transformed the gender landscape of British politics, making it possible and perhaps also necessary for him to feminise a party that was looking increasingly old fashioned and out of touch on gender issues.

Women in elected office

The 1997 Labour landslide was accompanied by a dramatic doubling of women's political representation from 60 to 120 MPs – that is, from nine to 18 per cent (in contrast, when Margaret Thatcher became Prime Minister in 1979, there were only 18 other women in the House of Commons – just 3 per cent of the total). This larger pool of women MPs enabled Blair to appoint an unprecedented five women to his first cabinet, rising to eight by the time he left office in 2007. Although the number of women in Brown's cabinets fell back to five and then down to four, this is still much higher than any previous administrations; for most of her time in office Thatcher was the only woman in her cabinet, and Major's first cabinet was entirely male.

Rather than a natural outcome of changing gender roles, the increase in women's political representation was the result of deliberate action within the Labour Party, culminating in its all-women shortlist policy in the run-up to the 1997 general election; far from being a specifically New Labour policy, this push for more women was the product of long-term campaigning by feminists within the party, combined with a perceived need to attract women voters (Short, 1996). Although in 1996 a tribunal found that the policy constituted illegal sex discrimination, it was in place long enough to produce dramatic differences between the parties a year later: in striking contrast to Labour's 101 women MPs, only 13 Conservative women were elected. In 2002, the Sex Discrimination (Election Candidates) Law permitted (but did not require) parties to use such measures (see Childs, 2002); although it was passed with Conservative front-bench support, only the Labour Party has used its provisions, and the gap between the two parties remains stark.

Today, it is perhaps difficult to understand how astonishing it was to suddenly have more than a handful of female politicians. Although the 1997 intake attracted some media ridicule and the nomenclature 'Blair's babes', their very numbers meant that they could not all be so easily dismissed; although by 2005 four out of five MPs were still men, women's political presence was not only 'normalised' but also widely expected. In this context, a parliamentary party with 181 men and only 17 women (just 8.6 per cent of the total) now looked decidedly odd and out of touch; this however was the parliamentary party that Cameron inherited in 2005.

Women-friendly policies and the machinery of government

As new leader, Cameron had to develop his party's policies in an environment in which Labour seemed to be taking the lead on 'women's issues' as well as women's representation. After 18 years in opposition, many in the Labour Party had by 1997 come to appreciate the need to attract women voters, and they were able to draw on academic research that identified clear differences between the sexes in terms of political priorities – with women significantly more likely than men to prioritise issues around health, education and the family, and men more concerned with the state of the economy and taxation. This message was pushed home by some very determined women within the Labour Party, including Clare Short and Harriet Harman, and by the 1997 the party appeared to be seriously addressing areas of concern such as childcare and the needs of women workers. Although it is notoriously difficult to show a direct causal link between the political presence of women and specific policy outcomes, the increase in the number of women MPs, including many who identified themselves as feminists with a role in representing women's interests, helped translate electoral promises into policy (Childs, 2004), and the years of Labour government saw a number of new measures that particularly benefited women. These included the development of the first national childcare strategy; the introduction of the national minimum wage; tightening up of the law to give more protection to victims of domestic violence; changes to state pension entitlement to take women's caring work into account; measures to help lone parents into employment; the introduction of child tax credits; and a number of provisions to help balance workplace and family commitments, including the extension of maternity leave and the introduction of paternity leave. In 2010, the Equalities Act also brought together and strengthened previous pieces of legislation aimed at combating discrimination on a number of grounds, including sex, age and disability.

The development of women-friendly policies was supported by the creation of the new post of Minister for Women (albeit unpaid and combined with another cabinet post) and the Women's Unit (later the Government Equalities Office). There were serious attempts at gender mainstreaming, with all departments from 1998 required to assess their policies for their gender impact (Durose and Gains, 2007). Labour ministers and MPs seeking to act for women could also draw on the resources provided by existing government machinery, particularly the Equal Opportunities Commission (which in 2007 became part of the wider Equality and Human Rights Commission) and the Women's National Commission (an umbrella advisory body, established in 1969 to represent the views of women and women's organisations to the government); outside groups such as the women's Budget Group (an independent organisation of researchers, economists, policy experts and activists committed to gender equality) and the Fawcett Society (a long-established feminist organisation) also provided important sources of expertise. These structures and links meant that if Cameron were serious in his commitment to feminisation, he would find supportive machinery and resources in place; the existence of expert groups also meant that he could readily be held to account if he reneged on his promises.

Although the Labour government did not seriously challenge the economic forces and gendered power structures that underpin unequal outcomes, even critical commentators have conceded that by treating equal pay and childcare as part of public policy, the Labour government had 'fundamentally altered the perspective of British political parties' (Rummer et al, 2007: 232) and that 'New Labour has taken a number of opportunities to address women's concerns and that as a consequence the policy framework in the UK has been significantly altered' (Annesley and Gains, 2007: 20). As with the drive to increase women's representation, this policy shift resulted from a combination of feminist pressure within the party and the search for electoral advantage amongst women voters.

Labour's electoral lead amongst women

Analysis of voting behaviour in the 1997, 2001 and 2005 elections indicates that the search for women's votes was successful, as a majority of women voted Labour in all three elections, with a shift away from the Conservatives that went well beyond the electoral swing amongst men. Whereas women had historically been more likely than men to vote Conservative, by 2005 this traditional pattern of voting behaviour had been reversed, with 4 per cent more women than men voting Labour, and 2 per cent fewer voting Conservative (Ipsos Mori, 2005). In other words, it was women's votes that defeated the Conservative Party under Michael Howard, and gave Tony Blair his third electoral success.

The omens for the future looked even more bleak for Conservatives, as the swing towards Labour had been particularly high amongst younger women: by 2005, 43 per cent of women voters aged 18 to 34 voted Labour in 2005 and only 21 to 22 per cent voted Conservative, who were the third choice for women in this age group, behind the Liberal Democrats. For men in the same age group the Labour lead over the Conservatives was narrow, at between 1 and 4 per cent (Fawcett Society, 2006; Ipsos Mori, 2006; Campbell and Childs, 2010). Although their higher than average turnout means that older women are electorally very important, this pattern suggested that the Conservative's traditional electoral lead amongst women might be literally dying out. In this context, feminising the party in terms of both women's political representation and policies to address women's concerns, could be seen as a political necessity, without which it would be condemned to permanent opposition.

Pressures and counter-pressures within the Conservative Party

The push for feminisation

While by the time of the 2005 election the Labour Party looked like a party that could represent women and was listening to their concerns, the Conservative Party looked more like an old-boy's club, out of touch with contemporary lifestyles and opposed to measures, such as the minimum wage, state support for childcare and family-friendly employment legislation, that increasingly enjoyed popular support from men as well as women. Its subsequent electoral defeat, and the gendered nature of the voting patterns behind this, highlighted the need to attract women voters both by increasing the numbers of Conservative women MPs and by developing more women-friendly policies. Such feminisation could also be seen as a break with the image of the Conservatives as the 'nasty party', part of a wider process of modernisation and ideological renewal that would bring the party into line with the needs of a rapidly changing society and distance Cameron from the unpopularity of his recent predecessors (Buckler and Dolowitz, 2009; Bryson and Heppell, 2010).

As with the earlier process of feminisation in the Labour Party, these pragmatic considerations were combined with pressure from women in both the parliamentary and extra-parliamentary party. The party's 2005 election defeat strengthened Conservative women's demand for both better representation and more input into policy-making, and they used both the long-established Conservative Women's Organisation (CWO) (http://www.conservativewomen.org.uk/women_parliament.asp) and a new group *women2win* (http://www.women2win.com/organisation.asp) to criticise the Conservative election manifesto's neglect of gender issues and the lack of women candidates in winnable seats. With members from all levels of the party and outside links with networks and expert groups including the Equal Opportunities Commission (EOC) and the Fawcett Society, these groups helped ensure that candidates in the 2005 leadership campaign discussed not only the need for more Conservative women in parliament but also policies around women's workplace needs and domestic responsibilities (Campbell et al, 2006; Childs, 2008).

In articulating the demand for better representation, some Conservative women used meritocratic, neo-liberal ideas to argue that ongoing discrimination against women is an uncompetitive restriction on individuals that also damages the party by excluding talent and reducing its electoral appeal. Others drew on more traditional Conservative ideas about women's role and the importance of the family, claiming that women's natural dispositions and/or experiences (particularly as mothers) give them distinct interests and a particular perspective on politics that deserves representation and that may bring a different style and approach to politics that will change it for the better (see Lovenduski, 2005).

A similar mix of arguments came together to support the demand that party policies should address the gender pay gap, the dearth of women in top jobs and the needs of working mothers. Here 'free-market feminists' insisted that there was a clear business case for ensuring that women's talents were not wasted or under-utilised, while wider social changes meant that by 2005 it was also no longer innovative or radical to suggest that women, including those with children, should be in paid employment, that they should expect to pursue careers without discrimination, and that they should be entitled to maternity leave to make this possible. The idea that fathers too should be entitled to spend time caring for their children was also increasingly seen as both natural and desirable (EOC, 2006), while any potential liberal/conservative clash on moral and social issues could be conveniently side-stepped via the mantra of 'choice' (Childs and Webb, forthcoming). In this context, Conservative acceptance of a changed gender order did not represent some wild and radical leap into the unknown; rather, it constituted an endorsement of what had become the new 'common sense' of society, and recent research finds that even traditionalists seem to be 'surprisingly progressive' on gender issues (Webb and Childs, 2011: 383).

Forces against feminisation

Widespread acceptance of the electoral necessity and/or desirability of feminisation did not, however, mean that it was universally supported by Conservative women, and the push for change came primarily from younger, London-based and business and career-oriented women (Childs et al, 2009). At a more general level, a number of writers have noted the ongoing strength of social conservatism within the party, and the consequent risks for a leader pursuing a more liberal agenda (Buckler and Dolowitz, 2009; Heppell and Hill, 2009; Hayton, 2010).

Although many party members now advocated an increase in women's political representation, this was not matched by support for the kind of practical measures that might ensure this, and there was widespread opposition to anything resembling quotas for election candidates, both because this seems like discrimination against men and because constituency activists resent central party interference in their selection processes (Childs et al, 2009). Similarly, Conservative claims for women in the workplace were combined with an insistence that women do not need any special favours, simply an acknowledgement of their abilities and an end to discrimination against them. While the open competition that this involves would spell an end to 'old boys' networks, it rules out any form of positive discrimination or quotas or measures to help women combine domestic and workplace responsibilities.

Combined with ideological hostility to state regulation and spending, such thinking meant that the 1979–1997 Conservative governments had refused to provide or fund childcare, to introduce a minimum wage, to extend maternity rights for women workers, to introduce paternity leave or to allow affirmative action to promote gender equality. Although by 2005, there had been some shift in party leadership thinking on these issues, business interests remained strongly opposed to enforcing 'family-friendly' conditions of employment through the state regulation, while the party's continuing commitment to privatisation and the outsourcing of public sector employment threatened the relatively favourable conditions of employment enjoyed by women in the sector. As the main users of welfare services and recipients of benefits (for their families as well as for themselves), women were also particularly vulnerable if the party's ongoing ideological commitment to reduced taxation and public spending involved welfare cuts. While the influence of business interests in the Labour Party was at least partially countered by the trade union movement, there was no such group in the Conservative Party to represent alternative interests and views.

Despite some shifts in attitudes and the assertion of women's perspectives, it seems clear that in 2005 the Conservative Party remained 'institutionally sexist', in that it 'reflect[ed] the needs of one sex at the agenda setting, formulation and implementation stages of the policy process' (Lovenduski, 2005: 53). The 2005 leadership campaign might have been 'unusual for both the quantity and quality of its rhetoric on women's representation and frequent references to women's issues' (Campbell et al, 2006: 18), but the party's new leader would inevitably face problems in translating any women-friendly promises into political outcomes. The following sections track the effects of these pressures and counter-pressures as Cameron moved from being a leadership contender to Leader of the Opposition and then Prime Minister of a coalition government.

Cameron's promises

The impact of Conservative women's push for feminisation was clear during the leadership campaign, when Cameron repeatedly stressed that he was aware of women's concerns, particularly in relation to political representation, and just two minutes into his leadership acceptance speech he identified the need to 'change the scandalous under-representation of women in the Conservative Party' (cited in Campbell et al, 2006: 18). In the early months of his leadership he consulted regularly with the Fawcett Society, whose feminist influence is apparent in his early policy statements on childcare, parental leave, the gender pay gap and rape. These policy developments marked a distinct break with earlier Conservative positions, and brought his party more in line with the new gender agenda established by the Labour government; more generally, his talk of 'compassionate conservatism' suggested a softer, more caring approach that might be expected to appeal to women voters.

Cameron soon also took some limited and mixed steps towards increasing women's voice in the party. In 2007 he made Theresa May, a self-described feminist, his shadow minister for Women and Equalities. He revived the post of Vice-Chairman for women's issues, adding responsibility for building up links with women outside the party to the post's earlier remit of increasing women's representation and ensuring that Conservative policies have 'women's interests and concerns uppermost' (Childs, 2008: 37). His appointee, Margot James, founded the Women's Policy Group, which produced a report that reads more like a feminist publication than a traditionally Conservative one (Conservative Party Women's Policy Group, 2008). James' post was, however, unpaid, and Cameron failed to establish formal channels of representation and accountability for Conservative women in the initial policy reviews that he set up to modernise the party across a very broad range of issues.

Meanwhile, Cameron's commitment to increasing the number of Conservative women MPs led to a series of reforms to the candidate selection process, of which the most important was probably the creation of an 'A-list' of priority candidates, at least 50 per cent of whom were female, from which local parties were required to select their shortlist. In defending this policy, which faced significant opposition in the party (Lovenduski, 2005; Campbell and Childs, 2010), Cameron drew on arguments about both women's ability and their experiences and interests, insisting that his party 'didn't pick more women candidates to try and look good ... [it] did it so we wouldn't lock out talent and fail to come up with the policies that modern families need' (Cameron, 2008d). By the time of the 2009 Speaker's Conference, a special parliamentary committee to investigate the under-representation of women, Cameron even appeared to support all-women shortlists; however, these were not used, and Childs and Webb have found that his statement in favour 'looks to have been mere rhetoric' (forthcoming). The more limited party reforms that were introduced fell far short of guaranteeing women's selection, and after the 2010 election only 16 per cent of Conservative MPs were women, compared to 32 per cent of Labour MPs; nevertheless, this was nearly double the percentage in 2005, an unprecedented 48 Conservative women MPs (Centre for Women and Democracy, 2010).

While he remained Leader of the Opposition, Cameron did not have to match his rhetorical commitments to detailed proposals, and his policies around employment and the family involved a careful balancing act that could appeal to both feminists and traditionalists within his party, and that also sought to win over the women voters who had been attracted by Labour policies without at the same time antagonising business interests. In particular, he advocated tax relief on childcare (Bennett, 2006), repeatedly talked about developing 'family-friendly' employment, took paternity leave when his own child was born and supported parents' right to ask for flexible working arrangements (Mulholland, 2007). With the rest of his front bench, he supported the 2006 Work and Families Act which extended maternity leave and enabled mothers to transfer a portion of this to their partner (Childs et al, 2009). Some Conservative backbenchers with business interests had spoken against this legislation, but at the 2008 Conservative Party Conference Cameron reiterated his commitment to flexible working by arguing that this was a means of strengthening the family that would also benefit business:

> It's because I want to strengthen families that I support flexible working. To those who say this is some intolerable burden on business, I say 'wrong'. Business pays the costs of family breakdown in taxes – and isn't it right that everyone, including business, should play their part in making Britain a more family-friendly country? Do you know what, if we don't change these antiquated business practices then women half the talent of the country are just put off from joining the workforce (Cameron, 2008d).

Such arguments address the concerns of working women, business interests and those with traditional attitudes to the family; traditionalists could also find succour in Cameron's frequently expressed endorsement of marriage as a central element of a stable society. However, as Kirby points out, Cameron was careful not to present this as a moral issue or a condemnation of single mothers. Rather, his favoured policy of rewarding marriage through the tax system was presented as an evidence-based method of mending Britain's 'broken society' and reducing the financial and social costs of family breakdown and fatherless households (Kirby, 2009). Although in 2003 he had voted against artificial insemination for all but married, heterosexual couples (Hayton, 2010), Cameron was now careful to insist that marriage rights should include gay people in civil partnerships. He also affirmed the right of both married and unmarried mothers of young children to stay at home; here he rejected Labour proposals that lone mothers of pre-school children who were in receipt of benefits should be required to prepare for entry into the labour market (although not actually to work), arguing that we must not 'make our broken society worse. We need to help families, not make life harder for them, and that especially applies to single-parent families who already have it hard enough' (reported by Sparrow, 2008). He also committed a future Conservative government to taking positive and practical measures to end violence against women, and he promised support for preventative education, police training and additional funding for rape crisis centres (Mulholland, 2008).

By the time of the 2010 election, the Conservative Party seemed to have largely accepted the gender agenda that had been established by the Labour government and was increasingly being demanded by women in the party. The main party manifestos were now competing for women's votes on much the same grounds, with their manifestos proffering 'a smorgasbord of issues relating to women's work/life balance, with the remaining, relatively minor [i]nter-party differences ... not, crucially, always in the direction one might expect'. For example, the Conservatives were slightly more generous than Labour and other parties in their promises around the right to request flexible working and the transfer of maternity/paternity leave between parents (Campbell and Childs, 2010: 762, 773). All main parties also promised action to address violence against women, with the Conservatives promising new rape crisis centres and stable, long-term funding for existing ones.

However, some clear party political differences remained, reflecting deep-seated economic and ideological disagreements about the role of the state and the public sector, the causes of the financial crisis and the extent to which public spending should be cut. Unlike the other main parties, the Conservatives insisted that early cuts in spending were essential, and indicated that spending on benefits such as tax credits, Child Trust Funds and Sure Start should be reduced by targeting it at poorer families. Their manifesto also re-stated Cameron's commitment to recognising marriage and civil partnerships in the tax system; interestingly, this policy seems very much Cameron's own rather than a product of consultation with women, and recent research on the attitudes of Conservative women MPs has found little explicit support for it (Childs and Webb, forthcoming).

Nevertheless, as Campbell and Childs reported at the end of 2010, 'the Conservatives came into government, alongside the Liberal Democrats, with their most detailed and thorough manifesto commitments for women' (2010: 761). The fate of these commitments as the party made the transition from opposition to government is discussed in the next section.

From opposition to coalition government: The first year

Any talk of feminisation at first sight seemed forgotten in the negotiations that produced the coalition government, as both the Conservative and Liberal Democrat negotiating teams were exclusively male. Nevertheless, there was no reason to suppose that Liberal Democrats, who had long argued for equal opportunities for women in both politics and employment, would oppose Cameron's feminisation agenda if he sought to pursue it. Although there was a potential tension between the party's liberal wing, which shared Cameron's individualistic and free market approach to equal opportunities, and its social democratic wing, which took a more collectivist approach that was more inclined to support positive action and preserve the public sector, there was also reason to expect that Liberal Democrats would try to moderate some aspects of Conservative policy that might negatively affect women. In particular, during the election campaign the party had rejected the need for cuts on the scale that the Conservatives proposed, and Nick Clegg had promised to 'work with Fawcett and others to ensure that both local and national deficit cutting proposals are assessed in terms of how they would impact on women – both regarding access to public services and women's incomes' (Fawcett Society, 2010). Groups such as Fawcett were further reassured by Clegg's rejection of Cameron's proposal to reward marriage in the tax system, which they feared would increase women's financial dependency on their husband, and which Clegg had described as 'patronising drivel that belongs in the Edwardian age' (Fawcett Society, 2010).

The 'programme for government'

Given their shared commitments and promises to women, it is unsurprising that the coalition 'programme for government' included a pledge to promote equal pay, take 'a range of measures' to end discrimination in the workplace, support the provision of free nursery care, provide flexible parental leave, extend the right to request flexible working and explore ways of improving the funding of rape crisis centres. Indeed, it seemed that such commitments were now the common stock of political discourse, articulated even in women's absence – although feminist critics felt that the workplace proposals were too reliant on voluntary compliance rather than effective regulation, and would have preferred the state to provide nursery care rather than supporting its provision by 'a diverse range of providers' (HM Government, 2010a: 18, 19). Meanwhile, the programme's proposal to introduce a transferable tax allowance for married couples was of course contrary to Liberal Democratic policy. Although it was agreed that they would have a right to abstain on the issue, the Fawcett Society declared itself 'shocked' by Clegg's apparent willingness to accept its inclusion without insisting on the right to speak and vote against it (Fawcett Society, 2010).

It was, however, the programme's proposal that defendants in rape trials should, like their accusers, be given a right to anonymity (HM Government, 2010a: 24), that attracted most opposition from women – not only from the Fawcett Society, external organisations and Labour women MPs, but also from female coalition backbenchers. Although the proposal had not been included in either party's manifesto, it was a long-standing Liberal Democratic policy. It was also fiercely opposed by those who believed that it would deter women from reporting rape and further reduce the appallingly low conviction rate for the crime. The strength and success of the campaign against it indicates both the impact that even a modest female presence can have and the gendered nature of the issue: in the Commons debate, women from all the main parties spoke against anonymity and men from all the main parties spoke for it, and, in one of the coalition's first u-turns, the proposal was abandoned in November 2010.

The programme's proposals on rape trials appeared to reflect the absence of women's voices in the development of its early policies, so that the limited nature of feminisation in the sense of women's political presence also meant largely un-feminised policies that failed to address women's concerns. This experience highlighted the danger that the welfare of many women might be seriously threatened if the deficit reduction programme, which the document said 'takes precedence over any of the other measures in this agreement', failed to take women's experience and interests into account. The paucity of women's voices was not improved by the alliance with the Liberal Democrats, who had only seven women out of 57 MPs (two fewer than in 2005), and Cameron appointed only four women to his first cabinet (Theresa May, Lady Warsi, Caroline Spelman and Cheryl Gillan). Nevertheless, the appointment of May to the senior post of Home Secretary looked like a very positive move. Cameron also made May Equalities Minister; although this doubling up of posts (which followed Labour precedents) might seem to downgrade her role in promoting equality, the appointment of such a strong feminist seemed to suggest that he took the role seriously.

Some positive results and their limitations

One of May's first steps was to establish an inter-ministerial group on equalities to coordinate policy across departments. An early policy statement from this group promised that 'Equality is not an add-on, but an integral part of this government's commitment to build a stronger economy and fairer society' and that the government would be 'leading by example and embedding equality in everything we do in government as an integral part of our policies and programmes' (HM Government, 2010c: 9, 24). The statement reiterated the government's commitment to tackling discrimination and promoting equal opportunities, which it argued could be best achieved through advocacy, consultation and voluntary measures rather than regulation.

May sought to improve communication between the Equalities Office and women through a new 'Women's Engagement' newsletter and launched a consultation on 'Strengthening Women's Voices in Government' which proposed that ministers directly engage with women and their organisations to provide 'the opportunity for a genuine two way dialogue on policies affecting women' (Women's Engagement, March 2011: 3). In her 'Foreword' to the first newsletter, May was also able to point to budgetary changes that lifted nearly one million of the lowest paid workers (many of whom are women) out of income tax, protected the lowest paid public sector workers from the public sector pay freeze and increased child tax credits for the poorest families (Women's Engagement, Jan/Feb 2010). The newsletter itself reported new funding for rape crisis centres and the establishment of a review, headed by Lord Davies, on the lack of women on the boards of top companies (just 12.5 per cent of board members of FTSE 100 companies are women). Davies' subsequent report strongly criticised existing recruitment and promotion practices and called for companies to aim for their boards to be 25 per cent female by 2015, with the threat of statutory quotas if these voluntary targets failed to produce results. The government welcomed his report and 'will engage with business in considering his recommendations' (Women's Engagement, March 2011: 6).

The coalition programme's commitment to more family-friendly employment was taken forward with the launch of a consultation plan in May 2011. This proposed extending the right to request flexible working to all employees and giving parents more choice in how to share parental leave between them. Launching the consultation, May identified a need to move away from 'an outdated nine to five model of the working day', insisting that flexible employment is in the interests of all and that it will 'help end the state-endorsed stereotype of women doing the caring and men earning the money when a couple start a family' (May, 2011). Meanwhile, many women benefitted from the restoration of the earnings link to state pensions, with the 'triple guarantee' that these will rise by the higher of earnings, prices or 2.5 per cent.

The coalition government also appeared to be taking issues around sexual and domestic violence seriously. Continuing initiatives begun by the Labour government, the Equalities Office produced a 'Call to End Violence Against Women and Girls' at the end of 2010, and an 'Action Plan' early the next year. This plan recognised the complexity of the issues and stressed the importance of education and prevention as well as helping victims and ensuring offenders are brought to justice; it also said that it would work through a wide range of partners from local communities, voluntary groups, local authorities and international organisations to achieve this.

Taken together, these changes suggest that feminisation of government policy is progressing in terms of both processes and outcomes. However, there are a number of problems. First, the effectiveness of the inter-ministerial group has been limited by the absence of any minister from the Treasury; as discussed in the next section, the impact of recent budgetary and spending decisions has been particularly damaging to many women. Secondly, while the attempt to reach out to women is of course welcome, the need to do this would have been much less urgent if the government had not first abolished the Women's National Commission (WNC) as part of its 'bonfire of the quangos'. As a *Guardian* report on its closure said, the 670 partners who had found a voice through the WNC 'included all sorts of views and groups, many of them so far outside the charmed circle of political power that they would otherwise be unseen and unheard' (Ashley, 2010). By May 2011, some feared that further changes to the machinery of government that would limit the effectiveness of action to promote equality were pending, as the Equalities Act was put out for discussion as a possible way of cutting unnecessary red tape. However, May has stated in parliament (5 May 2011) that the intention is not to abolish the Act, but to see how it is working in practice and whether it could be improved.

Thirdly, the proposed employment and workplace reforms around the Davies Report and family-friendly employment were characterised by an arguably over-optimistic dependence on voluntary compliance. While the proposed changes may indeed be profitable in the long run, as Cameron and May have claimed, they are likely to be opposed by those men who find that their expected smooth ride into top positions is threatened and by employers who fear that they will involve expense and inconvenience; here the proposals for more flexible working have been welcomed by the TUC but opposed by the CBI. As discussed in the next section, most gains by pensioners and low-paid workers have been more than cancelled by wider changes to the tax and benefits system and by cuts to public spending.

Fourthly, plans to combat violence against women run up against the impact of cuts in public spending and grants to voluntary agencies. Here the Action Plan states that although local authorities have difficult spending decisions to make, services to protect women 'should not be the easy cut' (HM Government, 2010c: 2). However, no action has been taken to ring-fence them, and in some areas services have been reduced. Meanwhile, groups whose funding has been lost or reduced include those providing services for victims of domestic violence and sexual trafficking, and the head of a leading women's refuge has handed back the OBE she was awarded for her work because she believes that funding cuts are making it impossible to provide an adequate service (Butler and Travis, 2011; Gentleman, 2011).

Given the coalition government's commitment to spending cuts, any programme that seriously attempts to combat the inequalities and injustices faced by many women is likely to encounter problems. While of course money cannot solve everything, effective action requires a level of resources that is not forthcoming from the private sector and which the voluntary sector is increasingly unable to provide. However, the next section shows that the changes introduced in recent budgets and spending reviews have not simply halted progress towards greater gender equality; rather, they have reversed it.

The impact of budgetary, spending and welfare reforms

Despite her positive statements about the government's commitment to gender equality, May was very aware that women's voices were not being heard as critical economic decisions were made. There were initially no women in the 'star chamber' set up by Chancellor George Osborne to decide where spending cuts should be made, and in the run-up to the emergency budget of June 2010, May wrote to Osborne, with a copy to Cameron, warning him that he risked breaking the law if he did not conduct a gender impact assessment of the budget (Dodd, 2010; *Stopgap*, 2010). In the event, Osborne did not do this, and it was left to the Shadow Equalities Minister, Yvette Cooper, to request a breakdown of the figures from the House of Commons library.

The figures provided by the library, which analysed the gender impact of budgetary changes in direct taxes and benefits, are shocking. Although they confirmed May's claim, discussed above, that some changes had benefitted some women, the overall figures show that women would pay for 72 per cent of the savings made in the budget, which raised nearly six billion pounds from women, and just over two billion pounds from men. The detailed calculations behind these headline figures are complex, but reflect the cumulative effects of changes to the tax credits and welfare benefits on which women rely more than men, and it was poorer women, particularly lone mothers and single female pensioners, who were most adversely affected; a disproportionate number of these poor women are of black or minority ethnic origin. Changes included a fall in the real value of child benefit, the abolition of the health in pregnancy grant, the limiting of the Sure Start maternity grant to the first child, cuts in housing benefit and child tax credits, and a general fall in the real value of benefits and pensions as the basis of uprating changed from the retail price index to the less generous consumer price index (the Commons library figures are available on www.yvettecooper.com/women-bear-brunt-of-budget-cuts; for further analysis, see Women's Budget Group, 2010a; TUC, 2010; Reed, 2011).

Osborne's October 2010 spending review announced drastic cuts in public expenditure, involving £18 billion in cuts to social security and welfare, involving hundreds of thousands of job losses in the public sector. Although this time there was an equalities impact assessment, this was very limited, and once again it is women who were most adversely affected, both because they are the main users of services and because they are the majority (65 per cent) of public sector employees. By mid-2011, cuts in local government spending in many areas of the country included reduced support for carers and those in need of caring services, cuts in early years provision, including Sure Start, and cuts in youth and after school clubs. These service cuts also involve redundancy for many women workers, while many others are faced with unaffordable childcare costs, as the tax credit that helped them pay for this has been withdrawn entirely from those who work fewer than 24 hours a week, and significantly reduced for the rest. As the Women's Budget Group found, this means that, combined with the impact of the emergency budget, the cuts 'represent an immense reduction in the standard of living and financial independence of millions of women, and a reversal in progress made towards gender equality' (Women's Budget Group, 2010b: 1–2; see also *Stopgap*, 2010; TUC, 2010). The group also found that the 2011 budget did not redress the imbalances that had been created, and concluded that 'gender equality is under threat, both in terms of income, and of jobs, and of ability to reconcile employment with the time to care for family, friends and neighbours' (Women's Budget Group, 2011: 2).

Other proposed changes in welfare provision will also have negative effects on many women. If separated parents cannot agree on child maintenance, the parent claiming maintenance (most commonly the mother) will now have to pay if they need the state to enforce a settlement and collect the money on their behalf. Lone parents in receipt of benefits (90 per cent of whom are women) will also be required to look for paid work when their youngest child is five. Although many women eventually stand to gain from a proposed new, higher, flat rate state pension, the unexpectedly fast equalisation and raising of the pensionable age for both men and women to 66 by 2020 has hit many women in their fifties: half a million will have to work over a year longer than they had planned, for some it will be two years. Here it is not the principle of equalisation that most women object to, but its acceleration, in breach of the coalition agreement. Like men, women also face cuts to work-based pensions, which will now be up-rated in line with the lower Consumer Price Index, rather than the Retail Price Index. Although the Department of Work and Pensions says that there will be 'no losers' under the proposed shift to a universal credit, this would go only to one partner in a couple, the main earner; in many cases, this means that the childcare and child elements of tax credits will go to fathers rather than mothers.

Conclusion

Before he became prime minister, Cameron's rhetoric suggested that he was committed to feminising his party, both in terms of increasing women's representation and in developing policies to address women's concerns. This rhetoric may have contributed to his success in halting the drift of women voters away from his party: while women were still 3 per cent more likely than men to vote Labour in 2010, and 4 per cent more likely to vote Liberal Democrat, their swing towards the Conservatives was much the same as men's, and it was only in the 25 to 35 year age group that more women voted Labour than Conservative (Ipsos Mori, 2010). Had he been serious in his commitment to feminisation, he would have found strong backing from some sections of his party and some supportive machinery and legislation in place. However, he would have also encountered strong opposition from business interests and other sections of his party.

One year into the coalition government, women seem to be the big losers. True, Cameron managed to get more women in his parliamentary party, and there is no reason to suppose that he does not believe that women should have the same political and workplace opportunities as men. In terms of political representation, however, Cameron has yet to introduce measures that would guarantee the selection of more women; meanwhile, coalition proposals to reduce the number of MPs will intensify competition and reduce the number of vacant seats that women might contest, and women are likely to be particularly uncomfortable with changes to the system of parliamentary expenses that will make it harder for MPs to live with their families during the week. In terms of feminised policy-making, by the end of 2010 the Fawcett Society, whose expertise Cameron appeared to seek when he became leader, reported that 'The government's plans thus far have shown a lack of consideration, understanding or possibly interest in women's equality' (*Stopgap*, 2010: 8). Although the right to request flexible work might look like a significant advance, it is meaningless for women who have lost their job, or been told that they risk losing benefits if they do not try to get a job, or who have had to give up work because they can no longer afford childcare or because cuts in care services mean that they cannot leave their elderly mother. Similarly, public expressions of support for women who are victims of sexual violence mean little when many of the services that might support them are facing cuts or closure.

The coalition government presents the cuts as a necessary means to the urgent end of cutting the budget deficit. However, whether this was the result of Labour politicians' profligacy or the greed and foolishness of bankers, one thing is clear: it was not the fault of the women who are now disproportionately paying for it. The wisdom of seeking to reduce the deficit so quickly is of course itself disputed, but even if the need for rapid reduction is accepted there are other, much less regressive, ways of achieving this: for example, the Women's Budget Group suggests that a 'Robin Hood' tax which some have argued should be placed on financial transactions could be turned into a 'Maid Marion' tax by using the revenue to avoid cuts that damage women (Women's Budget Group, 2010b). Such ideas, along with the voices of those who will suffer most, are not being heard as policies are developed.

By April 2011, even the appearance of progressive attitudes to women seemed to be disappearing, as Cameron told a female Labour MP, Angela Eagle, to 'Calm down dear' during a Commons debate, David Willets (the Universities Minister) blamed feminism for a lack of jobs for working class men, and Kenneth Clarke (the Justice Secretary) appeared to suggest that some forms of rape were less serious than others (for reports on these incidents see Edemariam, 2011; Mulholland, 2011; Travis and Watt, 2011). Apparently trivial in themselves, these remarks may indicate a more deep-seated lack of respect for women or understanding of the issues that affect them. However, they pale into insignificance in comparison with the tangible damage that is being done to so many women's lives. 'Feminisation' is not just about making the right noises and having a few more women's faces at top tables; it involves hard choices and a radical rethinking of political priorities. There is no sign that Cameron has been prepared to make these choices or rethink his priorities.

Acknowledgment

I would like to thank Professor Sarah Childs of Bristol University for constructive comments on an earlier draft of this chapter.

12
Liberal Conservatism: Ideological Coherence?

Stuart McAnulla

Introduction

Many commentators were startled by the formation of the coalition government in May 2010. Surprise was followed by the expectation that a process of ideological compromise would ensue as the Conservative and Liberal Democrat leaderships sought to agree with a common policy platform. In respects, this is indeed what has occurred during their first 15 months of government. However, the task of tracing the ideological character of the coalition is much more complicated than just looking for ways in which the difference has (or has not) been split between competing sets of ideas, or merely highlighting those areas in which the coalition partners share a common vision. For it is clear that both parties are themselves, as ever, 'coalitions' of actors with often distinct ideas. Also, in recent years it has arguably become particularly difficult to draw clear ideological dividing-lines between the main political parties. The coalition follows an extended period in office for a Labour government which made a virtue of its 'post-ideological' character. Insofar as the Blair administration had a guiding philosophy this was 'the third way', which sought to explicitly transcend traditional ideological dividing-lines, and combine a commitment to a 'dynamic market economy' with a pledge to pursue 'social justice' (Giddens, 1998; Blair, 1998).

Whilst in opposition, both the Conservatives and Liberal Democrats struggled to challenge a set of ideas which were carefully constructed as 'centrist' and pragmatic. The Conservatives were often painted as stuck in a now out-dated Thatcherite mind-set, and the Liberal Democrats were sometimes tempted to challenge Labour from the 'left' on issues such as taxation and public services. Only following David Cameron's election as party leader in 2005 did the Conservatives make a sustained effort to renew their ideological direction (O'Hara, 2007). Although Cameron had major successes in changing perceptions of the party, doubts persisted as to the content of his new Conservatism, and sections of the party were uncomfortable with perceived departures from Thatcherism. Nick Clegg's election as leader of the Liberal

Democrats in 2007 in part represented a new ascendancy for the so-called 'Orange Book' tendencies in the party (Marshall and Laws, 2004). Thus the party began to move in a more economically liberal direction, marking a break with the more social democratic tone of the previous leaderships of Ming Campbell, Charles Kennedy and Paddy Ashdown. Both parties had endured periods of ideological doubt, uncertainty and flux, which had in turn opened key actors (particularly the respective leaderships) to the potential influence of new or refreshed ideas. However, behind the efforts by these parties to stress their own 'centrist' credentials, there were still significant differences of opinion and emphasis, even between front-bench members of each party. Within the Conservatives, the 'modernising' tendencies of figures like Cameron and Osborne were viewed with scepticism by many traditionalists in the wider parliamentary party. Inside the Liberal Democrats, tensions endured between the economic-liberal and social-liberal wings of the party.

This chapter argues there have been three major strands to the ideological positions of the coalition to date. The first of these is the critique which is offered of post-war British politics, particularly the ideological positions pursued by the governments led by Margaret Thatcher. The key emphasis here is that neo-liberal economics have been necessary, but that on their own they are insufficient to create a strong society and effective politics. The second strand of significance is the *anti-statist* emphasis of the coalition, which seeks to downplay the extent to which central government can or should direct public services. The third main strand is the *'rolling-out' of society* which argues communities and individuals must be empowered through decentralised and localised forms of governance. Having outlined these positions, the chapter concludes by identifying the tensions within coalition ideology, and providing a tentative interpretation of the ideological locations of the governing parties.

The insufficiency of neo-liberalism and Thatcherism

An important aspect of Cameron's rebranding of the Conservative Party was the effort to demonstrate that the party had moved beyond Thatcherism. Commentators have debated how far this change was driven by perceived electoral necessity, as against a sense in which the party felt a genuine need to alter or refresh direction in the wake of societal change and contemporary public policy challenges (Bale, 2008b; Dorey, 2007). The presentation of Thatcherism as presenting hyper-individualism, social authoritarianism and an uncaring attitude to those suffering disadvantage has often been considered by senior Conservatives as a crass caricature (Willetts, 1992). However, it is a perception that gained widespread currency, and became the frame through which many people came to interpret the modern Conservative Party. There was also a tangible sense in which the party had struggled to move on from the Thatcher-Major years, and this was manifest in the inter-party splits that emerged between more socially-liberal 'modernisers' and Thatcherite traditionalists under different leaders between 1997 and 2005. At times both William Hague and Iain Duncan Smith made at least half-hearted efforts to distance themselves from the Thatcher era, but when placed under internal pressure both would end up siding with traditionalists. However, following a third successive election defeat, the case for more far-reaching reappraisal of the party's stance became overwhelming. The early years of Cameron's leadership were marked by overt attempts to distance himself from Thatcherism, even though he was careful to point out what he considered successful aspects of Thatcher's reign (Evans, 2010). Cameron did this through two strategies, the first of which was to explicitly distance himself from the perceived excessive individualism of Thatcherism, through stressing repeatedly that 'there *is* such a thing as society' (Cameron, 2008e). Relatedly he also drew upon the 'one nation' theme within Conservatism that Thatcher had arguably eschewed.

In more substantive terms Cameron's approach involved dispelling the idea that Conservatives aspired to privatise the NHS and that they were indifferent to post-material concerns such as the environment and global poverty. Initially, much of this manoeuvring was done rhetorically, with few clear ideas about what such commitments might practically mean. This left Cameron vulnerable to the charge that the announcements were mainly about good PR and electoralism rather than genuine changes in intellectual outlook. However, what has perhaps been underplayed about this period was the extent to which Cameron developed a sustained critique of Thatcherism. Many had previously considered a Conservative-Liberal Democrat government unlikely even in the context of a hung parliament, precisely because of many Tories continuing affection for Thatcherite policies. As is indicated below, a number of the changes under Cameron effectively brought the Conservatives closer to positions that could dovetail with the inclinations of certain Liberal Democrat stances.

There were two aspects of Thatcherite reforms in the 1980s which Cameron directly argued were mistaken. The first of these was on the issue of poverty. The 1980s had witnessed the growth of child poverty, with data suggesting that by 1990 one-third of children were growing up in homes bringing in less than half the median income. The issue was one which prompted critics to emphasise the socially divisive aspects of Thatcherite policies. Cameron came to argue that the Conservatives had been wrong to reject the concept of 'relative poverty' (Cameron, 2006e) and linked this to a wider argument that whilst Thatcher had brought necessary economic reform, the social aspect of her approach had been lacking. Philosophically, this involved the recognition that market reforms and general economic growth do not of themselves resolve embedded social problems and can, in aspects, exacerbate them. From this critique emerged the coalition's later pledge to keep New Labour's goals concerning the long-term elimination of child poverty.

The other aspect of Thatcherism which Cameron criticised is the centralisation of power which occurred during the 1980s. Though Thatcherism sought to 'roll back' state intervention in the economy, it was also concerned with asserting strong government from the centre. One aspect of this was to thwart efforts by left-wing councils to undermine the neo-liberal project of reform by creating upward pressures on public spending. Thus the government abolished significant tiers of local government and otherwise restricted the powers available to local authorities. There had always been tension within Thatcherism on this point as it appeared to give mixed messages as to the likely wisdom of decision-makers in central government. However, the belief of many neo-liberals was that such authoritarian steps were needed for the longer-term project of freeing people from municipal socialism and fostering greater individual freedom through the spread of the market. Yet Cameron believed that such state centralism had produced regrettable consequences (2007c). Conservative modernisers argued the difficulty with this approach was that it in effect took away power from the local institutions which help foster productive social bonds (Kruger, 2007: 2). By undermining such local organisation the belief was that the Conservatives unwittingly contributed to trends towards isolation and social disconnection. Decisions were being made at too great a distance from people to be sufficiently sensitive to the particular requirements of local communities. For Cameron, this 'top down' aspect of Thatcherism was continued with under subsequent Labour governments, fusing with the enduring statist tendencies even within New Labour. Thus Cameron sought to draw on the decentralising strands within traditional Conservatism to establish a clear difference with the Thatcherite view. In turn this paved the way for the development of Cameron's notion of the Big Society (see below).

There were further respects in which Cameron qualified the authoritarian aspects of strands of traditional Conservative and Thatcherite thinking. Although some Tories backed the New Labour's idea of introducing national ID cards as a means of counteracting crime and terrorism, Cameron balked at the plan, arguing that it would involve state infringement of basic liberties. In this regard, Cameron drew on more libertarian strands of conservatism which fear the way government may be tempted to abuse the information it collects centrally regarding its citizens. In addition, Cameron signalled departure from the more socially prescriptive, moralistic dimensions of traditional conservatism, through emphasising his support for gay rights. Whist attending a gay pride event he apologised for the Thatcher government's imposition of section 28 which banned public authorities from promoting homosexuality (Cameron, 2009c). On entering office, the coalition have continued with new Labour's reforms on gay rights and have been considering furthering these by allowing gay couples in civil partnerships to have full marriage rights. New measures on tackling homophobic bullying in schools have been announced and Cameron spoke out on promoting gay rights in Africa.

A perhaps more nuanced departure from Thatcherism could be found in Cameron's view of the public services. Thatcherite reforms of the public services drew heavily on ideas drawn from public choice theory. Thus the reforms made assumptions that public sector workers are likely to be self-interested, recalcitrant and often indifferent as to the quality of service experienced by consumers. Thus the Thatcherites sought to introduce quasi-markets and incentives into the public sector in order to stimulate the kind of competition that they believed could improve services. Cameron offered little suggestion that these reforms had been in error, but did argue against the assumptions that had been made regarding the motivations of public sector workers. Instead Cameron emphasised the dedication and self-sacrifice often involved in such occupations such as nursing and teaching. He also rejected the theme, popular amongst many neo-liberals, that the public sector is a drain on the 'productive' private sectors of the economy. Cameron argued public service employees provide the support and development individuals need to succeed, and thus are indeed effective 'wealth-creators' (Cameron, 2011b). Still, Cameron pledged no let-up in market-oriented reforms of public services. He did however gesture at stripping away some of the 'top down' bureaucracy which he argued hampered public sector employees from doing their jobs and were a legacy of previous government's failure to trust professionals to do their job effectively.

A wider critique of public choice assumptions was discernible in Cameron's engagement with 'Nudge' theory, associated with the American behaviouralist economists Richard Thaler and Cass Sustein (2009). 'Nudge' theory was formulated as a response to the perceived limitations of neo-classical economic theory in accounting for the complexities of decision-making. Whereas neo-liberals tend to assume actors will make rational self-maximising choices, Thaler and Sustein argue that people's decisions are affected by perceptions of how those around them are also behaving. Thus they propose that we cannot rely on the idea that individuals will make the optimal choices when it comes to matters such as making healthy food choices or preparing for their economic futures. Indeed it is suggested that people may, through habit or inertia, choose to behave or consume in ways that can be damaging for both them and the general good of society. Therefore, the idea that government should simply leave individuals to make free choices is insufficient. Equally, Thaler and Sustein highlight the weaknesses of government taking a top-down or authoritarian approach to enforce behaviour. Not only are such steps resented, they are viewed as ineffective as they take responsibility away from individuals who then do not learn to make good choices. Thaler and Sustein suggest a middle way of 'libertarian paternalism' is possible, through which government can encourage people to make benign choices, without insisting upon it (ibid: 5). Through providing information and shaping the 'choice architecture' of decision-making, people can be 'nudged' towards good behaviours, yet this is done in a way which preserves genuine liberty (ibid: 3, 81).

This philosophy attracted attention from both Cameron and George Osborne as it appears to offer a way of avoiding moral indifference towards people's behaviour, yet also eschewing the kind of heavy-handed moralism that arguably was a feature of Thatcherism (Osborne, 2008). After entering office, Cameron established a 'Nudge' unit, formally known as the Behavioural Insight Team, led by the behavioural economist David Halpern. The team was tasked with initially looking at ways of encouraging healthy living, before looking at other aspects of public policy. The unit has, for example, been looking at ways of helping smokers to quit (for example, through rewards) and how to improve numbers of organ donators (for example, through making people to decide whether to donate or not when applying for a driver's licence). As yet, the government's embrace of nudge theory is rather experimental, and Minister Oliver Letwin admitted that the philosophy may not yield the practical gains hoped for (Curtis, 2011a). However, despite criticism of the unit from some quarters, including environmentalists, it continues to work on ideas for promoting green behaviour, such as introducing car labelling to make energy efficiency more conspicuous.

Long before the general election of 2010, Cameron was aware that many of the above changes in effect brought the party closer to some of the ideological positions of the Liberal Democrats. Indeed through his pledge of commitment to public services, opposition to ID cards, support for gay rights and backing for decentralising power to localities he was making strands of liberal political philosophy prominent within his renewal of British conservatism. Indeed he was keen to highlight how he believes conservative and liberal modes of political thought compliment one another: 'we need a new liberal consensus in our country. Without Conservative stress on communal obligations and institutions, liberalism can become hollow individualism ... And without the liberal stress on individual freedom, Conservatism can become hollow individualism' (Cameron, 2007c).

Even at this stage, Cameron's pronouncements in support of 'liberal conservatism' had party-political intent, hoping either to attract liberal-leaning voters to the Conservatives, or perhaps helping to lay some groundwork for a possible post-election understanding between the parties. However, there was also content to the message, since his emphasis on decentralisation would appeal to traditional Liberals emphasis on localism, and the message on liberties would appeal to the Liberal Democrats emphasis on fiercely protecting individual rights against state power.

Anti-statism

It should be emphasised that for all Cameron's revisions, additions and qualifications of contemporary Conservative thinking, his ideological inclinations still bear huge resemblances to those favoured during the Thatcher-Major years. Put crudely, whilst for Cameron neo-liberal ideology is by itself insufficient, his broad philosophy is one which not only endorses much of the neo-liberal critique of the state, but seeks to push the project of state retrenchment further. Some commentators have been surprised by the anti-statism of the coalition government, arguing that this sits at odds with the Cameron's friendly rhetoric towards public services before the 2010 general election. Yet Cameron's scepticism towards the state and 'Big Government' were frequently made clear after his election as party leader six years ago. Indeed, it could plausibly be argued that no opposition party in modern times has fought to win political power with a philosophy which is so pessimistic as to the direct benefits which the state itself can produce. This emphasis drew not just on neo-liberal thought, but was buttressed and developed by other strands of political analysis. There are at last three dimensions to this view: i) a critique of monopoly provision; ii) a revitalised attack on 'dependency' on the welfare state; and, iii) retrenchment of New Labour's 'social investment' state.

Critique of monopoly provision

The last three decades of British politics have witnessed the widespread transfer of service provision from the government to the private sector. Famously, the Thatcher governments privatised key public utilities and allowed private companies to bid to run local services. Over time, particularly under New Labour, governments have also looked at ways of enabling voluntary and community groups to run some public services. The Thatcher governments drew on neo-liberal philosophy to argue that the state itself was always likely to be inefficient in its provision of services. This was taken to occur because the state had a monopoly on the running of these services, and hence lacked the kind of competition for custom and quality that would incentivise them to improve their provision. Lacking the profit motive, and external accountability, state providers would be too inclined to look after their own interests before that of consumers. New Labour largely held to this logic and also emphasised that voluntary groups could also be good alternative service providers, given their knowledge and expertise of issues within communities. Thus the Cameron coalition's effort to promote more diversity in service provision represents continuity with recent trends in British public policy. Cameron's rationale for this approach is perhaps distinctive only in that it provides a somewhat more localist and conservative justification for this policy direction than previous governments did. Cameron draws on Edmund Burke's idea that social issues can often be dealt with best by 'little platoons' of local volunteers rather than by larger institutions (Burke, 1789). The emphasis is on the idea that local communities can often best provide for themselves organically, through self-organisation. Hence Cameron's argument that 'Big Government' needs to be curtailed in order for the Big Society to flourish (Cameron, 2011b, 2011c). During Cameron's first year in office steps were taken to create new opportunities for local people to take control of services, such as enabling parents and communities to create 'free schools' which would not be subject to many of the standard regulations surrounding the provision of education. The coalition has also encouraged the creation of more faith schools, where local religious organisations can establish and manage schools dedicated to educating children within a particular religious context.

At the same time, at a national level the coalition has taken controversial steps to encourage further competition within major public services. Government followed through on the recommendations of the Browne review into Higher Education (established under New Labour) to legislate for the withdrawal of direct funds for teaching in Higher Education, to be replaced with funding through greatly increased tuition fees for new students. In theory, this would create more competition between universities on prices and quality for students, and in turn drive up teaching standards in the sector. It also appeared intended to create new providers of degree programmes, a goal which seemed to be on course to be realised when the philosopher A. C. Grayling announced plans for a new elite university that would charge high fees (Eagleton, 2011). The issue did, however, raise enormous problems for the Liberal Democrats who had pledged before the election to scrap tuition fees and to vote against any plan to increase them. For many in the party the issue was indeed one of ideological principle in that they believed increased fees would create more inequality of access to a service which many thought ought to be financed by the state. However, it appears that whilst this social democratic stance held sway within much of the party, the leadership of the Liberal Democrats had come to the view that this would not be a viable long-term position. Even as Liberal Democrat MPs publicly signed pledge cards not to vote for hikes in fees, senior Liberal Democrats had allegedly drawn up plans to negotiate away this policy in the event of a hung parliament (Watt, 2010b).

Further controversy emerged from a government white paper on NHS reform which sought to transfer control of budgets from health authorities to GP practices. One intention of this change was that it would enable GPs to contract out administration of such budgets to private providers, a step which many considered a form of back-door privatisation. Ministers argued the change would take control of purchasing away from top-down management to a level where there would be greater sensitivity to getting the best deal available for patients. However, the plans came under enormous criticism, including from medical professionals and also grassroot Liberal Democrats (Boffey, 2011a). The plans were eventually significantly watered-down, to the disdain of many Tories who believed the opportunity for substantially enhancing competition in the NHS was being lost.

Revitalised attack on welfare 'dependency'

In recent decades ideological debates on welfare have had two interrelated dimensions, namely the economic and the moral. Neo-liberal authors emphasised the idea that the provision of state welfare was a drain on the wealth-creating sectors of the economy as individuals and businesses had to contribute earnings they could otherwise have invested. Conservatives often argued that reliance on welfare was damaging to the moral character of individuals who could become too dependent on the welfare state for income. These views held sway within Conservative Party circles in the Thatcher-Major years and beyond. However, there was also a high degree of consensus between the two main political parties (Conservative and Labour) about the need to reform welfare to do more to help claimants out of dependency and into work. Whilst Cameron was in opposition, he sought to demonstrate that the Conservatives had a new commitment to social justice, and his shadow welfare minister, Iain Duncan Smith oversaw the production of a lengthy report on welfare issues (*Breakthrough Britain*, 2007). The report argued that Labour's approach was still hampered by looking too much towards the central state for solutions, but they also recognised the need for active partnerships between different sectors (including government) to tackle deep-rooted social problems. There were tangible differences in the moral messages Cameron promoted concerning welfare, yet these still identified dependency as a critical problem. Whereas Thatcherites had sometimes singled out particular groups (for example, single mothers) as living undesirable, possibly immoral lives on welfare benefit, Cameron *largely* avoided blaming specific groups or lifestyles. Instead of championing the traditional family to the exclusion of other ways of co-habiting, Cameron recognised diversity in living arrangements and different types of family make-up (including same sex couples). At the same time, Cameron criticised new Labour for 'shying away from saying anything meaningful about family' (Cameron, 2011e). Cameron maintains that families are the best context into which to bring up children and reserves strong moral judgement for parents who neglect their duties to children. He has repeatedly identified absent fathers as 'irresponsible' and contributing to social breakdown:

> I also think we need to make Britain a genuinely hostile place for fathers who go AWOL. It's high time runaway dads were stigmatised, and the full force of shame was heaped upon them. They should be looked at like drink drivers, people who are beyond the pale (ibid).

Thus in July 2011 the government was reported to be considering new penalties upon such fathers, including the immediate suspension of driving licences and passports, and direct deduction of child support payments from their bank accounts (*Mail on Sunday*, 3 July 2011).

The perceived imperative of cutting the public deficit quickly provided a test of the Conservatives contemporary attitude to welfare. Given the large portion of government spending devoted to welfare it was always likely to be targeted for significant cuts. However, for some, the nature of the cuts announced following the Comprehensive Spending Review in 2010 were evidence of the Conservatives enduring desire to strip away benefits from the 'undeserving'. Indeed Cameron told 'those intent on ripping off the system ...we will not let you live off the hard work of others' (Cameron, 2011d). Nick Clegg also declared his intention to look after the interests of 'alarm clock' Britain, those who 'worked hard' and did not rely on the state (Clegg, 2011a). Large cuts were announced for incapacity benefits, through which claimants for insurance-based benefits would now only be entitled to only a year's payment, before they would be subject to means-benefits tests. Only in severe cases would the benefit be retained, with other claimants moving on to work-related benefits. More generally, the approach of the coalition to welfare reform has been to continue with and step up the market-driven reform agenda established under New Labour following the publication of the Freud report (Driver, 2011; Freud, 2007). This has involved, for example, making more use of private and voluntary contractors to provide welfare-to-work services in what Cameron has described previously as a shift from 'state welfare to social welfare' (2006f).

Dismantling the 'social investment' state?

Some interpretations of New Labour's ideology argued that the party promoted what Anthony Giddens coined a 'social investment' state which would attempt to provide the education, training, welfare and support needed to ensure people could perform well in the market economy (Giddens, 1998: 118). Thus high levels of spending on areas such as education and health would be complimented by measures aimed at improving the social conditions that affect employability and community cohesion. Arguably, the coalition has projected a quite different role for the state, one which involves rolling-back of government initiatives and, in the prevailing context of cuts, significantly reducing state spending on social policies. One manifestation of this is in the coalition's decision to remove much of the infrastructure of regional government that had been established by New Labour. The Blair-Brown governments had viewed regional-level coordination and investment as a key way of developing skills and attracting business to particular areas. However, the coalition has largely viewed regional-level government as adding an unnecessary layer of state bureaucracy to public affairs. In this view regional administration has also acted as a mechanism which unhelpfully distances local people from the governance processes that affect them. Thus the coalition has stripped away much of the edifice of regional government. Additionally the government has abolished (or in some cases merged) a vast range of special purpose bodies, which again, in the Cameron view, are regarded as often faceless organisations which do not do enough to justify the large amounts of public spending devoted to them.

The coalition's commitment to a smaller state is reflected in their decision to try to cut the public deficit considerably more quickly than the Labour government has intended to do. Whereas Labour sought to deal with the issue over two terms, the coalition hopes to have tackled most of the debt by 2014–2015. Figures suggest that the level of state intervention will actually fall below that of the United States (Taylor-Gooby and Stoker, 2011: 14). Significant cuts in budgets for housing benefits, disability allowance and job-seekers allowance mean the economic impact on many of the least wealthy groups may be severe. The poorest 10 per cent of families with children are anticipated to face a 7 per cent cut in income by 2014–2015 (ibid: 8). Massive cuts in local government spending will also reduce state services and activities in local areas. The coalition stance on cuts reflects a neo-liberal belief that as the state is 'rolled back' the private sector will produce the demand and jobs required to produce economic growth. Indeed their economic approach may be thought 'more or less a Joseph-Thatcher economic perspective which proclaims the primacy of the market over the welfare state ... and reduces the efficacy of public administration to mere cost-benefit analysis' (Beech, 2011b). The coalition has introduced a raft of measures aimed at encouraging entrepreneurial activity, and sought to stimulate business growth through measures such as a cut in corporation tax. The cumulative picture of changes to taxes, benefits, and spending under the coalition indicate that the government has prioritised achieving economic growth through a resurgent private sector above all other objectives.

'Rolling-out' society

Cameron argues that post-war British politics has been bedevilled by two problems. The first of these is excessive statism, and the persistent tendency of governments to believe they can solve problems through legislation or technocratic management. The second of these is excessive individualism, and a tendency to assume that if people obtain sufficient income this will necessarily lead to positive social outcomes. For Cameron, the problem is that the focus on the state and the individual has been harmful to the dimension that lies between them: society. Even in the face of widespread scepticism, Cameron has continued to promote his notion of the Big Society (Cameron, 2011c, 2011d; Kisby, 2010; Barker, 2011). A range of intellectual strands appear to have influenced the thinking behind this concept.

The work of David Brooks, particularly his recent book *The Social Animal,* outlines reasons why people ought to be sceptical about the idea that government of administrators can exert clear control over the behaviour of the public (Brooks, 2011). Brooks opposes not only old-style statism but also the belief of many neo-liberals that behaviour can be shaped by treating individuals as rational, self-maximising actors who will act according to the incentives and punishments they are subjected to. For Brooks we are much more influenced by our emotions and the unconscious mind than we often believe, and our well-being is often shaped by the quality of our relationships than our bank-balance. Brooks recognises a lineage of ideas in British Enlightenment thinkers with their scepticism of rationalist political thought, but develops these themes further with reference to developments in neuroscience (Brooks, 2011: 234). Cameron endorses this perspective, arguing that government 'has sometimes seemed to carry on oblivious to the fact that we are human beings, behaving in ways ministers and officials can't possibly predict' (Cameron, 2011d). Though Brooks highlights human tendencies to laziness, ill-discipline and short-sightedness, his is a perspective which strikes a more optimistic note than some strands of traditional conservatism. Brooks highlights the way in which humans do better when engaged in communities and networks, that we are indeed social animals. In practical terms this implies that politicians ought to be at least concerned with promoting and measuring well-being in society as they are in improving economic growth. This kind of thinking inspired Cameron's announcement that the Office of National Statistics would develop an index for assessing levels of well-being across the nation (Cameron, 2010a).

Cameron has also been affected by the comparable communitarian perspective of 'Red Toryism', associated with the author Philip Blond (2009). Blond's particular focus is on notions of community and the way he believes state centralism and economic individualism has eroded community-life. He argues that both public and private sector monopolies on services are problematic because of their insensitivity to local needs. In Blond's view government should actively seek to empower local communities through decentralisation and through enabling the flourishing of local organisations that can do much to both tackle social problems and engage people in active local citizenship. Cameron's concept of the Big Society reflects similar thinking, with its pledge both to devolve power to community and voluntary groups and to pull-back the heavy-hand of central government. In this dimension there are ideological overlaps between the coalition governing parties, given the long-standing tradition within British liberalism for localism. The 'Toryism' within Red Toryism may be thought to come from the emphasis on people taking and exercising responsibility for what happens in both their communities and families. This has been a major theme in Cameron's discourse since becoming leader. However, Nick Clegg has insisted that responsibility and obligation are (against the perceptions of some, probably including Philip Blond!) also very much part of the Liberal Tradition: 'Freedom comes hand in hand with responsibility. As the Liberal leader Jo Grimond said "Freedom entails the acceptance of responsibility. Responsibility is meaningless without freedom"' (Clegg, 2011b).

Thus both Cameron and Clegg have spoken of the necessity of 'muscular liberalism', a liberalism which holds true to the liberal insistence on liberties, but which is not relativist or agnostic on moral issues (Clegg, 2011b). In substantive terms, this thinking has involved finding ways to allow people to take on responsibility within local communities, including through reforms of local government. For example, the coalition has removed the 'ring-fencing' around areas of local government budgets to allow more local determination of priorities and pooling of resources. Cameron claims to have removed many of the bureaucratic assessments of local government which he said had in the past driven them 'mad' (Cameron, 2011e). The coalition has also sought to give local people new opportunities to take control of local assets which may be under threat, such as Post Offices.

Tensions

A key question concerns to what extent government itself can guide a process which is specifically aimed at reducing the role of the state and encouraging local self-organisation. Arguably, achieving the Big Society seems to require what Kruger calls 'a sort of reverse alchemy' in which government tries to 'change state institutions into social ones ... artificial into natural matter' (Kruger, 2007: 8). The dilemmas thrown up by this were indicated when it was alleged that government had insisted that the Big Society should become a priority area for research in the budget of the *Arts and Humanities Research Council (AHRC)* (Boffey, 2011b). Academics argued that this amounted to the state interfering with academic freedom to promote an ideological and political agenda. Given the Big Society's emphasis on facilitating creativity free from state regulation, the government's approach could certainly be considered ironic. More generally, critics argued that the ostensible commitment to developing local institutions was undermined by approaches to deficit reduction which seemed to reflect an ideological preference for reducing the local state. The moral dimension of the Big Society also raises questions as to how far Cameron may be prepared to go in taking steps that could at points challenge commercial interests. His establishment of an independent review on the Commercialisation and Sexualisation of childhood raised the possibility of significant new regulations constraining the kind of product advertising that might be aimed at children (Cameron, 2010b). In line with Blond's 'Red Toryism' Cameron has rhetorically argued for the need to be tough on private monopolies as well as state monopolies (Cameron, 2011c). Yet there is as yet little evidence of what this might mean and the position stands in tension with wider pro-business stances, including apparent government willingness to consider allowing *NewsCorp,* owned by Rupert Murdoch, to buy-up shares to take full control of *BskyB*. This issue revealed real division within the coalition, when the Liberal Democrat Business Secretary, Vince Cable was revealed to have 'declared war' on the 'Murdoch Empire' (Winnett, 2010a). More generally, the Clegg-Cameron stances on major issues such as the speed of deficit-cuts; reform of public sector pensions; and greater use of market mechanisms are problematic for many on the social-liberal wing of the Liberal Democrats. At the beginning of 2011 Clegg himself highlighted a split within the progressive traditions in British politics between those 'old progressives' who value a powerful state and 'new progressives' who value powerful citizens (Clegg, 2011b). The distinction served to emphasise the extent of the shared ground between the philosophies of the two coalition leaders and their sceptical attitude towards the remaining aspects of post-war social democracy. Yet it also highlighted the gap between the Clegg-Cameron position and the more Labour-friendly instincts of many wider Liberal Democrats. Cameron's stance also sits uneasily with some of the attitudes of Thatcherite Conservatives, as was reflected in hostility to Cameron's toying with more 'liberal' policies on crime and his contentment with significant cuts in military spending.

Conclusion

The Cameron coalition has developed themes which are in many ways designed to differentiate their approach from that of Thatcherism. It was fortunate for the Conservatives that their shift in ideological emphasis overlapped with the views of Orange Book Liberal Democrats, who also wanted to disassociate' 'small state' liberalism from the authoritarian stances it had become linked with in the 1980s (Marshall and Laws, 2004). For all the ideological tensions highlighted above, Clegg and Cameron seem in strong agreement regarding the need for limited state intervention. Cameron's anti-statism draws on various traditions including Burkean, communitarian *and* Hayekian thought, alongside forms of contemporary behavioural economics. Clegg arguably endorses a form of 'liberalism in which the marketplace is the benchmark by which society will be judged ... the fundamental norm from which any departure in future would have to be justified' (Gray, 2010). Thus 'Liberal Conservatism' appears more than a politically convenient slogan, or uneasy fusion of ideas, but rather a term which does go someway towards capturing the ideological leanings of a large section of the contemporary British political elite. At the same time, it follows Labour's 'third way' in presenting itself as 'post-ideological' and beyond the supposedly dogmatic era of 'statism versus individualism' (McAnulla, 2010). However Cameron's Big Society does attempt to popularise a 'big idea' at a time when big ideas are assumed to be out of fashion. To the extent that the Big Society may be failing to resonate or excite, this does not necessarily result from a lack of thinking behind the concept. Indeed there is considerable experimentation within Cameron's approach which combines refreshed scepticism towards the state with novel attempts to use what remains of government influence to reshape behaviour. The overriding issue of cuts has forced the coalition to reveal more about its ideological preferences than might normally be the case at this stage in the development of a governing agenda. In the wake of an international crisis for neo-liberal economics Cameron has remained a steadfast believer in the need for balanced books and quick deficit reduction. Austerity is deemed the price worth paying to enable future economic growth. Cameron's approach does though acknowledge the insufficiency of market politics in securing fulfilled individuals and strong communities. Yet there remains ambiguity in what role the state and government can play in facilitating the Big Society. Should government's role be to take the lead on moral issues, or should it be one of subtly 'nudging' people into good choices? Should the state simply withdraw as far as possible from local institutions, or does it hold renewed responsibility for ensuring well-being and constraining corporate power within communities? As yet we still lack a fully defined sense of what a Cameronite state should look like.

13
Coalition Cohesion

Philip Norton

Anthony King (1976) identified different modes of executive-legislative relations. In the United Kingdom, the most visible is the *opposition mode*, in which the party in government is pitted against the party, or parties, in opposition. This mode, as King notes, is marked by conflict. Each side is usually united as it faces the other side. However, cohesion may not be total. As a result, one other mode, the *intra-party mode* – encompassing opposition within a party – is significant because the party in government rests on the support of those who occupy its benches rather than those who sit opposite. If its ranks show signs of dissent then it may be in trouble. The opposition mode has been the dominant mode for more than a century, though in recent decades the intra-party mode has assumed greater significance as government backbenchers have proved more willing to vote against their party (Norton, 1975, 1978, 1980; Cowley and Norton, 1999; Cowley, 2002, 2005).

The formation of a coalition government in May 2010 produced a novel situation in that another mode applied: the *inter-party mode* of executive-legislative relations. This encompasses the relationship of parties within a coalition. The potential for conflict between partners within a coalition has not existed in the UK since the exceptional conditions of wartime (see Norton, 1998) but is familiar to legislatures used to having coalition governments (see Andeweg et al, 2008; Norton, 2008: 239). The relationship of the two partners to the coalition, the Conservative and Liberal Democratic parties, became a focus of considerable media attention. Would conflict between the two jeopardise the continuation of the coalition?

In practice, the conflict in the first year of the coalition tended to be most significant within the context of the intra-party mode rather than the inter-party mode. The coalition witnessed unprecedented levels of dissent in the division lobbies in the House of Commons. Dissent was not confined to the House of Commons. In the House of Lords, some coalition peers also proved willing to dissent. The dissent was remarkable not only for its extent but also for its existence in the first session of a Parliament under a new government.

At the end of the year, in the wake of the referendum of 5 May 2011 on the Alternative Vote (AV), there were indications that the inter-party mode may also become significant, but supplementing rather than supplanting tensions within parties. For party leaders, the challenge became one of juggling the need to keep their respective parties together as well as maintaining the coalition. Under the coalition, the UK was witnessing a 'new politics' but possibly not in the way that was anticipated.

Inter-party conflict

The potential for inter-party conflict is inherent in the formation of a coalition. It was present in the negotiations leading up to the coalition (see Laws, 2010; Wilson, 2010; Norton, 2011a) and was addressed in those negotiations in two ways. One was to acknowledge existing conflicts and as far as possible identify a position that each would support or at least not oppose. This was most apparent in respect of electoral reform: the Liberal Democrats supported a system of proportional representation; the Conservatives wanted to retain the established first-past-the-post electoral system. Negotiations almost foundered on the issue (Wilson, 2010: 162; Laws, 2010: 104; see also Kavanagh and Cowley, 2010: 215; Stuart, 2011: 49–51). It was only resolved after the two leaders met to thrash out an agreement. The parties agreed to hold a referendum on the Alternative Vote and for party members to be free to campaign on whichever side they favoured. They also agreed that if the Browne report on higher education was unacceptable to the Liberal Democrats, 'then arrangements will be made to enable Liberal Democrat MPs to abstain in any vote' (HM Government, 2010a: 32).

The other way was by creating the mechanisms for resolving any disputes. *A Coalition Agreement for Stability and Reform* was published on 21 May 2010 outlining the arrangements for sharing information and consultation. A ten-member Cabinet Committee, the Coalition Committee, was appointed, chaired jointly by the Prime Minister and Deputy Prime Minister, and was scheduled to meet weekly, or as required, 'to manage the business and priorities of the Government and the implementation and operation of the Coalition agreement'. It was to consider any differences reported from other Cabinet Committees. Lower level, or day-to-day, disputes were to be resolved by an informal four-member Coalition Operation and Strategic Planning Group chaired jointly by Chief Secretary to the Treasury Danny Alexander (in his role providing support to the Deputy Prime Minister in the Cabinet Office) and Cabinet Office Minister Oliver Letwin. Though included in the Cabinet Office's list of Cabinet Committees, the list makes clear that this is 'an informal working group and not a Cabinet sub-Committee' (Cabinet Office, 2010). The group was scheduled to meet weekly, or as required, 'to consider and resolve issues relating to the operation of the coalition agreement, the longer term strategic planning of Government Business and to report as necessary to the Coalition Committee'.

In practice, these bodies were little used. The Coalition Committee, reported Cabinet Secretary Sir Gus O'Donnell, 'hasn't met that often' (Political and Constitutional Reform Committee, 2011: Ev 55). The structures to deal with the coalition, according to Rutter and Atkinson, 'have worked surprisingly well' (Rutter and Atkinson, 2011: 23). The coalition partners in the first year of the coalition hung together, with some tensions but with nothing that constituted an enduring or coalition-threatening conflict between the parties. The tension tended to be within the parties. This was predictable given the nature of the coalition agreement. On some issues, the parties either compromised (as on the referendum on AV) or more usually conceded a case (as with fixed-term Parliaments or deficit reduction) (see Laws, 2010: 117). The problem was marked in respect of constitutional issues, given that this was one sector in which the parties adopted mutually exclusive stances (see Norton, 2011b). The Liberal Democrats adhered to the liberal view of constitutional change (Norton, 1982: 275–9): they took the view that the political system was no longer appropriate to the needs of the United Kingdom and that a new constitutional settlement was required. The Conservatives adhered to the traditional, or Westminster, view of the constitution (Norton, 1982: 279–87) believing that the system was basically sound. There was little scope for identifying common ground: one side had to concede a case or the two had to reach a compromise that satisfied the principled position of neither.

In the negotiations, the Liberal Democrat view of the constitution prevailed. 'The Government', declared the coalition agreement, 'believes that our political system is broken. We urgently need fundamental political reform' (HM Government, 2010a: 26). As Ruth Fox has noted of the agreement, 'Overall the Conservatives got the better of the deal in the economic arena, and the Liberal Democrats the political and constitutional reform agenda' (Fox, 2010: 34). The agreement included provisions (see Bogdanor, 2011) that, ironically, had appeared in the Labour Party and/or Liberal Democrat manifestos (fixed-term parliaments, a referendum on the Alternative Vote electoral system) but which would never have been pursued by a Conservative government. One would thus anticipate that intra-party conflict was most likely to emerge in Tory ranks on constitutional issues and in Liberal Democratic ranks on economic or social issues. The reality quickly matched the expectation.

Intra-party dissent

The first session of a Parliament under a new government is notable usually for the extent of cohesion among the ranks of government supporters. The government brings forward key measures in the wake of election victory and its supporters willingly vote to pass them, usually with little or no dissent. The first sessions are notable honeymoon periods for leaders and backbenchers. This has been the case even in Parliaments in which the relationship between government and backbenchers subsequently turned sour, as for example under the Conservative government of Edward Heath: in the first session of the 1970–1974 Parliament, there were only seven divisions in which one or more Conservative MPs voted against the government; in the second session, the number was 128 (Norton, 1978: 40). In post-war Parliaments, where a new party has been returned to government, the percentage of divisions in which one or more government MPs have voted against their own side has ranged from 0 to 6 per cent. As Cowley and Stuart (2010b: 3) have written:

> The discipline of the election campaign is still strong; and the fact that that the government is implementing its manifesto is usually enough to prevent many MPs, even those who may disagree with the policies, from dissenting. There are also usually many new MPs, normally much less willing to defy the whips. The first session, then, is usually the calm before the storm.

In the new 2010 Parliament, there was no calm before the storm. In previous Parliaments, even in the most rebellious sessions, divisions in which government backbenchers rebelled were the exception rather than the norm. In the first year of the coalition Parliament, they were the norm rather than the exception. In the period up to the half-term recess in February 2011, no less than 110 divisions – 53 per cent of the total – had seen one or more coalition MP vote against the government (Cowley, 2011). That exceeds the total number of rebellions in the entire period from 1945 to 1959 and is unmatched by any other single session. A total of 76 Conservative MPs voted against the government on one or more occasions; that represents a quarter of the parliamentary party. A total of 28 Liberal Democrat MPs voted against on one or more occasions. The total may be smaller than that for the Conservatives, but is more significant when expressed as a proportion of the parliamentary party: it represents nearly half of the party and constitutes almost 85 per cent of all backbench MPs. By the end of March 2011, there had been 51 divisions in which one or more Liberal Democrat MPs had voted against the government.

The most persistent dissenters, though, were Conservatives: of the twenty MPs to vote most often against the government, only three were Liberal Democrats. The nine most rebellious were Conservatives, headed by Philip Hollobone, MP for Kettering, who voted against the whips on 59 occasions (Cowley, 2011). The only Liberal Democrat in the top ten was Michael Hancock, the controversial and somewhat eccentric Member for Portsmouth South (see Wright and Gysin, 2010).

The issue on which the backbenchers dissented are in line with expectations. As Cowley and Stuart noted of the period from May to November 2010, 'The issues to have caused the most frequent dissent so far this session has been the Coalition's plans for constitutional reform' (Cowley and Stuart,

2010b: 4). Of the 59 rebellions up to that point, the Parliamentary Voting System and Constituencies Bill accounted for 26 of them. The issue of European integration also continued to be a fault-line in Conservative politics. As part of its reform programme, the government introduced a European Union Bill, providing for referendums on any further changes in the powers of the European Union and attracting an array of opposition from different parts of the House, including its own supporters. A division, held on 23 March 2011, on a draft of the European Council decision to amend Article 136 of the Lisbon Treaty, saw 15 Tory MPs vote against the government, the fifteenth division on the issue of Europe that had attracted dissent by Conservative MPs.

As Cowley and Stuart note, Liberal Democrat MPs were more likely to vote against the government on issues such as the increase in VAT from 15 per cent to 17.5 per cent, the introduction of free schools and the expansion of academies. Since they penned their analysis, the first year also witnessed the most significant split in Liberal Democrat ranks, that on tuition fees. In the vote on 9 December 2010, 21 Liberal Democrats voted against the government, including former leaders Charles Kennedy and Sir Menzies Campbell, and only eight backbenchers voted in favour; the remaining backbench members, including deputy leader Simon Hughes, abstained or were absent. The dissent, though, was not exclusive to Liberal Democrat MPs: six Conservatives also voted against and two abstained.

A similar picture emerged with the government's Health and Social Care Bill, designed to abolish health authorities and transfer control of funding to GP commissioning boards. Though the Bill was given a Second Reading in the Commons in January 2011, it ran into criticism from Liberal Democrats, as well as from the Opposition and doctors. It was recognised that when the Bill reached the Lords, it would face opposition not only from the Labour benches but also from the Liberal Democrats, Baroness Williams – one-time Labour Cabinet minister and former Liberal Democrat leader in the Lords – having variously voiced her criticisms of the Bill. At the Liberal Democrat spring conference in Sheffield in March 2011, there was almost unanimous support for an amendment calling for councillors to have a central role in GP commissioning. Recognising that they faced defeat, the party leadership accepted this and another critical amendment; the acceptance came following a breakfast meeting between Baroness Williams and party leader Nick Clegg. As one report noted, 'the government's plans for a health service shakeup face a radical overhaul after the Liberal Democrat leadership was forced to bow to the strength of a grassroots rebellion fuelled by fear of privatisation and an undue emphasis on competition' (Wintour and Stratton, 2011a). As with student fees, some criticism also came from a number of Conservative MPs, including former GP and newly-elected Member for Totnes, Dr Sarah Wollaston. On 4 April, Health Secretary Andrew Lansley announced that he would use a 'natural break in the passage of the bill' to undertake further consultation.

The session was thus notable for the willingness of coalition MPs to vote against the government. The scale of the dissent was unprecedented. Nor was dissent confined to the House of Commons. The government had a much harder time getting its legislation through the House of Lords. Of 86 divisions held in the House up to the Whit recess in May 2011, the government lost 16 of them, in other words, approximately one in five. Two of the defeats were on amendments moved by Conservative peers, both former Cabinet ministers. There were 22 divisions in which one or more Liberal Democrats voted against the government and 19 in which one or more (usually more) Conservatives voted against. (There were also five divisions in which some Labour peers voted against the party line.) Of the 86 divisions, 33 witnessed coalition peers dissenting. (The figure is less than the sum of the divisions for the Tory and the Lib Dem rebellions in that several saw both Tory and Liberal Democrat peers voting against the Government.) As in the Commons, the measure attracting the most consistent dissent from Conservative peers was the Parliamentary Voting System and Constituencies Bill. Of the 16 divisions witnessing Conservative dissent, 12 were on the Bill; it also accounted for the two largest rebellions in each of which more than 20 Tory peers rebelled. Liberal Democrat peers were more likely to follow their counterparts in the Commons in voting against on social issues, such as fees, though one (The Viscount of Falkland) also variously rebelled on the Parliamentary Voting System and Constituencies Bill – he went on to move from the Liberal Democrat benches to the cross-benches. However, as we shall see, the correlation between government defeats and dissent by coalition peers was far from a strong one.

Does it matter?

Dissent by government MPs under the coalition has been unprecedented. But does it matter? At no point during its first year did the government lose a vote in the House of Commons. Though dissent was persistent, it was not notable for generating a large dissenting lobby. The most difficult vote was on tuition fees, when the government's majority fell from 83 to 21. The average for a Conservative dissenting lobby was seven, hardly a figure likely to trouble the whips (Cowley, 2011). Even on issues of European integration, where the average was 15 (revolts.co.uk, 24 March 2011), it was still well within what the coalition's overall majority could absorb. In terms of the size of dissenting lobbies, it was Labour that tended to produce the larger numbers, a feature of preceding Parliaments. Furthermore, the Tory dissenters were drawn from the party's right – the Liberal dissenters from the party's left, or social liberalism, wing (see Grayson, 2010) – and were operating essentially as discrete individuals rather than as part of some organised body or faction. Even on the issue of European integration, the Tory rebels were motivated by different reasons for their opposition to the government's policy.

In the House of Lords, most of the defeats suffered by the government were the product of cross-bench peers replacing the Liberal Democrats as the key swing voters in the House. Previously, the highly disciplined Liberal Democrats held the balance of power in the House (Russell and Sciara, 2007), but in the new Parliament, in which the two coalition parties notably outnumbered the Labour opposition, the mantle passed to the cross-benches. If cross-bench peers – constituting almost a quarter of the membership, but historically exhibiting a low turnout in votes – attended in relatively high numbers, and divided disproportionately against the government, then the government was in trouble. Of the 16 defeats suffered by the government, cross-voting by coalition peers made the difference in only six of them (that is, had the coalition peers who voted against cast their votes with the government, the coalition would not have lost), though abstentions by Tory peers may have contributed to a further three defeats. The cause of most defeats was cross-bench peers dividing disproportionately against the government, in some cases overwhelmingly so. In one defeat on the Public Bodies Bill, 84 cross-bench peers voted against the government and only three voted for. In another vote on the Parliamentary Voting System and Constituencies Bill, they divided 75/10 against the government. Even in the defeats where the votes of coalition peers made a difference, they would – with one exception – not have done so without the number of cross-bench peers who joined them in the lobby.

The government thus faced difficulties in the Upper House, though the principal threat in terms of voting behaviour came from the cross-benches rather than from its own. Its own supporters in the two Houses may express dissent but not usually on a scale – and in the Commons, not at all – to threaten the government's majority. However, the dissent in the session was nonetheless worrying to the coalition for three reasons. One was that it conveyed at times a divided coalition, or rather divided parties within the coalition, and – one observation on which politicians and psephologists are united – electors do not reward divided parties. Though most occasions of backbench dissent were given little or no media coverage, some – as on tuition fees and the Health and Social Care Bill – attracted significant attention, fuelling stories of tension within the ranks of the coalition. The conflicts within Liberal Democrat ranks leading up to the vote on tuition fees were extensively covered. Liberal Democrat MPs had signed a pledge before the general election not to raise tuition fees and here they were being asked to vote for an increase: the issue was described as 'toxic' for the party (Prince, 2010a). The vote took place in an atmosphere of tension within the chamber and with student demonstrators massed outside in Parliament Square. The Liberal Democrat Business Secretary, Vince Cable, acknowledged 'the coalition and his party had come through "a difficult test"' (BBC News online, 9 December 2010). It was a test that had acted as a magnet for the media.

The second reason was that, though those who voted against the party were not operating as organised entities, there was some indication that dissent may be finding some organisational manifestation or at least outlet. It was notable that some of the leading dissenters on the Tory benches were officers or members of the executive committee of the 1922 Committee, the body (in government) of the party's backbenchers (Goodhart, 1973; Norton, 1994). The session had got off to a bad start for the leadership, with the election as chair of the 1922 of Graham Brady, a former frontbencher who had resigned in opposition to the party's failure to support grammar schools. He was elected despite attempts by the leadership to facilitate the election of a candidate considered more supportive. David Cameron had pushed for ministers to be allowed to vote in elections for officers and executive members of the 1922. After this met stiff resistance, he conceded that the electorate should remain backbench members and Brady was elected by 126 votes to 85. Other independent-minded members of the parliamentary party were elected to other positions. Indeed, of the nine Tory MPs who were in the top ten of dissenters in subsequent months, five were officers or members of the executive. One of the most persistent, Christopher Chope, was joint secretary of the committee; Philip Davies, Peter Bone, Andrew Turner and Bernard Jenkin were members of the executive. Members who on occasion voted against the government included Brady and a joint vice-chairman, Charles Walker. When a vacancy occurred on the executive, the backbencher elected to fill it (in a five-way contest) was a new MP, Tracey Crouch, who had abstained in the vote on tuition fees.

The weekly meeting of the 1922 Committee also provided an outlet for backbenchers to express disquiet over coalition policy. Backbenchers used the opportunity to complain about the party's approach to the referendum on AV, believing that the party was not doing enough to raise funds for the No campaign. The Committee also established five policy committees (on the economy, home and constitutional affairs, foreign affairs, the public services, and the environment). Though they were not on the scale of the parliamentary party's infrastructure when it had previously been in government (Norton, 1994: 97–144), they nonetheless provided the means for reflecting on party policy separate from the coalition and for channelling any disquiet among backbenchers.

On the Liberal Democrat benches, a new series of parliamentary party committees was created, each co-chaired by an MP and a peer. Established in July 2010, each shadows a particular department and meets weekly, with some party officials also attending. Though the chairs are appointed by the party leader, they are viewed as a means of giving the party an independent voice on issues. Several of the co-chairs see their role as being 'a critical friend' of the government, being able to lobby 'publicly and privately for areas [we] think could be more fair' (quoted in Edgeworth, 2011: 19). They are sometimes referred to in the press as Liberal Democrat spokespersons on their particular subject, thus creating a separate party identity to ministers in the coalition. The committees are important in providing an institutional means of expressing a distinct view, one that may be at odds with that adopted by the government.

The third reason was that if it reflected what has been the pattern in previous Parliaments the government faced an even rougher ride in subsequent sessions. In the first year, government back-benchers in the Commons did not vote in such numbers as to threaten the government's majority, but about a third of them voted against the government, including, unusually, newly-elected members. They resisted the blandishment of the whips and faced highly negative comments from Cabinet ministers. Longer-serving Conservative MPs may also be less amenable to the appeals of the whips the longer they remain without ministerial office. The creation of the coalition resulted in a double-digit number of former Tory frontbenchers being omitted from the ranks of ministers.

Furthermore, the scope for rapid advancement was limited not only by the number of posts occupied by Liberal Democrat MPs (who, proportionate to the size of the parliamentary party, did well out of the allocation) but also by the *Coalition Agreement for Stability and Reform* which constrained the Prime Minister in any ministerial reshuffles, committing the coalition to maintaining the allocation of posts relative to the size of the parliamentary parties and with new ministerial appointments being made following consultation between the Prime Minister and Deputy Prime Minister, Liberal Democrat ministers being nominated by the Deputy Prime Minister and Conservative ministers by the Prime Minister. Furthermore, 'No Liberal Democrat Minister or Whip may be removed on the recommendation of the Prime Minister without full consultation with the Deputy Prime Minister'. David Cameron lacked the freedom of movement enjoyed by previous occupants of No. 10. Many Tory MPs were aware that their scope for promotion was limited and in some cases close to non-existent. When one newly-elected Conservative MP abstained in the vote on student fees, she is reported to have been castigated by Chancellor of the Exchequer George Osborne and told she had destroyed her chances of being promoted. She retorted that she had already done her calculations and recognised there was little scope for her being given ministerial office anyway. It was a response that reflected the politics of an unprecedented situation.

Evidence of increased tension was also apparent in the wake of the outcome of the referendum in May 2011. Liberal Democrats campaigned for a Yes vote, whereas Conservatives overwhelmingly – including Prime Minister David Cameron – campaigned for a No vote. Deputy Prime Minister Nick Clegg described opponents of electoral change as 'dinosaurs', defending the indefensible. 'Party sources indicated that he was referring as much to Mr Cameron as to senior Labour figures who are opposing change' (Watson, 2011a). David Cameron took to the public platform, including on one occasion with Labour former Cabinet minister Lord Reid, to argue the case for first-past-the-post.

In the wake of the decisive rejection of the Alternative Vote, Liberal Democrat resentment of the way in which the No campaign had been conducted was marked. There were complaints especially of the way in which the unpopularity of the party leader, Nick Clegg, had been exploited to encourage electors to vote No. 'The Tory tactics in the AV campaign, with the No camp warning that Clegg was a man who broke his promises, have left the minority party reeling' (Russell, 2011).

Tensions built up on both sides, with Tory MPs increasingly unwilling to make concessions and with Liberal Democrats demanding a more distinctive Liberal Democrat approach and some distancing from Tory policies. This was notable on health policy. As early as January 2011, Nick Clegg had said that there would be 'a natural reassertion of the separate identities in the coalition'. In the aftermath of the referendum, 'the new phrase doing the rounds was that the Coalition had to move onto a more "transactional" footing – joint business venture rather than marriage' (Paun, 2011: 15). The clash on the health service was the most immediate manifestation of the potential for inter-party conflict. 'It's the first sign that the political interests of the two coalition parties – and their leaders – are at odds. They will increasingly diverge between now and the next election' (Sylvester, 2011a). A claim by Nick Clegg that he would show that the Liberal Democrats were 'a moderating influence on the Conservatives' (Coates and Savage, 2011) generated particular resentment in Conservative ranks, from the Prime Minister down.

The increased tension between the parties found reflection in the division lobbies. Liberal Democrat resentment found an outlet in the Lords on the Police and Social Responsibility Bill. Thirteen Liberal Democrats voted for an amendment, moved by a Liberal Democrat peer, that undermined a key aim of the Bill (to introduce elected police commissioners), despite the fact that it was contained in the coalition agreement. On the Conservative side, six Tory peers supported a cross-bench amendment to the Fixed-term Parliaments Bill that effectively made the provisions of the Bill applicable in a future Parliament only if the Parliament voted to utilise them. The dissent in both cases resulted in government defeats. In the Commons, Tory MPs rallied behind embattled Health Secretary Andrew Lansley and also began to make clear their opposition to the coalition's plans for the future of the House of Lords.

The Liberal Democrat peers responsible for the defeat in the Lords, reported *The Independent,* 'admitted they defeated a flagship Tory plan for the public to elect police commissioners, partly to take revenge for the No campaign's personal attacks on Mr Clegg during the referendum on the voting system' (Grice, 2011a). It noted that the change of attitude was not confined to Liberal Democrat benches. 'There were signs that the Tories may not throw their full weight behind Mr Clegg's ambitious programme of constitutional reform. ... Senior Liberal Democrats fear the Tories are getting "cold feet", which could further undermine Mr Clegg's authority'. For many Conservatives, it was not so much a case of cold feet as one of actually being opposed to the proposals.

This was especially the case in respect of the government's proposals for the future of the House of Lords. All three party manifestos had contained some commitment for a largely or wholly elected House of Lords, albeit expressed in different forms and masking considerable opposition within the Conservative and Labour parties to an elected second chamber. The coalition's proposals were delayed – the coalition agreement prescribed that a draft Bill would be introduced by December 2010 but its publication was regularly put back – and when they were published, as a White Paper and draft Bill, in May 2011 (HM Government, 2011) they attracted a hostile reaction from Conservative (and Labour) members in both Houses (House of Commons Debates, 17 May 2011, cols 155–75; House of Lords Debates, 17 May 2011, cols 1268–89). The government proposed a House of 300 members with 80 per cent or 100 per cent elected by a system of proportional representation for single 15-year terms. The proposals added little to what had been proposed by the previous Labour government (see Ministry of Justice, 2008). Following the statement, Conservative MPs were reported to be lining up at the Chief Whip's Office to say they were not prepared to support the proposals. Among the most vehement opponents were some of the newly-elected members.

The government had committed itself to sending the draft Bill for pre-legislative scrutiny to a joint committee of the two Houses. It was anticipated that such pre-legislative scrutiny would take time: the joint committee was instructed to report by February 2012 but some parliamentarians expected it would take longer. If, in the light of the committee's report, the government persisted with the Bill, it was expected that it would face strong opposition in the House of Commons, where it would be introduced, and then the equivalent of parliamentary trench warfare in the House of Lords, with the potential for the coalition's legislative programme to be derailed by the time occupied by the Bill. However, there was uncertainty as to whether the Bill would ever reach that stage. The Liberal Democrats were seen as even keener than before to achieve a key measure of constitutional reform, given that there was to be no change to the method of electing MPs, and the Conservatives even more determined to thwart them. As the Chancellor of the Exchequer, George Osborne, was reported to have reminded colleagues, the coalition agreement did not commit the government to carry through the legislation (Watson, 2011b). It embodied only an agreement 'to establish a committee to bring forward proposals for a wholly or mainly elected upper chamber on the basis of proportional representation'.

The Deputy Prime Minister was left to promote legislation for which there was no obvious enthusiasm – and in some parts intense opposition – among the ranks of the Conservative MPs and peers. Having described opponents of electoral change as dinosaurs, Clegg was also reported to have used the same term to describe peers opposed to his plans for the second chamber. In the case of the Lords, the 'dinosaurs' included a good number of his own party's peers. House of Lords reform constituted an issue that for the coalition was toxic, holding out the possibility of intense conflict in terms both of inter-party and intra-party relationships.

Whereas the issue of the future of the Lords could be parked for a few months in a joint committee, no such luxury existed for the health reforms. The Health and Social Bill could be subject to no more than 'a natural' (albeit novel) break during its passage. Reports that the Prime Minister was prepared to humiliate his Health Secretary as 'the price of glueing the coalition back together' (Coates and Savage, 2011) appeared to anger Conservative backbenchers. One Conservative MP, 'thought to represent the views of a number of his colleagues', sent an e-mail to all his parliamentary colleagues identifying 'red lines' – 'the principles on which we will not budge' (BBC News Online, 27 May 2011). 'He told the BBC the voices of Tory MPs must be reflected as the proposals are scrutinised again and said he was surprised at the Lib Dems' position given they supported the bill during its initial passage through Parliament' (BBC News Online, 27 May 2011).

There were also potential conflicts brewing on immigration – the Prime Minister having signalled a desire to reduce annual immigration to 'tens of thousands' – and on the Human Rights Act, with some Conservatives becoming increasingly irritated by the interpretation of the European Convention on Human Rights by British judges. The coalition appointed a commission to examine a British Bill of Rights. 'The acid test', declared former Conservative leader Michael Howard (Lord Howard of Port Lympne), 'will be whether it can return to Parliament the supremacy that rightly belongs to it' (Howard, 2011). For the coalition, some conflicts were imminent and others being stored up for when various bodies reported.

Conclusion

The creation of a coalition added a new dimension to the analysis of cohesion in British parliamentary life. There was an additional level at which conflict could occur. The coming together of two parties to form a coalition was negotiated by the party leaderships. The two parties were thus formally committed to the coalition. They were, in effect, joined at the head but not at the hip (or, perhaps more appropriately in terms of the analogy, the heart). The leaders were committed to making the partnership work but had to persuade their parliamentary supporters to follow them. David Cameron had sought to keep his party's MPs on side during the negotiations, but they had not been required formally to give their approval. The Liberal Democrats had given approval through their party structures (Laws, 2010), but they had done so on the basis of parliamentary arithmetic rather than political ideology (Norton, 2011a: 251–6). Outside Parliament, there was no coalition at the electoral level: the parties fought elections as discrete entities.

In the first year of the coalition, the two parties held together. There were some tensions but, as we have seen, nothing to exercise significantly or regularly the mechanisms created for the purpose of resolving conflicts. The more notable and enduring conflict came within the parliamentary parties. The Coalition Committee of the Cabinet may have had little to do, but the whips in the two parties had a great deal to do in order to keep their supporters on side. They were successful in the Commons in carrying a majority in divisions, but ensuring complete cohesion in divisions was another matter. In the Lords, the whips failed to stave off defeats but generally managed to mobilise coalition peers in support of what the government brought forward. Nonetheless, in terms of the incidence of intra-party dissent, the House of Commons witnessed unprecedented levels of dissent – all the more remarkable (and worrying for the government) for occurring in the first session of a Parliament under a new government.

Though much of the coalition's controversial legislation had been enacted in the first year, the outcome of the AV referendum generated a new mood on both sides of the coalition. The benefit of the doubt was replaced by a mood of wariness if not outright distrust. 'Politics is about relationships as well as policies and there has been a breakdown of trust after the vicious referendum campaign' (Sylvester, 2011a). Some members of the government appeared semi-detached. The coalition of David Cameron and Nick Clegg had been likened to a civil partnership. The partnership post-referendum entered a new phase. The two were staying together for the sake of the coalition. Not all their parliamentary family were convinced that this was for the best. Doubts were especially apparent in the ranks of the Liberal Democrats. The lack of trust was expected to put pressure on the coalition's institutional framework. As one minister observed, much more use was likely to be made of the Coalition Committee (Russell, 2011). The whips were kept busy managing intra-party conflict. The Coalition Committee was on hand to manage inter-party conflict. Cohesion, clearly, was not what it was. That, arguably, was the reality of the new politics.

14
David Cameron as Prime Minister

Kevin Theakston

When David Cameron became prime minister on 11 May 2010 the prime-ministerial records books had to be updated. He was (at 43) the youngest prime minister since 1812. He was the first Old Etonian prime minister since 1964. He had got to the top after the shortest length of service as a Member of Parliament (nine years) since 1783. He was the first prime minister to have been a special adviser. And he was the first PM heading a coalition since 1945.

The coalition factor is the most important of these diverse facts because it has a crucial bearing on the scope, possibilities and constraints faced by Cameron in his premiership. The historical record shows that some of the most dominant and powerful British prime ministers have headed coalitions (notably Lloyd George and Churchill) as well as some of the weakest and most ineffective (such as Lord Aberdeen and Ramsay MacDonald). It is not that coalition necessarily reduces significantly the power and influence of the prime minister, but much depends on the party-political arithmetic involved and on external circumstances (the exceptional conditions of total war are obviously a big part of the story for Lloyd George and Churchill).

The advent of coalition government has certainly impacted on powers and responsibilities normally regarded as belonging to the prime minister alone. Under the *Coalition Agreement for Stability and Reform* the PM is obliged to consult and agree with the deputy prime minister, Nick Clegg, over the appointment, reshuffling and sacking of ministers. The PM hires and fires but must fully consult, and the allocation of posts between the parties in the coalition is expected to operate on a 'one-in, one-out' rule to maintain the agreed balance between the two coalition partners. The premier's patronage power in all governments is subject in practice to political constraints but – so long as the coalition lasts – this is a new formal limitation. A similar limitation on the PM's normal discretion is in relation to the establishment of Cabinet committees, the appointment of their members, and the framing of their terms of reference, which have to be agreed between the PM and the DPM. Principles and expectations are also spelt out about the functioning of government, including requirements for consultation and discussion among ministers, and clearing certain issues if necessary through the coalition committee to ensure both parties agree. Cameron had declared before the general election that he wanted a more collective Cabinet government style of policy-making and decision-taking. The imperatives and dynamics of coalition make that a necessity and affect the sort of role he can and needs to play as prime minister.

In terms of the political science models of the core executive or prime-ministerial 'predominance', however, the PM even in a coalition remains a 'resource-rich actor' in the executive (Bennister, 2011). Coalition may reshape some of the structures and levers of power the PM faces, and the trade-offs to be negotiated and managed may change in some respects, but personal and political skill is still needed to operate and steer in the political environment. The focus of this chapter is less on the question of whether or not Cameron is a 'powerful' PM – a debate about prime ministers where political scientists have, as it were, been chasing their own tails for a long time – and more on what he has to do as prime minister, how he does it and how well he does it. Borrowing from presidential studies, the focus is on Cameron's political skills and leadership style, using a six-point model derived from Fred Greenstein's (2001) study of US presidents, adapted to the institutional and political context of the British system. The argument, briefly, is that political and governmental leaders have to: communicate – organise – show political skill – set out policy aims and visions – process advice and take decisions – cope with the stress of the top job and show emotional intelligence. The model helps us understand the tasks and demands leaders face, the skills they have, their strengths and weaknesses, successes and failures, and the difference they make (Theakston, 2007, 2011).

Communication skills

In the run-up to the 2010 general election the Institute for Leadership and Management conducted a survey of 2,000 UK managers, asking them to rate the leadership skills of the three party leaders and to compare them to selected international leaders and to prominent business figures. On the five dimensions of leadership assessed in the poll, Cameron got his highest personal rating for his communication skills and was rated as the best of the party leaders on this aspect (scoring a mean of 6.22 on a ten-point scale, compared to Clegg's 5.52 and Brown's 3.91). He was rated a better communicator than Nicolas Sarkozy (5.64) and Angela Merkel (6.06), but compared less well to Richard Branson (8.11) and Barack Obama (8.20) (Institute for Leadership and Management, 2010).

There is wide agreement that Cameron excels at the public communication aspects of political leadership. He has been described as 'highly accomplished at the frontman aspect of being prime minister' (Rawnsley, 2011a), as 'the government's most effective communicator' (Kirkup, 2011b), and as 'an alpha-grade modern political performer' (Steavenson, 2010: 48). 'The communications side of the job presents him with no real problems' it has been said. 'Few governments have had such an effective advocate at the helm' (Kirkup, 2011a). 'He's a good salesman' admits Labour leader Ed Miliband (Beckett, 2011). Cameron is more like Blair than like Brown or Major in terms of media savvy, presentation skills, and knowing how to handle the media to sell and promote himself and his policies, and to reach out, connect with and persuade the wider public. Effectiveness as a communicator, message discipline and good media management are now not optional extras but crucial factors (necessary, albeit not sufficient) in the success of political and government leaders. Those who lack the presentational skills necessary in the modern political-media culture can pay a high price, as seen with Brown.

Cameron's media-handling and communication skills were honed in his apprenticeship as a party staffer and special adviser (when Gyles Brandreth [1999: 191] noted his 'fabulous turn of phrase') and as a corporate spin-doctor at Carlton Communications before he became an MP. And his brilliant no-notes speech at the party conference in 2005 had helped propel him to the leadership. But he has been at pains to argue that, while essential, 'getting your message across and explaining what you're about' and 'win[ning] the day-to-day battle of the media' are less important than 'the big strategic picture about your priorities in government'. A party leader and prime minister has to be more than a great salesman 'selling a clever message'. 'Spin and PR', he insists, 'will not get you where you want to go' (Jones, 2008: 73, 310).

While fluent, Cameron is not a great orator or rhetorician in the Churchillian style (Macintyre, 2010) and nor does he ape Blair's sometimes pulpit style (d'Ancona, 2011b). 'In the House of Commons he is not a great orator or speaker like William Hague', says one observer, 'but he can handle it well' (private information). He has long experience of preparing other Conservative leaders for Prime Minister's Questions (PMQs), was more than a match for Brown at PMQs before 2010, and now as prime minister is himself usually quick on his feet, sharp, confident and effective in those gladiatorial jousts. Sometimes, however, Ed Miliband and other Labour frontbenchers have been able to get under his skin and unsettle him, leading to suggestions that he can seem to lose his temper in the House and come across as an aggressive 'Flashman' figure (Wright, 2011). Chancellor George Osborne and Education Secretary Michael Gove apparently spend at least an hour with Cameron each Wednesday morning, rehearsing jokes and political put-downs to deploy at PMQs (Parker, 2011). In an early test, he was statesmanlike, assured and 'pitch perfect' in his parliamentary statement on the publication of the Saville report into the 'Bloody Sunday' (Freedland, 2010). Crucially, he has a 'softer edge' to his speaking style than Hague and Michael Howard had, meaning that he has been able to reach out beyond the Commons more effectively than his predecessors in the party leadership (Norton, 2009: 42). And like Blair, he is camera-friendly (Bale, 2010: 251) and good on television.

Organisational capacity

When Gordon Brown used to talk privately to Peter Mandelson (before the latter returned to government in 2008) about his problems as prime minister, Labour's Machiavelli would advise him that he needed not just 'good communications' but also 'good, confident people and organisation' and 'clear, bold policy' (Mandelson, 2010: 6) – advice that maps well on to Greenstein's model. Successful leadership for Greenstein (2001: 195–7) includes the ability to put together and then use a strong team of aides and advisers, and also the ability to design 'effective institutional arrangements' through which to govern and achieve results. Brown's failures on this front – including his reluctance or inability to delegate, his controlling and micro-managing methods, and his poorly-organised and sometimes dysfunctional Number 10 set-up – constituted something of a lesson in how not to organise and run a premiership (Theakston, 2011). Reacting against the build-up of prime-ministerial staff and the multiplication of advisory units under New Labour, the Conservative Opposition's Democracy Task Force had recommended in 2007 a 'smaller and simpler' operation at the centre of government. The prime minister, it said, still needed 'independent policy support – including longer-term thinking – and some progress-chasing capacity', but this should be clearly separate from the Cabinet Office, and there were warnings against 'the mingling of civil servants and special advisers within units' and against micro-management by the centre, and a proposal that the number of special advisers (in Number 10 and across government) should be reduced by 'at least half' (Democracy Task Force, 2007).

The Opposition talk of drastically cutting back on the number of special advisers did not translate into action in government, however. In March 2011 there was a total of 72 special advisers across the government (compared to 74 in the last year of the Brown administration), including 20 working in Number 10 for the prime minister and five for the deputy prime minister. There had been speculation before the election that Cameron and Osborne would have an integrated staff of political advisers (Watt and Wintour, 2009) but in the event the formation of the coalition led to the integration of Conservative and Liberal-Democrat staffers inside Number 10, advisers from each party sharing offices and working together in the various units (Stratton, 2010b). Nick Clegg has his official base as deputy prime minister in the Cabinet Office, but he has eyes and ears inside Number 10, four of the prime minister's special advisers actually being Liberal-Democrats appointed by the DPM.

Like Blair in 1997 and Brown in 2007, Cameron took into Number 10 the close-knit team of aides and advisers he had got used to working with and through before he became prime minister. The trusted inner core of his Opposition team was reassembled in government (Seldon, 2011a). Ed Llewellyn, whom he has known since Eton, is chief of staff but 'is not a domestic policy person' and operates largely as a foreign policy adviser to the prime minister, making the personal connections and lubricating the relations between Cameron and other leaders, particularly in the EU (personal information). Kate Fall, deputy chief of staff, functions as Cameron's 'gatekeeper' and is a close and influential aide. Steve Hilton has been described as the prime minister's chief 'policy guru' (Watt, 2011a), 'the director of blue skies thinking' (Wintour and Watt, 2011), and 'a wild Catherine wheel man of ideas' (private information). As strategy chief, he roams across the field, engaging in 'horizon scanning' (Stratton, 2010b), being the brains behind the Big Society, and is active in dreaming up ideas on public service reform. In Opposition it was claimed he 'commands Cameron's attention hourly. "If he could take just one call on a key decision," says an ally, "Steve's is the one he'd take"' (McElvoy, 2010). Reportedly, Hilton did not work well together with Andy Coulson, Cameron's director of communications from 2007 until he resigned in 2011. A close observer talks of 'Hilton being allowed to run amok'; with Coulson injecting a more 'feet on the ground' perspective (private information). Certainly, Coulson, the former tabloid editor with populist right-wing instincts, acted as something of a counterweight to Hilton, the long-term big picture thinker, in Cameron's team, and their relations were sometimes difficult. Coulson was replaced in March 2011 by Craig Oliver (formerly a TV editor, producer and executive), followed by the merger of the press offices in Number 10 and the Cabinet Office, and moves to extend the sway of the PM's media chief across the Whitehall press and communications operation generally in a way reminiscent of the days of Alastair Campbell and Bernard Ingham (Sherman, 2011).

Alongside the praetorian guard of Cameron's party and political aides, he has continued the one successful innovation that Brown made to the Downing Street set-up: Jeremy Heywood's appointment as permanent secretary and head of the prime minister's office, which has a staff of 178 civil servants. Close observers label Heywood 'the key official' in Number 10 and 'the indispensable man' (private information). Described as 'Mr Cameron's enforcer', he is said to be 'crucial both to the day-to-day running of the government and to its long-term reforms' (*Economist*, 2011), driving the delivery of key policy priorities, ensuring that the rest of Whitehall is kept aware of the prime minister's priorities and concerns, and (through the Number 10 implementation unit) monitoring departmental progress against their business plans and structural reform plans. 'Heywood spots the problems', it is said, 'and is called in to deal with them' (private information). Heywood – even more so than Cabinet Secretary Sir Gus O'Donnell – is the most powerful top civil servant adviser on the policy side (Rutter, 2011). The days when Cabinet Secretaries were powerful *eminence grises* to prime ministers seem long gone.

Blair rather marginalised his Cabinet Secretaries. There have been reports of tensions between the Cabinet Secretary and Cameron over the prime minister's attacks on Whitehall 'bureaucracy' and 'enemies of enterprise'. O'Donnell is a highly political civil servant, who has worked for three previous PMs. But arguably the key problem is his dual role as adviser to the prime minister and coordinator of government business while also being Head of the Civil Service, required while wearing that hat to stand up for the power, practices and perquisites of a Whitehall machine the prime minister and his party and strategy aides want to see reformed.

Newly elected prime ministers can rarely resist the temptation to play around with the machinery of government, reorganising the Whitehall departmental structure for a mixture of political, policy and presentational reasons, usually over-egging the supposed benefits and downplaying the disruption costs of their changes. Cameron was different, however, tinkering at the margins in 2010 rather than creating or abolishing whole departments. The Department for Children, Schools and Families was simply renamed the Department for Education; responsibility for some (but not all) constitutional issues was transferred from the Ministry of Justice to the Cabinet Office to come under the deputy prime minister; responsibility for the Olympics moved from the Cabinet Office to the Department of Culture, Media and Sport (DCMS); the Office for Budget Responsibility was created. Later, following a gaffe by Vince Cable, the media regulation functions of the Department for Business, Innovation and Skills were moved to the DCMS. Future reorganisations cannot be ruled out but Cameron was sensible not to rush immediately into large-scale action on this front.

One significant organisational change Cameron did make was to establish a National Security Council (NSC), together with a National Security Adviser (NSA) and supporting secretariat, based in the Cabinet Office (Sir Peter Ricketts, formerly permanent secretary of the Foreign Office, taking up the NSA post). Chaired by the prime minister, the NSC brings together the senior ministers with a role in national security, broadly defined, and – crucially – relevant experts, including the chief of the defence staff, the heads of the security and intelligence services, and others. It meets weekly, immediately after the full Cabinet, for an hour, with properly prepared agendas and papers. It has three ministerial sub-committees and a number of supporting and underpinning official groups. It had a series of meetings on the strategic defence review (Liaison Committee, 2010: 24) and looks at Afghanistan every fortnight (O'Donnell, 2011). Blair practiced 'sofa government' and sidelined the Foreign and Commonwealth Office (FCO); Cameron wants a more structured and collective approach in this field. William Hague has said the NSC is treated by the PM and other ministers as 'the true centre of decision making' on the matters it deals with (Foreign Affairs Committee, 2011: q.257). Cameron reportedly 'expects and wants a range of views, options and choices' fed into the NSC, with ministers exposed to 'different streams of reporting and thinking', including views and ideas from outside the government machine (Foreign Affairs Committee, 2011: qs.208, 210, 266). He apparently runs these meetings by first asking to hear the views of the officials and experts, followed by a policy discussion where ministers weigh in (O'Donnell, 2011). Like other modern prime ministers Cameron spends around half his time on foreign policy and national security issues (an aspect of the job that reportedly surprised him). His use of the NSC shows a more considered approach to the organisation of decision-making and to the structuring of advice than the more hole-in-the-corner and informal methods that arguably served some of his predecessors in Number 10 so ill.

After the first six or seven months of the new government there was, however, a clear sense in political, Whitehall and media circles that Cameron's Number 10 operation was under-resourced and under-powered. Tied in to criticisms of Cameron's personal style and approach, this 'capacity' issue was argued to be a factor in policy mistakes and political wobbles that had hit the government in late 2010 and early 2011. 'Under Labour', as one commentator put it, 'Downing Street became a big player in Whitehall, a large team of political advisers keeping ministers under close scrutiny and regularly intervening as policies were developed and implemented. Cameron's Number 10 has been a less fearsome machine' (Kirkup, 2011a). As a senior Whitehall figure observed, 'in the Blair years Number 10 advisers would be in touch with the department constantly and attend all key policy meetings here, less so under Brown, but not at all under Cameron' (private information). The Number 10 strategy unit was disbanded and the policy unit was run down after the election and had just two or three staff who did not shadow departments in the old way; there was felt to be insufficient policy expertise at the centre; and there were complaints that Number 10 was not getting to grips early enough with policy coming up from departments and with problems and issues. In some cases Number 10 was said to be engaging with departments virtually on the eve of the publication of policies and plans, only to be caught out by subsequent public or media criticisms and controversy.

Stymied by the pledge not to increase the number of political advisers, the response was to beef up the Number 10 machine by recruiting a new and expanded (ten-strong) team of civil servants and some outsiders from the private sector to staff a new policy and implementation unit, intended to be more proactive, to develop medium-term policy that goes beyond the coalition agreement published in 2010, to keep a closer watch on departmental policy-making, and to engage earlier and act as an early warning radar system spotting potential policy problems, with a new head of political strategy, Andrew Cooper, a former Tory official and pollster, appointed in February 2011 as a senior political adviser to the prime minister. The policy unit will be supported by a six-strong research and analysis unit, nicknamed 'boffins central' (Montgomerie, 2011). The aim is to extend and strengthen Number 10's grip on government policy-making – something prime ministers before Cameron have tried to do, of course, and with mixed results. Number 10 was regularly reorganised under Blair and Brown and it is likely that the Cameron experience will be no different – prime ministers never quite feel that the set-up is right, working properly or delivering what they want, and try out new advisers and new units from time to time. Cameron has acted fairly quickly to acknowledge and address perceived problems in this area; time will show whether and how his solution works.

Political skills and style

Prime ministers have varied greatly in terms of their skills and approaches as political operators, in the way in which they have dealt with their Cabinet colleagues and their parties, using persuasion, conciliation, negotiation, manipulation, brokerage or other methods to handle the problems they face and advance their goals. Some have been guileful and agile masters of the indirect approach; some have shown great tactical skill in balancing the factions and the competing personalities; some have interfered, controlled and constantly pulled things into Number 10 while others have been more detached and above the fray; some have used charm to win people over and avoid conflict while others have used more brutal and bullying methods. And of course the same prime minister may use different political methods at different times or in different situations during their premiership.

Insiders were impressed with Cameron's political skills even when he was a young special adviser, testifying to his 'astute political antennae' (Brandreth, 1999: 191), 'tactical nous' and 'rare political ability – an instinctive feel for opponents' weak spots and a ruthlessness in exploiting them' (Elliott and Hanning, 2009: 84). Observers of Cameron the political leader admit that he can be cunning (Jones, 2008: 9; Steavenson, 2010: 46). More emphasis, though, tends to be put on the way in which he is 'very good in small groups', like Blair using his courtesy, charm and social skills to great effect – 'but while Blair was a good actor, with Cameron it's more natural' (private information). Where Thatcher was abrasive, provocative, strident and confrontational, Cameron is a more emollient and consensual personality, something that helped in the 'detoxifying' of the Conservative brand in Opposition and now suits the coalition context. It can sometimes be politically useful to come across as the sort of person who seems to be more interested in settling an argument than picking a fight (Rawnsley, 2010b). Cameron certainly looks comfortable and at ease at the head of a coalition, and seems equipped to deal with the politics of a coalition, in a way that it is difficult to imagine Thatcher or Brown being.

Promising 'a different style of government', Cameron insisted before he became prime minister that he would 'restore the proper processes of government', which meant 'building a strong team', being inclusive and trusting his colleagues to get on with the job, taking decisions 'round the Cabinet table', and eschewing a presidential model of leadership for a chairmanship role (Cameron, 2006g, 2010c; Jones, 2008: 112). However, sceptics noted the shadow Cabinet collectively had not in practice counted for much in Opposition, the real decisions about policy and strategy being taken by Cameron, his inner group of advisers and a few top frontbenchers close to him, shadow ministers dealing with the leadership group bilaterally, while MPs and parliamentary groupings had little influence (Heffernan, 2010). Nevertheless, from the start of his premiership, Cameron again repeatedly emphasised his preference for a collective and collegiate approach (Liaison Committee, 2010).

'The coalition has brought back Cabinet government' it has been argued. 'The culture of coalition in which internal disagreement and compromise are unavoidable makes Thatcher-style leadership impossible' (Richards, 2011). 'The Cabinet does function as a Cabinet in the way it is supposed to in the textbooks', Business Secretary Vince Cable has said. 'We debate things across the table' (Oborne, 2010). Cameron has not, however, been holding particularly more, or more frequent, Cabinet meetings than the average for recent governments (O'Donnell, 2011). While Cabinet meetings are reportedly of a 'reasonable length with good discussions', it is 'not a decision-making body' (private information). Cabinet committees are key decision-making bodies, however, notably the NSC (see above), the Home Affairs Committee (chaired by Nick Clegg) and the Europe Committee (chaired by Foreign Secretary William Hague). The key group handling issues relating to the operation of the coalition and working out agreements on the big policy issues has not been the coalition committee, which has apparently met just once, but 'the Quad', consisting of Cameron and George Osborne for the Conservatives and Clegg and Danny Alexander (Chief Secretary to the Treasury) for the Liberal Democrats. This functions as an inner Cabinet and has had many meetings, dealing with the spending review and budget decision-making, for instance.

'Positive personal chemistry at the top' has been described as 'a sine qua non of effective coalition government' (Paun, 2010: 35). Cameron and Clegg were reported to get on well together and to have a close rapport: they meet a lot, talk on the phone and text each other, and are in contact by BlackBerry. An insider described them as 'incredibly respectful of each other to a degree not seen in other politicians' (private information). 'They don't agree on everything', said an adviser, but 'they can have a conversation' (Hurst, 2010). Clegg himself referred to a process of 'haggling, negotiating, arguing', and insisted that 'all the big judgements are genuinely jointly taken by David Cameron and myself' (Rawnsley, 2010a). Conservative ministers have been known to complain 'David is just indulging Clegg on this – we're not keen' (private information), and Tory backbenchers have voiced their frustrations too at what they see as disproportionate Liberal Democrat influence. The two top figures seem to get on better than Blair and Brown did, and Clegg has certainly been given more information and consultation about the budget than Blair usually got when Brown was at the Treasury. While the Cameron-Clegg relationship is the core one in the coalition, there are frequent occasions when ministers from both sides meet outside of the formal committee system to talk things through, discuss problems and manage inter-party relations. But after the coalitions first year, and with the weakening of the Liberal Democrat's political position after their big election losses and defeat on the AV referendum, there were reports that inter-party and ministerial relations – including those between Cameron and Clegg – would become more 'transactional', formal and business-like, with more airing of party differences and conflicts that might put relations under strain.

The other key personal and political relationship is between Cameron and George Osborne, the Chancellor of the Exchequer. They work collaboratively and are very close friends and political allies to a degree not seen in the modern history of prime minister-chancellor relations. Osborne is Cameron's 'closest lieutenant' and 'principal adviser: it's as simple as that', says one insider, and the advice ranges across all areas, not just the economy (Parker, 2011). Osborne is in fact the key figure on political strategy (Elliott and Hanning, 2009: 357). He spends a lot of time in and around Number 10, attending the two daily meetings there at 8.30 am and 4.00 pm with Cameron and the PM's inner team of aides and advisers (and which William Hague also often attends) that set the government's agenda and coordinate its message. Clegg does not attend those meetings, and – a sign of his status and clout – Osborne chairs them when Cameron is away (Brogan, 2010b; Parker, 2011).

Cameron's approach was described as relaxed, 'laid-back' or 'hands-off'. 'He's not up late at night or at 5.00 am sending emails', said a close observer. 'He does the big things and is very much the delegator. The criticism is that he's sometimes too detached' (private information). His declared preference for a 'chairmanship' rather than a 'chief executive' role (Jones, 2008: 108, 112) was identified as a factor in the government's difficulties and problems with issues like the controversial big NHS reorganisation, votes for prisoners and the U-turn on woodland sell-offs. Number 10, it was argued, should have spotted the snags and the PM should have intervened earlier. The implication was that there had been too much of a reaction against his predecessors' meddling and 'control-freakery'. There is 'a fine line between delegation and neglect' argued one commentator (d'Ancona, 2011a). 'David came into No. 10 as the most laissez faire Tory premier in history, letting ministers run their fiefdoms with an extraordinary degree of independence', a Conservative MP commented. 'But he has learned that this came at a high cost and he is now sorting this problem out' (Hennessy, 2011). The reinforcement of the Number 10 machine in early 2011 (see above) was part of the response here, with promises too of a more active leadership style on the part of the prime minister himself.

Policy vision

Taking a long view, most British prime ministers seem to have been pragmatists of one sort or another rather than vision-driven or highly ideological politicians. In modern conditions, however, parties and the mass media expect leaders to come up with a 'narrative', set out clear long-term goals and provide a strong sense of direction for their governments. Both Thatcher and Blair saw political leadership as involving winning the battle of ideas and pushing forward with their own policies and goals – which were *theirs* and not necessarily their parties' or Cabinets'. Major and Brown were less successful in this respect, neither of them being able to set out a clear sense of their priorities or a broad and convincing vision of what they stood for and wanted to achieve.

Cameron has often been described – and has described himself – as a non-ideological, practical, 'whatever works', type of Conservative, sceptical and pragmatic. 'I don't like grand plans and grand visions', he once said, accepting that having 'clear principles' was important but criticising leaders who had 'too much of a mission' or who were driven by 'some sort of messianic cause' (Jones, 2008: 43, 104, 110). 'I don't believe in isms', he announced (Steavenson, 2010: 45). He has been described in various ways: as like a centrist 'Macmillan Conservative' (Elliott and Hanning, 2009: 366), as the 'heir to Blair' (McAnulla, 2010), as a Thatcherite, a post-Thatcherite or as the heir to Thatcher (Evans, 2010), and as a combination of economic liberal and (socially) liberal conservative (Evans, 2009: 127). While some observers insist that 'he never goes the whole way on anything' (Steavenson, 2010: 47) – 'he believes things, but nothing too much' (Moore, 2008) – and some decry what they see as simple 'opportunism' (Elliott and Hanning, 2009: 366), others detect what they think is a definitely ideological approach and a clear agenda (Lee, 2009a: 11). On other accounts, however, changes in Conservative policy under him have been tactical and reactive, reflecting internal party dynamics and external developments (Williams and Scott, 2011), in line with Cameron's own argument that politicians should not cling to beliefs if changing circumstances render them obsolete (Lee, 2009b: 72).

A politician who, it is argued, 'understands strategy and how to implement it' (Bale, 2010: 20), Cameron can sometimes be cautious – '[doing] as little as he can get away with and as much as he can afford' (Bale, 2010: 20) – and at other times strikingly bold (Laws, 2010: 48, 51). But he is flexible and adaptable. He has 'a reverse gear' (Bale, 2009: 229) and has shown that he knows when and how to use it. As Tim Bale has said, 'Cameron has a tendency, when faced with serious opposition, to move back and rethink, the better to move around the obstacle. As long as his main point is achieved, he's happy to compromise around the margin if he has to' (Beckett, 2010). Anne Perkins (2010) notes that 'pragmatism is not the same as a lack of a sense of direction. It is merely flexibility about the means by which he gets there.'

From the start of his leadership Cameron was clear that he wanted to be as radical a social reformer as Thatcher had been an economic reformer (Jones, 2008: 315). Although purportedly suspicious of mission-driven leaders, he declared in 2008 that fixing the 'broken society' was his party's 'central mission' (Driver, 2009: 89) and in 2011 said that while it was the government's 'duty' to deal with the deficit, social recovery and the success of the Big Society was his 'mission and purpose' (Sylvester, 2011b). However imprecise and contested its policy implications, the Big Society is clearly Cameron's 'Big Idea' and a consistent theme of his leadership, not just a piece of political positioning (Rawnsley, 2011a), albeit an idea which even some close allies, such as George Osborne, have not been entirely sold on. Coalition freed Cameron from his party's right-wing die-hards – who were suspicious that he seemed far too comfortable with his enforced cohabitation with the Liberal-Democrats. But at the same time his government quickly established a radical momentum, with far-reaching policy initiatives on a number of fronts, going further and faster than Thatcher or Blair had done when they had come into office (Riddell, 2010). In Opposition Cameron had talked of the need to take difficult and tough decisions early on in order to effect change and get things done (Jones, 2008: 67–8), and that was what his government proceeded to do, though the risks and dangers of such an approach are obvious.

Cognitive style

Although Cameron is well educated, and the fifth prime minister since 1945 with a first class degree, no one describes him as an intellectual. He is said to pick up ideas quickly and to be intelligent but also to be pragmatic and 'philosophically incurious'. The interest seems to be in 'resolving problems' and 'making things happen' but not wanting to 'dig too deeply into philosophy' (Elliott and Hanning, 2009: 38, 42, 68, 362). Seldon (2009) describes him as 'philosophy-lite for a Conservative leader', a reactive politician whose agenda and ideas do not emanate from deep reading or profound convictions but have taken shape in response to events. A close observer describes him as 'a good examinee in the Oxford PPE style', suggesting breadth and quickness rather than depth (private information). In terms of cognitive style – how leaders process information and advice, their intellectual strengths and weaknesses, and how they approach decision-making – the nimble Cameron is certainly very different from his immediate predecessor in Number 10, who appeared to be obsessed by details, ponderous, inflexible and vacillating (Theakston, 2011). Having got those around him to outline the arguments on all sides of a question, he generally makes up his mind fairly quickly (Bale et al, forthcoming). Cameron has even more of a broad-brush style than Blair who could master details like a barrister when he needed to (private information). His approach is also different to Thatcher, who 'knew everything, was relentless, went at it – he's not like that' (private information). In

Opposition, his approach was described as tending to 'broad political canvases, not detailed policies' (Driver, 2009: 87), and as being primarily values-driven rather than policies-driven (Norton, 2009: 39). The issue is whether that style can be effective once in government.

Civil servants report that Cameron is a pleasure to work with: he is decisive but courteous, orderly, polite and well mannered. He is 'not a neurotic workaholic' (private information), though he is known to rise at 5.30 am to start his day by spending two hours working through his red boxes, dealing with his paperwork (Seldon, 2011b). But at the same time there are reports that 'an inattention to detail' and a 'failure to master briefs' has 'long worried some of his aides' (Montgomerie, 2010). Other insiders feel that he 'can sometimes act as if he believes his natural intellect is a substitute for hard graft.' 'He doesn't read enough' one was quoted as saying. 'He's so overwhelmingly sure of himself he thinks he can get by anyway. And quite often he does, but sometimes it can be a problem' (Kirkup, 2011a). 'Themes not details' are said to be his forte (private information). Cameron himself emphasises that 'being a good prime minister is about making the right judgements' (Jones, 2008: 104). Other PMs (such as Attlee) and observers of the premiership have often agreed that judgement rather than cleverness, and a clear mind rather than an original one, was what was needed in the occupant of Number 10. A more hands-on approach to policy development and decision-making – as opposed to a more detached Cabinet-chairman style – may, however, require a bit more from him in terms of prime-ministerial grind and homework.

Emotional intelligence

Cameron certainly scores highly in terms of the emotional intelligence now widely recognised to be an important component of successful political leadership. British prime ministers have varied greatly in terms of their temperament or the emotional intelligence dimension of personality and character. Historically, a surprisingly large proportion seems to have experienced significant levels of stress, anxiety, depression or other mental problems and disorders, which in some cases impacted negatively on their premierships (Davidson, 2011). Cameron, however, comes across as 'untroubled by inner demons' (Schama, 2010). He has been described as 'well-adjusted ... You search in vain ... for the chips [on the shoulder] that typically burden and motivate politicians' (*Economist*, 2010c). He has said himself that leadership 'requires the right temperament' (Cameron, 2010c), that 'character is far more important than policy' and that a good prime minister has to be a 'balanced' person (Jones, 2008: 104). The contrast with Gordon Brown is obvious, someone described by his predecessor as Labour leader and prime minister as having 'zero' emotional intelligence (Blair, 2010: 616). Deficiencies in emotional intelligence may not necessarily prevent a leader from governing successfully, but in Brown's case a more even temperament would have been an asset and helped him weather the demands of office and lead his government more effectively (Theakston, 2011). Cameron and Blair fit the model of the more emotionally literate leader that modern politics seems to require.

Compared to his three Conservative predecessors in Number 10, Cameron seems more emotionally secure, self-confident and comfortable with himself than Major; less wilful, headstrong, tempestuous and hectoring than Thatcher; and more rounded, affable and human than Heath. He has an easy manner, is optimistic, cool and calm under pressure, and can keep things in proportion; he is reportedly uninterested in calls through the night about next day's newspaper headlines (*Observer*, 2010). His biographers talk of his 'groundedness' and 'roundedness' (Elliott and Hanning, 2009: 46, 364). If it all sounds too good to be true, there are observers and critics who claim he can be petulant or niggardly at times, or even 'bumptious' and 'bullying', and that there can be flashes of a temper 'which can be fierce' (Elliott and Hanning, 2009: 367). But mostly, he appears to be able to handle the stress of the job (private information). Cameron is not, however, 'quite as nice as he looks', Michael Portillo has commented – adding, 'I'm pleased to know that' (Jones, 2008: 9). Underneath the personal charm and ease, it had been said, is a 'steely determination', someone who is 'as tough as nails' (Elliott and Hanning, 2009: 41), and 'a degree of dispassionate ruthlessness' (Jones, 2008: 18) or, put another way, 'the necessary coldness ... "the mask of command"' (Moore, 2008). There is, in other words, not only emotional intelligence but also the necessary emotional toughness to be effective in Number 10.

Conclusion

Cameron had been prime minister for only a few weeks when commentators started voicing the view that he seemed a 'natural' for the office and had made a strong personal start. 'Cameron is already proving to be a much better prime minister than Brown ever was', argued Martin Kettle (2010). 'He is showing himself as potentially the best all-round prime minister of the modern era.' In terms of the key leadership abilities, skills and characteristics Greenstein's model identifies, Brown can certainly be seen as someone not well equipped for the highest office, even allowing for the fact that he was very unlucky in the circumstances and problems he faced during his time in Number 10 (Theakston, 2011). However, Cameron was getting more critical reviews by the end of 2010 and in early 2011, related to his so-called 'laid-back' style, with Conservative MPs and pundits (and, privately, some ministers) calling for a more active and assertive approach from him.

The ideal British prime minister would, in terms of Greenstein's categories, possess an unlikely combination of skills and attributes. Individual PMs will always have their distinctive strengths and weaknesses under his headings, and their methods and their performance in relation to the leadership tasks they face is also likely to be variable over time as their term of office progresses. No one could or would get a proper picture of Thatcher's style and approach as prime minister, or Blair's, on the basis of an analysis made at the end of the first year in Number 10 (in 1980 and 1998 respectively). Cameron's premiership is a work in progress. He may well seem – and come to be – a very different type of prime minister after a number of years in office. Nevertheless at this stage he does seem to display key skills and abilities necessary for success in that office. He is a strong communicator; he has made some intelligent decisions about the organisation of advice and decision-making in government; he is a formidable political operator; he has a policy vision of sorts but has shown flexibility and pragmatism; he seems to be able to handle the intellectual and personal challenges of the premiership, and shows emotional intelligence. He faces, to be sure, huge political and economic challenges. But what he brings and is bringing to the premiership could be crucial in the coalition finding a way through these challenges and governing successfully.

15
Labour in Opposition

Timothy Heppell and Michael Hill

Every time we approach a general election, political commentators remind us of the old maxim that oppositions do not actually win elections; rather it is governments that lose them. Removals from office are thus to be attributed to the perceived failings of incumbent administrations, rather than the merits of the opposition as an alternative. For example, in 1979, the election of the Conservatives under Margaret Thatcher was a consequence of Labour under James Callaghan appearing to be economically incompetent in light of the Winter of Discontent. Equally, the election of New Labour under Tony Blair in 1997 was a consequence of the perceived economic incompetence of the John Major administration in light of their humiliating departure from the Exchange Rate Mechanism on Black Wednesday. That we have a Conservative administration, albeit in a coalition, is a by-product of the damage to the credibility of Labour and Gordon Brown caused by their perceived failings surrounding the banking collapse and the subsequent recession.

Whilst political commentators might feel comfortable with such an interpretation, academics have rightly questioned this thesis (Ball, 2005: 1–28). It is true that the electoral perception that a government is incompetent and thus vulnerable constitutes the *necessary* precondition for a potential change of government. However, that may not be *sufficient* – that is, just because a government is vulnerable to the charge of incompetence, does not mean that the opposition is going to be automatically swept into power. The party of opposition has to demonstrate that it is credible and worthy of replacing the incumbent administration (Norton, 2009: 31–3).

For example, the first-term Thatcher administration endured a painful recession and felt forced to implement hugely unpopular public expenditure cuts. However, Labour lacked all credibility as an alternative party of government and that saved Thatcher and the Conservatives. Pulling together the leadership limitations of Michael Foot; the fracturing away of parts of the right wing to form the Social Democratic Party; and their policy platform of unilateralism and further nationalisation, Denis Healey concluded that 'in that period the party acquired for itself a highly unfavourable image, based on disunity, extremism, crankiness and general unfitness to govern (Healey, 1990: 502). Similarly in 2005 New Labour and Tony Blair were vulnerable. Their inability to contribute to securing a swift resolution to the conflict in Iraq and the apparent absence of a post-invasion strategy and exit route, had led to serious questioning of the intelligence gathering and decision-making that justified war. Moreover, the internal unity of the Blair government was undermined by significant opposition among Labour MPs to Blair towards his approach to Iraq. That disunity was spreading in the second term as there were increasing divisions over education (tuition fees), health (foundation hospitals) and identity cards. However, although the necessary condition for the removal of the incumbent administration was there, the Conservatives in 2005, (under the leadership of Michael Howard), were simply 'not seen as electable' (Norton, 2009: 33).

With this necessary/sufficient distinction in mind, this chapter aims to assess how Labour has adapted to the transition from government to opposition, or what Haddon and Gruhn call a 'reverse transition' (Haddon and Gruhn, 2011: 64). It will consider the following themes. First, the chapter will assess the changes in personnel within the party at elite level by profiling the significance of the leadership election (May to September 2010) and the shadow Cabinet elections and subsequent portfolio allocations. Second, the chapter will consider the central strategic issues facing Labour in the aftermath of their removal from power. Running throughout the chapter will be an emphasis on impact through the use of opinion polling evidence to see how effective Ed Miliband has been as the new party leader in overcoming the factors that contributed to defeat in May 2010.

Changes in personnel: The leadership and shadow Cabinet

During the course of the protracted parallel negotiations between the Liberal Democrats and both the Conservatives and Labour, Gordon Brown had indicated his willingness to stand down as Labour Party leader by the autumn. Brown had reluctantly recognised that he was an obstacle to any potential Labour-Liberal Democrat coalition being made. In making the ultimate self sacrifice to ensure that Labour might remain in power somehow was an admission that the damage to his leadership credibility after three crisis dominated years as Prime Minister was irreversible (Norton, 2011a: 250). Had Labour somehow crafted a coalition deal with the Liberal Democrats, Brown intended to remain as party leader and Prime Minister until a newly elected Labour Party leader (selected that autumn through the Electoral College) could be proclaimed as the new Prime Minister. That this act of desperation was considered meant that should a Labour-Liberal Democrat coalition arrangement fail to materialise then it was inevitable that Brown would resign (Hickson, 2011: 257). Once this was evident, he resigned as Labour Party leader with immediate effect. Between May and September, Harriet Harman as the elected deputy party leader would serve as acting leader until a permanent successor was selected at the annual conference.

To enter the succession contest candidates needed to secure the backing of 12.5 per cent of the PLP (or 33 MPs) to pass the nominations threshold. Media attention initially focused around two candidates: David Miliband and Ed Balls. David Miliband was strongly associated with the Blairites and Balls with the Brownites. As such there was a concern about their unifying capability given that they were so closely associated with the rival factions which had so destabilised the New Labour project. Supporters of David Miliband were of the view that it was unlikely that his younger brother, Ed, would dispute the leadership against him, although it was noted that whilst associated with the Brownite faction he was far more acceptable to Blairites than Balls was (Hickson, 2011: 258). By entering the nomination contest Ed Miliband hived off support from Balls at the PLP level, and when nominations closed Balls only just passed the threshold for entry as did Andy Burnham and Diane Abbott. David Miliband secured 91 nominations to Ed Miliband on 63, although many supporters of the former Foreign Secretary had 'lent' their support to Abbott to ensure that she progressed to the Electoral College (Wickham-Jones and Jobson, 2010: 533). As David Miliband nominated Abbott many speculated that he wanted her on the ballot to fragment support on the left and to thus undermine the first round support base of his younger brother (Dorey and Denham, 2011: 295).

The contest largely failed to excite political commentators in the initial months. This was partly because their focus was primarily on the dynamics of the coalition, but also because there was a widely held view that David Miliband was going to win anyway. In addition to his lead with the PLP, he had the endorsement of the most constituency Labour parties (167 as compared to 147 for his younger brother). He had the strongest level of support from within the shadow Cabinet. Moreover, opinion polling data suggested that he led by 36 to 27 amongst those eligible to vote within the Electoral College (Wickham-Jones and Jobson, 2010: 534). Critically in addition to these positive indicators political commentators assumed that participants within the Electoral College would be influenced by YouGov data which showed that David led Ed by 47 to 19 per cent on the best alternative Prime Minister to Cameron. This poll also revealed that amongst those who had abandoned Labour in 2010, David Miliband led by 25 per cent as their preferred option (Watt, 2010c).

During the course of the campaign relations between the Miliband brothers and their respective campaigns deteriorated (Wintour et al, 2010 and Watt, 2010d). The 'human drama' of two brothers fighting for the leadership and their relationship appearing to suffer in an 'increasingly bitter contest' began to generate media interest (Wickham-Jones and Jobson, 2010: 533). That drama reached a climax as the Electoral College produced a desperately

Table 15.1 The Labour Party leadership election of 2010

	Round 1 %	Round 2 %	Round 3 %	Round 4 %
Diane Abbott	7.42			
Andy Burnham	8.68	10.41		
Ed Balls	11.79	13.23	16.02	
David Miliband	**37.78**	**38.89**	**42.72**	49.35
Ed Miliband	34.33	37.47	41.26	**50.65**

Source: Adapted from Kelly et al, 2010: 14.

close outcome of Ed Miliband winning by 50.65 to 49.35 per cent in the fourth round. That victory was secured even though it was the elder Miliband who had led in the earlier three rounds. As the votes of Abbot and Burnham were reallocated David Miliband retained his lead; but when the votes of Balls were reallocated that provided Ed Miliband with the narrowest of victories. Significantly of the three tranches of the Electoral College, Ed Miliband was the winner in only one: the trade union tranche (Wickham-Jones and Jobson, 2010: 534).

A critical question here would be what outcome did the Conservatives want? *The Guardian* claimed that Cameron was overheard (at a party held by Rupert Murdoch) stating that he was 'hoping' that it would be Ed Miliband, but that he 'feared' David Miliband' (Watt, 2010e). Opposing Ed rather than David Miliband, and the means by which the former won, provided clear political advantages for the Conservatives (Hasan and Macintyre, 2011: 241). They could claim that Ed Miliband had won due to the support of the trade unions, and thus seek to create an image of him being under their control (d'Ancona, 2010). It was rumoured that many New Labour Blairites who had supported David Miliband were aghast at the outcome for these reasons. It was described as a 'doomsday scenario' and a 'miracle for Conservative headquarters' (Kellner, 2010).

Another disadvantage of the outcome was its impact on the defeated pre-contest favourite. Psychologically being defeated by his less experienced and younger brother was hard for David Miliband to accept (Prince and Porter, 2010). Had he won it was widely assumed that Ed Miliband would have been willing to serve in his shadow Cabinet. However, after a short period of time for reflection, David Miliband decided not to stand for the autumn shadow Cabinet elections. His decision to retreat to the backbenchers contributed to an image of division and left the shadow Cabinet without one of the few high profile political heavyweights that the party still possessed. Those shadow Cabinet elections finalised a generational shift in Labour politics. From the outgoing Cabinet they lost Gordon Brown and Peter Mandelson, as well as

Alasdair Darling and Jack Straw, who both decided to bring their frontbench careers to an end. It also meant that the only member of the shadow Cabinet present in the shadow Cabinets of 1994–1997 and the first Blair Cabinet was Harriet Harman (Wickham-Jones and Jobson, 2010: 527).

Constructing the shadow Cabinet in the aftermath of the shadow Cabinet elections was the first big test for Ed Miliband as Labour Party leader (Watt and Wintour, 2010). A total of 49 Labour parliamentarians stood for the 19 places available and the outcome was described as a 'disappointment' for Ed Miliband. None of those elected in the top ten had him as their first preference for leader, and only five of the 19 elected had endorsed him as their first preference (Hasan and Macintyre, 2011: 257).

The critical appointment given the political terrain would be shadow Chancellor, which was the position he would have given to his elder brother had he been available (Hasan and Macintyre, 2011: 253). Given that two of the leading contenders – Ed Balls and Yvette Cooper – were married, Ed Miliband was concerned that the media would attempt to create another family drama around the one that he did not appoint. It was also reported that he wanted to avoid appointing the independently minded (and potentially divisive) Balls, as he wanted to prevent Balls from building up a rival power base that could replicate the Blair-Brown feuding of the previous generation (Kettle, 2011). His avoidance of Cooper and Balls meant he appointed Alan Johnson who had backed his eldest brother in the leadership election. Initially the appointment won some praise as a pragmatic form of party management – it represented a clear attempt to placate the majority of the PLP who had voted against him. Johnson had the additional advantage of experience and supposedly good communications skills (Wintour, 2010b). Moreover, it was felt that his impeccable working class credentials would contrast well to the elitist Cameron and Osborne as they engaged in massive public sector cuts (Hickson, 2010: 260).

However as it transpired it was a mistaken appointment that would last only a matter of months before Johnson resigned for personal reasons. The logic of the appointment was undermined by two problems. First, there was Johnson's honesty in admitting his limited knowledge of economic issues, which badly undermined his credibility (Brogan, 2011). Second, there were his substantive policy disagreements with Ed Miliband (Gammell, 2011). For example in the critical period leading up to the Commons divisions on tuition fees (December 2010) there was a clear difference between Ed Miliband who argued for a graduate tax, and Johnson (a former Education Secretary) who was implacably against one. This difference of opinion, and another on whether the 50p tax rate should be made permanent (Johnson opposed this), was openly displayed on the BBC *Politics Show* in November 2010 (Meikle, 2010; Bennett, 2010).

The subsequent decision to appoint Balls as shadow Chancellor after the resignation of Johnson produced some negative media comment. In policy terms there was a question as to whether they could work effectively together as there were disagreements between the two on the issue of cuts – Balls being more sceptical about the need to commit to a clear timetable (Freedland, 2011). In personal terms it was widely rumoured that there was a lack of trust between them and that Balls had struggled to disguise his disdain for Ed Miliband (Rawnsley, 2011b; see also Hasan and Macintyre, 2011). Finally in political terms was Balls a sensible tactical appointment to make? Critics argued that by being forced into this decision, which he had been so keen to avoid only three months later, this represented a 'terrible moment' for Ed Miliband and a 'crisis' (Brogan, 2011). An intellectual bruiser, Balls might provide a 'more focused and ruthless parliamentary message' (Kettle, 2011) than Johnson, but his strong association to Brown could leave him vulnerable to Conservative attacks. As Brogan acknowledged 'the Chancellor will be dusting down the over-flowing dossier of evidence incriminating Balls in the economic disaster we are in ... In the long term, the Tories will be delighted to have a key architect of Labour's economic policy in government in charge' (Brogan, 2011).

Beyond questions around portfolio allocation within the shadow Cabinet the critical concern has to be how effectively Ed Miliband has adapted to his role – in his first year has he looked like a Prime Minister in waiting? Initial media reaction to his election was dominated by the fact that he had defeated his elder brother on a disputed mandate and what this symbolised – the trade union beholden 'Red Ed' imagery (Hasan and Macintyre, 2011: 262–3). Thereafter he has suffered from sustained criticism from the Conservative press. They have retained an unhealthy interest in his lifestyle choices. Tabloid editors have become fixated by the following: the fact that his name was not listed on the birth certificate of his eldest child; the fact that he and his long time partner were not married; the suggestion that their subsequent marriage was an act of political calculation not love; his weight and his need for nasal surgery to aid his sleep, or according to his critics to address his 'annoying' voice (Prince, 2010b; Cannon, 2011).

In presentational terms Ed Miliband represents an improvement on Gordon Brown (Hasan and Macintyre, 2011: 276). However, concerns exist about his ability to exploit the weaknesses and divisions within the coalition, notably over the furore over sentencing which had exposed a gap between Cameron and his Justice Secretary, Kenneth Clarke, but also over the difficulties that Andrew Lansley was experiencing over healthcare reform (Letts, 2011). For the PLP effectiveness at Prime Ministers Questions is a key weapon through which to raise party morale – this after all was an environment in which Cameron frequently exposed and embarrassed Brown (Jones, 2010: 107). In this forum Ed Miliband has been competent at best and as Kevin Theakston noted in his earlier chapter he has got under the skin of Cameron. But he lacks the parliamentary precision and forensic exposure of policy flaws that characterised the approach of John Smith. Nor does he possess the quick thinking wit and repartee of a Harold Wilson. He has still to develop that method of constructing questions with an inbuilt and effective sound bite for the evening news – the technique that Blair mastered and Cameron then followed.

Too often in the early months of his leadership tenure Cameron was able to end their confrontations with the type of brutal put downs that win plaudits from political commentators. For example, in December 2010 Cameron exploited press speculation that Labour strategists were concerned about Ed Miliband's low public profile, by ending that confrontation with: 'three months and people are beginning to ask "When's he going to start?".' In the same month when Ed Miliband attempted to expose the Thatcherite inclinations running through the heart of the coalition, Cameron retorted with 'I'd rather be a child of Thatcher than a son of Brown'. It might not be quite on the put down scale of Lloyd Bentsen-Dan Quayle, but it did result in press comment about how Ed Miliband's 'inability to compete with the Prime Minister' was 'producing a sense of deep trepidation' on the Labour benches (Gimson, 2010). Sensing that mood, Cameron has repeatedly found reasons to refer to David Miliband in his responses. For example, when Ed Miliband attempted to question that morality of dumping policy and blaming his ministerial colleagues (the March 2011 U-turn on the proposed selling off of state-owned forests), Cameron responded with: 'in a minute he is going to give me a lesson on family loyalty' before observing that: 'when the opposition considers his [Ed Miliband's] performance it could be time for a bit of 'Brother, where art thou' (Hasan and Macintyre, 2011: 275).

In addition to concerns about his presentational limitations there are also question marks amongst Labour elites about his political judgement. A good example of this would be his participation in the 'March for an Alternative' TUC rally in March 2011. Whilst he officially accepted the need for cuts but disputed the scale and speed with the coalition, he attended and thereby endorsed a rally which was in reality against the principle of cuts. In his speech he spoke of the 'mainstream majority' in attendance, and compared their fight to other great struggles – 'the suffragettes who fought for votes for women and won ... the civil rights movement in America that fought against racism and won ... the anti-apartheid movement that fought the horror of that system and won' (Padley, 2011). Whilst the rhetoric could be described as over-blown, there was also the question as to whether attending the rally had been sensible politics. As Hennessy and Kite noted:

> It was the timing that Labour's high command had been dreading. At the very moment their party leader began his speech at the anti-cuts rally in Hyde Park, anarchists wearing masks and waving red flags began attacking shops and banks in Oxford Street. For several minutes, live television pictures of the violence were accompanied by words from Ed Miliband. The speech could not have been further away in tone from the actions of the mindless minority. Nevertheless, the warning privately expressed by some

> in Labour's high command that Ed Miliband should not be anywhere near Saturday's events appeared to have been vindicated (Hennessy and Kite, 2011).

Such press criticisms were also reflected in early polling data conducted to assess how Ed Miliband compares to Cameron as a potential Prime Minister. On a range of leadership based evaluations Ed Miliband trailed Cameron – capable leader (26 per cent Ed Miliband to 57 per cent Cameron); good in a crisis (15 per cent Ed Miliband to 41 per cent Cameron); understands the problems facing Britain (40 per cent Ed Miliband to 51 per cent Cameron); and honesty (Ed Miliband 24 per cent to 33 per cent Cameron) (Worcester et al, 2011: 263). On the critical question of who is best equipped to be Prime Minister Ed Miliband (23 per cent) trailed Cameron (38 per cent) even six months in as leader of the opposition (ibid: 264). Polling data that focused on Ed Miliband alone produced some worrying indicators for Labour. When asked to confirm whether they liked or disliked Ed Miliband 36 per cent liked him, and 51 per cent do not like him (ibid: 272).

Critically by May 2011 there was increasing concern that the electorate doubted the wisdom of the Labour Party in selecting the younger of the Miliband brothers. With 51 per cent of those questioned stating that they thought Ed Miliband was 'doing badly' (as against 32 per cent disagreeing with the statement), YouGov asked whether an alternative leader would enhance the position of Labour. On whether alternatives would do better or worse than Ed Miliband it was reassuring that the findings for Balls, Cooper and Harman were actually inferior: Balls was –11 (better minus worse); Cooper was –21; and Harman was –20. However, David Miliband was +35, and critically amongst projected Conservative and Liberal Democrat voters (whom Labour need to attract and defect to them) his lead was even greater – +44 amongst current projected Conservative voters; and +43 amongst current projected Liberal Democrat voters. In an age of valence politics, in which the charisma and likeability of the party leader are crucial, then it is clear that the personal ratings of Ed Miliband, relative to Cameron and indeed his brother, must improve if he is to hope to propel Labour back into power in 2015 (see YouGov, 2011).

Changes in strategy: Transcending New Labour?

However, focusing on changes in personnel, and specifically Ed Miliband as the new party leader, can be limiting. There is also a need to focus in on strategic choices facing Labour in opposition – specifically is the New Labour project to be abandoned, modified or continued? (Norton, 2011a: 258). Attempts to disavow New Labour generate elemental passions within the party. It was evident in the insights of Lord Mandelson who claimed that 'if you shut the door on New Labour you are effectively slamming the door in the faces of the millions of voters who voted for our party because we were New Labour ... if he [Ed Miliband] wants to create a pre-New Labour future for the party, then he and the rest of them will quickly find that that is an electoral cul-de-sac' (Winnett, 2010b).

Such comments by the architects of the New Labour project tended to support the position of the Conservative press who have sought to interpret any disavowal of New Labour as a 'lurch to the left' and a 'return to Old Labour' (Dorey and Denham, 2011: 296). Those New Labour architects are keen to protect their project and keen to reaffirm the strategic logic of their position. Their core narrative had revolved around a commitment to quality public services and enhancing social justice whilst at the same time prioritising economic efficiency – that is, the Third Way triangulation strategy that had created an electoral base of traditional working class supporters and new middle class voters. Their claim is that what made this core narrative effective as an electoral strategy was its ability to respond to the middle class desire for quality public services without appearing to require increases in direct taxation. Through this their core narrative of the Third Way and the electoral strategy of investment under New Labour or cuts under the Conservatives provided the party with an era of 'dominance' both intellectually and electorally (Beech, 2008: 1).

Central to the viability of this had been the fact that until their third term in office, Labour could emphasise how the economy had maintained steady growth and low inflation rates and that they had presided over falling unemployment. The prudence that they had displayed during their first term in office helped to establish their credibility with the financial markets and sustain their image of economic competence with the electorate, most notably the middle classes (Gamble, 2010: 648). After 1999 New Labour felt able to increase public spending which was a consequence of a rising tax yield flowing from the proceeds of economic growth (Heffernan, 2011: 167). However, the increases in public expenditure were dependent on continuing economic growth, which was in part reliant on corporate tax receipts from the finance sector where an active policy of minimal regulation was being followed (Beech, 2009a: 528).

However, the impact of the financial crash during their third term, and the response of the Brown administration, effectively 'terminated' New Labour. The banking crisis 'discredited' the economic and regulatory policies that New Labour had supported in the previous decade (Moran et al, 2011: 89). As their model of economic management unravelled and the tax yield fell as the economy went into recession, the Brown government followed up their bailing out of the banking sector by 'resorting to old fashioned methods of radical pump priming of the economy', which 'racked up unprecedented levels of public debt'. Despite this they 'continued to spend monies on social programmes when recession meant state revenues were in retreat' (Heffernan, 2011: 167).

However, even before the economic downturn unfolded there was evidence of a fracturing of that New Labour electoral coalition. This was evident from the reduction in support once in office, which was largely overlooked as they secured significant or acceptable parliamentary majorities – 13.6 million (1997); 10.7 million (2001); 9.5 million (2005) and then 8.6 million in the defeat of 2010 (Kavanagh and Cowley, 2010: 351; Heffernan, 2011: 163).

This reduction reflected the increasing disconnection between New Labour and the traditional working class base of the party. This was seen to be attributed to scepticism about their record on poverty reduction and income differentials as well as crime and immigration. Running parallel to working class scepticism were increasing doubts from amongst the middle classes who had transferred their allegiance to Labour in 1997. Liberal progressives felt alienated by policies such as ASBOs, ID cards and extending pre-charge detention for terrorist suspects, alongside their reservations about Iraq and Afghanistan (Coates, 2008: 3–16; Heffernan, 2011: 164). If such middle class voters became attracted to the Liberal Democrats so evolving electoral attitudes aided the changes of the Conservatives winning back some of those middle class defectors to New Labour. As government spending increased from 40.1 per cent of Gross Domestic Product in 1997 to 44.1 per cent after a decade of Labour governance, so there was a discernable shift in electoral attitudes on the balances between taxation and spending (Fielding, 2010: 658). By the time of their third term, the electorate was increasingly moving towards favouring reductions in taxation over further increases in spending. When combining the evolving scepticism within the different component parts of the New Labour coalition – that is, their traditional working class core base and their 1997, 2001 and 2005 middle class swing supporters – Fielding observed that by their third term New Labour was 'already losing the support of swing voters' and 'having made but a modest difference to the lives of most core supporters', the impending financial crisis would threaten to 'completely unravel the New Labour coalition' (Fielding, 2010: 658).

The option of framing electoral competition around Labour investment or Conservative cuts seemed defunct in an age of economic austerity. The banking collapse and recession undermined Labour's core narrative, their reputation for economic competence and thereby their electoral strategy. It would leave Ed Miliband with an uncomfortable legacy based around a reputation for economic incompetence and an ideational crisis about the meaning and identity of the Labour Party (Heffernan, 2011: 163).

Ed Miliband is thus left with the task of decontaminating the New Labour brand, and understandably for presentational reasons he has been keen to emphasise renewal and the transcending of New Labour (Heffernan, 2011: 175). When standing for and winning the party leadership he showed a willingness to repudiate many of the alignments around which the New Labour project had been created (Wickham-Jones and Jobson, 2010: 526). He has acknowledged the mistakes of the New Labour era in policy terms. In foreign policy terms he criticised the decision to align with the Americans in the Iraq war, whilst in economic policy terms he acknowledged that they had over-privileged the financial services and failed to address income differentials (Miliband, 2010a). On the issue of how New Labour thinking should influence the development of the party in opposition his rhetoric has been clear:

> Today our danger is to defend traditionalist New Labour solutions on every issue because this will consign us to defeat. It is my rejection of this New Labour nostalgia that makes me the modernising candidate at this election ... It is the New Labour comfort zone that we must escape: the rigidity of old formulae that have served their time, the belittling of any attempt to move on from past verities and the belief that more of the same is the way to win (Miliband, 2010b).

Other key figures within the shadow Cabinet have expressed similar sentiments about the need to transcend New Labour. Andy Burnham identified the need to address immigration and the way in which the BNP had exploited the issue (Burnham, 2010). He noted that the party was in denial and had to move beyond their concern about raising the issue as it was 'the biggest doorstep issue in constituencies where Labour lost' (Riddell, 2010) Ed Balls reaffirmed this view. He felt that Labour had stopped listening to the concerns of traditional Labour voters and immigration was one of their primary concerns as it impacted directly on their wages and living conditions. Acknowledging this and responding to it was vital if Labour was 'to rebuild trust with the British people' (Balls, 2010).

The rhetoric of key elites, from Ed Miliband to Burnham and Balls, and even David Miliband, acknowledge the need to form a new post New Labour narrative and electoral strategy. The first year in opposition has seen an incremental move away from assessing the limitations of New Labour towards a new post New Labour narrative with themes such as the 'British promise' (the expectation that children should have more life opportunities than their parents generation) and the 'squeezed middle' becoming more prevalent (Hasan and Macintyre, 2011: 294). In this context the embryonic thinking around the concept of 'Blue Labour' is gaining increasing attention. The primary intellectual influences upon Blue Labour include Maurice Glasman, a political theorist at London Metropolitan University; Marc Stears a political philosopher from University College, Oxford and Jonathan Rutherford, a Professor of Cultural Studies at Middlesex University, and the editor of *Soundings*. Significantly, Ed Miliband is described as being broadly supportive of their thinking and to be close to embracing the concept as a way of defining his leadership (Helm, 2011).

Central to their thinking is a focus on reclaiming the support of working class voters by adopting a more social conservative mindset on issues such as immigration and crime, whilst adopting an essentially economically interventionist position. To simplify it in definitional terms Goodhart described it as a marriage between the *Daily Mail* and the *Guardian* (Goodhart, 2011). In economic terms their critique of New Labour focuses on their uncritical view of the market economy and their failure to recognise the destructiveness of neo-liberalism and globalisation which has severed the connection between Labour and its community traditions. Their approach also embraces a critique of the top-down overly bureaucratic mentality of New Labour which contributed to the perception of an unresponsive state (Wintour, 2011).

However, it is their positioning on issues surrounding immigration that could be the most dangerous politically. Of New Labour Glasman has stated that they 'lied to the people about the extent of immigration ... and there's been a massive rupture of trust' (Hasan, 2011). To address that rupture Blue Labour seeks to embrace the fundamental conservatism of the working class by offering a 'conservative socialism', which defends traditional institutions and social relationships. Thus they aim to bind together traditionally small c conservative attitudes around family, faith and work ethic, with their own traditional emphasis on community and solidarity (Rooksby, 2011). Critics have focused on the aspects that engage with immigration. They argue that it smacks of making concessions to address the threat of the BNP and that in doing so the discourse has similarities with that of the BNP – for example, 'white working class'; 'influx of immigrant labour creating resentment' (Rooksby, 2011). Such reservations were intensified when Glasman appeared to suggest that they should involve English Defence League supporters within the party (Rooksby, 2011). Despite this Ed Miliband has recently (May 2011) endorsed Blue Labour thinking by providing a preface to their edited e-book entitled *The Labour Tradition and the Politics of Paradox* (Glasman et al, 2011).

The extent to which Labour will embrace this as their narrative in opposition remains to be seen. What is clear, however, is that even after a year of opposition the Labour Party has only made limited impact in terms of overcoming some of the negative images that had contributed to defeat. Of critical importance to improving the position of Labour will be the public battle to define responsibility for the negative economic climate in which the coalition are currently governing. The Conservatives, and indeed the Liberal Democrats within the coalition, have sought to blame the legacy of New Labour in economic terms as a means of justifying the subsequent need to initiate a significant cuts agenda (Moran et al, 2011: 89). YouGov polling data showed that more of the electorate disagreed that the Conservatives were cutting for ideological reasons (37 felt they were; 45 felt that they were not). Establishing in the minds of the electorate that the cuts agenda is ideologically motivated, rather than economically necessary is hugely important in political terms. At the point of the first anniversary of the coalition, Labour still trailed the Conservatives on the question of 'who is best equipped to manage the economy?' (Conservatives 38 per cent; Labour 24 per cent); whilst on the question of 'who is to blame for the cuts?' the Conservatives are viewed as responsible by 23 per cent but 38 per cent felt it was a necessary consequence of the failures of the previous Labour administration (Eaton, 2011).

Although the underlying trends identified above illustrate enduring doubts about Labour, especially in terms of economic competence, the party has managed to secure and sustain a small lead in the voting intentions polling data. The poll of polls showed Labour at around 33 per cent in June 2010; whilst similar poll of polls for October and November showed them just two percentage points behind the Conservatives. Both parties were polling an average of 40 per cent in the December poll of polls, and Labour have secured a lead in the poll of polls in the opening months of 2011 (Worcester et al, 2011: 276).

However, despite this Labour endured a mixed performance in the first crucial test of the leadership of Ed Miliband – the May local elections; the Welsh Assembly and Scottish Parliament elections and the AV referendum (Watt, 2011b). The Welsh elections produced a satisfactory outcome as they secured 30 of the 60 assembly seats and were able to form an administration in their own right, rather than continue in coalition (Morris, S., 2011). The English local council election results did see Labour making gains (with a 26 increase in the number of local councils under their control) but their 57 councils fell short of the 157 councils under Conservative control. Moreover, most of the advances that Labour did make were at the expense of the Liberal Democrats rather than the Conservatives. The Scottish Parliament elections proved to be a disappointment. In what had been traditionally a Labour heartland they saw the SNP secure 69 of the 129 seats as compared to Labour on 37. In the aftermath of defeat Ed Miliband would order review into the Scottish Labour Party, as a campaign insider admitted that 'it was a total disaster at all key levels of policy, organisation, personnel and message' (Watt, 2011b).

The AV referendum was also an uncomfortable experience for Labour. Ed Miliband argued for a 'yes' vote and campaigned hard for it. He did not receive too much internal party, or media criticism in the aftermath of the no verdict, as the attention of the political class was on the Liberal Democrats performance and divisions and Labour's poor showing in Scotland. During the course of a campaign Ed Miliband suffered from public criticism of his stance from within his own shadow ministerial team and from heavyweight former Cabinet ministers from the Blair era. The shadow Health Secretary, John Healey, described AV as 'perverse' and likely to be beneficial to only the BNP and the Liberal Democrats (Grice, 2011b). The former Home Secretary, David Blunkett noted that 'the Labour No campaign now includes over half of Labour's MPs, four out of five councillors, and thousands of Labour activists.' Moreover, Blunkett (who like fellow former Cabinet heavyweights, John Reid and Margaret Beckett, campaigned hard for the No camp) admitted to being worried about the attitude of the Labour leadership and Yes camp towards them. He felt that their accusation that those who were on the No camp for Labour were 'Conservative stooges' had the capacity to 'create underlying tensions that will need to be healed' (Chapman, 2011).

The AV campaign and its immediate aftermath shed some light onto the tactics that the Labour Party are developing *vis-à-vis* the Liberal Democrats. They appear to have adopted a view that Nick Clegg is politically toxic, and that the weakness of his leadership position and the huge condemnation that has been directed at him, means that Labour can secure political capital by attacking Clegg personally more than the Liberal Democrats as a party. During the course of the AV campaign Ed Miliband was prepared to align himself with senior Liberal Democrats and shared a platform with the Business Secretary Vince Cable, and the Liberal Democrat Party President, Tim Farron. He was prepared to emphasise the need to avoid the two progressive parties opposing each other again and allowing Conservative dominance as was the case in the twentieth century (Porter, 2011). However, he refused to share a platform with Nick Clegg, and would later comment that 'I know this referendum is far harder to win because of Nick Clegg's broken promises. But we can't reduce the second referendum in British political history to the betrayal of one man' (Wintour and Stratton, 2011b). Having described the Clegg era as an 'aberration' and that the Liberal Democrats were not likely to take a historic and decisive turn to aligning themselves with the Conservatives, Ed Miliband encouraged them to think again about the merits of propping up a Conservative administration. In seeking to offer the possibility of future cooperation between the two parties, Ed Miliband symbolically asked Liberal Democrat ministers to abandon the government by playing to their progressive consciences:

> Do they want Tory policies or progressive ones? .... If they are in favour of new politics they should start by keeping their promises and reflecting the will of those who put them into parliament. If they are not in favour of these Tory policies they should stand up for what they believe or leave the cabinet. They can come and work with us. My door is always open (Helm and Boffey, 2011).

Conclusion

Labour entered opposition in the knowledge that the political, economic and intellectual climate, and the individuals that had shaped the New Labour years, had been removed. Ed Miliband has inherited a difficult legacy. Overcoming the central dilemmas of electoral perceptions of economic mismanagement and incompetence, and resolving the ideational questions of New Labour is not made easier by the financial position of the party. By the time of the 2010 general election Labour was still best described as cash strapped. After a year of opposition they carry a £10 million debt, and were increasingly reliant on the trade unions for their financial support. Whereas 51 per cent of their funding came from the trade unions just before losing office, that figure was 87 per cent by May 2011 (Curtis, 2011b).

Despite these difficulties some political commentators have suggested that Labour have made a relatively good transition from government to opposition. Such assertions are based on historical comparisons. For example, Hickson notes that after earlier defeats, Labour have been engulfed by 'deep and damaging ideological splits between its left and right wing factions', and that 'one good reason to be optimistic was that this did not occur after the 2010 defeat and its unlikely to do so' (Hickson, 2011: 256). Moreover, the defeat that Labour suffered was not as bad as was feared. In percentage terms their return (29 per cent) was their second worse since the 1920s. However, their parliamentary representation (at 258) left them just short of the 271 that they secured under Neil Kinnock in 1992 (on 34 per cent), and 258 is considerably higher than the Conservatives secured in 1997 when their 31 per cent vote share provided only 165 MPs. Significantly upon entering opposition Labour have avoided the flat-lining that the Conservatives suffered in the 1997 to 2005 period – unlike William Hague and Iain Duncan Smith, Ed Miliband can claim to have made some positive impact in the standing of the party in terms of opinion polling data (Worcester et al, 2011: 276–7).

However, polling leads are no guarantee of future electoral success. Neil Kinnock had occasions when he held a lead over both Margaret Thatcher and John Major, but lost both the forthcoming elections of 1987 and 1992. The Conservatives under David Cameron had regular double digit leads in 2008 and 2009 but the prospect of a working majority dissolved in the months leading up to the 2010 general election (Rawnsley, 2011c). Ultimately, the future of Labour and Ed Miliband will be determined by events beyond their control, 'not the least the state of the economy and the success or otherwise – and the popularity or otherwise – of the coalition's austerity measures' (Norton, 2011a: 259). All that they can do is ensure that they fulfil the *sufficient* condition identified in the introduction of this chapter – that is, be seen to offer a viable and credible alternative party of government and Prime Minister – and hope that the coalition government provide the *necessary* condition – that is, a record of governing incompetence for the opposition to expose and exploit.

Acknowledgement

We would like to express our appreciation to Peter Dorey and Andrew Denham for providing a copy of their *British Politics* paper on the Labour Party Leadership Election prior to its publication.

16
Conclusion

Timothy Heppell and David Seawright

The introduction to this edited collection emphasised the potential value of using the Bulpitt statecraft model to aid our understanding of the transition from opposition to coalition government for the Conservatives under David Cameron. In basic terms statecraft can be interpreted as the art of winning elections (the politics of support) and governing competence (the politics of power) (Bulpitt, 1986: 19–39). A winning electoral strategy (propelling the party from opposition into government), will then require the sustaining of political argument hegemony (that is the dominance of elite debate) and evidence of governing competence. These dimensions, alongside successful party management, will then feed into another winning electoral strategy, thus confirming the success of the statecraft strategy (Bulpitt, 1986: 21–2). Our conclusion offers an audit of the Conservatives statecraft strategy at the point of the anniversary of their first year in office in terms of these dimensions.

Cameron and the Conservatives: Questions of party management

The last Conservative Prime Minister before Cameron, John Major, had his Prime Ministerial tenure disfigured by his inability to effectively manage party tensions surrounding European policy and the legacy of Thatcherism. This was a significant factor (although not the only factor) in the collapse of the mode of statecraft that had propelled the Conservatives to four successive election victories between 1979 and 1992 (Stevens, 2002: 119–50). When political leadership comparisons are made, Cameron is often considered against Margaret Thatcher and Tony Blair rather than John Major who has been widely derided as a weak and ineffective party manager (Evans, 2010: 225–343; McAnulla, 2010: 286–314). In party management terms, however, comparing Cameron with Major illustrates the centrality of context. When Cameron was faced with the dilemma of whether to seek to govern as a minority administration or as a coalition the memory of the paralysis of the Major administration was an influence. Amongst a myriad of considerations was the fear of being seen to be beholden to right-wing backbenchers whose loyalty to him was questionable and who were critical of him for his failure to deliver an outright victory (Stuart, 2011: 48). Not only could a minority administration face difficulties in parliament if Labour and Liberal Democrats voted together against them, but it would have faced the humiliation of parliamentary defeats and an image of disunity caused by rebellions by their own right wing. Norton notes that the fear of being held hostage by their own right wing, and the damage it could create to the image of Cameron as Prime Minister, was a dominant thought amongst Cameron's advisors notably Steve Hilton (Norton, 2011a: 254).

In this context, it is interesting to consider the comparative parliamentary rebellion rates experienced by Major and Cameron. Major operated with a small and dwindling majority and experienced a 13 per cent rebellion rate over the course of the five year Parliament (Cowley, 1999: 19–20). The rebellion rate amongst Conservative parliamentarians alone in the early stages of the Cameron coalition has been at around the 35 per cent mark, and when compared to the Conservative rebellion rate in the 2005–10 Parliament in opposition, there has also been a threefold increase (Cowley and Stuart, 2010b: 3). This suggests that Cameron has struggled with party management issues in the transition from opposition to government, and that he should be deemed a poorer party manager than Major. But here is the crux. First of all whilst political anoraks may get excited by parliamentary rebellions, what really matters to the electorate is the perception of division as portrayed through the media. That manifests itself either through sustained media commentary on intra-party divisions or through maverick backbench parliamentarians regularly appearing on the television and radio to showcase their opposition to the party leadership (Cowley, 1997: 20). Against this yardstick it could be argued that Cameron and the Conservatives can be deemed to have dealt with the challenges of party management relatively effectively. Cameron has avoided the savaging that Major experienced because whereas the divisive issue of the Major era – Europe – defined the Conservatives as disunited, the dominant disputes of the coalition era have divided the Liberal Democrats and Labour respectively.

The internal party unity and electoral credibility of the Liberal Democrats was savaged by university tuition fees. Their manifesto included a pledge to scrap unfair university tuition fees and every Liberal Democrat MP elected had signed a pledge stating that they would vote against any increase in fees. The subsequent decision of the coalition (in November 2010) to permit the increasing of university tuition fees up to a cap of £9,000 prompted widespread criticism and large-scale protests leading to some rioting. The departmental responsibility for piloting the legislation through Parliament also created more problems for the Liberal Democrats as it fell to Vince Cable at Business, Innovation and Skills to promote a policy which he clearly did not feel comfortable doing (Evans, 2011: 57). After flirting with the idea of abstaining on his own legislation, Cable voted in favour, but the media attention was on the 21 Liberal Democrats who voted against the government (and the eight abstainers), rather than the small number of Conservative backbenchers who opposed. Had they been a majority government, political commentators would have been focused in on the fact that the former Conservative Party leadership candidate, David Davis, had rebelled. As it was, all the focus of attention and criticism was on Nick Clegg and the Liberal Democrats for contradicting their manifesto commitment and their disunity (Lee, 2011: 15).

A similar analysis can be applied to the referendum on AV. Although many Conservatives were concerned about the concession of offering a referendum the negative media publicity from this fell primarily on the other parties. The Conservatives were unified in the opposition and the No campaign became closely associated with Cameron much to the chagrin of the Liberal Democrats. The Liberal Democrats were solidly in the Yes campaign, despite AV falling short of the type of electoral reform that they craved. Its association with them, and specifically with Clegg, meant that its subsequent rejection was seen as a 'humiliating disaster' for him and raised question marks about his leadership from activists (Hasan and Macintyre, 2011: 289). Meanwhile, as was mentioned in Chapter 15, on the issue of AV Labour was divided. The No vote and the fact that Ed Miliband was trying to face down a 'sizable and vocal opposition' amongst both his back and frontbenchers resulted in some short term political damage (Hasan and Macintryre, 2011: 290).

Thus far the reputation of Cameron and the Conservatives has not been badly damaged by the evidence of high dissension levels or media perceptions of divisions. However, the dynamics within the coalition and how they evolve carry with them real dangers for Cameron, and the potential exists for backbenchers making more impact by indiscipline through the media than in Parliament. Around the point of the first year anniversary two illustrations confirm this – healthcare reform and sentencing. The apparent *volte face* on the speed and scale of reform to the National Health Service has prompted criticism on the Conservative backbenchers. Of particular concern for Conservatives who believe that enhancing choice, competition and the involvement of the private sector must be progressed immediately was the reason for delay. The suggestion that it was a consequence of Liberal Democrat involvement irritated Conservatives, who complained about the 'gloating' of Clegg and accused Cameron and Health Secretary, Andrew Lansley, of 'caving in to Liberal Democrats' even though their coalition partners were politically weak (given their polling position and the outcome of the May elections and the AV referendum) (Watt, 2011c). Almost simultaneous to the accusation of a U-turn on healthcare reform at the behest of Liberal Democrat influence, Cameron was also incurring the wrath of social conservatives on the parliamentary right on the issue of sentencing. They felt that dominance on law and order demanded that the leadership commit to longer sentences for serious offenders. They were therefore deeply concerned about the position of Kenneth Clarke as Justice Secretary and the proposal that there could be a 50 per cent sentence reduction for all guilty pleas. With the likes of Philip Davies and Nadine Dorries becoming high profile in their condemnation, Cameron orchestrated a retreat in the face of potential rebellion (Shipman, 2011).

Cameron and the Conservatives: The Big Society and the quest for political argument hegemony

To what extent have the Conservatives obtained political argument hegemony? This involves manufacturing political debate with the objective of ensuring that the Conservatives are perceived to be the more plausible party for addressing public policy concerns: in other words attempting to organise your own core values into the political domain while simultaneously forcing the core values of Labour out of that domain, thus mobilising bias in your favour. Therefore, the successful execution of statecraft enables the Conservative leadership to secure the primacy of their policy prescriptions but it also enables them to define the political terrain over which political arguments occur (Hickson, 2005: 181).

Taylor argues that central to the formulation of a viable statecraft strategy is the articulation of a narrative of what the party stands for – the narrative conceptualises the political world for the electorate and has to do so in a communicable way (Taylor, 2005: 152). The narrative – the way in which the electorate can interpret Cameron and the Conservatives – has caused considerable debate. In the process of their transition from opposition to government, a number of identifiers have been ascribed to the Conservatives to differentiate them from their Thatcherite past. In the pre-economic crisis era in opposition some academics commented that the Cameron approach could be described as 'one-nation'; 'compassionate', 'civic' and 'progressive'; and then later it could be seen through the label of 'Red Toryism' or 'liberal conservatism' (Dorey, 2007, 2011; O'Hara, 2007; Beech, 2009b, 2011b; Blond, 2010). Such adaptations were also informed by symbolic gestures to confirm change – for example, the emphasis on feminisation and the environment, or the prioritising of international aid (Bryson and Heppell, 2010; Carter, 2009; Dunne et al, 2011). The unifying theme to these disparate themes became the Big Society narrative, which constitutes the Cameron attempt to secure dominance of elite debate or political argument hegemony.

There is a degree of scepticism towards the political value of the Big Society as the core narrative around which Cameron Conservatism is aiming to base itself. As was emphasised in Chapter 3 it simply failed to connect during the 2010 general election campaign, and yet despite this it 'remains central' to the

Conservative agenda 'despite being routinely lambasted and even declared dead on several occasions' (Brown and Blatchford, 2011: 42). Ultimately it can be argued that it has suffered from the following three main limitations, which are undermining its capacity to act as the internally unifying and externally appealing core narrative that Cameron wants and needs:

(1) The Big Society is treated with suspicion within Conservative ranks. The manner in which it has attempted to differentiate itself with Thatcherism by repudiating the 'no such thing as society' claim is antagonistic to the parliamentary right and to a large ground swell of Conservative activists.
(2) Although it may irritate Conservative activists the wider electorate remain unsure as to what it means. Whilst Cameron has sought to give it greater definitional detail by emphasising public sector reform; the empowering of communities and the encouragement of social action, it still remains clouded in clichés and vagueness.
(3) The Big Society narrative has political dangers attached to it when placed within the context of the comprehensive spending review, in the sense that it could be seen as 'a smokescreen for public service cuts through the promotion of volunteering as a cut-price alternative to state provision' (Mycock and Tonge, 2011: 56).

Therefore, how the Big Society becomes viewed by the electorate will be critical to the credibility of the Conservatives. Their capacity to obtain and sustain political argument hegemony is dependent on the ability (or lack of it) of Labour to successfully expose that alternative interpretation of the Big Society narrative. Can Labour establish and retain an electoral belief that the Big Society narrative is an opportunistic and ideologically (that is, Thatcherite) driven project to implement swinging public sector cuts? The challenge for Cameron and the Conservatives is to counter the accusation that the Big Society is simply a cover for cuts. Will they be able to convince the electorate that fundamentally rethinking the role of the state and the nature of public service delivery is both necessary and indeed desirable (Brown and Blatchford, 2011: 42–5)? Ultimately, however, debates on whether the Big Society narrative is a cover for cuts will be considered within the context of debates surrounding the competence or otherwise of the Cameron-led coalition. Should the economic strategy be deemed to have been necessary *and* effective then the Big Society narrative might become seen as 'short-hand for a new settlement between British citizens and their state, much as the Welfare state captured the new dispensation after World War Two' (Pattie and Johnston, 2011: 404). However, should the economic strategy come to be seen as flawed and a failure (cutting too much and too quickly and prompting a double dip recession) then the Big Society narrative might 'prove to be just another empty phrase touted by a party in opposition to present a picture of itself as fresh and forward looking', (such as Harold Wilson and the 'white heat of technological revolution'), which gradually fades from view (Pattie and Johnston, 2011: 405).

Cameron and the Conservatives: Governing competence and reducing the risks of policy failure

The end of our introduction cited the insights of Richard Hayton who suggested that the decision to enter the coalition *could* come to be seen as an 'astute piece of high politics' and a prelude to a period of Conservative dominance (Hayton, forthcoming, a). By high politics Hayton was referring to the statecraft emphasis on the Conservative desire to define (and restrict) what constitutes high politics. The logic of this is clearly outlined by Hickson, who comments that 'minimising the number of policy areas' that a Conservative government can be deemed to be 'responsible for' will limit the 'number of controversies in which it could become embroiled in'. By a narrow definition of high politics, Conservative governments should aim to depoliticise issues, thus limiting their responsibilities and broadening their governing autonomy, whilst enhancing perceptions of their competence, and improving their re-election chances (Hickson, 2005: 181).

For Cameron and the Conservatives a central theme underpinning their approach to government has been the discourse of there is no alternative. Cameron has been comfortable with the idea of reducing his government's culpability by reiterating the '[inherited] problem of Britain's over-centralised system of government, the emergence of a broken society and the legacy of the Labour Party's profligacy, which led to the creation of a budget deficit that placed the UK economy in peril' (Kerr et al, 2011: 203).

It is at this juncture that we can return to the concept of high politics and suggest that the Cameron approach, and the Big Society narrative, can be best seen within the context of depoliticisation and an attempt to redefine the parameters of high politics. As Christopher Byrne, Emma Foster and Peter Kerr mentioned in Chapter 2 depoliticisation does constitute a core plank to the Cameron governing strategy, and involves a deliberate strategy of *attempting* to place responsibility for decision-making 'at one remove' from government (Burnham, 2001; Flinders and Buller, 2006). As Kerr et al have noted elsewhere this can be viewed as a form of statecraft which is designed 'primarily to service the continuation of power and the maintenance of political office by reducing the risks of policy failure' thereby potentially allowing them 'to distance themselves from accountability while enhancing their electoral prospects' (Kerr et al, 2011: 200).

Not only can the Conservatives governing strategy be seen within the context of depoliticisation to reduce the risks of policy failure, but it can also be seen as the politics of deflection (Lee, 2011: 9–13). Deflection incorporates a number of dimensions. In an inter-party context it implies apportioning blame for the economic conditions that they have inherited on the economic mismanagement of New Labour and the insatiable demand for public sector budget increases that were created between 1997 and 2010 (Beech, 2011b: 271–6). In an inter-party (but intra-governmental) context, it involves the sharing of responsibility with the Liberal Democrats for the retrenchment of the state (Laws, 2010: 51, 200). The sharing of responsibility enables Cameron to narrate their political strategy around the politics of necessity and national interest with far greater conviction. This is of particular significance given that during the course of the general election campaign the Liberal Democrats had sided with Labour on the dangers of cutting too much and too soon, but when negotiating with the Conservatives they 'succumbed' to the latter's view on the necessity of cutting the deficit straightaway (Russell, 2010: 515). A majority Conservative administration engaging in a similar political strategy would be seen to be more ideologically motivated: Liberal Democrat endorsement legitimates the strategy and ensures that the so-called progressive alliance is on opposing sides of this debate (Lee, 2011: 10). Indeed, governing as part of a coalition allows Cameron some political leeway in terms of his own party and specifically his right wing. When he chooses to disassociate his government from the concerns or images of the socially conservative right this can be attributed to the necessities of coalition politics (Snowdon, 2010: 415).

Cameron and the Conservatives: Another winning electoral strategy?

Will depoliticisation and deflection work? Does the performance of the Conservatives suggest that the Cameron configured form of statecraft can provide them with the basis for electoral hegemony? That is a difficult question to answer as events will unfold over the next few years that may alter the assumptions that exist at the end of their first year in office. What can be said at this juncture is that their statecraft strategy is a high risk approach the success of which will be largely (but not exclusively) determined by the performance of the economy leading up to 2015.

At the point of the first anniversary of the coalition very few discernable trends in terms of party competition can be seen, other than the hugely negative impact of the coalition upon the Liberal Democrats in the opinion polls (Paun, 2011: 10). As David Denver noted in Chapter 4, Labour have established and sustained a small opinion polling lead once in opposition. But as Chapter 15 highlighted, the personal ratings for Ed Miliband remain poor and they still trail the Conservatives as the party best equipped to manage the economy. The Conservatives (or the coalition) do appear to have gained a grudging acceptance that fiscal readjustment is necessary (McCrae, 2011: 36). However, engagement with their core narrative – the Big Society – remains weak (Worcester et al, 2011: 260). The Conservatives have remained relatively close to their general election return of 36 per cent throughout the first year, with Labour support being largely interpreted as being at the expense of the Liberal Democrats. Whilst Cameron's personal ratings have declined he remains an asset to the Conservatives, Miliband is less popular than the party he leads (Hasan and Macintyre, 2011: 290). Asked which party has benefitted the most from the transition to coalition politics 14 per cent say the Liberal Democrats; 19 per cent say Labour; 24 per cent say the coalition parties jointly; and 36 per cent say the Conservatives (Nye, 2011: 74).

What we can say is for the Conservatives themselves and for British politics the transition to coalition government could become viewed as a critical juncture. In Chapter 5, Andrew Gamble concluded that the strategy for deficit reduction carried with it huge risks, but that Cameron and Osborne hope that their economic and electoral strategies can run hand-in-hand. That is to say that they will if they do have a narrative of economic growth to promote, then their status as being superior to Labour in terms of economic management will be retained and re-election will follow. An assumption is made here. If there is evidence of their remedial economic strategy being seen to work then they will reap the electoral dividend and not the Liberal Democrats (Russell, 2010: 522). Conservative strategists are hoping that Cameron's 'embrace of the Liberal Democrats will prove to be fatal for the latter, leaving the country no option, unless it is prepared to give Labour another try, to elect a Conservative majority government next time around' (Bale and Sanderson-Nash, 2011: 250).

Perceptions of economic competence and cohesion between and within the coalition partners will be critical to the future success of the coalition overall and the Conservatives specifically as the dominant partner. The years leading up to the supposed next general election on 7 May 2015 could result in one of four possible scenarios emerging. First, evidence of governing failure, especially in the economic sphere places such pressures on Liberal Democrats that they react to the impact on their popularity by abandoning the coalition and returning to the opposition benches, leaving the Conservatives to attempt to govern as a minority administration until the end of the Parliament. Second, the fragmentation of the coalition could involve leftward leaning Liberal Democrats abandoning the coalition, and for differing reasons, some right-wing Conservatives withdrawing their support. Third, the coalition survives the difficulties that will confront them over the years leading up to 2015 and then gives way to traditional electoral competition. Fourth, the coalition survives but the two parties come to believe that they have a vested interest in presenting themselves to the electorate through a mutually supporting electoral arrangement or a formal pact. Conservative MP Nick Boles has been at the forefront of advocating a formal pact, allowing Conservative candidates a free run against other parties where the Conservative is the more likely victor and vice versa where the Liberal Democrats are stronger than the Conservatives. The view of the two parties seeking to plan a two term coalition arrangement is something that has secured the qualified endorsement of John Major (Boles, 2011: 193; Snowdon, 2011: 195–6).

Should the coalition's high risk economic strategy not deliver evidence of economic improvement the statecraft strategy that Cameron has crafted (stumbled upon) may unravel. Should they suffer from a double dip recession, and increasing electoral disenchantment and declining living standards and possibly increasing public sector strike activity, what will Cameron and Osborne do? Engaging in a readjustment of their economic strategy would not be seen as pragmatic – it would be portrayed as a U-turn. To back down on their deficit reduction strategy may well incur the wrath of the financial markets but it would also carry with it seismic political implications (Elliott, 2011). The parliamentary right of the Conservative Party, long suspicious of Cameron, would be apoplectic and in fear of this eventuality they have already begun comparing Cameron to Edward Heath, whose 1970–1974 administration incurred the derision and despair of the right for its economic policy U-turn. Not only would the internal cohesion of the Conservatives be damaged but their external appeal would be undermined as their claim to economic credibility would be questioned. Ed Balls would berate them and assert that the deficit reduction plan had been a 'reckless gamble' and they had been forced to back down. Backing down on the speed and scale of the deficit reduction plan would also legitimate Labour as an opposition party by validating the position that Balls has taken (Johnson, 2011). In such a scenario Labour may well acquire a lead in terms of the party of economic competence, and as such the Conservatives would be struggling to claim to have dominance of elite debate – that is, political argument hegemony. As their governing competence is questioned and they cannot claim to possess political hegemony, so internal party,divisions of party strategy will intensify – in effect the Cameron statecraft strategy could unravel, leading to either a majority Labour administration post-2015 or a Lib-Lab coalition.

However, should such eventualities be avoided, and the end of the coalition occurs with the Conservatives being elected as a majority administration in 2015, (or the re-election of another Con-Lib coalition), then academics will want to reflect on the success of the statecraft strategy deployed by Cameron and the Conservatives. We can offer a series of possible interpretations through which academics may come to view that transition from opposition to coalition should the Conservatives secure re-election:

(1) A return to pragmatic Conservatism constructed to stall the development of a centre-left progressive realignment

This scenario recognises the strategic reasons why Cameron was so keen to form a coalition with the Liberal Democrats after failing to secure a majority. The fear for the Conservatives was the possibility of a Labour-Liberal Democrat coalition being formed. After all when the Conservatives were last in power the Liberal Democrats had ended their position of equidistance (1995) having taken a strategic decision to position themselves as an anti-Conservative Party. They had devoted their energies towards forging greater cooperation between themselves and Labour, and then leader Paddy Ashdown and Blair discussed the benefits of the realignment of the left. Between 1994 and 1997 the two parties resembled an anti-Conservative alliance (Russell, 2010: 512). Ultimately, however, the size of the parliamentary majority that New Labour secured made the need to develop the project with the Liberal Democrats less important (Russell and Fieldhouse, 2005: 39–41).

The project, and the close relationship that was being fostered between the Liberal Democrats and Labour, tied into a long cherished aspiration (indeed assumption) among progressives that eventually there would be an electoral outcome that would permit/require the formation of a Lib-Lab coalition. The significance of this, and the dangers implicit within were not lost on Cameron and leading Conservative strategists. The now ironic hung parliament party election broadcast reflected their fears that in a hung parliament situation the natural inclination of the Liberal Democrats would be to aim to form a coalition with Labour (Evans, 2011: 58–9). They knew that for such progressives, who had aimed to foster greater cooperation between the Liberal Democrats and Labour, there was a clear objective 'to mobilise the supposedly natural anti-Tory majority in the electorate to lock the Conservatives out of power, possibly forever' (Bale and Sanderson-Nash, 2011: 249).

A scenario in which a Lib-Lab coalition could be formed carried with it the risks of electoral reform that could be hugely disadvantageous to the Conservatives. Offering a referendum on AV to finalise a coalition deal with the Liberal Democrats, was a compromise worth making by Cameron to prevent a Lib-Lab deal being formed (even though the parliamentary arithmetic looked hugely problematic) (Russell, 2010: 514). Hayton argues that the subsequent conduct of Cameron should be viewed as an act of pragmatic statecraft. By persuading the Liberal Democrats to coalesce with the Conservatives Cameron, he argues, created a roadblock to their vision of a permanent realignment of British politics along progressive centre left lines. Moreover, by then defeating them on the AV referendum, Cameron has protected the long-term electoral competitiveness of the Conservatives (Hayton, forthcoming, a). Thus the coalition was simply a defensive protective measure on behalf of Cameron and the Conservatives.

(2) *The completion of the decontamination of the Conservative brand thus enabling the coalition to be seen as a realignment of the centre right*

The realignment of the centre-right argument is the second way in which the transition of the Conservatives from opposition to government under Cameron may come to be viewed. This viewpoint may come to emphasise how the aspiration and assumption that a progressive alliance would occur in a hung parliament scenario was not only stalled by Cameron but manipulated by him. Cameron turned a hugely negative situation for himself and his party and transformed it into an opportunity to forge a realignment of the centre right (Gamble, 2010: 644).

This interpretation suggests that Cameron has been genuinely committed to the 'modernisation' of the Conservatives and the objective of transcending their Thatcherite legacy. In this context Hayton suggests that it was Clegg who handed Cameron his 'clause IV' moment (Hayton, forthcoming, a). Whilst Boles may talk of electoral pacts and the combining of the best bits of liberalism and conservatism 'for the rest of this decade' (Boles, 2011: 190), it may be more plausible to see the re-alignment of the centre right not as collaboration and cooperation with the Liberal Democrats but in terms of exploitation and erosion. The dynamics of party competition may be transformed by the realignment of the centre right, as Hayton observes:

> Cameron might hope, for example that it will split Liberal Democrat support (and perhaps even the party itself), with a chunk of third party voters returning to the Conservative fold. If he can broaden the Conservative appeal to once again regularly command the support of over 40 per cent of the electorate, Cameron will have laid the ground for another lengthy period of Conservative electoral dominance (Hayton, forthcoming, a).

The two interpretations shed light on how the parties may be positioned in relation to each other and how Cameron was seeking to retain the electoral competitiveness of the Conservatives. The other two interpretations consider how their policy agenda and political constraints will come to be viewed. Will the Cameron era become viewed as a continuation of the New Labour agenda or a reaffirmation of Thatcherism?

(3) A continuation of aspects of the New Labour agenda reaffirming the triangulation of Conservatism to altered political terrain and confirming Cameron as the 'heir to Blair'

During the opposition years Cameron did acknowledge that the New Labour emphasis on combining social justice and economic efficiency constituted common ground in British Politics, and therefore he was seen as having moved the Conservatives closer to the stances of New Labour, and making them appear more centrist (McAnulla, 2010: 294, 300, 306). Indeed, prior to the onset of the recession it can be argued that there was a clear convergence between the two parties (Lee, 2009c: 44–59; Lee, 2009b: 60–79). When Cameron first acquired the party leadership the Conservatives operated on the assumption that as the economy had been growing for more than a decade and Labour were being endorsed for their economic competence, there was no political capital to be gained by challenging them on their economic record (Lee, 2009c: 58). That being the case the focus should not be economic, but social, with the implication being that Labour had presided over social decline (Lee, 2009c: 45). Through their focus on the social it was clear that Cameron was seeking to 'reach out' beyond his core constituency and 'establish credibility on issues long considered the territory of opponents' – that is, eliminating poverty through raising quality of life for all; fighting social injustice; tackling environmental threats; human rights and improving the quality of public services (McAnulla, 2010: 295). Ensuing rhetoric on the environment; on feminisation; on championing the National Health Service; supporting state schools; attacking 'fat cat' salaries; defending professional autonomy in the public sector, constituted 'reach out' rhetoric that was designed to symbolise how the Conservatives were disassociating themselves from the age of Thatcher and the ideology of Thatcherism. These rhetorical devices and policy positions were also entirely consistent with New Labour discourse and reflected a desire to compete with New Labour on public expenditure, and negate the investment versus cuts strategy that had propelled Blair through three successful election campaigns. Cameron had pledged to increase public expenditure, especially on health and education, to break that association with Thatcherism, and demonstrate that the Conservatives were genuine in their desire to 'tackle social fragmentation and inequality' and thereby mend what they defined as 'broken Britain' (Dorey, 2009: 260).

This attempt to fight on the ideological territory laid out by New Labour showed that the Conservatives were seeking to expropriate (or negate) opposition dominance on key electoral variables. This had been a core element of the New Labour strategy under Blair in the early years – say for example, law and order – and thus Cameron was deploying similar triangulation methods as used by Blair and third way acolytes (McAnulla, 2010: 292). Just as New Labour and the third way aimed to transcend the old definitions of left and right then so Cameron and the Conservatives are seeking to 'encourage people from a plethora of political traditions to identify with the modern Conservative leadership' (McAnulla, 2010: 297). In this context Cameron has reaffirmed the political strategies of New Labour and Blair and can claim to be the true 'heir to Blair'; after all constructing a coalition with the Liberal Democrats and persuading them to endorse his political strategy represents the type of 'big tent' politics associated with Blair (Geddes and Tonge, 2010: 866).

However, those 'comfortable narratives' that Cameron used in the 2005–2007 period appeared to 'assume, indeed necessitate', continued economic growth (Dorey, 2009: 261). Competition about how to share the proceeds of growth morphed in an argument about the scale and speed of deficit reduction, and this debate defined the final stages before the general election and has continued to inform party competition and debate in the first year of the coalition. However, despite this it can be argued that the transition from Labour to a Conservative-dominated coalition administration still has been characterised by some areas of policy continuity; and that these continuities could become embedded and might come to form the basis of a viable continuity with New Labour argument.

For example, recent articles by both Page and Pattie and Johnston have noted the continuities between New Labour and Cameron and the Conservatives in terms of poverty and social justice (Page, 2010: 51; Pattie and Johnston, 2011: 418–20). On their approach to addressing poverty Page notes that the Cameron strategy, like that of New Labour before them, places the focus on market participation (Page, 2010: 153). Meanwhile, Pattie and Johnston note that elements that would inform the Big Society narrative – an enhanced role for the voluntary sector and social enterprises alongside an emphasis on public sector reform – did form part of the New Labour agenda (Pattie and Johnston, 2011: 419–20). Noting on how New Labour's plans for more diverse and decentralised mode of public services floundered, Pattie and Johnston conclude that the Big Society:

> Contains distinct echoes of New Labour's agenda – only partially realised – for the restructuring of public services. New Labour had intended, for instance, greater involvement of citizens and voluntary groups in decision-making and provision of services. But intentions were sidetracked somewhat by events and by internal disputes within the Labour government. While the Blairite wing of the party wanted to push the reform agenda further, the Brownite wing was much more reluctant to let go the levers of state control ... Blair was later to describe the stalling of the public service reform agenda as one of his greatest regrets from his time in office. ... In some ways, the Big Society makes the case, as it can be seen as an attempt to take on some of Blair's unfinished business (Pattie and Johnston, 2011: 407).

(4) The continuation of Thatcherism but modernised and triangulated to reflect the altered post-New Labour political terrain

Whilst acknowledging the comparisons between the rhetoric, discourse and ideology of Cameron and New Labour McAnulla argues that the notion of consensus has to be treated with caution (McAnulla, 2010: 286–314). He argues that the third way form of politics that Cameron and the Conservatives have advanced – from opposition and through into the transition into coalition government – differs significantly from New Labour in philosophical terms (McAnulla, 2010: 301, 306). Given the antipathy of Cameron and the Conservatives to the state, it may be best to view their approach as a continuation or modification of Thatcherism (Kerr et al, 2011: 196–200; Seawright, 2010: 168).

This interpretation suggests that Cameron and the Conservatives could be accused of exploiting the current economic crisis to impose a new limited-state strategy and neo-liberal narrative in an 'age of austerity'. Hayton suggests that they are exploiting a unique opportunity to roll back the frontiers of the state and implement a level of welfare reform that both the Thatcher and Major administrations felt unable to embark upon (Hayton, forthcoming, c). This interpretation requires a distinction to be made between the rhetoric of Cameron (particularly in the early years of opposition and the age of prosperity) and the positions adopted and implemented in government (Griffiths, 2011: 26). That is to say that Cameron is advancing a Thatcherite strategy but presenting it rhetorically in a more palatable form. The Big Society is 'nothing more than recycled Thatcherite slogan' in an 'inverted form'; rather than use the Thatcherite discourse of 'rolling back the frontiers of the state' Cameron has deployed the more original 'rolling forward of society' approach through his Big Society narrative (Kerr et al, 2011: 197). As Beech argues the early stages of government suggest that their commitment to neo-liberalism 'trumps other competing concerns' and this should not be ignored amongst the altered political moderation *vis-à-vis* the environment, international aid or NHS funding (Beech, 2010: 1382; Beech, 2011b: 278). The approach of Cameron and the Conservatives demonstrates their lack of faith in the ability of the state to achieve positive social ends and their Thatcherite belief in the merits of a smaller state and marketised provision in public services (Griffiths, 2011: 23).

However, these arguments about continuation with either New Labour or Thatcherism could be seen to be problematic, as they are partial in terms of the policy areas selected to demonstrate continuation and many of the political methods may not fit clearly into the narratives being outlined. It may therefore be better to envisage the current Conservative approach by the signifier of the Big Society, and recognise that Thatcherism and the Third Way should be viewed as three distinct hegemonic projects which uphold neo-liberalism (Kerr et al, 2011: 197). That implies that the political discourse of New Labour can be applied to give further momentum to Thatcherism. A good example of this would be the way in which Cameron utilises the New Labour emphasis on freedom of information for Thatcherite purposes. For the centre left the rationale for freedom of information is rooted in enhancing the quality of our democracy. Cameron exploits this by utilising populist rhetoric of power to the people by arguing that freedom of information should be used to empower citizens to scrutinise government finances; presumably with the aim of identifying questionable expenditure commitments as a means of legitimising the needs for cutting spending (Kerr et al, 2011: 199).

This suggests that the Cameron era amounts to a new form of progressive Thatcherism based on a reaffirmation of neo-liberalism but rebranded to reflect the post-New Labour political terrain. The positioning of Cameron and the Conservatives is what makes the dynamics of party politics in the coalition age so intriguing for political scientists (Quinn, 2011: 411). After one year of coalition politics the Conservatives have stabilised their existing support base whilst witnessing a reduction in the support of the junior coalition partners, the Liberal Democrats (Evans, 2011: 56). The performance of the economy over the forthcoming years will be crucial to the viability of the Cameron statecraft strategy. Should a perception of competence be established and maintained then the other dimensions of successful statecraft will be retained – party management and political argument hegemony. Cameron and the Conservatives know that the current circumstances remain problematic for Ed Miliband. If Miliband decides to downgrade his recognition of the necessity of cuts and increases his attack on the austerity strategy of Cameron and Osborne, and the economy then improves in the latter part of the Parliament then this may alter the dynamics of party competition in the way that Cameron and the Conservatives want. The age of 'new politics' may actually showcase a growing divide between a Thatcherite-orientated Conservative Party alongside the neutered and marginalised Liberal Democrats, and a pre-Blair Labour Party.

Bibliography

Achato, L., Eaton, M. and Jones, C. (2010) *The Migrant Journey. Research Report 43* (London: Home Office).

Al Jazeera (2011) *How Tunisia's Revolution Began*, 26 January, available at: http://english.aljazeera.net/indepth/features/2011/01/2011126121815985483.html.

Andeweg, R., de Winter, L. and Müller, W. C. (2008) 'Parliamentary Opposition in Post-Consociational Democracies: Austria, Belgium and the Netherlands', *The Journal of Legislative Studies*, 14(1/2): 77–112.

Annesley, C. and Gains, F. (2007) 'Feminising Politics and Policy: The Impact of New Labour', in Annesley, C., Gains, F. and Rummery, K. (eds) *Women and New Labour* (Bristol: The Policy Press).

APPG (All Party Parliamentary Group on Migration) (2011) *APPG Migration Briefing 1 – Student Immigration Reforms and Their Anticipated Economic Impact*, 2 March 2011, available at: http://www.appgmigration.org.uk/reports.

Ashcroft, M. (2005) *Smell the Coffee: A Wake-up Call for the Conservative Party* (London: Michael Ashcroft).

Ashcroft, M. (2010) *Minority Verdict: The Conservative Party, the Voters and the 2010 Election* (London: Biteback).

Ashley, J. (2010) 'Policy Shouldn't Be Decided By Those Who Shout Loudest', *Guardian*, 17 October.

Aughey, A. (2010a) 'Fifth Nation: The United Kingdom Between Definite and Indefinite Articles', *British Politics*, 3(5): 265–85.

Aughey, A. (2010b) 'Anxiety and Injustice: The Anatomy of Contemporary English Nationalism', *Nations and Nationalism*, 16(3): 506–24.

Aughey, A. (2011) 'The Con-Lib Coalition Agenda for Scotland, Wales and Northern Ireland', in Lee, S. and Beech, M. (eds) *The Cameron-Clegg Government. Coalition Politics in an Age of Austerity* (Basingstoke: Palgrave Macmillan).

Bale, T. (2008a) 'Turning Round the Telescope: Centre-Right Parties and Immigration and Integration Policy in Europe', *Journal of European Public Policy*, 15(3): 315–30.

Bale, T. (2008b) 'A Bit Less Bunny Hugging and a Bit More Bunny Boiling? Qualifying Conservative Party Change Under Cameron', *British Politics*, 3(3): 270–99.

Bale, T. (2009) '"Cometh the hour, cometh the Dave": How Far is the Conservative Party's Revival All Down to David Cameron?' *The Political Quarterly*, 80(2): 222–32.

Bale, T. (2010) *The Conservative Party from Thatcher to Cameron* (Cambridge: Polity).

Bale, T. (forthcoming) 'David Cameron 2005–2010', in Heppell, T. (ed.) *Leaders of the Opposition: From Churchill to Cameron* (Basingstoke: Palgrave).

Bale, T. and Sanderson-Nash, E. (2011) 'A Leap of Faith and a Leap in the Dark', in Lee, S. and Beech, M. (eds) *The Cameron-Clegg Coalition: Coalition Politics in the Age of Austerity* (Basingstoke: Palgrave).

Bale, T. and Webb, P. (2011) 'The Conservative Party', in Allen, N. and Bartle, J. (eds) *Britain at the Polls 2010* (London: Sage).

Bale, T., Hampshire, J. and Partos, R. (2011) 'Having One's Cake and Eating It Too: Cameron's Conservatives and Immigration', *The Political Quarterly*, 82(3): 398–404.

Bale, T., Hanley, S. and Szczerbiak, A. (2010) 'May Contain Nuts? The Reality Behind the Rhetoric Surrounding the British Conservatives' New Group in the European Parliament', *The Political Quarterly*, 81(1): 85–98.

Ball, S. (2005) 'Factors in Opposition Performance: The Conservative Experience since 1867', in Ball, S. and Seldon, A. (eds) *Recovering Power: The Conservatives in Opposition since 1867* (Basingstoke: Palgrave).
Balls, E. (2010) 'We Were Wrong to Allow So Many Eastern Europeans in Britain', *Observer*, 6 June.
Barker, A. (2010) 'Five Elephant Traps for Cameron in India', *Financial Times Westminster Blog*, 27 July 2010, available at: http://blogs.ft.com/westminster/2010/07/five-elephant-traps-for-cameron-in-india/.
Barker, R. (2011) 'Big Societies, Little Platoons and the Problems with Pluralism', *The Political Quarterly*, 82(1): 50–5.
Barnes, E. (2011) 'Race for the Swing Vote', *Scotland on Sunday*, 20 February.
Bartle, J. And Crewe, I. (2002) 'The Impact of Party Leaders in Britain: Strong Assumptions, Weak Evidence', in King, A. (ed.) *Leaders' Personalities and the Outcomes of Democratic Elections* (Oxford: Oxford University Press).
BBC News (2010a) 'David Cameron Launches Indian Trade Drive', 28 July, available at: http://www.bbc.co.uk/news/uk-politics-10784317.
BBC News (2010b) 'Benefits System Overhaul "to Make Work Pay"', 11 November, available at: http://www.bbc.co.uk/news/uk-politics-11728546.
BBC News (2011) *British Military Officers to be Sent to Libya*, 19 April, available at: http://www.bbc.co.uk/news/uk-13132654.
Beckett, A. (2010) 'Is David Cameron the Master of the U-turn?' *Guardian*, 8 December.
Beckett, A. (2011) 'Ed Miliband: Welcome to My World', *Guardian*, 19 March.
Beech, M. (2008) 'New Labour and the Politics of Dominance', in Beech, M. and Lee, S. (eds) *Ten Years of New Labour* (Basingstoke: Palgrave).
Beech, M. (2009a) 'No New Vision: The Gradual Death of British Social Democracy', *The Political Quarterly*, 80(4): 526–32.
Beech, M. (2009b) 'Cameron and Conservative Ideology', in Lee, S. and Beech, M. (eds) *The Conservatives Under David Cameron: Built to Last?* (Basingstoke: Palgrave).
Beech, M. (2010) 'Change, Compromise and the Coalition: British Politics in 2010', *West European Politics*, 33(6): 1378–88.
Beech, M. (2011a) 'British Conservatism and Foreign Policy', *British Journal of Politics and International Relations*, 13(3): 348–63.
Beech, M. (2011b) 'A Tale of Two Liberalism', in Lee, S. and Beech, M. (eds) *The Cameron-Clegg Coalition: Coalition Politics in an Age of Austerity* (Basingstoke: Palgrave).
Bennett, R. (2006) 'Cameron Pledges Tax Breaks on Childcare for All', *The Times*, 20 June.
Bennett, R. (2010) 'Shadow Ministers Undermine Miliband with Doubts Over 50p Tax Rate', *The Times*, 29 November.
Bennister, M. (2011) Written evidence to the Political and Constitutional Reform Committee inquiry into *The Role and Powers of the Prime Minister* (London: House of Commons).
Berman, G. and Keep, M. (2011) *The Local Government Finance Settlement 2011–2013* (London: House of Commons Library).
BIS (Department for Business, Innovation and Skills) (2010) *A Strategy for Sustainable Growth* (London: BIS).
Blair, T. (1998) *The Third Way: New Politics for The New Century* (London: Fabian Society).
Blair, T. (1999) 'Doctrine of International Community', 24 April, Number 10 website, available at: http://www.number10.gov.uk/Page1297.
Blair, T. (2010) *A Journey* (London: Hutchinson).
Blond, P. (2009) 'The Rise of the Red Tories', 28 February, *Prospect*, 155: 32–6.

Blond, P. (2010) *Red Tory: How Left and Right Have Broken Britain and How We Can Fix It* (London: Faber).

Bochel, H. (2010) 'One Nation Conservatism and Social Policy, 1951–64', *Journal of Poverty and Social Justice*, 18(2): 123–34.

Bochel, H. and Defty, A. (2010) 'Safe as Houses? Conservative Social Policy, Public Opinion and Parliament', *The Political Quarterly*, 81(1): 74–84.

Boffey, D. (2011a) 'Liberal Democrat Grassroots Insist on Changes to Proposed Health Reforms', *Guardian*, 9 April.

Boffey, D. (2011b) 'Academic Fury Over Order to Study the Big Society', *Observer*, 27 March.

Bogdanor, V. (2010) 'The West Lothian Question', *Parliamentary Affairs*, 63(1): 156–72.

Bogdanor, V. (2011) *The Coalition and the Constitution* (Oxford: Hart Publishing).

Boles, N. (2010) *Which Way's Up? The Future for Coalition Britain and How to Get There* (London: Biteback).

Boles, N. (2011) 'The Coalition', *Public Policy Research*, 17(4): 189–94.

Boorstin, D. J. (1992) *The Image: A Guide to Pseudo-Events in America*, first published in 1961 (New York: Vintage).

Boulton, A. and Jones, J. (2010) *Hung Together* (London: Simon & Schuster).

Bradbury, J. (2006) 'Territory and Power Revisited: Theorising Territorial Politics in the United Kingdom After Devolution', *Political Studies*, 54(3): 559–82.

Bradbury, J. (2010) 'Jim Bulpitt's Territory and Power in the United Kingdom and Interpreting Political Development: Bringing the State and Temporal Analysis Back In', *Government and Opposition*, 45(3): 318–44.

Brandreth, G. (1999) *Breaking the Code: Westminster Diaries 1990–1997* (London: Weidenfeld and Nicolson).

Breakthrough Britain (2007) *Ending the Costs of Social Breakdown*, final report of the Conservative Social Justice Policy Group chaired by Right Hon. Ian Duncan Smith, available at: http://www.centreforsocialjustice.org.uk/client/downloads/overview.pdf.

Brewer, M., Browne, J. and Jin, W. (2010) *Universal Credit: A Preliminary Analysis (IFS Briefing Note 116)* (London: Institute for Fiscal Studies).

Brogan, B. (2010a) 'Beware the Seductive Charms of Clegg – He, Too, is a Politician', *The Daily Telegraph*, 15 April.

Brogan, B. (2010b) 'David Cameron Didn't Want an Easy Life – And He's Not Getting One', *Daily Telegraph*, 22 December.

Brogan, B. (2011) 'Alan Johnson's Resignation: A Disaster on All Fronts for Red Ed', *Daily Telegraph*, 20 January.

Brooks, D. (2011) *The Social Animal: A Story of How Success Happens* (London: Short Books).

Brown, A. and Blatchford, K. (2011) 'The Big Society', in Paun, A. (ed.) *One Year On: The First Year of the Coalition Government* (London: Institute for Government).

Bryson, V. and Heppell, T. (2010) 'Conservatism and Feminism: The Case of the British Conservative Party', *Journal of Political Ideology*, 15(1): 31–50.

Buckler, S. and Dolowitz, D. (2009) 'Ideology, Party Identity and Renewal', *Journal of Political Ideologies*, 14(1): 11–30.

Bulpitt, J. (1982) 'Conservatism, Unionism and the Problem of Territorial Management', in Magwick, P. and Rose, R. (eds) *The Territorial Dimension in United Kingdom Politics* (Basingstoke: Macmillan Press).

Bulpitt, J. (1986) 'The Discipline of the New Democracy: Mrs Thatcher's Domestic Statecraft', *Political Studies*, 34(1): 19–39.

Bulpitt, J. (1989) 'Walking Back to Happiness: Conservative Central Governments and Elected Local Authorities in the 1980s', in Crouch, C. and Marquand, M. (eds) *The New Centralism* (London: Basil Blackwell).

Bulpitt, J. (2008) *Territory and Power in the United Kingdom. An Interpretation* (Colchester: ECPR Press).

Burgess, C. (2011) '"The Election Will Be Won By People Not Posters" ... Advertising and the 2010 General Election', in Wring, D., Mortimore, R. and Atkinson, S. (eds) *Political Communication in Britain: The Leader Debates, the Campaign and the Media in the 2010 General Election* (Basingstoke: Palgrave).

Burke, E. (1789) *Reflections on the Revolution in France*, edited by Clark, J. C. D. (2001) (Stanford, California: Stanford University Press).

Burnham, A. (2010) *The Labour Leadership: How Important is it that the Party has a Distinctive Ideology?*, available at: http://www.fabians.org.uk/publications.

Burnham, P. (2001) 'New Labour and the Politics of Depoliticisation', *British Journal of Politics and International Relations*, 3(2): 127–49.

Butler, D. and Stokes, D. (1974) *Political Change in Britain*, 2nd edition (Basingstoke: Macmillan).

Butler, P. and Travis, A. (2011) 'Sex Trafficking Charity Loses Out to Salvation Army Over £6m contract', *Guardian*, 11 April.

Cabinet Office (2010) *Cabinet Committee System* (London: The Cabinet Office).

Cabinet Office (2011) *Applying Behavioural Insight to Health*, available at: http://www.cabinetoffice.gov.uk/sites/default/files/resources/403936_BehaviouralInsight_acc.pdf.

Cameron, D. (2005) speech: 'A Voice for Hope, for Optimism and for Change' (leadership election victory speech), 6 December.

All speeches referenced for David Cameron below, where otherwise stated, are available at: http://www.conservatives.com/News/Speeches.aspx.

Cameron, D. (2006a) speech: 'Chamberlain Lecture on Communities', 14 July.

Cameron, D. (2006b) speech: 'I Will Never Take Scotland for Granted', 15 September.

Cameron, D. (2006c) speech: 'A New Approach to Foreign Affairs – Liberal Conservatism', 11 September.

Cameron, D. (2006d) speech: 'Modern Conservatism', speech at Demos, 30 January.

Cameron, D. (2006e) speech: 'Tackling Poverty is a Social Responsibility', 24 November.

Cameron, D. (2006f) speech: 'From State Welfare to Social Welfare', 14 December.

Cameron, D. (2006g) speech: 'The Best is Yet to Come', Conservative Party conference speech, 4 October.

Cameron, D. (2006h) speech: 'The New Global Economy', 22 May.

Cameron, D. (2006i) speech: 'It's Time to Share Power with the People', 6 May.

Cameron, D. (2007a) speech: 'The EU: A New Agenda for the 21st Century', to the Movement for European Reform, Brussels, 6 March.

Cameron, D. (2007b) speech: 'Cameron: I'll Give EU a Vote', *The Sun*, 26 September.

Cameron, D. (2007c) speech: 'A Liberal Conservative Consensus to Restore Trust in Politics', 22 March.

Cameron, D. (2007d) speech: 'Stronger Together', 10 December.

Cameron, D. (2007e) speech: 'The Conservative Approach to Improving Public Services', 26 January.

Cameron, D. (2008a) speech: 'A New Political Force in Northern Ireland', 6 December.

Cameron, D. (2008b) speech: 'Democracy Should be the Work of Patient Craftsmanship', 3 September.

Cameron, D. (2008c) speech: 'Fixing Our Broken Society', speech in Glasgow, 7 July.

Cameron, D. (2008d) speech: 'to Conservative Party Conference', 1 October 2008.

Cameron, D. (2008e) speech: 'to Campaign for Preservation of Rural England', 12 May.

Cameron, D. (2009a) speech: 'to Welsh Conservative Party Conference', 29 March.

Cameron, D. (2009b) speech: 'A European Policy that People Can Believe In', London, 4 November.

Cameron, D. (2009c) speech: 'at London Gay Pride Event', 30 June.
Cameron, D. (2009d) speech: 'The Age of Austerity', 26 March.
Cameron, D. (2009e) speech: 'to Conservative Spring Forum', 19 March.
Cameron, D. (2009f) speech: 'Government Launches "Big Society" Programme', 18 May.
Cameron, D. (2009g) speech: 'People Power – Reforming Quangos', 6 July.
Cameron, D. (2010a) speech: 'on Well-Being', 25 November, available at: http://www.number10.gov.uk/news-type/speeches-and-transcripts/.
Cameron, D. (2010b) speech: 'on Families and Relationships', 10 December, available at: http://www.number10.gov.uk/news-type/speeches-and-transcripts/.
Cameron, D. (2010c) 'My Credo for My Country', *Daily Telegraph*, 2 April.
Cameron, D. (2010d) speech: 'Our Big Society Agenda', 19 July.
Cameron, D. (2010e) speech: 'The Big Society', 10 November.
Cameron, D. (2011a) speech: 'The Action We are Taking will Protect the Libyan People', 18 March.
Cameron, D. (2011b) speech: 'on Modern Public Services', 17 January, available at: http://www.number10.gov.uk/news-type/speeches-and-transcripts/.
Cameron, D. (2011c) speech: 'on Big Society', 14 February, available at: http://www.number10.gov.uk/news-type/speeches-and-transcripts/.
Cameron, D. (2011d) speech: 'on the Big Society', 23 May, available at: http://www.number10.gov.uk/news-type/speeches-and-transcripts/.
Cameron, D. (2011e) speech: 'at the Local Government Association', 28 June, available at: http://www.number10.gov.uk/news-type/speeches-and-transcripts/.
Campbell, A. (2010) 'Has the Political Poster Virtually Had Its Day?' *The Times*, 22 February.
Campbell, A. and Stott, R. (2007) *The Blair Years: Extracts from the Alistair Campbell Diaries* (London: Hutchinson).
Campbell, R. and Childs, S. (2010) '"Wags", "Wives" and "Mothers" – But What about Women Politicians?' *Parliamentary Affairs*, 63(4): 760–77.
Campbell, R., Childs, S. and Lovenduski, J. (2006) 'Women's Equality Guarantees and the Conservative Party', *The Political Quarterly*, 77(1): 18–27.
Cannon, E. (2011) 'I'm Sorry Ed, but Nose Surgery May Not Solve Your Sleep Problems', *Daily Mail*, 1 May.
Carmichael, P. (1996) 'The Changing Territorial Operating Code of the United Kingdom: Evidence from Northern Ireland', *Public Administration*, 74(3): 413–33.
Carswell, D. (2011) 'A Giant Leap Forward for Europe – and Our Government Just Agreed', 26 March, available at: http://www.talkcarswell.com/show.aspx?id=1855.
Carter, N. (2009) 'Vote Blue, Go Green? Cameron's Conservatives and the Environment', *The Political Quarterly*, 80(2): 233–42.
CBI (2011) CBI Press release, 16 February, available at: http://www.cbi.org.uk/ndbs/press.nsf/0363c1f07c6ca12a8025671c00381cc7/5ade62c325697b1e80257838006153c0?OpenDocument.
Centre for Women and Democracy (2010) '"Derisory" Increase in Women MPs', available at: http://www.cfwd.org.uk/.
Chapman, J. (2011) 'Labour at War Over AV', *Daily Mail*, 28 March.
Charmley, J. (1996) *A History of Conservative Politics 1900–1996* (Basingstoke: Macmillan).
Childs, S. (2002) 'Concepts of Representation and the Passage of the Sex Discrimination (Election Candidates) Bill', *Journal of Legislative* Studies, 8(3): 90–108.
Childs, S. (2004) *New Labour's Women MPs* (London: Routledge).

Childs, S. (2008) *Women and British Party Politics: Descriptive, Substantive and Symbolic Representation* (London and New York: Routledge).
Childs, S., Webb, P. and Marthaller, S. (2009) 'The Feminisation of the Conservative Party: Party Members' Attitudes', *The Political Quarterly*, 80(2): 204–13.
Childs, S. and Webb, P. (forthcoming) *Gender and the Conservative Party: From Iron Ladies to Kitten Heels* (Basingstoke: Palgrave Macmillan).
CIPFA (2011) 'Survey Shows Growing Fears of Council Finance Chiefs Over Budgets', available at: http://www.cipfa.org.uk/press/press_show.cfm?news_id=61280.
Clarke, H., Sanders, D., Stewart, M. and Whiteley, P. (2004) *Political Choice in Britain* (Oxford: Oxford University Press).
Clarke, H., Sanders, D., Stewart, M. and Whiteley, P. (2009) *Performance Politics and the British Voter* (Cambridge: Cambridge University Press).
Clegg, N. (2011a) Parenting speech, 17 January, available at: http://www.dpm.cabinetoffice.gov.uk/speeches.
Clegg, N. (2011b) Deputy Prime Minister's speech on the open, confident society, 3 March, available at: http://www.dpm.cabinetoffice.gov.uk/speeches.
Coates, D. (1994) *The Question of UK Decline* (London: Harvester Wheatsheaf).
Coates, D. (2008) 'Darling, It is Entirely My Fault! Gordon Brown's Legacy to Alistair and Himself', *British Politics*, 3(1): 3–21.
Coates, S. (2010) 'Tories Puzzled by Policy Pyramid', *The Times*, 18 March.
Coates, S., Elliot, F. and Mostrous, A. (2010) 'We Can't Go On Like This ... Tories Rehire Saatchi Brothers for Election Campaign', *The Times*, 26 March.
Coates, S. and Savage, M. (2011) 'Cameron Ready to Humiliate His Tory Health Minister as Sacrifice to Appease Clegg', *The Times*, 9 May.
Cockerell, M., Hennessy, P. and Walker, D. (1984) *Sources Close to the Prime Minister: Inside the Hidden World of the News Manipulators* (London: Macmillan).
Cohen, N. (2001) 'WITHOUT PREJUDICE: Is Blair Bush's Poodle? That's Unfair to Poodles', *Observer*, 25 February.
Collings, D. and Seldon, A. (2001) 'Conservatives in Opposition', *Parliamentary Affairs*, 54(4): 624–37.
Conservative Party (2001a) *Time for Common Sense* (London: Conservative Party).
Conservative Party (2001b) *Your Life, Your Council* (London: Conservative Party).
Conservative Party (2005) *The Conservative Election Manifesto 2005: Are You Thinking What We're Thinking?* (London: Conservative Party).
Conservative Party (2008a) 'Summary excerpt from *Devolution in Wales: The Way Ahead* by Rt Hon Lord Roberts of Conwy' (London: Conservative Party).
Conservative Party (2008b) *Repair Plan for Social Reform* (London: Conservative Party).
Conservative Party (2009) *Control Shift. Returning Power to Local Communities* (London: Conservative Party).
Conservative Party (2010) *Invitation to Join the Government of Britain: The Conservative Manifesto of 2010* (London: Conservative Party).
Conservative Party Women's Policy Group (2008) *Women in the World Today*, available at: http://www.conservatives.com/.
Constitution Committee, House of Lords (2011) *European Union Bill*, 13th Report, Session 2010–11, HL Paper 121 (London: The Stationery Office).
Cowley, P. (1997) *The Parliamentary Conservative Party* (Hull: Centre for Legislative Studies).
Cowley, P. (1999) 'Chaos or Cohesion: Major and the Parliamentary Conservative Party', in Dorey, P. (ed.) *The Major Premiership* (Basingstoke: Palgrave).
Cowley, P. (2002) *Revolts and Rebellions* (London: Politico's).
Cowley, P. (2005) *The Rebels* (London: Politico's).

Cowley, P. (2011) 'Rebels and Causes', *Ballots & Bullets*, available at: http://notts-politics.rg/2011/02/21/rebels-and-causes/.

Cowley, P. and Norton, P. (1999) 'Rebels and Rebellions: Conservative MPs in the 1992 Parliament', *British Journal of Politics & International Relations*, 1(1): 84–105.

Cowley, P. and Stuart, M. (2010a) 'Where Has All the Trouble Gone? British Intra-Party Divisions During the Lisbon Ratification', *British Politics*, 5(2): 133–48.

Cowley, P. and Stuart, M. (2010b) 'A Coalition with Wobbly Wings: Backbench Dissent since May 2010', available at: www.revolts.co.uk.

Crouch, C. (2008) 'What Will Follow the Demise of Privatised Keynesianism?' *The Political Quarterly*, 79(4): 476–87.

Crozier, M., Huntington, S. P. and Watanuki, J. (1975) *The Crisis of Democracy: Report on the Governability of Democracies to the Trilateral Commission* (New York: NYUP).

Curtice, J. (2009) 'Is There an English Backlash? Reactions to Devolution', in Park, A., Curtice, J., Thomson, K., Phillips, M. and Clery, E. (eds) *British Social Attitudes: The 25th Report* (London: Sage).

Curtis, P. (2011a) 'Nudge Unit Not Guaranteed to Work says Oliver Letwin', *Observer*, 20 February.

Curtis, P. (2011b) 'Labour Party Counts on Unions as Other Donors Fall Away', *Guardian*, 25 May.

Curtis, P., Stratton, A. and Watt, N. (2010) 'William Hague Hid Lord Ashcroft's Tax Status for Months', *Guardian*, 4 March.

Cutts, D., Ford, R. and Goodwin, M. (2011) 'Anti-Immigrant, Politically Disaffected or Still Racist After All? Examining the Attitudinal Drivers of Extreme Right Support in Britain at the 2009 European Elections', *European Journal of Political Research*, 50(3): 418–40.

d'Ancona, M. (2010) 'David Cameron Has Just Won the Next General Election', *Sunday Telegraph*, 26 September.

d'Ancona, M. (2011a) 'Downing Street's Backroom Boys Want to Save the Tories from Themselves', *Daily Telegraph*, 19 February.

d'Ancona, M. (2011b) 'David Cameron's True Character Will Be Revealed on the World Stage', *Daily Telegraph*, 26 February.

Davidson, J. (2011) *Downing Street Blues: A History of Depression and Other Mental Disorders in British Prime Ministers* (Jefferson: McFarland).

Davies, A. J. (1996) *We the Nation: The Conservative Party and the Pursuit of Power* (London: Abacus).

de Bruxelles, S. (2011) 'Wales "Comes of Age" as Voters Back More Powers for Assembly', *The Times*, 5 March.

Democracy Task Force (2007) *An End to Sofa Government* (London: Conservative Party).

Democracy Taskforce (2008) *Answering the Question: Devolution, The West Lothian Question and the Future of the Union* (London: Conservative Party).

Denham, A. and O'Hara, K. (2007) 'The Three "Mantras": "Modernization" and the Conservative Party', *British Politics*, 2(2): 167–90.

Denham, A., Dorey, P. and Garnett, M. (2011) *From Crisis to Coalition: The Conservative Party 1997–2010* (Basingstoke: Palgrave).

Denver, D. (1998) 'The Government That Could Do No Right', in King, A., Denver, D., McLean, I., Norris, P., Norton, P., Sanders, D. and Seyd, P. (eds) *New Labour Triumphs: Britain at the Polls* (New York: Chatham House).

Denver, D. and Fisher, J. (2009) 'Blair's Electoral Record', in Casey, T. (ed.) *The Blair Legacy: Politics, Policy, Governance and Foreign Affairs* (Basingstoke: Palgrave Macmillan).

Denver, D. and Garnett, M. (forthcoming) 'The Popularity of British Prime Ministers', *British Journal of Politics and International Relations.*

Direct Democracy (2005) *Direct Democracy: An Agenda for a New Model Party* (London: direct-democracy.co.uk).

Dodd, V. (2010) 'Budget Cuts Could Break Equality Laws, Theresa May Warned Chancellor', *Guardian*, 3 August.

Dodds, K. and Elden, S. (2008) 'Thinking Ahead: David Cameron, the Henry Jackson Society and British Neo-Conservatism', *British Journal of Politics and International Relations*, 10(3): 347–63.

Dorey, P. (1999) 'Despair and Disillusion Abound: The Major Premiership in Perspective', in Dorey, P. (ed.) *The Major Premiership* (Basingstoke: Palgrave).

Dorey, P. (2003) 'Conservative Policy Under Hague', in Garnett, M. and Lynch, P. (eds) *The Conservatives in Crisis* (Manchester: Manchester University Press).

Dorey, P. (2007) 'New Direction or Another False Dawn? David Cameron and the Crisis of British Conservatism', *British Politics*, 2(2): 137–66.

Dorey, P. (2009) 'Sharing the Proceeds of Growth: Conservative Economic Policy Under David Cameron', *The Political Quarterly*, 80(2): 259–69.

Dorey, P. (2010) 'Faltering Before the Finishing Line: The Conservative Party's Performance in the 2010 General Election', *British Politics*, 5(4): 402–35.

Dorey, P. (2011) *British Conservatism: The Politics and Philosophy of Inequality* (London: I. B. Tauris).

Dorey, P. and Denham, A. (2011) 'O Brother, Where Art Thou? The Labour Party Leadership Election of 2010', *British Politics*, 6(3): 286–316.

Driver, S. (2008) 'Poverty, Social Justice and the Labour Government, 1997–2007', *Benefits: The Journal of Poverty and Social Justice*, 16(2): 157–67.

Driver, S. (2009) '"Fixing Our Broken Society": David Cameron's Post-Thatcherite Social Policy', in Lee, S. and Beech, M. (eds) *The Conservatives Under Cameron: Built to Last?* (Basingstoke: Palgrave Macmillan).

Driver, S. (2011) 'Welfare Reform and Coalition Politics in the Age of Austerity', in Lee, S. and Beech, M. (eds) *The Cameron-Clegg Government* (Basingstoke: Palgrave Macmillan).

Driver, S. and Martell, L. (1998) *New Labour: Politics After Thatcherism* (Cambridge: Polity).

Driver, S. and Martell, L. (2002) *Blair's Britain* (Cambridge: Polity).

Duncan Smith, I. (2004) *Britain's Conservative Majority* (London: Centre for Social Justice).

Dunne, M., Hall-Matthews, D. and Lightfoot, S. (2011) 'Our Aid'*: UK International Development Policy Under the Coalition Political Insight*, 2: 29–31.

Durose, C. and Gains, F. (2007) 'Engendering the Machinery of Governance', in Annesley, C., Gains, F. and Rummery, K. (eds) *Women and New Labour* (Bristol: The Policy Press).

Eagleton, T. (2011) 'AC Grayling's Private University of Odious', *Guardian*, 6 June.

Eaton, G. (2011) 'How Unpopular are the Cuts Now', *The New Statesman*, 25 March.

Economist, The (2010a) 'How Broken is Britain?' 4 February.

Economist, The (2010b) 'Through a Glass Darkly', 4 February.

Economist (2010c) 'Bagehot: The Love-In', 15 May.

Economist (2011) 'Britain's Most Important Civil Servant: The Unsung Radical', *The Economist*, 10 February.

Edemariam, A. (2011) 'Dear, Oh Dear, Oh Dear', *Guardian*, 28 April.

Edgeworth, P. (2011) *Shadowing Their Own Government? An Analysis of the Roles and Functions of Liberal Democrat Parliamentary Party Committees since the 2010 General*

Election, unpublished undergraduate thesis, University of Hull: Department of Politics and International Studies.
Elliott, F. and Hanning, J. (2009) *Cameron: The Rise of the New Conservative* (London: Harper Perennial).
Elliot, F. and Watson, R. (2010) 'How Cameron's Secret Kitchen Cabinet Had to Rethink Party's Plans for Power', *The Times*, 8 May.
Elliot, F., Watson, R. and Coates, S. (2010) 'Tactics Overhauled for Round 2', *The Times*, 17 April.
Elliott, L. (2011) 'Fiscal U-turn would be a Tricky Manoeuvre', *Guardian*, 27 June.
Energy-pedia (2011) *Libya: US Sanctions Hit Libyan Oil Flows*, 8 March, available at: http://www.energy-pedia.com/article.aspx?articleid=144446.
EOC (2006) *Sex Equality and the Modern Family: The New Political Battleground* (Manchester: Equal Opportunities Commission).
Equalities Office (2010) 'Call to End Violence Against Women and Girls', available at: http://www.homeoffice.gov.uk/publications.
European Scrutiny Committee (2010) *The EU Bill and Parliamentary Sovereignty*, 10th Report, Session 2010–11, Vol.1, HC 633-I, House of Commons (London: The Stationery Office).
European Scrutiny Committee (2011) *The EU Bill: Restrictions on Treaties and Decisions Relating to the EU*, 15th Report, Session 2010–11, HC 682, House of Commons (London: The Stationery Office).
Evans, E. (2011) 'Two Heads are Better than One: Assessing the Implications of the Conservative-Liberal Democrat Coalition for British Politics', *Political Science*, 63(1): 45–60.
Evans, M. (2009) 'Cameron's Competition State', in Lee, S. and Beech, M. (eds) *The Conservatives Under David Cameron: Built to Last?* (Basingstoke: Palgrave).
Evans, S. (2008) 'Consigning Its Past to History? David Cameron and the Conservative Party', *Parliamentary Affairs*, 61(2): 291–314.
Evans, S. (2010) '"Mother's Boy": David Cameron and Margaret Thatcher', *British Journal of Politics and International Relations*, 12(3): 325–43.
Fawcett Society (2006) 'Women's Representation in British Politics', available at: http://www.fawcettsociety.org.uk/index.asp?PageID=786.
Fawcett Society (2010) 'Women's Equality in the New Coalition – Policy Red Line or Expendable?' available at: http://www.fawcettsociety.org.uk/index.asp?PageID=1150.
Fielding, S. (2010) 'Labour's Campaign: Things Can Only Get ... Worse?' *Parliamentary Affairs*, 63(4): 653–66.
Finlayson, A. (2003) *Making Sense of New Labour* (London: Lawrence and Wishart).
Flinders, M. and Buller, J. (2006) 'Depoliticisation: Principles, Tactics and Tools', *British Politics*, 1(1): 293–318.
Foreign Affairs Committee (2011) 'The Role of the FCO in UK Government', Oral evidence (London: House of Commons).
Foucault, M. (2008) *The Birth of Biopolitics* (Basingstoke: Palgrave Macmillan).
Foucault, M. (2009) *Security, Territory, Population* (Basingstoke: Palgrave Macmillan).
Fox, L. (2005) 'Speech to the Conservative Conference', *Guardian*, 5 October.
Fox, R. (2010) 'Five Days in May: A New Political Order Emerges', in Geddes, A. and Tonge, J. (eds) *Britain Votes 2010* (Oxford: Oxford University Press).
Freedland, J. (2010) '100 Days of the Coalition Government', *Guardian*, 18 August.
Freedland, J. (2011) 'Alan Johnson's Resignation Offers Plenty for Labour Worriers', *Guardian*, 20 October.
Freeman, G. P. (1995) 'Modes of Immigration Politics in Liberal Democratic States', *International Migration Review*, 24(4): 881–902.

Freud, D. (2007) 'Reducing Dependency, Increasing Opportunity, Options for the Future of Welfare to Work: An Independent Report to the Department for Work and Pensions', available at: http://www.dwp.gov.uk/docs/welfarereview.pdf.

Forsyth, J. and Nelson, F. (2011) 'Pushing Back at Brussels: The Prime Minister on Europe and Other Problems', *The Spectator*, 9 July.

Fox, R. (2010) 'Five Days in May: A New Political Order Emerges', *Parliamentary Affairs*, 63(4): 607–22.

Gamble, A. (1988) *The Free Economy and the Strong State: The Politics of Thatcherism* (Basingstoke: Macmillan).

Gamble, A. (1995) 'The Crisis of Conservatism', *New Left Review*, 214: 3–25.

Gamble, A. (2010) 'New Labour and Political Change', *Parliamentary Affairs*, 63(4): 639–52.

Gammell, C. (2011) 'Alan Johnson – The Gaffes as Shadow Chancellor', *Daily Telegraph*, 20 January.

Geddes, A. and Tonge, J. (2010) 'An Absorbing Hanging', *Parliamentary Affairs*, 63(4): 866–73.

Gentleman, A. (2011) 'Women's Refuge Chief Returns OBE in Protest Over Cuts', *Guardian*, 15 February.

Giddens, A. (1998) *The Third Way* (Cambridge: Polity).

Gimson, A. (2010) 'David Cameron Slaughtered Ed Miliband', *Daily Telegraph*, 1 December.

Glasman, M., Rutherford, J., Stears, M. and White, S. (eds) (2011) *The Labour Tradition and the Politics of Paradox* (Oxford London Seminars: Soundings).

Glover, J. (2010) 'Desire for Change, But Only a Narrow Tory Lead', *Guardian*, 16 March.

Goodhart, D. (2011) 'Labour Can Have Its Own Coalition Too', *The Independent*, 20 March.

Goodhart, P. (1973) *The 1922* (London: Macmillan).

Gray, J. (2010) 'Progressive, like the 1980s', *London Review of Books*, 32(20): 3–7.

Grayson, R. (2010) 'Yellows in Peril: The Struggle for the Soul of Liberalism', *New Statesman*, 12 July.

Great Britain (2011) *Budget Responsibility and National Audit Act 2011* (London: The Stationary Office).

Green, A. (2010) 'David Cameron Must Now Show that He is Serious About Reducing Immigration', *Conservative Home Comment*, 8 November 2010, available at: http://conservativehome.blogs.com/platform/2010/11/sir-andrew-green-.html.

Green, D. (2010) 'The Real Immigration Question', speech to the Royal Commonwealth Society, 6 September, available at: http://www.homeoffice.gov.uk/mediacentre/speeches/Damian-Green-real-immigration.

Green, D. (2011) 'Reforming the Immigration System', speech to the Reform think tank, 1 February, available at: http://www.homeoffice.gov.uk/mediacentre/speeches/immigrationreform.

Green, J. (2010) 'Strategic Recovery? The Conservative Party Under David Cameron', *Parliamentary Affairs*, 63(4): 667–88.

Greenstein, F. (2001) *The Presidential Difference: Leadership Style from FDR to Clinton* (Princeton, NJ: Princeton University Press).

Grice, A. (2011a) 'Lib Dem Rebels Threaten Cameron-Clegg Unity Rift', *The Independent*, 13 May.

Grice, A. (2011b) 'Shadow Cabinet Revolt as Miliband Launches AV Bid', *The Independent*, 16 March.

Griffiths, S. (2011) 'The Retreat of the State: Conservative Modernisation and the Public Services', *Public Policy Research*, 18(1): 23–9.

Groom, B. and Rigby, E. (2010) 'Employers Face Bumpy Ride as Growth Slows', *Financial Times*, 22 October.
Guardian (1997) *Robin Cook's Speech on the Government's Ethical Foreign Policy*, 12 May, available at: http://www.guardian.co.uk/world/1997/may/12/indonesia.ethicalforeignpolicy.
Haddon, C. and Gruhn, Z. (2011) 'The Opposition', in Paun, A. (ed.) *One Year On: The First Year of the Coalition Government* (London: Institute for Government).
Hague, W. (1998) 'Leader's Speech, Bournemouth 1998', available at: http://www.britishpoliticalspeech.org/speech-archive.htm?speech=144.
Hague, W. (1999) 'Hague Addresses Conservative Spring Conference', available at: http://replay.web.archive.org/19990420150116/http://www.conservative-party.org.uk/newspags/03131239.htm.
Hague, W. (2006) speech: 'Foreign Affairs May be the Greatest of all Challenges for the Next Government of this Country', 3 October.
Speeches referenced for William Hague since 2000 in this bibliography below are available at: http://www.conservatives.com/News/Speeches.aspx.
Hague, W. (2007a) speech: 'Constructive Responsible Foreign Policy', 3 March.
Hague, W. (2007b) speech: 'Vital Steps in the Middle East: What the British Government Should Do Now', 2 July.
Hague, W. (2009a) speech: 'A 21st Century Partnership with the Commonwealth', 4 February.
Hague, W. (2009b) speech: 'The Future of British Foreign Policy', 21 July.
Hague, W. (2009c) 'Renewing and Reinforcing Our Role in the World', 8 October.
Hague, W. (2010a) speech: 'The Biggest Risk for Britain is Five More Years of Brown', to the Royal United Services Institute, London, 10 March.
Hague, W. (2010b) speech: 'The Change This Country Needs', 27 February.
Hague, W. (2010c) speech: 'Britain's Foreign Policy in a Networked World', 1 July.
Hampshire, J. (forthcoming) *The Politics of Immigration: Contradictions of the Liberal State* (Cambridge: Polity).
Harding, J. and Watson, R. (2010) 'Cameron Fights to Keep Campaign on Track as Yellow Peril Threatens to Pip Him at the Post', *The Times*, 22 April.
Hasan, M. (2011) 'Memo to Blue Labour: Tone Down the Nostalgia', *New Statesman*, 20 April.
Hasan, M. and Macintyre, J. (2011) *Ed: Ed Miliband and the Re-making of the Labour Party* (London: Biteback).
HASC (Home Affairs Select Committee) (2011) 'Home Affairs Committee Publishes Report on Student Visas', 17 March, available at: http://www.parliament.uk/business/committees/committees-az/commonsselect/home-affairs-committee/news/110317-student-visas-release/.
Hay, C. (1999) *The Political Economy of New Labour* (Manchester: Manchester University Press).
Hay, C. (2010) 'Chronicles of a Death Foretold: The Winter of Discontent and the Construction of the Crisis of British Keynesianism', *Parliamentary Affairs*, 63(3): 446–70.
Hay, C. and Farrall, S. (2011) 'Establishing the Ontological Status of Thatcherism by Gauging Its "Periodisability": Towards a "Cascade Theory" of Public Policy Radicalism', *British Journal of Politics and International Relations*.
Hayton, R. (2010) 'Conservative Party Modernisation and David Cameron's Politics of the Family', *The Political Quarterly*, 81(4): 492–500.
Hayton, R. (forthcoming, a) 'The Conservative Party', in Baldini, G. and Hopkin, J. (eds) *Cameron's Britain: UK Politics and the 2010 Election* (Manchester: Manchester University Press).

Hayton, R. (forthcoming, b) 'Iain Duncan Smith: Leadership Without Authority', in Heppell, T. (ed.) *Leaders of the Opposition from Churchill to Cameron* (Basingstoke: Palgrave Macmillan).

Hayton, R. (forthcoming, c) *Reconstructing Conservatism? The Conservative Party in Opposition, 1997–2010* (Manchester: Manchester University Press).

Hayton, R. and Heppell, T. (2010) 'The Quiet Man of British Politics: The Rise, Fall and Significance of Iain Duncan Smith', *Parliamentary Affairs*, 63(3): 425–55.

Healey, D. (1990) *The Time of My Life* (London: Penguin).

Heffernan, R. (2010) 'The Predominant Party Leader as Predominant Prime Minister? David Cameron in Downing Street', paper to the American Political Science Association annual meeting.

Heffernan, R. (2011) 'Labour's New Labour Legacy: Politics After Blair and Brown', *Political Studies Review*, 9(2): 163–77.

Helm, T. (2010) 'Tory Discontent Begins to Boil Over After "Heir to Blair" Fails to Seal Victory', *Observer*, 9 May.

Helm, T. (2011) 'Maurice Glasman: The Peer Plotting Labour's New Strategy from His Flat', *Observer*, 16 January.

Helm, T. and Boffey, D. (2011) 'Ed Miliband Calls on Lib Dem Ministers to Quit Cabinet', *Observer*, 8 May.

Hennessy, P. (2010) 'Poll Blow for Clegg as Voters Think Twice', *Sunday Telegraph*, 2 May.

Hennessy, P. (2011) 'Forest Fiasco Minister Faces New Humiliation', *Daily Telegraph*, 19 February.

Hennessy, P. and Kite, M. (2011) 'Embarrassment for Labour Leader as Riots Start as He Speaks at Cut Rally', *Daily Telegraph*, 26 March.

Heppell, T. and Hill, M. (2009) 'Transcending Thatcherism? Ideology and the Conservative Party Leadership Mandate of David Cameron', *The Political Quarterly*, 80(3): 388–99.

Hickson, K. (2005) 'Inequality', in Hickson, K. (ed.) *The Political Thought of the Conservative Party since 1945* (Basingstoke: Palgrave).

Hickson, K. (2009) 'Conservatism and the Poor: Conservative Party Attitudes to Poverty and Inequality since the 1970s', *British Politics*, 4(3): 341–62.

Hickson, K. (2010) 'Thatcherism, Poverty and Social Justice', *Journal of Poverty and Social Justice*, 18(2): 135–45.

Hickson, K. (2011) 'The End of New Labour? The Future of the Labour Party', in Lee, S. and Beech, M. (eds) *The Cameron-Clegg Government: Coalition Politics in an Age of Austerity* (Basingstoke: Palgrave).

HM Government (2010a) *The Coalition: Our Programme for Government* (London: The Cabinet Office).

HM Government (2010b) *Scotland Bill: Explanatory Notes* (London: The Stationary Office).

HM Government (2010c) *The Equality Strategy – Building a Fairer Britain* (London: Government Equalities Office).

HM Government (2011) *House of Lords Reform Draft Bill*, Cm 8077 (London: The Stationery Office).

Home Office (2010a) 'Immigration Minister Damian Green Visits India', 23 August, available at: http://www.homeoffice.gov.uk/media-centre/news/damian-green-india-visit.

Home Office (2010b) 'We Welcome the Brightest and Best', 2 September, available at: http://www.homeoffice.gov.uk/media-centre/news/brightest-and-best.

Home Office (2010c) 'Migrants Marrying UK Citizens Must Now Learn English', available at: http://www.homeoffice.gov.uk/media-centre/press-releases/migrants-learn-english.

Home Office (2011) *Report to Parliament on the Application of Protocols 19 and 21 to the Treaty on the Functioning of the European Union (TFEU) ('the Treaties') in Relation to EU Justice and Home Affairs (JHA) Matters (1 December 2009–30 November 2010).* Cm. 8000 (London: The Stationery Office).

Honeyman, V. (2010a) 'Gordon Brown and International Policy', in Lee, S. and Beech, M. (eds) *Gordon Brown; A Policy Evaluation* (London: Routledge).

Honeyman, V. (2010b) 'David Cameron and International Policy', in Lee, S. and Beech, M. (eds) *Cameron and the Conservatives* (Basingstoke: Palgrave Macmillan).

Howard, M. (2004) 'Speech to the News Corporation Conference in Cancun', Mexico, 19 March, available at: news.bbc.co.uk/2/hi/uk_news/politics/3551121.stm.

Howard, M. (2011) 'Parliament Protects Our Freedoms, Not Judges', *The Times*, 23 February.

Howarth, D. and Stavrakakis, Y. (2000) 'Introducing Discourse Theory and Political Analysis', in Howarth, D., Norval, A. J. and Stavrakakis, Y. (eds) *Discourse Theory and Political Analysis* (Manchester: Manchester University Press).

Hurst, G. (2010) 'Unlikely Duo Thrive Thanks to Abundance of Text Appeal', *The Times*, 3 July.

Institute for Leadership and Management (2010) *Politics: Leadership Matters* (London: Institute for Leadership and Management).

Ipsos Mori (2005) *How Britain Voted in 2005*, available at: http://www.ipsos-mori.com.

Ipsos Mori (2006) *Historical Trends in Women's Voting*, available at: http://www.ipsos-mori.com.

Ipsos Mori (2010) *Trend. How Britain Voted in 2010*, available at: http://www.ipsos-mori.com.

JCWI (2010) (Joint Council for the Welfare of Immigrants/Immigration Law Practitioners Association), 'Letter to Damian Green, 1 October 2010', available at: http://www.jcwi.org.uk/.

Jamieson, K. H. and Birdsell, D. S. (1988) *Presidential Debates: The Challenge of Creating an Informed Electorate* (Oxford: Oxford University Press).

Johnson, P. (2011) 'Is Osborne Right?' *Prospect Magazine*, 22 June.

Johnston, R., McLean, I., Pattie, C. and Rossiter, D. (2009) 'Can the Boundary Commissions Help the Conservative Party? Constituency Size and Electoral Bias in the United Kingdom', *The Political Quarterly*, 80(4): 479–94.

Jones, D. (2008) *Cameron on Cameron: Conversations with Dylan Jones* (London: Fourth Estate).

Jones, N. (2010) *Campaign 2010: The Making of the Prime Minister* (London: Biteback).

Katz, R. S. and Mair, P. (1995) 'Changing Models of Party Organisation and Party Democracy: The Emergence of the Cartel Party', *Party Politics*, 1(1): 5–28.

Kavanagh, D. and Cowley, P. (2010) *The British General Election of 2010* (Basingstoke: Palgrave).

Kellner, P. (2010) 'How He Won', *The Sunday Times*, 26 September.

Kelly, R. (2001) 'Conservatism Under Hague: The Fatal Dilemma', *The Political Quarterly*, 72(2): 197–203.

Kelly, R., Lester, P. and Durkin, M. (2010) *Leadership Elections: Labour Party* (London: House of Commons, Library, Parliament and Constitution Centre).

Kerr, P., Byrne, C. and Foster, E. (2011) 'Theorising Cameronism', *Political Studies Review*, 9(2): 193–207.

Kettle, M. (2010) 'A Man of Grace. Cameron Has Been Good for Britain', *Guardian*, 8 July.

Kettle, M. (2011) 'Labour's Recent History May Be About to Repeat Itself', *Guardian*, 20 January.

King, A. (1976) 'Modes of Executive-Legislative Relations: Great Britain, France and West Germany', *Legislative Studies Quarterly*, 1(1): 11–34.

Kirby, J. (2009) 'From Broken Families to the Broken Society', *The Political Quarterly*, 80(2): 243–7.

Kirkup, J. (2011a) 'Laid-back David Cameron Should Tighten His Grip', *Daily Telegraph*, 7 February.

Kirkup, J. (2011b) 'David Cameron to Become More Hands-On', *Daily Telegraph*, 7 February.

Kirkup, J. (2011c) 'David Cameron Says He is a "Eurosceptic" Following EU "Deal"', *Daily Telegraph*, 29 October.

Kirkup, J. and Whitehead, T. (2010) 'David Cameron Hints at Relaxing Immigration Cap', *The Daily Telegraph*, 25 October.

Kisby, B. (2010) 'The Big Society: Power to the People?' *The Political Quarterly*, 81(4): 484–91.

Kite, M. (2010) 'Dissecting a Broken Dream', *The Sunday Telegraph*, 9 May.

Kruger, D. (2007) *On Fraternity: Politics Beyond Liberty and Equality* (London: Civitas).

Lambert, R. (2011) 'Coalition Government "by No Means Firing on All Cylinders"', CBI News release 24 January, available at: http://www.cbi.org.uk/ndbs/press.nsf/0363c1f07c6ca12a8025671c00381cc7/f84f9fe2a2c4cf2f802578220030e5ca?OpenDocument.

Laclau, E. (1996) *Emancipation(s)* (London: Verso).

Laws, D. (2010) *22 Days in May: The Birth of the Lib Dem-Conservative Coalition* (London: Biteback).

Lee, S. (2009a) 'Introduction: David Cameron's Political Challenges', in Lee, S. and Beech, M. (eds) *The Conservatives Under David Cameron: Built to Last?* (Basingstoke: Palgrave).

Lee, S. (2009b) 'Convergence, Critique and Divergence: The Development of Economic Policy Under David Cameron', in Lee, S. and Beech, M. (eds) *The Conservatives Under David Cameron: Built to Last?* (Basingstoke: Palgrave).

Lee, S. (2009c) 'David Cameron and the Renewal of Policy', in Lee, S. and Beech, M. (eds) *The Conservatives Under David Cameron: Built to Last?* (Basingstoke: Palgrave).

Lee, S. (2011) 'We Are All in This Together: The Coalition Agenda for British Modernisation', in Lee, S. and Beech, M. (eds) *The Cameron-Clegg Coalition: Coalition Politics in the Age of Austerity* (Basingstoke: Palgrave).

Lee, S. and Beech, M. (eds) (2011) *The Cameron-Clegg Government: Coalition Politics in the Age of Austerity* (Basingstoke: Palgrave).

Letts, Q. (2011) 'Miliband Had His Big Chance: He Funked It', *Daily Mail*, 9 June.

Letwin, S. (1992) *The Anatomy of Thatcherism* (London: HarperCollins).

Liaison Committee (2010) 'Oral Evidence of the Prime Minister', 18 November, HC 608-i, 2010–11 (London: House of Commons).

Liberal Democrats (2010) *Liberal Democrat Manifesto 2010* (London: Liberal Democrat Party).

Lidington, D. (2010) speech: 'to the UK Association for European Law', 25 November.

Local Government Association (2011) *Local Government Finance Report 2011–12* (London: Local Government Association).

Lovenduski, J. (2005) *Feminizing Politics* (Cambridge: Polity Press).

Lynch, P. (2009) 'The Conservatives and the European Union: The Lull Before the Storm', in Lee, S. and Beech, M. (eds) *The Conservatives Under David Cameron. Built to Last?* (Basingstoke: Palgrave Macmillan).

Lynch, P. and Whitaker, R. (2008) 'A Loveless Marriage. The Conservatives and the European People's Party', *Parliamentary Affairs*, 61(1): 31–51.

MAC (Migration Advisory Committee) (2010) *Consultation by the Migration Advisory Committee on the Level of an Annual Limit on Economic Migration to the UK* (London: MAC).

Macintyre, B. (2010) 'Cameron Must Address His Rhetorical Deficit', *The Times*, 8 June.

MacNab, S. (2011) 'Tory Backs Devolved Corporation Tax', *The Scotsman*, 29 March.

Mandelson, P. (2010) *The Third Man: Life at the Heart of New Labour* (London: Harper Press).

Marshall, P. and Laws, D. (2004) *The Orange Book: Reclaiming Liberalism* (London: Profile Books).

Mason, P. (2009) *Meltdown: The End of the Age of Greed* (London: Verso).

May, T. (2010) 'The Home Secretary's Immigration Speech', 5 November, available at: http://www.homeoffice.gov.uk/media-centre/speeches/immigration-speech.

May, T. (2011) 'Launch of the Modern Workplaces Consultation', 16 May, available at: http://www.homeoffice.gov.uk/media-centre/speeches/modern-workplaces.

Maynard, G. (1988) *The Economy Under Mrs Thatcher* (Oxford: Blackwell).

McAnulla, S. (2010) 'Heirs to Blair's Third Way? David Cameron's Triangulating Conservatism', *British Politics*, 5(3): 286–314.

McCrae, J. (2011) 'Fiscal Consolidation', in Paun, A. (ed.) *One Year On: The First Year of the Coalition Government* (London: Institute for Government).

McCrum, R. R. (2010) 'Jitters Strike Cameron as He Nears Finishing Line', *The Observer*, 1 May.

McElvoy, A. (2010) 'David Cameron's Secret Weapon: Tories Architect Steve Hilton', *Sunday Times*, 11 April.

McLean, I. (2010) *What's Wrong with the British Constitution?* (Oxford: Oxford University Press).

McLean, I. and McMillan, A. (2005) *State of the Union: Unionism and the Alternatives in the United Kingdom since 1707* (Oxford: Oxford University Press).

Meikle, J. (2010) 'Alan Johnson Performs U-turn on Graduate Tax', *Guardian*, 8 December.

Miliband, E. (2010a) 'I'll Make Capitalism Work for the People', *Observer*, 29 August.

Miliband, E. (2010b) 'Change to Win' Statement, available at: http://edmiliband.org/learnmore/we-needto-change-to-win-eds-fabian-essay/.

Miller, W. L. and Mackie, M. (1973) 'The Electoral Cycle and the Asymmetry of Government and Opposition Popularity', *Political Studies*, 21(3): 263–79.

Ministry of Justice (2008) *An Elected Second Chamber: Further Reform of the House of Lords*, Cm 7438 (London: The Stationery Office).

Mitchell, J. (2006) 'Devolution's Unfinished Business', *The Political Quarterly*, 77(4): 465–74.

Montgomerie, T. (2010) 'The Breakneck Coalition', *New Statesman*, 9 August.

Montgomerie, T. (2011) 'The New 10 Downing Street', ConservativeHome blog, available at: http://conservativehome.blogs.com/thetorydiary/2011/02/the-new-10-downing-street.html.

Moore, C. (2008) 'David Cameron: Thoroughly Modern Dave or the Most Traditional Tory Leader Ever?' *Daily Telegraph*, 26 September.

Moore, C. (2010) 'Politics is the Loser in These TV Debates', *The Daily Telegraph*, 19 April.

Moran, M., Johal, S. and Williams, K. (2011) 'The Financial Crisis and Its Consequences', in Allen, N. and Bartle, J. (eds) *Britain at the Polls 2010* (London: Sage).

Morgan, J. (2010) 'UK as a Whole Will Suffer if a Big Mistake is Made on Student Visas, V-C Warns', *Times*, 2 December.

Morris, J. (2011) 'How Great is Britain?' *British Journal of Politics and International Relations*, 13(3): 326–47.

Morris, N. (2010) 'May Plans to Cut Student Visas By Up to 120,000', *The Independent*, 24 November.

Morris, S. (2011) 'Labour Looks to Rule Welsh Assembly', *Guardian*, 6 May.

MRN (Migrants' Rights Network) (2011) 'Discussing the Economic Impact of Curbing Foreign Student Numbers at a Cross-Party Meeting in Parliament', 5 March, available at: http://www.migrantsrights.org.uk/blog/2011/03/discussing-economic-impact-curbing-foreign-student-numbers-cross-party-meeting-parliame.

Muir, R. (2010) 'Coalition: A New Era in British Politics', *Public Policy Research*, 17(1): 17–23.

Mulholland, H. (2007) 'Tories Would Extend Flexible Working to All Parents, says Cameron', *Guardian*, 14 June.

Mulholland, H. (2008) 'Cameron Promises to Tackle Violence Against Women', *Guardian*, 22 December.

Mulholland, H. (2011) 'Minister Blames Feminism Over Lack of Jobs for Working Men', *Guardian*, 2 April.

Mundell, D. (2010) 'We Want to Use Devolution to Take Scotland Forward, Not Keep It in the Past', available at: http://www.conservatives.com/News/Speeches/2010/10/David_Mundell.

Mycock, A. and Tonge, J. (2011) 'A Big Idea for the Big Society? The Advent of National Citizen Service', *The Political Quarterly*, 82(1): 56–66.

Nelson, D. (2010) 'Mission to India: UK Stalks Sub-Continent's Economic Tiger', *Daily Telegraph*, 25 July.

New Local Government Network (2011) *Shared Necessities: The Next Generation of Shared Services* (London: New Local Government Network).

Newman, J. (2001) *Modernising Governance: New Labour, Policy and Society* (London: Sage).

NIESR (2011) *Report* (London: NIESR, 5 May).

Northern Ireland Executive, Scottish Government and Welsh Assembly Government (2010) 'Joint Declaration from the Devolved Administrations', available at: http://wales.gov.uk/docs/newsroom/2010/documents/101007jointdeclarationen.doc.

Norton, P. (1975) *Dissension in the House of Commons 1945–74* (London: Macmillan).

Norton, P. (1978) *Conservative Dissidents* (London: Temple Smith).

Norton, P. (1980) *Dissension in the House of Commons 1974–1979* (Oxford: Clarendon Press).

Norton, P. (1982) *The Constitution in Flux* (Oxford: Martin Robertson).

Norton, P. (1994) 'The Parliamentary Party and Party Committees', in Seldon, A. and Ball, S. (eds) *Conservative Century* (Oxford: Oxford University Press).

Norton, P. (1998) 'Winning the War but Losing the Peace: The British House of Commons During the Second World War', *The Journal of Legislative Studies*, 4(3): 33–51.

Norton, P. (2001) 'The Conservative Leadership Election', *British Politics Group Newsletter*, Fall 2001: 11–16.

Norton, P. (2008) 'Making Sense of Opposition', *The Journal of Legislative Studies*, 14(1/2): 236–50.

Norton, P. (2009) 'David Cameron and Tory Success: Bystander or Architect?' in Beech, M. and Lee, S. (eds) *Built to Last? The Conservatives Under David Cameron* (Basingstoke: Palgrave).

Norton, P. (2011a) 'The Politics of Coalition', in Allen, A. and Bartle, J. (eds) *Britain at the Polls 2010* (London: Sage).

Norton, P. (2011b) 'The Con-Lib Agenda for the "New Politics" and Constitutional Reform', in Lee, S. and Beech, M. (eds) *The Cameron-Clegg Government: Coalition Politics in an Age of Austerity* (Basingstoke: Palgrave Macmillan).

Nutt, T. (2006) 'The Child Support Agency and the Old Poor Law', *History and Policy*, October 2006, available at: http://www.historyandpolicy.org/papers/policy-paper-47.html.

Nye, R. (2011) 'Public Opinion', in Paun, A. (ed.) *One Year On: The First Year of the Coalition Government* (London: Institute for Government).

Oborne, P. (2010) 'Cameron's Masterly Inactivity is Putting Us Back on Course', *Daily Telegraph*, 23 December.

Observer (2010) 'What Exactly Does Prime Minister David Cameron Do?' 5 December.

O'Donnell, G. (2011) Evidence to the Iraq (Chilcot) Inquiry, 28 January.

OBR (Office for Budget Responsibility) (2011) *Economic Outlook* (London: HM Treasury).

O'Hara, K. (2007) *After Blair: David Cameron and the Conservative Tradition* (Cambridge: Icon).

Oliver, J. (2010a) 'You Can't Airbrush This, Dave: The Incredible Shrinking Tory Lead', *The Sunday Times*, 28 February.

Oliver, J. (2010b) 'Let Me Roll Up My Sleeves and Take Decisions', *The Sunday Times*, 2 May.

Oliver, J. and Smith, D. (2010) 'Clegg Nearly as Popular as Churchill', *The Sunday Times*, 18 April.

Osborne, G. (2008) 'Nudge, Nudge, Win Win: Why are Conservatives Hooked on These New Economic Psychological Ideas? Because They Work', *Guardian*, 14 July.

Osborne, G. (2010) 'June Budget Report Statement to the House of Commons', 22 June, available at: http://www.direct.gov.uk/prod_consum_dg/groups/dg_digitalassets/@dg/@en/documents/digitalasset/dg_188595.pdf.

O'Shaughnessy, N. (2005) 'The British General Election of 2005: A Summary Perspective', *Journal of Marketing Management*, 21(9–10): 907–23.

Owen, G. (2000) *From Empire to Europe* (London: HarperCollins).

Owen, G. and Lowther, W. (2010) 'Obama Aide Prepping Cameron for TV Clash', *Daily Mail*, 11 April.

Padley, B. (2011) 'Colleagues Defend Miliband Rally Speech', *The Independent*, 27 March.

Page, R. M. (2010) 'David Cameron's Modern Conservative Approach to Poverty and Social Justice: Towards One Nation or Two?' *Journal of Poverty and Social Justice*, 18(2): 147–60.

Parker, G. (2011) 'Osborne's Long Game', *Financial Times Magazine*, 19 March.

Parker, G. and Boxell, J. (2010) 'Fears Force Immigration Cap Rethink', *Financial Times*, 25 June.

Parker, G. and Pignal, S. (2010) 'Tories to Steer Clear of Instant Conflict with the EU', *Financial Times*, 9 March.

Pattie, C. and Johnston, R. (2011) 'How Big is the Big Society?' *Parliamentary Affairs*, 64(3): 403–24.

Paun, A. (2010) *United We Stand? Coalition Government in the UK* (London: Institute for Government).

Paun, A. (2011) 'Governing in Coalition', in Institute for Government, *One Year On: The First Year of Coalition Government* (London: Institute for Government).

Paun, A. and Hazell, R. (2010) 'Hung Parliaments and the Challenges for Westminster and Whitehall: How to Make Minority and Multiparty Government Work', *The Political Quarterly*, 8(2): 213–22.

Perkins, A. (2010) 'A Two-Nation Tory', *Guardian*, 18 August.

Pickles, E. (2010) 'Response to the LGA Offer', available at: http://www.communities.gov.uk/speeches/newsroom/lgaoffer.

Pickles, E. (2011a) 'National Council for Voluntary Organisations Annual Conference 2011', available at: http://www.conservatives.com/News/Speeches/2011/03/Eric_Pickles_We_will_let_councils_make_their_own_decisions.aspx.

Pickles, E. (2011b) 'We Will Let Councils Make Their Own Decisions', available at: http://www.conservatives.com/News/Speeches/2011/03/Eric_Pickles_We_will_let_councils_make_their_own_decisions.aspx.

Pierre, J. and Peters, B. G. (2000) *Governance, Politics and the State* (Basingstoke: Palgrave).

Pierson, P. (1994) *Dismantling the Welfare State* (Cambridge: Cambridge University Press).

Political and Constitutional Reform Committee, House of Commons (2011) *Lessons from the Process of Government Formation After the 2010 General Election*, Fourth Report, Session 2010–11, HC 528 (London: The Stationery Office).

Porter, A. (2011) 'Ed Miliband: Change to AV system Will Freeze Out the Tories', *Daily Telegraph*, 30 March.

Prince, R. (2010a) 'Liberal Democrats "in a Mess" Over Tuition Fees', *Daily Telegraph*, 5 December.

Prince, R. (2010b) 'Ed Miliband "Too Busy" to Marry Pregnant Girlfriend', *Daily Telegraph*, 27 September.

Prince, R. and Porter, A. (2010) 'Ed Miliband: In Victory He Asked "What Have I Done to David?"' *Daily Telegraph*, 27 September.

Quinn, T. (2011) 'From New Labour to New Politics: The British General Election of 2010', *West European Politics*, 34(2): 403–11.

Rallings, C. and Thrasher, M. (2007) *British Electoral Facts* (Aldershot: Ashgate).

Rallings, C. and Thrasher, M. (2009) *Local Elections Handbook 2009* (Local Government Chronicle Elections Centre, University of Plymouth).

Rallings, C. and Thrasher, M. (2010) 'Majority Missed by a Whisker', *Sunday Times*, 9 May.

Rallings, C., Thrasher, M. and Johnston, R. (2002) 'The Slow Death of a Governing Party: The Erosion of Conservative Local Electoral Support in England, 1979–97', *British Journal of Politics and International Relations*, 4(2): 271–98.

Ramsden, J. (1999) *An Appetite for Power: A History of the Conservative Party since 1830* (New York: HarperCollins).

Randall, N. (2009) 'No Friends in the North? The Conservative Party in Northern England', *The Political Quarterly*, 80(2): 184–92.

Rawnsley, A. (2010a) 'Nick Clegg: We've Released the Inner Liberal in Many Tories', *Observer*, 19 September.

Rawnsley, A. (2010b) 'David Cameron's Ambivalent Relationship With the Lady in Blue', *Observer*, 10 October.

Rawnsley, A. (2011a) 'The Spotlight Begins to Shine On the Coalition's Flaws and Faultlines', *Observer*, 13 February.

Rawnsley, A. (2011b) 'Cameron Loses a Tainted Friend, Miliband Promotes a Tricky Rival', *Guardian*, 23 January.

Rawnsley, A. (2011c) 'To Have a Hope of Power Labour Must Turn from Dull into Dynamic', *Observer*, 15 May.

Reed, H. (2011) 'How the Government Has Got It Wrong on Gender Equality', *Fabian Review*, Spring, 4–5.

Rentoul, J. (2011) 'Big Society Cover for Cuts: Poll', *The Independent*, 12 February.

Rhodes, R. (1997) *Understanding Governance: Policy Networks, Governance, Reflexivity, and Accountability* (Buckingham: Open University Press).

Richards, S. (2011) 'The "Heirs to Blair" are Nothing Like Him', *The Independent*, 20 January.

Riddell, M. (2010) 'Andy Burnham Interview', *Daily Telegraph*, 27 May.

Riddell, P. (2011) 'Fast Forward', *Public Service Magazine*, Spring 2011.

Ridge, S. (2011) 'Pickles Under Fire from Tory-Led Councils', available at: http://news.sky.com/skynews/Home/Politics/Conservative-Led-Councils-Tell-Communities-Secretary-Eric-Pickles-Cuts-Could-Be-Devastating/Article/201102315938145.

Robinson, N. (2008) 'Europe – Ticking Time Bomb? Nick Robinson's Newslog', 28 October, available at: http://www.bbc.co.uk/blogs/nickrobinson/2008/10/europe_ticking.html.

Rooksby, E. (2011) 'Don't Underestimate Toxic Blue Labour', *Guardian*, 21 May.

Rosindell, A. (2010) 'Interview with Andrew Rosindell, Conservative MP', *The Politics Show*, BBC 1, 13 June, cited in *JCWI/ILPA*, 'Briefing re: Statement of Changes in Immigration Rules (Cm 7944)', 25 October 2010, available at: http://www.jcwi.org.uk/.

Rummery, K., Gains, F. and Annesley, C. (2007) 'New Labour: Towards an Engendered Politics and Policy?' in Annesley, C., Gains, F. and Rummery, K. (eds) *Women and New Labour* (Bristol: The Policy Press).

Russell, A. (2010) 'Inclusion, Exclusion or Obscurity? The 2010 General Election and the Implications of the Con-Lib Coalition for Third-Party Politics in Britain', *British Politics*, 5(4): 506–24.

Russell, A. and Fieldhouse, E. (2005) *Neither Left Not Right: The Liberal Democrats and the Electorate* (Manchester: Manchester University Press).

Russell, J. (2011) 'The Gloves are Off as the Lib-Dems Switch Tactics', *Evening Standard*, 9 May.

Russell, M. and Sciara, M. (2007) 'Why Does the Government Get Defeated in the House of Lords? The Lords, the Party System and British Politics', *British Politics*, 2(3): 299–322.

Rutter, J. (2011) 'How the Most Powerful Mandarins Spend Their Time', Institute for Government blog, 17 March, available at: http://www.instituteforgovernment.org.uk/blog/2187/how-the-most-powerful-mandarins-spend-their-time/.

Rutter, J. and Atkinson, D. (2011) 'Number 10 and the Centre', in Institute for Government, *One Year On: The First Year of Coalition Government* (London: Institute for Government).

Ryley, J. (2009) 'Who'll Show Up for the TV Election Showdown?' *The Times*, 2 September.

Salmond, A. (2010) 'A Missed Opportunity to Govern for the Whole of These Islands', *The Times*, 12 May.

Sanders, D. (2005) 'The Political Economy of UK Party Support, 1997–2004: Forecasts for the 2005 General Election', *Journal of Elections, Public Opinion and Parties*, 15(1): 47–71.

Sanders, D. (2006) 'Reflections on the 2005 General Election: Some Speculations on How the Conservatives Can Win Next Time', *British Politics*, 1(1): 170–94.

Schama, S. (2010) 'David Cameron Talks to Simon Schama', *Financial Times Magazine*, 2/3 October.

Schwartz, T. (1974) *The Responsive Chord* (New York: Anchor Books).

Seawright, D. (1999) *An Important Matter of Principle. The Decline of the Scottish Conservative and Unionist Party* (Aldershot: Ashgate).

Seawright, D. (2002) 'The Scottish Conservative and Unionist Party: The Lesser Spotted Tory', in Hassan, G. and Warhurst, C., *Tomorrow's Scotland* (London: Lawrence & Wishart).

Seawright, D. (2010) *The British Conservative Party and One Nation Politics* (New York: Continuum).

Seawright, D. (forthcoming) '"Cameron 2010": An Exemplification of Personality Based Campaigning', *Journal of Political Marketing*.

Seldon, A. (2009) 'What Sort of Prime Minister Would David Cameron Be?' *Daily Telegraph*, 5 September.

Seldon, A. (2011a) 'Inside Cameron's Number 10', *Parliamentary Brief*, April.

Seldon, A. (2011b) 'A Year On and the Loser is Now the Master', *Sunday Times*, 1 May.

Seldon, A. and Snowdon, P. (2005) 'The Barren Years 1997–2005', in Ball, S. and Seldon, A. (eds) *Recovering Power: The Conservatives in Opposition since 1867* (Basingstoke: Palgrave).

Sherman, J. (2011) 'Whitehall Fears New Era of Spin Under Cameron's Media Chief', *The Times*, 23 March.

Shipman, T. (2011) 'MPs Back Sentencing Reforms', *Daily Mail*, 30 June.

Short, C. (1996) 'Women and the Labour Party', *Parliamentary Affairs*, 49(1): 17–25.

Sky News (2010) 'David Cameron Interviewed on Sunday Live with Adam Boulton', *Sky News*, 4 April.

SJPG (2006) *Breakdown Britain* (London: Social Justice Policy Group).

SJPG (2007) *Breakthrough Britain: Ending the Costs of Social Breakdown (Overview)* (London: Social Justice Policy Group).

Smith, M. J. (2010) 'From Big Government to Big Society: Changing the State-Society Balance', *Parliamentary Affairs*, 63(4): 818–33.

Snowdon, P. (2010) *Back from the Brink: The Extraordinary Fall and Rise of the Conservative Party* (London: Harper Press).

Snowdon, P. (2011) 'Audacious Gamble Presents Great Risks for Both Governing Parties', *Public Policy Research*, 17(4): 194–7.

Sparrow, A. (2008) 'David Cameron Attacks Labour's "Shameful" Lone Parent Plan', *Guardian*, 16 December.

Steavenson, W. (2010) 'Born to Lead, But Where?' *Prospect*, May.

Stephens, P. (1996) *Politics and the Pound: The Conservatives' Struggle With Sterling* (Basingstoke: Macmillan).

Stevens, C. (2002) 'Thatcherism, Majorism and the Collapse of Tory Statecraft', *Contemporary British History*, 16(1): 119–50.

Stopgap (2010) 'The Fawcett Society Magazine: "Cutting Women Out?" A Stopgap Special on the Way Cuts Will Hit Women', Winter.

Stratton, A. (2010a) 'Vince Cable: Abolition of Development Agencies was "Maoist and Chaotic"', *Guardian*, 12 November.

Stratton, A. (2010b) 'Coalition's First 100 Days: Tory and Lib Dem Aides Share Much in Common', *Guardian*, 18 August.

Streeter, G. (ed.) (2003) *There is Such a Thing as Society* (London: Politicos).

Stuart, M. (2011) 'The Formation of the Coalition', in Lee, S. and Beech, M. (eds) *The Cameron-Clegg Government: Coalition Politics in an Age of Austerity* (London: Palgrave Macmillan).

Sylvester, R. (2011a) 'Lib Dems Must Now Decontaminate Themselves', *The Times*, 10 May.

Sylvester, R. (2011b) 'A Facebook Policy Met by Baffled Faces', *The Times*, 15 February.

Taggart, P. and Szczerbiack, A. (2008) 'Theorising Party-Based Euroscepticism: Problems of Definition, Measurement and Causality', in Taggart, P. and Szczerbiack, A. (eds) *Opposing Europe. The Comparative Party Politics of Euroscepticism, Volume 2* (Oxford: Oxford University Press).

Taylor, A. (2005) 'Economic Statecraft', in Hickson, K. (ed.) *The Political Thought of the Conservative Party since 1945* (Basingstoke: Palgrave).
Taylor, A. (2010) 'British Conservatives, David Cameron and the Politics of Adaptation', *Representation*, 46(4): 489–96.
Taylor-Gooby, P. (2001) 'Welfare Reform in the UK: The Construction of a Liberal Consensus', in Taylor-Gooby, P. (ed.) *Welfare States Under Pressure* (London: Sage).
Taylor-Gooby, P. and Stoker, G. (2011) 'The Coalition Programme: A New Vision for Britain or Politics as Usual?' *The Political Quarterly*, 82(1): 4–15.
Thaler, H. R. and Sustein, C. (2009) *Nudge: Improving Decisions about Health, Wealth and Happiness* (London: Penguin).
Theakston, K. (2007) 'What Makes for an Effective British Prime Minister?' *Quarderni Di Scienza Politica*, 14(2): 39–61.
Theakston, K. (2011) 'Gordon Brown as Prime Minister: Political Skills and Leadership Style', *British Politics*, 6(1): 78–100.
Travis, A. (2011) 'Ministers Fail to Agree on How to Cut Number of International Students', *Guardian*, 3 March.
Travis, A. and Watt, N. (2011) 'Clarke Forced to Apologise for Rape Comments', *Guardian*, 18 May.
Transtlantic Trends (2011) *Transatlantic Trends: Immigration 2010*, German Marshall Fund of the United States, available at: http://trends.gmfus.org/immigration/doc/TTI2010_English_Key.pdf.
TUC 'The Gender Impact of the Cuts', November 2010, available at: www.tuc.org.uk/genderimpactofcuts.
UKBA (2008) *Marriage Visas: The Way Forward* (London: UKBA).
UKBA (2010a) *Limits on Non-EU Economic Migration: A Consultation* (London: UKBA).
UKBA (2010b) *Consultation on Limits on Non-EU Economic Migration: Consultation Questionnaire Results* (London: UKBA).
UKBA (2010c) 'Government Sets First Annual Limit for Non-European Workers', 23 November, available at: http://www.ukba.homeoffice.gov.uk/sitecontent/news-articles/2010/nov/78-first-annual-limit/.
UKBA (2010d) 'Annual Limit for Tier 1 and Tier 2 Visa Applications', 24 November, available at: http://www.ukba.homeoffice.gov.uk/sitecontent/newsfragments/35-t1-t2-annual-limits.
UKBA (2010e) *The Student Immigration System: A Consultation* (London: UKBA).
UKBA (2011) 'Government Rolls Out Red Carpet for Entrepreneurs and Investors', press release, available at: http://www.homeoffice.gov.uk/media-centre/press-releases/entrepeneurs-investors-uk.
UN Security Council (2011) *Security Council Approves 'No-Fly Zone' Over Libya, Authorizing 'All Necessary Measures' to Protect Civilians, by Vote of 10 in Favour with 5 Abstentions*, 17 May, available at: http://www.un.org/News/Press/docs/2011/sc10200.doc.htm.
UUKA (Universities UK, the Wellcome Trust and the Association of Medical Research Charities) (2010) 'Briefing for Lords Debate on the Government's Proposed Limit on Non-EU Economic Migration', 21 October 2010, available at: http://www.universities-uk.ac.uk/ParliamentaryActivities/Documents/UUKAMRCWellcomeImmigration.pdf.
UUK (2011) 'Universities UK Responds to Home Secretary's Statement on Student Visas', press release 22 March, available at: http://www.universitiesuk.ac.uk/Newsroom/Media-Releases/Pages/UniversitiesUKrespondstoHomeSecretary'sstatementon-studentvisas.aspx.
UK Parliament (2011) 'MPs Identify "Convincing Case" for Lower Rate of Corporation Tax in Northern Ireland', available at: http://www.parliament.uk/business/committees/

committees-a-z/commons-select/northern-ireland-affairs-committee/news/corporation-tax-report-substantive/.
Vickers, R. (2011) 'The Con-Lib Agenda for Foreign Policy and International Development', in Lee, S. and Beech, M. (eds) *The Cameron-Clegg Government* (Basingstoke: Palgrave).
Watson, R. (2010) 'Enter the Outsider', *The Times*, 16 April.
Watson, R. (2011a) 'Coalition Under Strain as Clegg Condemns Anti-AV "Dinosaurs"', *The Times*, 22 April.
Watson, R. (2011b) 'Two Little Words May Mean Chamber of Horrors', *The Times*, 9 May.
Watt, N. (2010a) 'David Cameron's India Trip May Be "Undermined" by Immigration Policy', *Guardian*, 25 July.
Watt, N. (2010b) 'Revealed: Lib Dems Planned Before Election to Abandon Tuition Fees Pledge', *Guardian*, 12 November.
Watt, N. (2010c) 'David Miliband is Voters' Choice for Labour Leader, says Poll', *Guardian*, 3 September.
Watt, N. (2010d) 'David Miliband Attack Risks Rift With Brother', *Guardian*, 25 August.
Watt, N. (2010e) 'Cameron: David Miliband Greatest Threat to the Conservatives', *Guardian*, 27 August.
Watt, N. (2011a) 'David Cameron Set to Appoint Andrew Cooper as Downing Street Director of Strategy', *Guardian*, 15 February.
Watt, N. (2011b) 'Elections 2011: Ed Miliband Puts on a Brave Face After Mixed Results for Labour', *Guardian*, 7 May.
Watt, N. (2011c) 'NHS Reform is Safe: Andrew Lansley Makes Private Plea for Tory Support', *Guardian*, 13 June.
Watt, N. and Wintour, P. (2009) 'David Cameron Plans Mini "West Wing" to Avoid Blair-Brown Rifts', *Guardian*, 3 July.
Watt, N. and Wintour, P. (2010) 'Leader Shows Ruthless Streak Over Shadow Chancellor Post', *Guardian*, 9 October.
Webb, P. and Childs, S. (2011) 'Wets and Dries Resurgent? Intra-Party Alignments Among Contemporary Conservative Party Members', *Parliamentary Affairs*, 64(3): 383–402.
Webster, P. and Foster, P. (2010) 'Party Leaders Agree to 4½ Hours of TV Debates in US-style Election Gamble', *The Times*, 22 December.
Wickham-Jones, M. and Jobson, R. (2010) 'Gripped by the Past: Nostalgia and the 2010 Labour Party Leadership Contest', *British Politics*, 5(4): 525–48.
Willetts, D. (1992) *Modern Conservatism* (London: Penguin).
Willetts, D. (2005) 'A Tory Community', *Prospect*, 115(October): 73–4.
Williams, S. and Scott, P. (2011) 'The Nature of Conservative Party Modernization Under David Cameron: The Trajectory of Employment Relations Policy', *Parliamentary Affairs*, 64(3): 513–29.
Wilson, G. (2011) 'PM Backtracks on Migrant Cuts', *The Sun*, 20 April.
Wilson, R. (2010) *5 Days to Power* (London: Biteback Publishing).
Winnett, R. (2010a) 'Vince Cable: I Have Declared War on the Murdoch Empire', *Daily Telegraph*, 21 December.
Winnett, R. (2010b) 'Labour Leadership Race: Miliband Battle Turns into Civil War', *Daily Telegraph*, 31 August.
Wintour, P. (2010a) 'Anglo-French Defence Agreement Hailed by Leaders', *Guardian*, 2 November.
Wintour, P. (2010b) 'Ed Miliband Keeps Ed Balls and Yvette Cooper from Labour's Economic Heart', *Guardian*, 8 October.

Wintour, P. (2011) 'Miliband Speech to Engage With Blue Labour Ideals', *Guardian*, 21 April.

Wintour, P. and Stratton, A. (2011a) 'NHS Reforms Face Overhaul After Liberal Democrats' Rebellion', *Guardian*, 13 March.

Wintour, P. and Stratton, A. (2011b) 'Miliband and Clegg Dispute Causes Cancellation of Alternative Vote Event', *The Guardian*, 13 March.

Wintour, P., Stratton, A. and Watt, N. (2010) 'Labour Leadership Race', *Guardian*, 24 September.

Wintour, P. and Watt, N. (2011) 'Downing Street Flounders as Aides Struggle to Formulate Strategic Direction', *Guardian*, 7 February.

Wolf, M. (2011a) 'Britain's Experiment in Austerity', *Financial Times*, 8 February.

Wolf, M. (2011b) 'Why British Fiscal Policy is a Huge Gamble', *Financial Times*, 28 April.

Women's Budget Group (2010a) 'A Gender Impact Assessment of the Coalition Government Budget, June 2010', available at: http://www.fawcettsociety.org.uk/ index.asp?PageID=1164.

Women's Budget Group (2010b) 'The Impact on Women of the Coalition Spending Review 2010', available at: http://www.wbg.org.uk/.

Women's Budget Group (2011) 'The Impact on Women of the Budget 2011', available at: http://www.wbg.org.uk/.

Women's Engagement (2010–11) Newsletters from the Government Equalities Office, available at: http://www.equalities.gov.uk/publications_and_research.aspx.

Worcester, R., Mortimore, R., Baines, P. and Gill, M. (2011) *Explaining Cameron's Coalition: How It Came About* (London: Biteback).

Wright, O. (2011) 'Cut Out the Flashman Act, Aides Tell David Cameron', *The Independent*, 11 May.

Wright, S. and Gysin, C. (2010) 'Five Female Assistants – and All from Russia: How Lothario MP Became Obsessed with Eastern European Women', *MailOnline*, 7 December, available at: http://www.dailymail.co.uk/news/article-1336173/Lib-Dem-MP-Mike-Hancock-obsessed-Russian-women.html.

Wring, D. (2011) 'Introduction', in Wring, D., Mortimore, R. and Atkinson, S. (eds) *Political Communication in Britain: The Leader Debates, the Campaign and the Media in the 2010 General Election* (Basingstoke: Palgrave).

Wring, D. and Ward, S. (2010) 'The Media and the 2010 Campaign: The Television Election?' *Parliamentary Affairs*, 63(4): 802–17.

YouGov (2011) 'Government Tracker Data, June 2011', available at: http://today.yougov.co.uk/sites/today.yougov.co.uk/files/yg-archives-pol-st-results-10-120611.pdf.

Index